The Justice Motive in Adolescence and Young Adulthood

Individuals experience unfairness on a daily basis, from everyday inconveniences to fundamental societal problems. There are, however, great differences in individual reactions to unfairness and in striving for justice. This book is the first to build a conceptual bridge between justice psychology and developmental psychology. It shows how these differences can be explained by the justice motive, or just world hypothesis, which states that people need to believe in a just world in which everybody gets what they deserve.

The first section of the book explores how and why the justice motive develops, with a particular focus on direct transmission, parenting and the impact of the family structure. The second and third sections describe the impact of the justice motive on development in adolescence and young adulthood, on school and career development. The authors show that the justice motive is an important resource for sustaining mental health during adolescence and young adulthood, helping young people to enhance their school careers and to cope with critical life-events such as imprisonment. The final chapters focus on the justice motive as a buffer during the initial stages of unemployment, protecting young adults' mental health and helping them to make the school-to-work transition successfully. The changing meaning of the justice motive across the lifespan is also explored.

The Justice Motive in Adolescence and Young Adulthood summarises studies from across Europe, giving the reader significant new insights into justice psychology and important aspects of youth development.

Claudia Dalbert is Professor of Psychology at the Martin Luther University of Halle-Wittenberg, Germany. She has written numerous articles and books about the justice motive, including *The Justice Motive as a Personal Resource: Dealing with Challenges and Critical Life Events* (2001). **Hedvig Sallay** is Assistant Professor at the University of Debrecen, Hungary. Her research has been concerned primarily with parenting and its consequences in adolescence.

Routledge research international series in social psychology
Edited by W. Peter Robinson
University of Bristol, UK

This series represents a showcase for both the latest cutting-edge research in the field, and important critiques of existing theory. International in scope, and directed at an international audience, applied topics are well represented. Social psychology is defined broadly to include related areas from social development to the social psychology of abnormal behaviour. The series is a rich source of information for advanced students and researchers alike.

Routledge is pleased to invite proposals for new books in the series. In the first instance, any interested authors should contact:

Professor W. Peter Robinson
Department of Experimental Psychology
University of Bristol
8 Woodland Road
Bristol BS8 1TN
E-mail: P.Robinson@bristol.ac.uk

1 **Cooperation in Modern Society**
Promoting the welfare of communities, states and organizations
Edited by Mark van Vugt, Mark Snyder, Tom R. Tyler and Anders Biel

2 **Youth and Coping in Twelve Nations**
Surveys of 18–20-year-old young people
Edited by Janice Gibson-Cline

3 **Responsibility**
The many faces of a social phenomenon
Hans-Werner Bierhoff and Ann Elisabeth Auhagen

4 **The Psychological Origins of Institutionalized Torture**
Mika Haritos-Fatouros

5 **A Sociocognitive Approach to Social Norms**
Edited by Nicole Dubois

6 Human Rights as Social Representations
Willem Doise

7 The Microanalysis of Political Communication
Claptrap and ambiguity
Peter Bull

8 The Justice Motive in Adolescence and Young Adulthood
Origins and consequences
Edited by Claudia Dalbert and Hedvig Sallay

Also available in International Series in Social Psychology, now published by Psychology Press

Children as Consumers
A psychological analysis of the young people's market
Barrie Gunter and Adrian Furnham

Adjustment of Adolescents
Cross-cultural similarities and differences
Ruth Scott and William Scott

Social Psychology and Education
Pam Maras

Making Sense of Television
The psychology of audience interpretation
Sonia Livingstone

Stereotypes During the Decline and Fall of Communism
Gyorgy Hunyady

Understanding the Older Consumer
The grey market
Barrie Gunter

Adolescence: From Crisis to Coping
A thirteen nation study
Edited by Janice Gibson-Cline

Changing European Identities
Social psychological analyses of social change
Edited by Glynis M. Breakwell and Evanthia Lyons

Social Groups and Identities
Developing the legacy of Henri Tajfel
Edited by W. Peter Robinson

Assertion and its Social Context
Keithia Wilson and Cynthia Gallois

Children's Social Competence in Context
The contributions of family, school and culture
Barry H. Schneider

Emotion and Social Judgements
Edited by Joseph P. Forgas

Game Theory and its Applications
In the social and biological sciences
Andrew M. Colman

Genius and Eminence
Edited by Robert S. Albert

The Psychology of Gambling
Michael Walker

Social Dilemmas
Theoretical issues and research findings
Edited by Wim Liebrand, David Messick and Henk Wilke

The Theory of Reasoned Action
Its application to AIDS-preventive behaviour
Edited by Deborah Terry, Cynthia Gallois and Malcolm McCamish

The Economic Psychology of Everyday Life
Paul Webley, Carole B. Burgoyne, Stephen E.G. Lea and Brian M. Young

Personal Relationships Across the Lifespan
Patricia Noller, Judith Feeney and Candida Peterson

Language in Action: Psychological Models of Conversation
William Turnbull

Rival Truths: Common Sense and Social Psychological Explanations in Health and Illness
Lindsay St Claire

The Justice Motive in Adolescence and Young Adulthood

Origins and consequences

Edited by Claudia Dalbert and Hedvig Sallay

LONDON AND NEW YORK

First published 2004
by Routledge
2 Park Square, Milton Park, Abingdon, Oxfordshire OX14 4RN

Simultaneously published in the USA and Canada
by Routledge
29 West 35th Street, New York, NY 10001

Routledge is an imprint of the Taylor & Francis Group

© 2004 Editorial matter and selection, Claudia Dalbert and Hedvig
Sallay; individual chapters, the contributors

Typeset in Baskerville by Wearset Ltd, Boldon, Tyne and Wear
Printed and bound in Great Britain by MPG Books Ltd, Bodmin

All rights reserved. No part of this book may be reprinted or
reproduced or utilised in any form or by any electronic, mechanical,
or other means, now known or hereafter invented, including
photocopying and recording, or in any information storage or
retrieval system, without permission in writing from the publishers.

British Library Cataloguing in Publication Data
A catalogue record for this book is available from the British Library

Library of Congress Cataloging in Publication Data
The justice motive in adolescence and young adulthood / origins
and consequences / edited by Claudia Dalbert and Hedvig Sallay.
      p. cm.
   Includes bibliographical references and index.
   1. Justice in adolescence. 2. Justice in young adults. I. Dalbert,
Claudia. II. Sallay, Hedvig.
BF724.3.J87 2004
155.5′1825–dc22

2004000708

ISBN 0-415-31677-4

Contents

List of figures	x
List of tables	xi
Notes on contributors	xiv

1 Introduction   1

HEDVIG SALLAY AND CLAUDIA DALBERT

PART 1
The development of the belief in a just world   9

2 Parenting and young adolescents' belief in a just world   11

CLAUDIA DALBERT AND MATTHIAS RADANT

3 The development of the belief in a just world: the impact of being raised in a one-parent or an intact family   26

HEDVIG SALLAY AND CLAUDIA DALBERT

4 Transmission of the belief in a just world in the family   43

UTE SCHÖNPFLUG AND LUDWIG BILZ

5 Transformation of the justice motive? Belief in a just world and its correlates in different age groups   64

JÜRGEN MAES AND MANFRED SCHMITT

viii *Contents*

PART 2
The belief in a just world as a resource for mental health and coping in adolescence   **83**

6 **Belief in a just world, subjective well-being and trust of young adults**   85
ISABEL CORREIA AND JORGE VALA

7 **Belief in a just world, personality and well-being of adolescents**   101
CLAUDIA DALBERT AND JOZEF DZUKA

8 **The implications and functions of just and unjust experiences in school**   117
CLAUDIA DALBERT

9 **Two facets of the belief in a just world and achievement behaviour at school**   135
JÜRGEN MAES AND ELISABETH KALS

10 **Belief in a just world as a resource for different types of young prisoners**   153
KATHLEEN OTTO AND CLAUDIA DALBERT

PART 3
Belief in a just world and career development   **173**

11 **Belief in a just world as a resource for unemployed young adults**   175
CLAUDIA DALBERT

12 **Belief in a just world and young adults' ways of coping with unemployment and the job search**   189
VERA CUBELA ADORIC

13 **Entering the job market: belief in a just world, fairness and well-being of graduating students**   215
HEDVIG SALLAY

14 **Belief in a just world and adolescents' vocational and social goals**   231
DOROTHEA DETTE, JOACHIM STÖBER AND
CLAUDIA DALBERT

15 **Developmental trajectories and developmental functions of the belief in a just world: some concluding remarks**   248
CLAUDIA DALBERT AND HEDVIG SALLAY

Index   263

Figures

2.1	Latent path model for parenting, beliefs in a just world, and just family climate as perceived retrospectively by young adults	16
2.2	Latent path model for personal belief in a just world and just family climate as perceived by young adolescents and parenting as perceived by their mothers and fathers	21
4.1	Female and male students' own and their parents' belief in a just world	52
4.2	Belief in a just world of father, mother and child as dependent on child's age	53
5.1	Justice beliefs in four different age groups	68
10.1	Change in the perceived justice of the trial as a function of personal belief in a just world and detention	161
10.2	Change in moral justification as a function of personal belief in a just world and time in prison	162
10.3	Change in feelings of guilt as a function of personal belief in a just world and age at first conviction	163
10.4	Change in anger-control as a function of personal belief in a just world and the number of offences in the criminal career	165
10.5	Change in anger-out as a function of personal belief in a just world and violent crimes	166
10.6	Change in prospects of success in personal goals as a function of personal belief in a just world and the number of offences in the criminal career	167
12.1	General and personal BJW in unemployed individuals with differing numbers of unsuccessful job applications	200
12.2	Relationship between general and personal BJW and the self-reported frequency of unfair treatment at the workplace and in the job search	202
14.1	The prediction of the probability of success in adolescents' vocational and social goals	242

Tables

2.1	Personal belief in a just world (BJW) and just family climate (JFC) of children and their parents	19
3.1	Second-order factor analysis of maternal parenting in one-parent families	32
3.2	Second-order factor analysis of parenting in intact families	33
3.3	Regression of general and personal BJW and just family climate on maternal parenting and family situation	35
3.4	Regression of general and personal BJW and just family climate on parenting in intact families	37
4.1	Child's belief in a just world as dependent on parental concordance of their belief in a just world	54
4.2	Multiple regressions of the child's belief in a just world (BJW) on father's and mother's belief in a just world	57
5.1	Correlations of justice beliefs with indicators of subjective well-being and mental health	70
5.2	Correlations of justice beliefs with indicators of an idealistic world-view	72
5.3	Correlations of justice beliefs with indicators of socio-political orientation	73
6.1	Correlations between BJW and internal locus of control in different studies	90
6.2	Study 1: Correlations between belief in a just world, internal locus of control, optimism, satisfaction with life and self-esteem	93
6.3	Study 1: Regression from satisfaction with life and self-esteem on optimism, locus of control and belief in a just world	93
6.4	Study 2: Correlations between belief in a just world, optimism, satisfaction with life and self-esteem	94
6.5	Study 2: Multiple regression analysis with optimism and belief in a just world as predictors and satisfaction with life and self-esteem as criteria	95

xii *Tables*

6.6	Study 3: Correlations between belief in a just world, happiness, interpersonal trust, institutional trust and perceptions of social justice	96
7.1	Correlations in Study 1	106
7.2	Well-being on gender, extraversion, neuroticism, general and personal BJW and the interactions of both BJWs with both personality dimensions in Study 1	108
7.3	Correlations in Study 2	110
7.4	Well-being on gender, extraversion, neuroticism, general and personal BJW and the interactions of both BJWs with both personality dimensions in Study 2	110
9.1	Partial correlational analysis: two BJW facets with pupil's aims in learning and aspiration levels	143
9.2	Partial correlational analysis: two BJW facets with achievement-oriented emotions	144
9.3	Partial correlational analysis: two BJW facets with self-ascribed capacities and learning styles	145
9.4	Partial correlational analysis: two BJW facets with attributions for success and failure	147
9.5	Partial correlational analysis: two BJW facets with life satisfaction	148
10.1	Total effects of personal and familial background, criminal career and personal belief in a just world on justice judgements and outcome variables	158
10.2	Regression models for justice of trial, moral justification, feelings of guilt, anger-control, anger-out and prospects of success in personal goals	160
12.1	Factor structure of the General Belief in a Just World Scale in employed and unemployed participants	199
12.2	Correlations of the BJW with reactions towards unfair treatment in the job search (unemployed) and at the workplace (employed)	203
12.3	Correlations between reactions towards unfair treatment in the job search, separately for participants low and high in general and personal BJW	204
12.4	Correlations between reactions towards unfair treatment at the workplace, separately for participants low and high in general and personal BJW	205
12.5	Beta weights of perceived unfairness and self-blame in explaining discontent with unfair treatment in the job search (unemployed) and at the workplace (employed) in the groups of participants high and low in personal BJW	207

Tables xiii

13.1	Means (*M*), standard deviations (*SD*) and bivariate correlations for BJW and SWB	224
13.2	Regression of SWB on BJW, anticipated fairness at the workplace, time point, gender and job situation and their interactions	225
14.1	Means, standard deviations and bivariate correlations	240

Contributors

Vera Cubela Adoric is Senior Lecturer in Social Psychology at the University of Zadar, Croatia. Her research focuses on the role of perceived responsibility and of self- and world-views in reactions to traumatised and underprivileged people and in coping with negative interpersonal and life events.

Ludwig Bilz received his diploma in psychology from the Martin Luther University, Halle-Wittenberg in 2002. He is research assistant at the Department of Educational Science at the Technical University of Dresden, Germany. His research interest lies in socialisation and value transmission. Currently his research is concerned primarily with health and health behaviours of adolescents.

Isabel Correia is Assistant Professor working at the ISCTE, Lisbon, Portugal. Her research has been concerned primarily with threat to belief in a just world and secondary victimisation of innocent victims by observers. Her other interest lies in discrimination and social influence.

Claudia Dalbert is Professor of Psychology at the Martin Luther University, Halle-Wittenberg, Germany. Her research focuses on justice motive theory. Currently she is investigating the differentiation between an implicit and a self-attributed justice motive and how the justice motive develops. Her other interest is concerned with the tolerance of uncertainty.

Dorothea E. Dette is a research assistant at the Institute of Psychology at the University of Erlangen-Nuremberg, Germany. Her current research interest concerns the influence of work and family variables on well-being and life satisfaction in early adulthood, as well as the pursuit of personal goals and the role of the belief in a just world.

Jozef Dzuka is Assistant Professor of Psychology working at the University of Presov, Slovakia. His research has been concerned primarily with motivation. Currently his research is focused on theoretical modelling and empirical testing of subjective well-being.

Contributors xv

Elisabeth Kals is Professor of Psychology at the Catholic University of Eichstätt-Ingolstadt, Germany. Her main research interests cover social and educational psychology with a focus on communication, mediation, environmental and health issues.

Jürgen Maes teaches educational, social, tourism and media psychology at the Department of Educational and Applied Psychology at the University of Trier, Germany. His research aims at understanding the process of adjustment to societal change, the role of individual justice conceptions in social conflicts, and the connection between justice and mental health.

Kathleen Otto is a PhD student at the Department of Educational Psychology at the Martin Luther University, Halle-Wittenberg, Germany (dissertation scholarship, state of Saxony-Anhalt). Besides justice beliefs she is interested in individual and vocational predictors supporting geographic and job mobility of employed and unemployed people.

Matthias Radant is a psychology student at the Martin Luther University, Halle-Wittenberg, Germany. He has been collaborating on projects researching the just world belief and uncertainty tolerance in the Department of Educational Psychology.

Hedvig Sallay is Assistant Professor of Psychology at the University of Debrecen, Hungary. Her research has been concerned primarily with parenting and its consequences in adolescence. Currently she is examining different correlates of the just world belief. Her other interest lies in self- and identity development in adolescence.

Manfred Schmitt is Professor of Social Psychology at the University of Koblenz-Landau, Germany. His research interests include social justice, emotion, empathy, prejudice, helping, depression, moderators of the consistency among trait indicators, and structural equation models for multitrait–mulitstate–multimethod data. His current research is devoted to long-term effects of relative deprivation, justice sensitivity and the cognitive mechanisms shaping individual differences in justice behaviour.

Ute Schönpflug is currently adjunct member of the Institute of Cognitive Science in Boulder, Colorado, USA and book review editor of the *Journal of Cross-Cultural Psychology*. Her research interests are in cultural transmission and developmental aspects of text processing.

Joachim Stöber is Scientific Assistant at the Department of Educational Psychology of the Martin Luther University, Halle-Wittenberg, Germany. His current research is examining personal goals in high school students and the effects of parental and teacher support on motivation, prosocial behaviour and well-being.

xvi *Contributors*

Jorge Vala is Professor of Psychology at ISCTE (Instituto Superior de Ciências do Trabalho e da Empresa), Lisbon, Portugal. His current research projects analyse the association between perceptions of social justice and racial discrimination and the social validation of everyday knowledge.

1 Introduction

Hedvig Sallay and Claudia Dalbert

This book aims to combine developmental psychology with a traditional social psychological topic: the justice motive theory. Since the first paper on 'the belief in a just world' (BJW) was published by Melvin Lerner in 1965, there has been steady international interest in the concept (Furnham, 2003). There is now no doubt that the BJW serves important functions. Thus, it is timely to explore how and why this belief develops and how it impacts on development, in particular on development in adolescence and young adulthood.

A short history of the concept

The BJW hypothesis states that everyone gets what they deserve, that good things tend to happen to good people, and that bad people are punished for their behaviour by negative outcomes. In the 38 years since Lerner published his first paper on the belief in a just world in 1965, several studies have been conducted to test the hypothesis that people need to believe that they live in a just world. The number of studies on BJW has increased gradually over the past decades (Maes, 1998), indicating that new directions in this research field are continuing to develop, contributing to different areas of psychological research.

According to Maes (1998), eight stages can be distinguished in the development of BJW research, starting with the identification of the phenomenon, followed by the elaboration of the nature of the observed effect. In the third phase, a self-report measure was developed and the first correlational research was conducted. During the extended fourth stage, experimental and correlational studies were used to validate the scale. In the fifth stage, the construct was found to be multidimensional, and the subdimensions identified helped to resolve the equivocal findings of previous research. In the sixth phase, researchers aimed to develop even better scales, and this led to the seventh phase, in which doubts were cast on the original concept, especially its conceptual and psychometric status. According to Furnham (1990), the last phase can be called 'acceptance and text-bookisation', meaning that the concept

2   *H. Sallay and C. Dalbert*

was accepted scientifically and now features in several textbooks on personality.

Recently, Furnham (2003) reviewed the BJW research conducted in the 1990s. He underlined that, compared to earlier research, which concentrated mainly on the negative side of the BJW, namely victim derogation, more recent research has involved a shift in emphasis, with BJW now being seen as a healthy coping resource with many psychological benefits. This book represents a further step in this direction, showing that BJW is an important personal resource that impacts on development in adolescence and young adulthood, and in different spheres of life.

The functions of BJW

According to Dalbert (2001), the belief in a just world serves three important functions: (a) it endows individuals with the confidence that they will be treated fairly by others; (b) it provides a conceptual framework which makes it possible for people to interpret the events of their personal life in a meaningful way; and (c) it is indicative of the personal obligation to behave fairly. Thus, this belief can be considered an important resource which enables people to deal successfully with the challenges of everyday life and to cope with critical life-events.

Previous studies have demonstrated the different functions of the BJW. The first function – allowing individuals to believe that they will be treated fairly in life – is of great relevance to people engaged in everyday activities, and is an important precondition for their actions. Individuals who 'play fair' in their interactions with others can expect others to be fair to them as well. BJW thus endows individuals with a stable trust in the fairness of the world. Trust is an emotional orientation. Individuals high in BJW show more trust in others (Zuckerman and Gerbasi, 1977), and they expect their investments to be fairly rewarded in the future. According to the findings of Tomaka and Blascovich (1994), the more strongly people believe in a just world, the less stressed and threatened they are by achievement situations, and the better their results.

The second function of the BJW – encouraging people to see the world as meaningful and thus to find meaning in life – means that the belief in a just world can be interpreted as a positive illusion. People high in BJW do not believe that events in the complex social world around them are entirely random, but that they are reliable and predictable (Lerner and Miller, 1978). When individuals are confronted with an injustice, either observed or experienced, this threatens their just-world belief, and they are motivated to try to restore justice either psychologically (e.g. by minimising the injustice) or behaviourally (e.g. by compensating the injustice). This belief increases their feelings of control and competence, which make it possible for them to have a positive outlook on their future and to view their past life in a positive way (Lipkus and

Introduction 3

Siegler, 1993). This results in stable mental health and positive subjective well-being.

Much of the empirical work on the second function of the BJW has dealt with reactions to victims, especially victim blaming. In a series of studies, Montada (1998) demonstrated the close relationship between BJW and reactions to different kinds of 'victims' (e.g. disabled people, AIDS patients, rape victims). Strong believers in a just world are more likely to make more internal attributions or to blame the victim. In other words, high believers interpret negative outcomes as being less unjust, and thus experience more positive and fewer negative emotions. Later on, laboratory studies (Hafer and Olson, 1998; Hafer, 2000a) revealed that the BJW is also relevant to personal misfortune, as high believers perceive less unfairness in their own lives and thus show less discontent than those with a weak BJW. The implications of internal attributions of experienced unfairness for the victims' mental health are still unclear, however (Dalbert, 2001).

Finally, the third function of the BJW is that it is indicative of the personal obligation to behave fairly. The strength of the BJW varies between individuals (Rubin and Peplau, 1975). The stronger the BJW, the more justice-motivated a person's reactions. For example, the more strongly people believe that they live in a just world, the more they are likely to help innocent victims (Bierhoff *et al.*, 1991; DePalma *et al.*, 1999). Furthermore, strong believers in a just world are highly motivated to achieve their goals by just means – by acting fairly they respect the terms of the personal contract, which in turn assures them of being fairly rewarded (Hafer, 2000b). In most cases, justice-motivated actions lead to positive outcomes such as coping behaviour and enhanced well-being (Dalbert, 2001). Unjust behaviour, in contrast, is censured by a decrease in self-esteem – but only for those high in BJW (Dalbert, 1999).

As this short history and review of work on the BJW demonstrates, the concept of BJW is now well established. A succession of studies has demonstrated its importance in all aspects of life. With this in mind, our knowledge on the meaning and functions of the belief in a just world could be greatly enhanced by exploring developmental questions: How does the belief emerge and develop during different periods of life? Which factors impact on the development of the BJW during the socialisation process? What are the long- and short-term developmental consequences of being high or low in BJW? This volume unites studies from different parts of Europe, all of which aim to explore the development and the developmental functions of the BJW, particularly in adolescence and young adulthood.

4   H. Sallay and C. Dalbert

About this book

The chapters of the book are grouped into three parts. The first part comprises studies describing the possible developmental trajectories of the belief in a just world. Dalbert and Radant explore how different parenting dimensions contribute to the development of the belief in a just world. The findings of their cross-sectional study with early adolescents and their parents in Germany show that the perception of a fair family climate seems to result from a combination of nurture and restriction. In contrast, the BJW only appears to be strengthened by nurture, which the authors define as a harmonious family climate with a low rate of conflicts and manipulation. No direct transmission from the parents' BJW to the BJW of the child was observed. As this was a first study exploring the antecedents of the BJW, further studies are still needed to validate these results. The study by Sallay and Dalbert extends this line of research by comparing the just-world beliefs of those brought up in intact families with one-parent families in Hungary. Their cross-sectional study with young adults again shows that a supportive family environment, which is not characterised by either conflicts or inconsistent parenting styles, strengthens the BJW. Comparison of the two family types reveals that one-parent families tend to be more conflict-ridden than intact families. Moreover, the BJW of young adults who were brought up by their mothers alone seems to be weaker than the BJW of those who grew up with both parents. Schönpflug and Bilz test the direct transmission between parents' and child's BJW more closely in a German sample. Their findings show that direct transmission from the parents' to the child's BJW may occur, but only under specific circumstances, e.g. when the child accepts the parents as role models, or when there is a high level of similarity between the parents' BJWs. The last chapter in this part reveals that the BJW has different functions for different age groups. Maes and Schmitt analyse cross-sectional data collected in Germany and show that the BJW decreases in adulthood, but increases again in old age. The change in the strength of the BJW across the life-span seems reasonable when taking into account the different functions it has for different age groups. While the BJW has the function of promoting trust and confidence during adolescence and young adulthood, it serves rather to help individuals reflect positively on their experiences in 'mature' adulthood. In old age, the BJW acquires the function of comforting and consoling, and even religious integration.

Following this exploration of how the BJW is formed in the family context and develops across different ages, the second part of the book gives an insight into how the BJW serves as a developmental resource helping individuals to resolve developmental tasks and sustain mental health in adolescence and young adulthood. Correia and Vala analyse the relationship between BJW, subjective well-being and trust in young adults in Portugal. Findings of two questionnaire studies unambiguously show

Introduction 5

that the BJW uniquely impacts on life satisfaction, but not on self-esteem, when controlling for optimism and internal locus of control. Their third study, based on a representative sample of young adults in Portugal, demonstrates that BJW is positively associated with institutional, but not interpersonal trust. Dalbert and Dzuka investigate the impact of BJW on mental health, described in terms of subjective well-being, in German and Slovakian adolescents, and test whether the adaptive relationship between BJW and well-being holds when controlling for the global personality dimensions, neuroticism and extraversion. This question was addressed because neuroticism has been shown to be negatively associated with both BJW and well-being. Their three studies confirm that BJW and well-being have a unique relationship, even when controlling for the global personality. Moreover, BJW sometimes seems to work as a buffer protecting the mental health of those with deficits in their global personality structure, i.e. those low in extraversion. In the next chapter, Dalbert reviews studies about justice concerns in school. She outlines the implications of (unjust) experiences in school and highlights how these experiences are shaped by the belief in a just world (BJW). Finally, she describes the consequences of the BJW and (un)just experiences in school for a successful school career and personality development, namely its functions for the students' legal socialisation, their feelings of empowerment, their achievement motivation and achievement and, lastly, their well-being. Maes and Kals also explore the school context, and focus on the role that justice beliefs – in particular the belief in immanent justice and ultimate justice – play in learning processes. According to the belief in immanent justice, there is a direct link between good behaviour and good luck and between bad behaviour and bad luck. According to the belief in ultimate justice, in contrast, all current injustices will be resolved or compensated in the long run. The authors demonstrate that the belief in ultimate justice enhances coping and adaptation. The role of the belief in immanent justice seems to be more ambiguous, as it only serves as a resource for adolescents with consistently good learning outcomes. Otto and Dalbert investigate the three functions of the BJW in a sample of young prisoners in a German detention centre. Their results show that, compared to those with a weak BJW, strong believers in a just world experience fewer disciplinary problems during imprisonment, perceive their trial and their sentence as more just, feel more guilty about their crime and are less likely to justify or excuse their crime, report more anger control and less overt anger, and are more convinced that they will succeed in attaining their personal goals. However, these adaptive functions seem to hold only for young prisoners with a less serious criminal career (e.g. first-time prisoners or those first convicted later in adolescence).

Finally, the third part deals with the impact of the BJW on career development in young adulthood. Most chapters in this part focus on the issue of unemployment, which is shown to be a serious problem for young

6   *H. Sallay and C. Dalbert*

adults in Croatia, Germany, Slovakia and Hungary. Each chapter addresses different aspects of the topic, thus helping readers to gain a broad understanding of the phenomena, irrespective of the country in question. Dalbert reviews previous studies on BJW and its impact on coping and mental health for those who have recently entered unemployment. She argues that the BJW is a personal resource which helps unemployed young people to cope with their situation and, in particular, to avoid ruminating about their fate. Consequently, persons strong in BJW enjoy better mental health in the early stages of unemployment and are thus better able to engage in problem-focused coping. Leaving school and applying for their first job is a decisive point in young people's lives, and the BJW may enable them to cope with this task more successfully. Cubela Adoric focuses on the stability of the BJW in a sample of young Croatian adults (particularly those experiencing long-term unemployment before gathering any kind of previous job experience at all), and also employed young adults. She investigates how repeated experiences of unfairness during the job search or at the workplace weaken the BJW and how the BJW is associated with the affective and cognitive responses to these unfair experiences. The key result of this study is that the BJW remains relatively stable despite frequent rejections, but that repeated experiences of unfair treatment during the job search or at the workplace diminish the BJW. Sallay's study, which focuses on graduating students who have or have not yet found a job, was conducted in 1999 and 2001, following the rapid political and societal changes in Hungary. In addition to the BJW, this study also considers anticipated fairness at the workplace. The fairer subjects anticipated their future workplace to be, the more positive their attitudes towards life, the fewer personal problems they mentioned, the higher their self-esteem, and the less depressed they were. This effect was above and beyond the well-documented positive impact of BJW on well-being. Thus, the impact of BJW on subjective well-being can be seen as mediated by the anticipated fairness at the workplace. Finally, Dette *et al.* concentrate on the BJW's impact on career development outside the field of early unemployment. They focus on the BJW's functions for the goal perspectives of German school-leavers. Previous research suggests that expected success is a central predictor of goal investment. As one function of the BJW is to provide trust in being treated fairly by others, the authors expected the BJW to be positively associated with the perceived probability of success in vocational and social personal goals. The expected adaptive relationship between the BJW and belief in successful goal attainment was indeed observed for social and vocational goals, and holds even when controlled for global personality dimensions or goal-specific predictors, e.g. social self-efficacy for social goals.

With its aim of integrating studies on the development of just world belief from various European countries, this volume will be of interest to a diverse group of advanced students of psychology, researchers and practi-

Introduction 7

tioners. Social psychologists can learn more about the meaning and functions of the BJW: in particular, how its meaning and its relationship with other constructs – e.g. conservatism or tolerance – changes over the lifespan, how it impacts on mental health, in school or during early career development, and how unique these effects are when compared with broad personality dimensions such as neuroticism. Readers interested in the developmental perspective will learn more about transmission processes in the family, the familial conditions facilitating the development of a strong BJW, and how the BJW functions as a resource during adolescence and young adulthood, as individuals cope with normative developmental tasks such as succeeding at school or establishing personal vocational goals, or with critical life events such as early unemployment. Researchers in the fields of social and developmental psychology can expect to find conceptual advances and innovations that will enrich their own work. We hope all of them will enjoy exploring this exciting issue of the development of the belief in a just world.

References

Bierhoff, H.W., Klein, R. and Kramp, P. (1991) 'Evidence for the altruistic personality from data on accident research', *Journal of Personality*, 59: 263–80.

Dalbert, C. (1999) 'The world is more just for me than generally: About the Personal Belief in a Just World Scale's validity', *Social Justice Research*, 12: 79–98.

Dalbert, C. (2001) *The Justice Motive as a Personal Resource: Dealing with Challenges and Critical Life Events*, New York: Kluwer Academic/Plenum Publishers.

DePalma, M., Madey, S.F., Tillman, T.C. and Wheeler, J. (1999) 'Perceived patient responsibility and belief in a just world affect helping', *Basic and Applied Social Psychology*, 21: 131–7.

Furnham, A. (1990) 'The development of single trait personality theories', *Personality and Individual Differences*, 11: 923–9.

Furnham, A. (2003) 'Belief in a just world: Research progress over the past decade', *Personality and Individual Differences*, 34: 795–817.

Hafer C.L. (2000a) 'Do innocent victims threaten the belief in a just world? Evidence from a modified Stroop task', *Journal of Personality and Social Psychology*, 79: 165–73.

Hafer, C.L. (2000b) 'Investment in long-term goals and commitment to just means drive the need to believe in a just world', *Personality and Social Psychology Bulletin*, 26: 1059–73.

Hafer, C.L. and Olson, J. (1998) 'Individual differences in beliefs in a just world and responses to personal misfortune', in Montada, L. and Lerner, M.J. (eds), *Responses to Victimizations and Belief in the Just World*, New York: Plenum Press.

Lerner, M.J. (1965) 'Evaluation of performance as a function of performer's reward and attractiveness', *Journal of Personality and Social Psychology*, 67: 219–25.

Lerner, M.J. and Miller, D.T. (1978) 'Just world research and the attribution process. Looking back and ahead', *Psychological Bulletin*, 85: 1030–51.

Lipkus, I.M. and Siegler, I.C. (1993) 'The belief in a just world and perceptions of discrimination', *Journal of Psychology*, 127: 465–74.

8　H. Sallay and C. Dalbert

Maes, J. (1998) 'Eight stages in the development of research on the construct of belief in a just world?', in Montada L. and Lerner M.J. (eds), *Responses to Victimizations and Belief in a Just World*, New York: Plenum Press.

Montada, L. (1998) 'Belief in a just world: a hybrid of justice motive and self-interest', in Montada L. and Lerner M.J. (eds), *Responses to Victimizations and Belief in a Just World*, New York: Plenum Press.

Rubin, Z. and Peplau, L.A. (1975) 'Who believes in a just world?', *Journal of Social Issues*, 31(3): 65–89.

Tomaka, J. and Blascovich, J. (1994) 'Effects of justice beliefs on cognitive and psychological and behavioral responses to potential stress', *Journal of Personality and Social Psychology*, 67: 732–40.

Zuckerman, M. and Gerbasi, K.C. (1977) 'Belief in internal control or belief in a just world: The use and misuse of the I-E scale in prediction of attitudes and behavior', *Journal of Personality*, 45: 356–78.

Part I

The development of the belief in a just world

2 Parenting and young adolescents' belief in a just world

Claudia Dalbert and Matthias Radant

Until the age of 7 or 8, children typically believe in immanent justice, and are convinced that wrongdoings are automatically punished (Piaget, 1932/1997). As they grow older, however, children slowly abandon this belief in immanent justice and realise that things sometimes happen at random, and that the good may be punished while wrongdoers are not. In response to this realisation, children develop a belief in a just world. Because of their cognitive development, older children and adults have no difficulty in identifying random events. Nevertheless, they sense that a random fate is unjust, and when given the possibility to justify a negative fate by reasoning that it was self-inflicted, for example, they will embrace the chance to do so. Thus, the belief in a just world (BJW) can be interpreted as a more mature version of children's belief in immanent justice – as the belief that people in general deserve their fate, but accompanied by the cognitive ability to identify causality and randomness (Dalbert, 2001).

Besides this general developmental trajectory, there is great variability in the strength of individuals' beliefs in a just world. Some people are convinced that the world is a just place. Others seriously doubt there is any justice at all. This raises the question of which conditions promote the development of the belief in a just world and which conditions hinder its development. Throughout this book, we argue that the BJW is an important resource which promotes successful development during adolescence and young adulthood. The conditions that foster the development of the BJW are thus of particular interest. By identifying these conditions, we may be able to pinpoint ways of promoting the development of a strong BJW.

Several studies have found evidence for genetic as well as environmental components of variance in social attitudes (e.g. Abrahamson *et al.*, 2002; Scarr and Weinberg, 1981). Overall, the influence of hereditary factors is estimated to increase with age (e.g. Plomin *et al.*, 1997). One explanation for this is that individuals tend to seek out environments that are compatible with their own genetic predispositions. As individuals enter adolescence and adulthood, they are granted substantially more freedom to choose their environmental surroundings than in childhood.

12   C. Dalbert and M. Radant

As a consequence, the impact of genetic factors increases with age. During childhood and early adolescence, in contrast, social attitudes tend to be shaped largely by one's familial experiences. Thus, parents are of special importance for children's development and can also be assumed to play a key role in the foundation of their children's justice beliefs. Against this background, we conducted two studies to investigate the relationship between BJW and parenting.

Familial influences on the BJW

In our main study, we investigated the direct association between the BJW of children aged about 12 years and the BJW of their parents. The first question here is how findings of significant associations between the two – or a lack of such associations – are to be interpreted. A positive correlation between the parents' and the child's BJW could indicate either a genetic influence on the development of the child's BJW or an environmental influence of the shared familial situation. If, on the other hand, no significant relationship were found between the parents' and the child's BJW, this would not necessarily mean that no genetic factors impact on the BJW. Rather, hereditary factors may not become apparent until later in life, when adolescents increasingly surround themselves with people and experiences compatible with their genetic dispositions. In sum, it would not be possible to interpret either finding in an unambiguous manner. Thus, it would seem more promising to try to identify characteristics of the familial situation which foster the development of children's BJW. This would point to ways of promoting children's BJW, but would not imply that these are the only qualities impacting on the BJW. Therefore, we focused on parenting as an important aspect of the familial situation and investigated its relationship with the BJW.

In order to explore the impact of parenting on the development of the BJW, we applied a three-factor model of parenting which has already been successfully implemented in cross-cultural studies (Sallay and Dalbert, 2002) and in another developmental study about the impact of being raised in a one-parent family as compared with an intact family (Sallay and Dalbert, Chapter 3 in this volume). In this model, three independent dimensions of parenting are distinguished: nurture, restriction and parenting with the aim of autonomy (Holden and Edwards, 1989). 'Nurture' is regarded as the emotional quality of the family with a harmonious atmosphere and fewer conflicts. In the present studies, nurture was assessed (reverse-coded) as a conflict-ridden family. 'Restriction' describes the instrumental part of parenting and is defined here as a family orientation toward strict rules and rule reinforcement, where breaking rules has aversive consequences. It was assessed in terms of a rule-oriented family. The third factor describes the importance of the parenting aim of autonomy, which may vary independently of both other factors. Nurture and restriction, but not the parenting aim of autonomy, are assumed to be important for the development of BJW.

BJW endows individuals with the trust in fairness, that they will be treated fairly by others (e.g. Tomaka and Blascovich, 1994) and that they will not fall victim to an unforeseeable fate (e.g. Dalbert, 2001). The firmer their belief in a just world, the more people can rely on or trust in being treated fairly by others. Trust is an emotional orientation. Growing up in a harmonious family with a low rate of conflict and interpersonal manipulation can be expected to promote trust. Children who live in families in which each member cares for the others, and attempts at emotional manipulation are rare, can be more confident in being treated fairly by the other family members. As a consequence, they may have a stronger belief that the events in their lives are generally just. It was therefore hypothesised that a positive emotional orientation in the family – nurture – is important for the development of a strong BJW.

The belief that the world is a just place in which everyone gets what they deserve and deserves what they get may be strengthened by personal experience of justice. If a child repeatedly experiences unfairness in the family, his or her BJW may be weakened. The more often a child is treated fairly by other family members, and the more often he or she observes that all members of the family try to behave fairly, the more convinced the child will become that the world is a just place and that he or she can count on being treated fairly most of the time. Thus, the impact of a harmonious family may be mediated by the evaluation of the family climate as a just one. If parenting that creates a harmonious family leads children to the specific perception that their family is a just one, this may have a particularly positive effect on the belief in a personal just world.

Justice is often defined by rules, and breaking the rules is seen as unfair. Children's beliefs that they live in a fair family and are treated fairly may thus also be enhanced by growing up in a family with a strong rule-orientation. Moreover, children who grow up in rule-oriented families have been shown to be high in authoritarianism (Goch, 1997), and a positive relationship between BJW and authoritarianism has frequently been observed in adult samples (Furnham and Procter, 1989). Hence, it can be assumed that a strong rule-orientation in the family promotes the perception of the family climate as a fair one and boosts the BJW. Yet some evidence casts doubt on this hypothesis. There are marked differences between the BJW and authoritarianism. Authoritarianism is more strongly correlated with hostility and pessimism than BJW and, in contrast to authoritarianism, BJW is positively correlated with a positive outlook and a positive mood level (Dalbert, 1992; Lerner, 1978). Therefore, it is far from clear that BJW and authoritarianism can be attributed to the same kind of upbringing.

In sum, our studies aimed to test the following hypotheses: the personal BJW is assumed to be stronger, (a) the more rule-oriented the family,

14   C. Dalbert and M. Radant

(b) the less conflict-ridden the family, and (c) the fairer the family climate. Because providing trust is seen as an important feature of the BJW, (d) we expect families low in conflicts – as compared to those high in rule-orientation – to represent an especially conducive environment for the BJW and its enhancement. In our main study, we explored the association between the BJW of parents and that of their young adolescent children.

Parenting and BJW: a pilot study

We conducted a first questionnaire study aimed at testing our hypothesis that nurture is a critical dimension for the development of the BJW and the perception of a just family climate. The study was conducted anonymously as part of a larger questionnaire study administered at the end of university lessons. Our subjects were $N = 230$ female university students, none of them majoring in psychology. Their ages ranged between 19 and 50 years ($M = 24.09$, $SD = 4.74$). We measured both the general and the personal dimension of the BJW, the perception of a just family climate, and several parenting dimensions that have been shown to reflect the nurture and restriction dimensions of parenting across cultures (Sallay and Dalbert, 2002). We administered the 7-item *Personal Belief in Just World Scale* (Dalbert, 1999; Alpha = 0.81), the 6-item *General Belief in Just World Scale* (Dalbert *et al.*, 1987; Alpha = 0.68), the 4-item *Just Family Climate Scale* (Dalbert, 1993; Alpha = 0.90; see Appendix for item wording). Parenting was measured with a short version of the Family Socialisation Questionnaire (Dalbert and Goch, 1997), which consisted of selected items from the FTDS (Schneewind *et al.*, 1985) tapping the family climate and the parenting aims and attitudes of fathers and mothers separately. In this study, parenting was assessed in retrospect, and subjects were asked to think back to the time when they were 16 years old. Note that the Just Family Climate Scale was presented as part of the Family Socialisation Questionnaire and thus also tapped the family climate retrospectively, at age 16. Factor analyses revealed that the items describing the mother and the father on the same dimensions formed one common factor. Thus, the father and mother items for each dimension were summarised to form a single parent score. In total, six parenting dimensions were measured: *Rule-Oriented Family Climate* (7 items; Alpha = 0.84; sample item: 'In our family, we had to stick to the rules relatively strictly'), *Conflict-Ridden Family Climate* (7 items, Alpha = 0.87; sample item: 'There were a lot of hassles in our family'); *Constant Parenting Attitude* (4 items; Alpha = 0.67; sample item: 'When my father forbade me something, I could do what I liked, he wouldn't change his mind'); *Manipulative Parenting Attitude* (6 items; Alpha = 0.80; sample item: 'Sometimes my mother complained that I made her life too hard'); *Parenting Aim Autonomy* (8 items; Alpha = 0.82; sample item: 'My mother let me decide how to spend my pocket money');

Parenting Aim Conformity (8 items; Alpha = 0.80; sample item: 'My mother wanted me to write nicely'). All items were rated on a 6-point Likert scale with endpoints 1 ('totally disagree') and 6 ('totally agree'). When more than one item was missing, the whole variable was defined as missing. The unweighted scale means were used as scale values, with high values indicating a strong construct.

We tested our hypotheses using confirmatory factor analyses with LISREL 8.12 (Jöreskog and Sörbom, 1994). The covariance matrix was analysed for all models. We specified a six-factor model with random error based on earlier information about the second-order factor structure (Sallay and Dalbert, 2002). Thus, we differentiated three latent dependent variables – personal and general BJW and just family climate, all of which were defined by their odd–even subscales – and three latent independent variables. The latent factor rule-oriented family was defined *a priori* by the three dimensions rule-oriented family climate, parenting aim conformity, and constant parenting attitude. The latent factor conflict-ridden family was defined *a priori* by the two dimensions conflict-ridden family climate and manipulative parenting attitude. The latent factor parenting with the aim of autonomy was defined by the mothers' and fathers' subscales of the dimension parenting aim autonomy. This model resulted in a reasonable fit of the data ($\chi^2_{50} = 143.05$; $GFI = 0.92$; $RMR = 0.074$). Closer inspection of the standardised residuals revealed that the latent factor rule-oriented family was also partly composed of the dimension manipulative parenting attitude. Thus, a loading from rule-oriented family to manipulative attitude was allowed, significantly improving the model fit. Additionally, the second loading of the two factors which were defined by their odd–even subscales (personal BJW, just family climate, but not general BJW) and of parenting with the aim of autonomy, could be fixed to 1.00 without a significant decrease in model fit. Further inspection revealed that the three paths from the three independent factors to general BJW and the remaining two paths from parenting with the aim of autonomy, to personal BJW and just family climate were not significant. Thus, these five paths were fixed to 0, without significantly decreasing the model fit. No further paths – for example, from rule-oriented family or conflict-ridden family to personal BJW – could be fixed to 0. However, the paths from rule-oriented family and conflict-ridden family to personal BJW could be fixed to be equal. The model finally accepted resulted in a satisfactory fit of the data ($\chi^2_{57} = 131.09$; $GFI = 0.92$; $RMR = 0.070$).

The accepted model is depicted in Figure 2.1 and provides us with five interesting results. As expected, (a) parenting with the aim of autonomy did not predict any of the three justice dimensions and could thus be dropped from further studies. Again in line with our hypotheses, (b) a conflict-ridden family significantly decreased the just family climate and the personal BJW; moreover, (c) its impact on just family climate was stronger than on personal BJW and its effect on general BJW was not

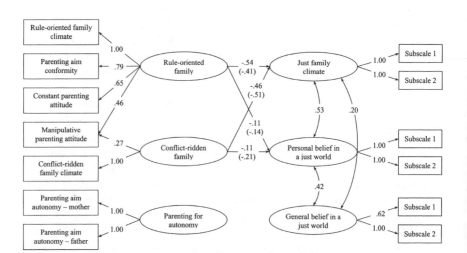

Figure 2.1 Latent path model for parenting, beliefs in a just world, and just family climate as perceived retrospectively by young adults (two-headed arrows depict correlations, one-headed arrows depict paths; the numbers in parentheses are standardised path coefficients; $\chi^2_{58} = 131.09$; $GFI = 0.92$; $RMR = 0.070$).

significant. This pattern of results points to a mediating model, with nurture – defined here as being low in conflict-ridden families – strengthening the perception of the family climate as a just one, which in turn partly mediates the effect of nurture on the personal BJW. In the same vein, the more intimate the justice factors were, the more closely they were correlated. More specifically, just family climate and personal BJW were more strongly correlated with each other than either of these factors were with general BJW. This also lends support to the assumption that the experience of nurture and a just family climate promotes the development of personal BJW, whereas the general BJW develops largely independently of actual experiences in the family. Furthermore, (d) it emerged that a rule-oriented family impacted significantly, but negatively, on both just family climate and personal BJW. This was in contradiction to our expectations. We had hypothesised that a strong rule-orientation would increase the experience of justice, and not the reverse. In retrospect, we speculate that this surprising result is a consequence of our design. We asked young adults to recall their experiences at age 16. Rule-orientation may have a different function for children and younger adolescents than it does for young adults (such as our subjects) or older adolescents (as referred to in our instruction). Adolescence and young adulthood can be seen as a potentially turbulent time in which young people have to develop their own philosophy of life and personal goals, become independent of their family of origin, form social relations with

Parenting and young adolescents' BJW 17

their peers, and lay the foundations for starting a family of their own. At this stage of life, a strong rule-orientation in the family may be perceived as a hindrance to one's personal development rather than a framework for ensuring justice. If this interpretation is correct, a study with children or young adolescents would enhance our understanding of how a rule-oriented family impacts on the development of personal BJW. (e) Finally, close inspection of the standardised residuals revealed that the two parenting factors rule-oriented family and conflict-ridden family were less clearly defined in this sample than in other studies (Sallay and Dalbert, 2002; Sallay and Dalbert, in this volume). In particular, a manipulative parenting attitude was expected to be a defining dimension of conflict-ridden families. However, it actually emerged to be more relevant to rule-oriented families. To some extent, these differences between our present study and other studies may be attributed to the fact that we used a confirmatory approach to test the hypothesised three-factor model of parenting, whereas previous studies have used exploratory factor analyses. Moreover, the finding that young adults recalling their teenage years described rule-oriented families as manipulative is also consistent with our theory that the meaning of a rule-oriented family may change during development. Additional studies are needed to inspect the factor structure of rule-oriented and conflict-ridden families in more detail.

In sum, this first study provided evidence to support our hypothesis that nurture is especially important for the development of a belief in a personal just world. The more our participants remembered their families as conflict-ridden, the less they recalled a just family climate, and the weaker their current personal BJW. Moreover, the pilot study raised two questions. The impact of a rule-oriented family was not entirely clear from the results of this study, and the structure of the parenting factors was called into doubt, with a manipulative parenting attitude emerging – contrary to expectations – to be part of the rule-oriented family factor.

Parenting and BJW of young adolescents

We conducted a second study to replicate the main findings of the first one and to shed light on the open questions concerning the structure of the parenting factors and the impact of a rule-oriented family. As discussed above, measuring parenting experiences in retrospect by asking young adults to recall their teenage years did not provide a clear insight into the role of a rule-oriented family. The end of childhood and the beginning of adolescence seems to be a crucial period for the development of BJW. Thus, examining this important period of life may provide us with a deeper insight into the development of BJW. Another aim of our second study was to gain a better idea of parenting in the family and to reduce method variance in our results. One way to improve the validity of a measure is to ask more than one person for their subjective impressions

18   C. Dalbert and M. Radant

and to aggregate these measures ('multi-method': Campbell and Fiske, 1959; Dalbert, 1991). For parenting, this implies interviewing the mother and father as well as their child or children. Moreover, covariance may be overestimated when all information is provided by the same person (i.e. the child).

We thus conducted a second study with young adolescents and their parents to explore parenting at the time of the assessment. The mothers' and the fathers' variables were taken as separate measures of parenting describing the independent factors. In contrast, only the children's variables were used as measures for the dependent justice dimensions. Hence, the independent and dependent variables did not share method variance, in particular the common variance of being rated by the same judge. Moreover, parenting was estimated by the common variance of the mothers' and the fathers' description of each parenting dimension. This procedure should increase the construct validity of the parenting.

The young adolescents were assessed at school during lesson time. Afterwards, they were given two questionnaires in separate envelopes, to be completed independently by their mother and father and brought back to school. One hundred and four families participated in the study. The children's ages ranged from 10 to 14 years ($M = 11.6$, $SD = 0.75$); 35 were boys and 69 were girls. Their mothers were aged between 30 and 54 years ($M = 40.4$, $SD = 4.9$), and their fathers between 26 and 55 years ($M = 42.8$, $SD = 5.9$). The same instruments were applied as in the first study, with the exception of parenting with the aim of autonomy and the general BJW. Thus, five parenting dimensions (*Rule-Oriented Family Climate:* 4 items, Alphas: mothers = 0.79; fathers = 0.71; *Conflict-Ridden Family Climate* 5 items, Alphas: mothers = 0.68; fathers = 0.77; *Constant Parenting Attitude* 2 items, Alphas: mothers = 0.50; fathers = 0.22; *Manipulative Parenting Attitude* 3 items, Alphas: mothers = 0.65; fathers = 0.73; *Parenting Aim Conformity:* 4 items, Alphas: mothers = 0.69; fathers = 0.61), *Personal BJW* (7 items, Alphas: children = 0.84; mothers = 0.87; fathers = 0.85) and *Just Family Climate* (4 items, Alphas: children = 0.76; mothers = 0.66; fathers = 0.52) were measured.

The descriptive statistics for the family members' personal BJW and perceptions of a just family climate are reported in Table 2.1. Children differed significantly from their mothers and fathers with respect to personal BJW, with children revealing a significantly stronger BJW than their parents (tested with an ANOVA with the repeated measurement factor BJW: $F = 5.527$, $p = 0.005$). We interpret these mean differences, which are consistent with previous findings about the age curve of the BJW (Dalbert, 2001), as evidence of a developmental trajectory. BJW decreases slightly, but significantly, from childhood to young adulthood. Note that parents still expressed a belief that their life was personally just, with means leaning towards the positive end of the scale. Moreover, there was a significant intercorrelation between the parents' BJWs, but neither

Table 2.1 Personal belief in a just world (BJW) and just family climate (JFC) of children and their parents ($N > 95$; mean M, standard deviation SD, correlation)

	M	SD	1	2	3	4	5	6
1 BJW child	4.70_a	0.87	1.00					
2 BJW mother	4.45_b	0.82	0.09	1.00				
3 BJW father	4.35_b	0.86	−0.01	0.55***	1.00			
4 JFC child	$4.85_{a'}$	0.87	0.69***	0.21*	0.07	1.00		
5 JFC mother	$4.80_{a'}$	0.72	0.13	0.25*	0.15	0.25*	1.00	
6 JFC father	$4.75_{a'}$	0.67	0.13	0.12	0.31**	0.24*	0.55***	1.00

Notes
All variables ranged from 1 to 6, with a high number indicating a strong construct. Means which do not share the same subscript differ significantly.
* $p < 0.05$.
** $p < 0.01$.
*** $p < 0.001$.

parental BJW correlated with that of the child. Thus, no direct transmission of the personal BJW from mothers and fathers to their child was observed. This makes the question of how parenting impacts on children's BJW all the more important.

Mothers, fathers and children did not differ significantly in the perceived justice of the family climate which, on the whole, was perceived as just. The perceptions of the parents intercorrelated more strongly ($Z = 1.793$; $p = 0.036$, one-tailed; Meng *et al.*, 1992; Stöber, 2000) than either of their perceptions did with that of the child, although both parent–child correlations for just family climate were significant. Thus, we can identify a direct relationship between mothers' and fathers' perceptions of just family climate and their children's perception of this variable. In addition to these within-trait features, we observed significant correlations between BJW and just family climate for each respondent. This is the first evidence for our hypothesis that a just family climate is associated with the level of personal BJW. Finally, the more the mother believed in a personal just world, the more the child perceived the family climate as just. This last result may indicate an indirect transmission from the mothers' BJW to the children's BJW, mediated by the children's perception of a just family climate.

In a second step, the impact of parenting on the child's personal BJW and perception of a just family climate was again tested using confirmatory factor analyses with LISREL 8.12 (Jöreskog and Sörbom, 1994). We specified a four-factor model with random error, analogous to the model specified in Study 1. Thus, we differentiated two latent independent variables – rule-oriented family and conflict-ridden family – and two latent dependent variables, personal BJW and just family climate. As indicators for the justice dimensions, the children's scales were divided into

20   C. Dalbert and M. Radant

odd–even subscales. The latent factor rule-oriented family was defined *a priori* by the three dimensions, rule-oriented family climate, parenting aim conformity and constant parenting attitude. The latent factor conflict-ridden family was defined *a priori* by the two dimensions, conflict-ridden family climate and manipulative parenting attitude. Each parenting dimension was described by the fathers' and the mothers' scales separately. Thus, the rule-oriented family dimension was described by six scales, and the conflict-ridden family dimension by four scales. This model resulted in a good fit of the data ($\chi^2_{71} = 143.62$; *GFI* = 0.84; *RMR* = 0.089). Closer inspection of the standardised residuals revealed that the latent factor rule-oriented family was partly composed of the dimension conflict-ridden family climate. Thus, loadings from the factor rule-oriented family to conflict-ridden family climate – as described by the mother and the father – were allowed, significantly improving the model fit. Additionally, the second loading of the two dependent factors defined by odd–even subscales (personal BJW, just family climate) could be fixed to 1.00. For the parenting dimensions, the second loadings could either be fixed to 1.00 or set to be equal to the loading on the other parent's variables. These constraints did not significantly reduce model fit. Further inspection of the standardised residuals revealed that most of the residuals > 2.00 occurred for the covariance of the two related parenting dimensions (father/mother), indicating a method factor produced by applying the same scales for both parents. As a consequence, the related error terms were allowed to correlate stepwise, beginning with the greatest residual. This resulted in a model with correlated error terms for three of the five parenting dimensions, and with a significantly better fit. Further inspection revealed that the path from rule-oriented family to BJW was not significant; it was thus fixed to 0. The model finally accepted resulted in a very good fit of the data ($\chi^2_{76} = 88.31$; *GFI* = 0.89; *RMR* = 0.076).

The accepted model is depicted in Figure 2.2. As expected and already observed in Study 1, (a) a conflict-ridden family significantly decreased the perception of a just family climate and the level of personal BJW. Moreover, (b) its impact on just family climate was stronger than on personal BJW. Additionally, and in contrast to Study 1 but in line with our hypotheses, (c) a rule-oriented family had a positive impact on just family climate, but (d) not on personal BJW. Furthermore, (e) the conflict-ridden families' impact on just family climate was slightly stronger than that of the rule-oriented families. (f) Just family climate and personal BJW were strongly correlated, even more so than in the pilot study. (g) Again, rule-oriented families and conflict-ridden families could not be defined as totally independent. In this study, however, it was the conflict-ridden family climate which also partly defined a rule-oriented family. Note, however, that the impact of the factor rule-oriented family on a conflict-ridden family climate was negative, whereas the corresponding impact of the factor conflict-ridden family was positive. This means that rule-

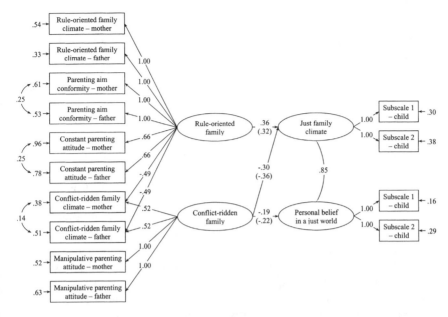

Figure 2.2 Latent path model for personal belief in a just world and just family climate as perceived by young adolescents and parenting as perceived by their mothers and fathers (two-headed arrows depict correlations, one-headed arrows depict paths; the numbers in parentheses are standardised path coefficients; $\chi^2_{76} = 88.31$; $GFI = 0.89$; $RMR = 0.076$).

oriented families were also characterised by low levels of conflict-ridden family climate, whereas conflict-ridden families typically scored high on the conflict-ridden family climate scale.

The more rule-oriented and the less conflict-ridden the families were, the more the children perceived the family climate as just, and the more they believed in a personally just world. A harmonious, non-conflict-ridden family environment was particularly important in enhancing both the perception of a just family climate and the personal BJW. Families low in conflicts – compared to those high in rule-orientation – had been expected to provide an especially conducive environment for the BJW and its enhancement. The difference between the impact of the two dimensions was not as distinct as had been expected, however. This may be partly because the two factors could not be defined as completely independent. Both were partly defined by the fathers' and the mothers' perceptions of a conflict-ridden family climate. In contrast to Study 1, however, a rule-oriented family did reveal the expected positive effects on the just family climate. This supports our interpretation that the unexpected finding of negative effects in Study 1 resulted from the assessment procedure (retrospective; concerning teenage years).

22 C. Dalbert and M. Radant

Discussion

The results of both studies indicate that nurture is the crucial factor in the development of personal BJW. Nurture was defined as a low level of conflict in the family, more specifically as a harmonious family climate with few conflicts and little manipulation as assessed by both parents. The more harmonious the family – the fewer conflicts the adolescents experienced and the less they felt manipulated by their parents – the stronger their belief in a personally just world in which events tend to be just. The impact of familial experiences on the development of personal BJW may be partly mediated by the perception of the family climate as a just one. There is a clear difference between just family climate and the personal BJW, however. The perception of the family climate as a just one seems to increase when the family is described as less conflict-ridden and more rule-oriented. A description of the family as rule-oriented thus has an impact on the perception of the family climate as just, and this impact is only slightly weaker than that of a conflict-ridden family. However, the rule-oriented family has no direct impact on the personal BJW. Overall, this pattern of results supports our hypothesis that nurture is more important than restriction for the development of personal BJW.

A closer look at the relationships between the three justice factors provides further insights into the development of justice beliefs. For young adolescents, just family climate and personal BJW were strongly correlated. At $r_{latent} = 0.85$, the correlation was even stronger than in the university student sample, where it was $r_{latent} = 0.53$. This can be interpreted as follows. The younger the individuals are, the more important their experiences in the family are for the development of their justice beliefs. This results in a huge overlap between the perception of a just family climate and the personal BJW. As the individuals grow older, other areas of life such as peer contacts and school may become more influential in shaping their justice beliefs. In contrast, the belief in a generally just world, in which all people tend to be treated fairly, was only modestly associated with the personal BJW, and even less so with just family climate. Thus, the general BJW seems to be less closely linked to experiences in the family.

We may speculate that the general BJW is more closely associated with experiences in other areas of life and, potentially, observations of what happens to other people in the world. Furthermore, the ability to engage in abstract reasoning develops in adolescence; younger children's reasoning is more concrete. The general BJW consists of more abstract schemata of the world and may be shaped not only by experiences, but also by observations, whereas the personal BJW seems to be based rather on one's concrete experiences. Thus, we would like to argue that children first establish their belief in a personal just world and later differentiate the general BJW from this personal BJW. To more fully explore this line of reasoning, it would be interesting to compare the impact of a just family climate with the impact of a just school climate and just peer contacts and the amount of observed injustice on the personal and general BJW of different age groups.

Comparison of the two studies clearly shows that retrospective studies may sometimes be misleading. The implications of parenting seem to differ when described by different age groups or for different periods of development. In the adolescence study, a rule-oriented family could be defined more independently from a conflict-ridden family. Moreover, the impact of a rule-oriented family on the development of the BJW seems to differ in the two studies. Our interpretation is that retrospective evaluations of rule-orientation are misleading because the implications of this kind of family structure are different for children or young adolescents on the one hand and older teenagers or young adults on the other.

Conclusion

A fair family climate seems to result from a combination of nurture and restriction. The belief in a personal just world, in which one is usually treated justly, however, is more strongly and more consistently associated with nurture, defined here as a harmonious family climate with fewer conflicts and less manipulation. Thus, only specific familial experiences seem to be important in strengthening the personal BJW. Future studies should examine this relationship more closely. Furthermore, the pattern of associations between just family climate and personal and general BJW suggests that general BJW is more strongly shaped by experiences outside the family and by observations concerning the fates of others than personal BJW is. Empirical studies are needed to substantiate this hypothesis.

Acknowledgements

We thank Irene Goch for providing us with the data for Study 2.

Appendix

Items of the Just Family Climate Scale (Dalbert, 1993)

1   At home, things are just.
2   At home, important decisions that are made are usually just.
3   At home, injustice is the exception rather than the rule.
4   At home, justice finally prevails.

24   C. Dalbert and M. Radant

References

Abrahamson, A.C., Baker, L.A. and Caspi, A. (2002) 'Rebellious teens? Genetic and environmental influences on the social attitudes of adolescents', *Journal of Personality and Social Psychology*, 83: 1392–408.

Campbell, D.T. and Fiske, D.M. (1959) 'Convergent and discriminant validation by the multitrait–multimethod-matrix', *Psychological Bulletin*, 56: 81–105.

Dalbert, C. (1991) 'Multimodales Messen und konvergente Validität: Entwicklung eines Strukturgleichungsmodells zur Überprüfung einer Multitrait–Multimethod-Matrix [Multimethod assessment and convergent validity: Development of a structural equation model to test a multitrait–multimethod-matrix], *Diagnostica*, 37: 97–108.

Dalbert, C. (1992) 'Der Glaube an die gerechte Welt: Differenzierung und Validierung eines Konstrukts' [The belief in a just world: Differentiation and validation of a construct], *Zeitschrift für Sozialpsychologie*, 23: 268–76.

Dalbert, C. (1993) *Just Family Climate Scale*, Martin Luther University of Halle-Wittenberg, Department of Educational Psychology.

Dalbert, C. (1999) 'The world is more just for me than generally: About the Personal Belief in a Just World Scale's validity', *Social Justice Research*, 12: 79–98.

Dalbert, C. (2001). *The Justice Motive as a Personal Resource: Dealing with Challenges and Critical Life Events*, New York: Kluwer Academic/Plenum Publishers.

Dalbert, C. and Goch, I. (1997) 'Gerechtigkeitserleben und familiale Sozialisation' [Justice experiences and familial socialization], in Langfeldt, H.-P. (ed.), *Informationen, Programm, Abstracts*, Landau: Verlag Empirische Pädagogik.

Dalbert, C., Montada, L. and Schmitt, M. (1987) 'Glaube an eine gerechte Welt als Motiv: Validierungskorrelate zweier Skalen' [The belief in a just world as a motive: Validity correlates of two scales], *Psychologische Beiträge*, 29: 596–615.

Furnham, A. and Procter, E. (1989) 'Belief in a just world: Review and critique of the individual difference literature', *British Journal of Social Psychology*, 28: 365–84.

Goch, I. (1997) *Entwicklung der Ungewißheitstoleranz. Die Bedeutung der familialen Sozialisation* [The development of the uncertainty orientation: The importance of the familial socialization], Regensburg: S. Roderer Verlag.

Holden, G.W. and Edwards, L.A. (1989) 'Parental attitudes toward child rearing: Instruments, issues, and applications', *Psychological Bulletin*, 106: 29–58.

Jöreskog, K.G. and Sörbom, D. (1994) *Lisrel 8*, Chicago: Scientific Software International.

Lerner, M.J. (1978) '"Belief in a just world" versus the "authoritarianism" syndrome . . . but nobody liked the Indians', *Ethnicity*, 5: 229–37.

Meng, X.-L., Rosenthal, R. and Rubin, D.B. (1992) 'Comparing correlated correlation coefficients', *Psychological Bulletin*, 111: 172–5.

Piaget, J. (1932/1997) *The Moral Judgment of the Child*, Glencoe, IL.: Free Press.

Plomin, R., Fulker, D.W., Corley, R. and DeFries, J.C. (1997) 'Nature, nurture, and cognitive development from 1 to 16 years', *Psychological Science*, 8: 442–7.

Sallay, H. and Dalbert, C. (2002) 'Women's perception of parenting: A German–Hungarian comparison', *Applied Psychology in Hungary*, 3–4: 55–64.

Scarr, S. and Weinberg, R. (1981) 'The transmission of authoritarianism in families: Genetic resemblance in social-political attitudes', in Scarr, S. (ed.), *Race, Social Class, and Individual Differences*, Hillsdale, NJ: Erlbaum.

Schneewind, K., Beckmann, M. and Hecht-Jackl, A. (1985) *Das Familiendiagnostische*

Testsystem (FDTS): Konzeption und Überblick, Forschungsberichte Universität München, Institut für Psychologie, Robert 1/1985.

Stöber, J. (2000) *CCC-I/II* [Computer software], Martin Luther University of Halle-Wittenberg, Department of Educational Psychology.

Tomaka, J. and Blascovich, J. (1994) 'Effects of justice beliefs on cognitive, psychological, and behavioral responses to potential stress', *Journal of Personality and Social Psychology,* 67: 732–40.

3 The development of the belief in a just world
The impact of being raised in a one-parent or an intact family

Hedvig Sallay and Claudia Dalbert

Introduction

The last four decades have seen massive changes in patterns of family life of a kind that have substantial implications for children (Hess, 1995). Divorce rates have soared in most countries, and sizeable proportions of children live in one-parent families and/or experience parental remarriage. A key question is what sort of implications this has for the children's psychological development. There is abundant evidence that parental divorce or separation is associated with an increased psychological risk for the children. For example, divorce has proved to be a meaningful predictor of physical illness (Sherwood and Siegel, 1989), and to lead to decreased levels of developmental achievement and individual resilience (Runyin and Jackson, 1988). However, there is equally strong evidence to suggest that the main risk resides in the discord, tensions and conflicts that surround divorce, rather than the parental separation as such.

Despite these changes in family patterns, the family is still considered to be the most important agency of socialisation. Internalised parental norms, world beliefs and values may have a strong impact on later behavioural outcomes. In our study, we explored the impact of family patterns and parenting on the belief in a just world (BJW). Lerner (1980) proposed that people need to believe that the world is a just place, where individuals get what they deserve. This trust in being treated fairly by others serves important functions and thus helps to promote mental health. Studies have confirmed the complex role of the belief in a just world in seeking and avoiding social contact (Lerner and Agar, 1972), altruism (Miller, 1977), coping with life crises (Simmons and Lerner, 1968), attributions in education (Richey and Richey, 1978), and even job satisfaction (Stephan and Holahan, 1982). Individuals thus feel the need to maintain their belief that the world is a just place, and this prompts them to respond to observed injustice in various ways: by helping, by blaming victims for their bad luck, or by derogating innocent victims (e.g. Lerner and Simmons, 1966). The belief in a just world is an interindividually varying disposition (Rubin and Peplau, 1973), which

The development of the BJW   27

can be measured by just world scales (e.g. Dalbert *et al.*, 1987). Recent studies have shown that the general belief in a just world can be differentiated from the personal belief in a just world (Lipkus *et al.*, 1996). The general BJW reflects the belief that the world is generally a just place, while the personal BJW reflects the belief that one's own fate is just and that the events in one's life are deserved. The general and the personal belief in a just world share a common variance in reflecting a belief in a meaningful world.

A lot has been learned about the meaning of the BJW over the past decades. Nonetheless, studies regarding the antecedents or the origin of justice-related beliefs are still rare. To fully understand the complex impact of just world beliefs, however, it seems necessary to explore their development during the socialisation process. Therefore, the present study was conducted to investigate the impact of parenting on the development of just world beliefs and to compare these relationships among individuals who grew up in different family situations. In particular, we compared one-parent families, i.e. individuals brought up by their mother only, with intact families, i.e. individuals brought up by their mother and father.

Socialisation in one-parent families and in intact families

On the societal level, families in Hungary have been undergoing transition over the past decades. Family members have always found mutual help and support within the family in critical periods of life. However, the post-1990 changes have had two major effects on family life. First, families have become more open, and have more opportunities to participate in various areas of social life (e.g. going to church on Sundays, taking part in different programmes organised by civic organisations). Second, a significant proportion of families have started their own businesses. For them, mutual interests and common goals in executing plans strengthen family cohesion, and contribute to their children's future plans and career orientation by offering them safe jobs in the future.

In general, the number of divorces has risen rapidly over the past decades partly because women's increased labour force participation gives them more control over resources and empowers them to exercise more influence in family decision-making (Burns and Scott, 1994). The family changes most relevant to children's immediate experiences relate to how their parents treat them. There are fundamental differences between one-parent and intact families, and several studies have identified short- and long-term consequences of being brought up in a one-parent or an intact family. For example, analysis of six nationally representative US data sets by McLanahan and Sandefur (1994) has demonstrated that children growing up in single-parent households have twice the risk of dropping out of high school, being out of work and becoming a teenage mother.

28   *H. Sallay and C. Dalbert*

Children brought up in one-parent families spend much less time with their father – one-third see them once a week, another third not at all – and they are twice as likely to have to move house and school, losing friends in the process (McLanahan and Sandefur, 1994). However, the long-term outcome depends on the circumstances of the custodial parent after the separation and on the quality of the relationship with each parent (Garmezy and Masten, 1994).

Growing up with a single parent has been found to have three detrimental effects. In general, disrupted families have (a) fewer financial resources to devote to upbringing and education, (b) less time and energy to nurture and supervise children, and (c) reduced access to community resources that supplement parents' efforts (McLanahan, 1999). In sum, single mothers who feel unable to cope with the strain of being the only resident parent may have difficulties in fulfilling their parental role adequately.

Studies show that parenting styles are changing in many parts of the world, becoming less authoritarian and more responsive to the children. Stable middle-class families are shifting towards authoritative parenting, in which parental responsiveness and control are combined (Schlegel and Barry, 1991). To gain a better understanding of this process, we investigate the parenting of children growing up in different family situations. Three independent dimensions of parenting are distinguished: nurture, restriction and parenting with the aim of autonomy (Holden and Edwards, 1989; Sallay and Münnich, 1999). Restriction within a family is associated with constant parenting attitudes, conformity and power (e.g. Aunola et al., 2001), that is, with a rule-oriented family climate where constant parenting attitudes and conformity as a parenting aim are considered to be typical (Sallay and Dalbert, 2002). Nurture within the family implies a harmonious atmosphere, where parents are supportive rather than manipulative, and the parenting style is consistent. In one-parent families, mothers have to struggle with a more stressful parenting situation, often assuming the role of the father as well. Thus, the parenting of mothers in intact families may differ from that of mothers in one-parent families. In particular, we expect nurture to be lower in one-parent than in intact families.

When analysing parenting within nuclear families, differences between mothers and fathers also have to be taken into consideration. Empirical results have shown that mothers engage in more child monitoring, but mixed results for warmth and consistent discipline have prevented any conclusions being drawn regarding mother–father differences in these respects (Maccoby and Martin, 1983). Conrade and Ho (2001) conducted a study with college students who reported retrospectively on their mothers' and fathers' parenting. Their results showed that mothers, rather than fathers, were perceived to be authoritative and permissive. When considering the extent to which parents differentiated between

The development of the BJW   29

their sons and daughters, significant differences were found for authoritarian, authoritative and permissive styles. Fathers were perceived to be more likely to have an authoritarian style by male respondents. Mothers were perceived to be more likely to have an authoritative style by female respondents, and to have a permissive style by male respondents. These results clearly indicate that mother–father differences in parenting exist, and that the gender of the child is an important factor here.

Parenting and BJW

It was Piaget (1932) who provided the first evidence showing that children typically interpret the world in line with a belief in immanent justice. This immanent belief is accompanied by a moral realism. The other characteristic of this stage of heteronomous morality is the absolute value of the judgements held by the child. Children regard events and occurrences as either totally right or totally wrong, and assume that everyone else shares their judgements. At a later stage in life, when the child has developed an autonomous concept of morality, these immanent justice beliefs change, transforming into the belief in a just world (Karniol, 1980). The need to construct and defend a belief in a just world arises as a result of cognitive development (Dalbert, 2001). Children gradually realise that the world is not always as just as described in fairy tales, but that events are often random and even unfair. Internalised parental norms and values, as well as experiences and observations of justice in the family, may have a pervasive effect on their evaluation of the fairness of events in their lives and in turn, impact on the formation of their beliefs in a just world.

Justice beliefs inevitably develop gradually, and personal experiences in the family play an important role in this process. Developmental studies indicate that the process begins at a very early age, when children start to play together and disputes arise between them, prompting parents to intervene and solve the conflicts (Brody et al., 1992). Ihinger (1975) proposed that parents who coherently and consistently enforce a set of rules governing their children's interactions will decrease the extent of both conflicts among children and challenges to parental rules. Family norms of equity and fairness will develop, and children will learn about sharing, reciprocity and the rights of others. To be effective in establishing family norms of equity, Ihinger suggests that parents should address issues raised in children's disputes and adopt consistently enforced positions on those issues. In this way, children learn the principles of justice. Grusec and Goodnow (1994) also argued that the internalisation of parental standards includes a process whereby children determine the acceptability of what the parent says and does in a discipline encounter. Further evidence was found for this view in later studies (e.g. Ross et al., 1994). Thus, we expect rule-orientation within the family to strengthen the belief in a just world. Furthermore, BJW increases the confidence in being treated fairly

30   *H. Sallay and C. Dalbert*

by others. Growing up in a harmonious family with a low rate of conflict and interpersonal manipulation can be expected to promote trust. Therefore, these kinds of emotional experiences in the family can also be considered to enhance the belief in a just world. Rule-orientation and conflicts in the family may impact on the BJW directly or indirectly, mediated by the fairness perceptions in the family itself.

Perceptions about the legitimacy of parental treatment can be a rich source of information about how children conceptualise family relationships. Recently, Kowal and her colleagues (Kowal *et al.*, 2002) conducted a study exploring adolescents' perceptions of the fairness of parental preferential treatment and their socio-emotional well-being. In this study, siblings were interviewed independently about their parents' distribution of affection and control. The results demonstrated that children are more likely to display behavioural problems and poorer socio-emotional well-being when they perceive parental resources as being distributed inequitably or unfairly. Consequently, the experience of being treated fairly in the family may also have a significant impact on the development of the belief in a just world.

The present study aimed at exploring the relationships between parenting and BJW in one-parent and intact families. The following hypotheses were tested. (1) Maternal parenting differs in one-parent and intact families; in particular, nurture is lower in one-parent families. Compared to those raised in one-parent families, individuals who grew up in intact families (2) perceive the family climate as more just and (3) reveal a stronger belief in a general and personal just world. (4) Nurture and restriction increase both the general and the personal BJW. (5) The impact of parenting on BJW is mediated by the fairness perception in the family.

Method

Sample

The research questions were addressed in a questionnaire study conducted in north-east Hungary. The sample comprised 390 participants (mean age: 26.3 years), enrolled in different faculties of a university and a college. Fifty-five participants were raised in one-parent families (24 males and 31 females): the others ($N=335$, of whom 156 were males and 179 females) were brought up in intact families. Participants filled in the questionnaires anonymously at the end of their psychology courses.

The development of the BJW 31

Instruments

Justice constructs

The *general BJW* was measured with the six items of the General Belief in a Just World Scale (Alpha = 0.67; Dalbert *et al.*, 1987). The Hungarian version of this scale had already been implemented successfully in a previous study (Dalbert and Katona-Sallay, 1996). The *personal BJW* was measured with the Hungarian version of the seven items from the Personal Belief in a Just World Scale (Alpha = 0.88; Dalbert, 1999). The experience of a just family climate was studied with the Hungarian version of the Just Family Climate Scale (Alpha = 0.82; Dalbert, 1993; for a list of items, see Dalbert and Radant, in this volume). Students responded to all items on a 6-point Likert scale ranging from 1 ('totally disagree') to 6 ('totally agree'). The items belonging to each scale were averaged to give a measure of each just world belief and the parenting dimensions.

Parenting

The young adults' perceptions of parenting practices were measured retrospectively using the Hungarian version of the four item Family Socialisation Questionnaire (Dalbert and Goch, 1997), which covers the family climate as well as parenting aims, attitudes and styles (for sample items, see Dalbert and Radant, in this volume). The Hungarian version has already been successfully piloted (Sallay and Dalbert, 2002). At the beginning of the questionnaire, participants were instructed to think back to the time when they were young adolescents aged 12–14, and to complete the questionnaire in line with their memories of family life at this time. With the exception of the family climate dimensions, each scale includes parallel items for the mother and father. Because one-parent families (where mothers brought up their children alone) were compared with intact families (where mothers and fathers lived and raised their children together) in the present study, separate scales were constructed for mothers and fathers, and students from one-parent families responded to those tapping maternal parenting only.

The following nine dimensions were included: *Rule-Oriented Family Climate* (4 items; Alpha = 0.82); *Conflict-Ridden Family Climate* (5 items; Alpha = 0.75); *Constant Parenting Attitude* (for mothers in intact families: 2 items, $r = 0.57$, $p \leq 0.01$; for fathers in intact families: 2 items, $r = 0.78$, $p \leq 0.01$; for mothers in one-parent families: 2 items; $r = 0.73$, $p \leq 0.01$); *Manipulative Parenting Attitude* (for mothers in intact families: 3 items, Alpha = 0.78; for fathers in intact families: 3 items, Alpha = 0.81; for mothers in one-parent families: 3 items; Alpha = 0.82); *Parenting Aim Autonomy* (for mothers in intact families: 3 items, Alpha = 0.59; for fathers in intact families: 3 items, Alpha = 0.81; for mothers in one-parent families:

32 H. Sallay and C. Dalbert

3 items; Alpha = 0.61); *Parenting Aim Conformity* (for mothers in intact families: 3 items, Alpha = 0.56; for fathers in intact families: 4 items, Alpha = 0.72; for mothers in one-parent families: 2 items; $r = 0.61$, $p \leqslant 0.01$); *Inconsistent Parenting Style* (for mothers in intact families: 2 items, $r = 0.77$, $p \leqslant 0.01$; for fathers in intact families: 2 items, $r = 0.79$, $p \leqslant 0.01$; for mothers in one-parent families: 2 items; $r = 0.79$, $p \leqslant 0.01$); *Supportive Parenting Style* (for mothers in intact families: 3 items, Alpha = 0.87; for fathers in intact families: 3 items, Alpha = 0.81; for mothers in one-parent families: 3 items; Alpha = 0.73); *Reproving Parenting Style* (for mothers in intact families: 2 items, $r = 0.57$, $p \leqslant 0.01$; for fathers in intact families: 2 items, $r = 0.78$, $p \leqslant 0.01$; for mothers in one-parent families: 2 items; $r = 0.75$, $p \leqslant 0.01$). The items were rated on a 6-point Likert-type scale with the endpoints 1 ('not typical at all') to 6 ('absolutely typical'). Demographic data were collected at the end of the questionnaire.

Results

Parenting patterns in one-parent and intact families

Separate second-order factor analyses were run for parenting practices in the one-parent families and in the intact families to explore the underlying structures. A two-factor solution emerged for the one-parent families (eigenvalues > 1: 3.151, 1.570), explaining a total of 57 per cent of the variance in the mothers' parenting. The results are given in Table 3.1. The first factor, explaining 39 per cent of the variance, described nurture (reverse coded), and was characterised by a conflict-ridden family climate, manipulative parenting attitudes and inconsistent parenting styles, a lack of parental support, and rejection of the parenting aim of autonomy. The second factor, explaining 18 per cent of the variance, depicted restriction,

Table 3.1 Second-order factor analysis of maternal parenting in one-parent families (factor loadings > 0.30)

Parenting dimensions	Factor 1	Factor 2
Conflict-ridden family climate	**0.68**	–
Parenting aim autonomy	**−0.80**	–
Manipulative parenting attitude	**0.77**	0.43
Supportive parenting style	**−0.73**	–
Inconsistent parenting style	**0.68**	0.48
Reproving parenting style	0.41	–
Rule-oriented family climate	–	**0.88**
Constant parenting attitude	–	**0.84**
Parenting aim conformity	–	**0.52**

Note
Factor loadings > |0.50| are depicted in **bold**.

The development of the BJW   33

and was characterised by a rule-oriented family climate, the parenting aim of conformity and a constant parenting attitude.

For intact families, a four-factor solution emerged (eigenvalues > 1: 5.432, 2.819, 1.538, 1.212), explaining a total of 69 per cent of the variance (see Table 3.2). The first factor again depicted nurture in a similar way to that described for maternal parenting in one-parent families. Moreover, the parenting of mothers and fathers was equally well described by this factor. Only two exceptions emerged. The parenting aim of autonomy did not load on this factor for either parent, but formed an independent fourth factor, explaining 7 per cent of the variance. In addition, the parenting aim of conformity, particularly that of the fathers, loaded on this factor instead of on the restriction factor, as had been expected and indeed observed for the one-parent families. However, the mothers' parenting aim of conformity had a higher loading on the second factor, which depicted restriction in the family and explained 18 per cent of the variance. Interestingly, apart from the rule-oriented family climate, only the mothers' parenting practices were characteristic of restriction. This factor was similar to the restriction factor observed in one-parent families, with the exception of the mothers' reproving parenting style, which loaded weakly on the nurture factor in the one-parent families, but was not that important overall. In the intact families, the mothers' reproving parenting style was characteristic for restriction in the family. The third factor, explaining 9 per cent of the variance, described a similar factor for the fathers' parenting, namely a constant parenting attitude and a reproving parenting style.

Table 3.2 Second-order factor analysis of parenting in intact families (factor loadings > 0.30)

Parenting dimensions	Factor 1	Factor 2	Factor 3	Factor 4
Conflict-ridden family climate	**0.77**	–	–	–
Manipulative parenting attitude (father)	**0.80**	–	–	–
Manipulative parenting attitude (mother)	**0.64**	0.44	–	–
Inconsistent parenting style (father)	**0.81**	–	–	–
Inconsistent parenting style (mother)	**0.75**	–	−0.43	–
Supportive parenting style (father)	**−0.66**	–	–	**0.53**
Supportive parenting style (mother)	**−0.72**	–	–	0.45
Parenting aim conformity (father)	**0.61**	0.33	0.48	–
Parenting aim conformity (mother)	**0.50**	**0.58**	–	–
Rule-oriented family climate	–	**0.55**	–	–
Constant parenting attitude (mother)	–	**0.72**	–	–
Reproving parenting style (mother)	−0.31	**0.72**	–	–
Constant parenting attitude (father)	–	–	**0.84**	–
Reproving parenting style (father)	–	0.30	**0.77**	–
Parenting aim autonomy (father)	–	–	–	**0.85**
Parenting aim autonomy (mother)	–	–	–	**0.84**

Note
Factor loadings > |0.50| are depicted in **bold**.

34   H. Sallay and C. Dalbert

Mean differences between family types and gender

Two-way ANOVAs with the family situation (one-parent or intact families) and gender (male or female) were conducted for each parenting dimension, just family climate, and both BJWs separately. Concerning parenting, significant main effects were observed only for conflict-ridden family climates ($F_{(1,388)} = 3.912$; $p = 0.049$), and mothers' constant parenting attitudes ($F_{(1,387)} = 10.1021$; $p = 0.002$). Individuals brought up in one-parent families described a more conflict-ridden family climate ($M = 3.16$, $SD = 1.02$) and a more constant parenting attitude ($M = 3.91$, $SD = 1.16$) than those brought up in intact families ($M = 2.85$, $SD = 1.10$; $M = 3.40$, $SD = 1.02$). Both BJWs differed between family types, but only general BJW differed between males and females. Subjects from one-parent families showed a higher level of general BJW ($F_{(1,382)} = 5.756$; $p = 0.017$; $M = 3.52$, $SD = 0.83$) than subjects from intact families ($M = 3.25$, $SD = 0.90$), and males endorsed the general BJW ($F_{(1,382)} = 8.586$; $p = 0.004$; $M = 3.36$, $SD = 0.85$) less strongly than females ($M = 3.56$, $SD = 0.84$). Furthermore, individuals raised in one-parent families endorsed the personal BJW ($F_{(1,245)} = 8.473$; $p = 0.004$; $M = 3.05$, $SD = 1.12$) less strongly than those raised in intact families ($M = 3.68$, $SD = 1.06$). No significant differences between family types or gender were observed for just family climate.

Mean differences between mothers' and fathers' parenting in intact families

Paired-samples t-tests showed three significant differences in the evaluation of mothers' and fathers' parenting. Subjects perceived their mothers' parenting as more manipulative ($t(327) = 4.204$, $p < 0.001$; $M_{mother} = 3.08$, $SD_{mother} = 1.24$; $M_{father} = 2.76$, $SD_{father} = 1.54$), but perceived their fathers to emphasise the parenting aim of autonomy more ($t(329) = -3.428$, $p < 0.001$; $M_{father} = 3.70$, $SD_{father} = 1.30$; $M_{mother} = 3.49$, $SD_{mother} = 1.15$), and their mothers to stress the parenting aim of conformity more ($t(330) = 2.702$, $p < 0.001$; $M_{mother} = 3.45$, $SD_{mother} = 1.09$; $M_{father} = 3.30$, $SD_{father} = 1.28$).

Comparing one-parent and intact families

In a next step, we tested which maternal parenting dimensions were associated with a just family climate and with both BJW dimensions, and compared these patterns for one-parent and intact families. A moderated stepwise ($p \leqslant 0.05$) regression was run separately for each BJW and for just family climate. In each analysis, family situation and gender were entered in the first block, maternal parenting dimensions in the second block, just family climate in the third block (for BJW only), and the interaction terms between gender and family situation on the one hand, and those of parenting and just family climate with gender and family situation on the other hand in the final block. Interaction terms which were not significant and variables which were neither part of an interaction nor revealed a significant main effect were deleted from the regression equation. Additionally, main effects were only accepted when the predictors showed a significant bivariate correlation with the dependent variable. Results are depicted in Table 3.3.

General BJW was predicted by three main effects and an interaction effect, explaining a total of 12 per cent of the variance. The more just subjects perceived the family climate to be, the more strongly they endorsed the general BJW. Females and those brought up in one-parent families

Table 3.3 Regression of general and personal BJW and just family climate on maternal parenting and family situation (accepted models, $p < 0.05$)

Predictor	R	R^2	b	t	p
General belief in a just world ($F_{total} = 9.780$; $df = 5/376$; $p < 0.000$)					
Gender	0.13	0.02[a]	0.22	2.70	0.007
Family situation	0.17	0.03[a]	1.05	2.77	
Just family climate	0.29	0.09[c]	0.19	3.95	0.000
Conflict-ridden family climate	0.29	0.09	0.07	–	–
Family situation × Conflict-ridden family climate	0.34	0.12[c]	−0.41	−3.57	0.000
			2.39		
Personal belief in a just world ($F_{total} = 35.062$; $df = 6/237$; $p < 0.001$)					
Family situation	0.20	0.04[b]	−0.58	−3.95	0.000
Gender	0.20	0.04	−1.19	–	–
Inconsistent parenting style	0.60	0.37[c]	−0.24	−6.77	0.000
Just family climate	0.65	0.42[c]	0.32	6.03	0.000
Parenting aim autonomy	0.66	0.43[a]	−0.35	–	–
Gender × Parenting aim autonomy	0.69	0.48[c]	0.39	4.29	0.000
			4.21		
Just family climate ($F_{total} = 81.476$; $df = 7/379$; $p < 0.001$)					
Family situation	0.05	0.00	−0.88	–	–
Gender	0.05	0.00	0.21	–	–
Supportive parenting style	0.69	0.48[c]	0.29	–	–
Conflict-ridden family climate	0.77	0.59[c]	−0.42	−9.06	0.000
Inconsistent parenting style	0.77	0.59	0.01	–	–
Family situation × Supportive parenting style	0.77	0.60[b]	0.22	2.69	0.008
Gender × Inconsistent parenting style	0.78	0.61[a]	−0.11	−2.48	0.014
			4.34		

Notes
Family situation (0 = intact families; 1 = one-parent families); Gender (0 = males; 1 = females).
+ $p < 0.10$.
a $p < 0.05$.
b $p < 0.01$.
c $p < 0.001$.

36 H. Sallay and C. Dalbert

were also high in general BJW. Moreover, the less conflict-ridden the subjects perceived their family to be, the more they endorsed the general BJW. The latter was especially true of one-parent families ($b = -0.34$) as compared to intact families ($b = 0.07$). Personal BJW was predicted by three main effects and one interaction effect, explaining a total of 48 per cent of the variance. The more just subjects perceived their family climate to be, and the less inconsistent their mothers' parenting style was, the more they endorsed the personal BJW. Those brought up in intact families were also high in personal BJW. The more the mothers emphasised the parenting aim of autonomy, the less subjects endorsed the personal BJW. However, the latter was only true for males ($b = -0.35$), but not for females ($b = 0.04$). The just family climate was predicted by one main effect and two interactions, explaining a total of 61 per cent of the variance. The less conflict-ridden the family climate was perceived to be, the more subjects perceived the family climate to be just. Moreover, the more subjects remembered their mothers to have been supportive – especially in one-parent families ($b = 0.51$) as compared to intact families ($b = 0.29$) – the more they considered the family climate to be just. Conversely, the more the mothers' parenting style was perceived as inconsistent, the less the family climate was considered to be just. However, this was only true for females ($b = -0.10$) and not for males ($b = 0.01$).

Parenting within the intact families

We also analysed the relationship between parenting aims, attitudes, just family climate and just world beliefs in intact families, with the aim of comparing the impact of the mothers' and the fathers' parenting respectively. Comparable moderated regression analyses were run, the only differences being that both mothers' and fathers' parenting were included and no dummy for family exists. Results are depicted in Table 3.4. The general BJW was predicted by just family climate only, explaining 4 per cent of the variance. The more just subjects considered their family climate to be just, the more strongly they endorsed the general BJW. Four main effects were revealed for personal BJW, explaining a total of 41 per cent of the variance. The less inconsistent the parenting styles of both parents, the less mothers emphasised conformity as a parenting aim, and the more just the family climate, the more strongly subjects endorsed the personal BJW. Just family climate in intact families was predicted by four main effects and one interaction effect, explaining a total of 64 per cent of the variance. The less the family climate was seen as conflict-ridden and the more subjects felt supported by both parents, the more they perceived the family climate as just. Moreover, the less they evaluated both parents' parenting styles as inconsistent, the more they saw the family climate as just. With respect to the fathers' parenting style, however, the latter was especially true for females ($b = -0.25$) as compared to males ($b = -0.08$).

Table 3.4 Regression of general and personal BJW and just family climate on parenting in intact families (accepted models, $p < 0.05$)

Predictor	R	R^2	b	t	p
General belief in a just world ($F_{total} = 11.537$; $df = 1/323$; $p < 0.001$)					
Just family climate	0.19	0.04	0.13	3.40	0.001
			2.97		
Personal belief in a just world ($F_{total} = 40.299$; $df = 4/237$; $p \leqslant 0.001$)					
Inconsistent parenting style (mother)	0.57	0.32[c]	−0.20	−5.26	0.000
Inconsistent parenting style (father)	0.62	0.38[c]	−0.11	−2.72	0.007
Just family climate	0.63	0.40[a]	0.15	2.47	0.014
Parenting aim conformity (mother)	0.64	0.41[a]	0.11	−2.01	0.045
			4.28		
Just family climate ($F_{total} = 80.758$; $df = 7/323$; $p \leqslant 0.001$)					
Supportive parenting style (mother)	0.68	0.46[c]	0.15	3.27	0.001
Inconsistent parenting style (father)	0.76	0.57[c]	−0.06	–	–
Conflict-ridden family climate	0.78	0.61[c]	−0.25	−4.68	0.000
Supportive parenting style (father)	0.79	0.62[a]	0.14	3.02	0.003
Inconsistent parenting style (mother)	0.79	0.63[a]	−0.08	−2.10	0.037
Gender	0.79	0.63	0.40		
Gender × Inconsistent parenting style (father)	0.80	0.64[c]	−0.17	−3.76	0.000
			4.22		

Notes
+ $p < 0.10$.
a $p < 0.05$.
b $p < 0.01$.
c $p < 0.001$.

The more the females remembered their fathers' parenting style as inconsistent, the less they saw the family climate as just.

Discussion

First of all, we analysed parenting patterns within one-parent families and intact families by means of factor analyses. Within the one-parent families, we observed the expected factor solution discriminating between nurture – as indicated by high endorsements of harmonious family climate and maternal support, and low endorsements of manipulative parenting attitude and inconsistent parenting style – and restriction, as reflected by high endorsement of rule-oriented family climate, constant parenting attitude and the parenting aim of conformity. However, one important difference was observed for the one-parent families as compared to intact families and cross-cultural analyses (Sallay and Dalbert, 2002), namely that the parenting aim of autonomy did not form an independent factor, but was part of the nurture factor. Thus, in the one-parent families in this sample, high nurture was characterised by rejection of the parenting aim of autonomy.

38   *H. Sallay and C. Dalbert*

In the intact families, we were interested in comparing the impact of the mothers' and the fathers' parenting on parenting patterns. Previous studies (e.g. Dalbert and Radant, in this volume; Forehand and Nousi-ainen, 1993) have shown that the parenting styles of mothers and fathers are closely related, suggesting that the two parents in an intact family tend to have similar styles. In the present study, we identified the three expected parenting patterns – labelled nurture, restriction and parenting for autonomy – and maternal and paternal parenting described each factor equally well, with one unambiguous exception. Maternal restriction and paternal restriction were clearly depicted by two independent factors. In other words, mothers and fathers in intact famil-ies seem to have an equal impact with respect to nurture and parenting with the aim of autonomy. However, the impact of the two parents with respect to restriction in the family, i.e. a constant parenting attitude and a reproving parenting style, was perceived separately and can thus vary independently.

Previous studies exploring parenting in one-parent and intact families did not reveal any fundamental differences in maternal parenting (e.g. Dunlop *et al.*, 2001). However, we observed two parenting-related differ-ences between one-parent and intact families. One-parent families were evaluated as more conflict-ridden and mothers in these families were per-ceived to have more constant parenting styles. Thus, a lower level of nurture was accompanied by more restriction. Moreover, subjects raised in one-parent and intact families differed significantly in their level of general and personal BJW. Those brought up in intact families showed a significantly higher level of personal BJW, but a lower level of general BJW than those who grew up in one-parent families. The latter result was totally unexpected, but suggests that the belief in a personal just world and the belief in a general just world seem to have different meanings. Why being brought up in a one-parent family strengthens the belief that the world is, overall, a just place, is worthy of closer examination.

The results of the multiple regression analyses provide a detailed account of how just world beliefs relate to parenting in one-parent and intact families. Besides the surprising positive impact of being raised in a one-parent family on the general belief in a just world, a just family climate seems to enhance the belief in a general just world in both family types. Furthermore, a conflict-ridden climate only seems to weaken the general BJW in one-parent families. Besides being raised in an intact family, a just family climate and consistency in parenting seem to promote a personal BJW in both family types. Finally, the perception of the family climate as just was promoted by a harmonious family climate and parental support and consistent parenting further strengthened the just family climate, particularly for females in both family types.

Overall, the results of this study unambiguously underline the import-ance of nurture as opposed to restriction for the formation of beliefs in a

The development of the BJW 39

just world. A conflict-ridden family climate and an inconsistent parenting style were both part of the nurture factor (reverse coded) and were significantly associated with both BJWs. Moreover, the experience of a just family climate inevitably plays a mediating role between nurture – in terms of a conflict-ridden family climate, a supportive and an inconsistent parenting style – and the BJWs. This mediation model holds for both family types.

What does this mean for the formation of just world beliefs of adolescents living in one-parent families? Our results confirm that the family climate in one-parent families is more discordant than that in intact families. As a consequence, the family climate is at risk of being seen as less just, and both perceptions may weaken the development of the BJW. However, our results show that it is not as simple as the mediating model may imply. First of all, the one-parent families and the intact families did not differ in their perception of justice in the family climate, although they did differ in their perceptions of the level of conflict. One explanation may be that certain parenting efforts within the one-parent families buffer against the effects of the higher conflict level. Maternal support may serve as such a buffer. Maternal support did not differ between family types, but it was especially important in strengthening the perception of a just family climate in one-parent families. However, why the personal BJW is lower for those brought up in one-parent families than in intact families, given that it does not seem to be a matter of more conflicts or a less just climate experienced in the family, is an open question that needs further clarification.

Some shortcomings of this study should also be mentioned. First of all, it was retrospective in nature, and thus leaves unclear whether differences in parenting result in different levels of just world beliefs, or whether different levels of just world beliefs lead to different memories of parenting. Moreover, to fully understand the role of one-parent families in the development of just world beliefs, other variables should also be taken into consideration: for example, the duration of single motherhood, the relationship between the child and the father of origin (if they keep regular contact or have no contact at all), the number of siblings, and the possible presence of a stepfather. Most importantly, in line with our assumptions, we observed that individuals raised in one-parent families believed less that the events in their own life are fair, but more that the world is a generally just place. Although critical life-events do not have a strong impact on just world beliefs (Dalbert, 2001), growing up in a one-parent family inevitably does. Shedding further light on the development of just world beliefs will be a challenge for future studies.

This chapter represents an attempt to outline the role of the family situation and parenting in the development of just world beliefs. The results presented here confirm that parenting and the experience of being treated fairly in the family contribute to the development of just

40   H. Sallay and C. Dalbert

world beliefs in the socialisation process. Children form impressions and gather experiences in their interactions with peers, siblings and other family members. Later, from about 12 years of age according to Piaget (1952), cognitive development is characterised by the onset of logical thinking and problem solving. This ability is not only apparent in formal logical tasks, but can also be observed in the evaluation of social interactions. Young adolescents observe and experience unfairness in the lives of others and in their own lives, in contact with their peers, siblings and parents. According to Dalbert (2001), the differentiation of the general and personal belief in a just world takes place during adolescence. The former states that people generally get what they deserve, while the latter reflects the belief in being treated fairly in one's own life. Whatever injustices children face, they are motivated to defend their belief that the world is a just place. But how can parents contribute to the development of this belief? Our study showed that parents should provide support, avoid conflicts and maintain a consistent parenting style. In intact families, moreover, the very same parental practices of mothers and fathers provide for a just family climate and promote the development of the belief in a personal just world.

References

Aunola, K., Vanhatalo, O. and Sethi, R. (2001) 'Social background, values and parenting', *Psykologia*, 36: 148–58.

Brody, G.H., Stoneman, Z., McCoy, J.K. and Forehand, R. (1992) 'Contemporaneous and longitudinal associations of sibling conflict with family relationship assessments and family discussions about sibling problems', *Child Development*, 63: 391–400.

Burns, A. and Scott, C. (1994) *Mother-headed Families and Why They Have Increased*, Hillsdale, NJ: Erlbaum.

Conrade, G. and Ho, R. (2001) 'Differential parenting styles for fathers and mothers: Differential treatment for sons and daughters', *Australian Journal of Psychology*, 53: 29–35.

Dalbert, C. (1993) *Just Family Climate Scale*, Martin Luther University of Halle-Wittenberg, Department of Educational Psychology.

Dalbert, C. (1999) 'The world is more just for me than generally: About the Personal Belief in a just world scale's validity', *Social Justice Research*, 12: 79–98.

Dalbert, C. (2001) *The Justice Motive as a Personal Resource: Dealing with Challenges and Critical Life Events*, New York: Kluwer Academic/Plenum Publishers.

Dalbert, C. and Katona-Sallay, H. (1996) 'The "belief in a just world" construct in Hungary', *Journal of Cross-Cultural Psychology*, 27: 293–314.

Dalbert, C., Montada, L. and Schmitt, M. (1987) 'Glaube an eine gerechte Wet als Motiv: Validierungskorrelate zweier Skalen' [Belief in a just world: Validity correlates of two scales], *Psychologische Beitrage*, 29: 596–615.

Dalbert, S. and Goch, I. (1997) 'Gerechtigkeitserleben und familiale Socialisation' [Justice experiences and family socialisation], in Langfeldt, H.-P. (ed.), *Informationen, Programm, Abstracts* (Information, programme, abstracts), Landau: Verlag Empirishe Paedagogik, p. 60.

The development of the BJW   41

Dunlop, R., Burns, A. and Bermingham, S. (2001) 'Parent–child relations and adolescent self-image following divorce: A 10 year study', *Journal of Youth and Adolescence*, 30: 117–34.

Forehand, R. and Nousiainen, S. (1993) 'Maternal and paternal parenting: Critical dimensions in adolescent functioning', *Journal of Family Psychology*, 7: 213–21.

Garmezy, N. and Masten, A.S. (1994) 'Chronic adversities', in Rutter, M., Taylor, E. and Hersov, L. (eds), *Child and Adolescent Psychiatry: Modern Approaches, 3rd edn*, Oxford: Blackwell Scientific Publications.

Grusec, J.E. and Goodnow, J.J. (1994) 'Impact of parental discipline methods on the child's internalization of values. A reconceptualization of current points of view', *Developmental Psychology*, 30: 4–19.

Hess, L.E. (1995) 'Changing family patterns in Western Europe: Opportunity and risk factors for adolescent development', in Rutter, M. and Smith, D.J. (eds), *Psychological Disorders in Young People: Time Trends and Their Cause*, Wiley: Chichester.

Holden G.W. and Edwards, L.A. (1989) 'Parental attitudes toward child rearing: Instruments, issues, and applications', *Psychological Bulletin*, 106: 29–58.

Ihinger, M. (1975) 'The referee role and norms of equity: A contribution toward a theory of sibling conflict', *Journal of Marriage and the Family*, 37: 515–24.

Karniol, R. (1980) 'Behavioral and cognitive correlates of various immanent justice responses in children: Deterrent versus punitive moral systems', *Journal of Personality and Social Psychology*, 43: 811–20.

Kowal, A., Kramer, L., Krull, J.L. and Crick, N.R. (2002) 'Children's perceptions of the fairness of parental preferential treatment and their socioemotional well-being', *Journal of Family Psychology*, 16: 297–306.

Lerner, M. (1980) *The Belief in a Just World: A Fundamental Delusion*, New York: Plenum.

Lerner, M. and Agar, E. (1972) 'The consequences of perceived similarity: Attraction and rejection, approach and avoidance', *Journal of Experimental Research in Personality*, 6: 69–75.

Lerner, M. and Simmons, C.H. (1966) 'The observer's reaction to the "innocent victim": Compassion or rejection?', *Journal of Personality and Social Psychology*, 4: 203–10.

Lipkus, I.M., Dalbert, C. and Siegler, I.C. (1996) 'The importance of distinguishing the belief in a just world for self versus others', *Personality and Social Psychology Bulletin*, 22: 666–77.

Maccoby, E.E. and Martin, J.A. (1983) 'Socialization in the context of the family: Parent–child interaction', in Hetherington, E.M. (ed.), *Socialization, Personality, and Social Development: Vol.4. Handbook of child psychology*, New York: Wiley.

McLanahan, S.S (1999) 'Father absence and the welfare of children', in E.M. Hetherington (ed.), *Coping with Divorce, Single Parenting, and remarriage: A Risk and Resiliency Perspective*, Mahwah, NJ: Lawrence Erlbaum Associates, pp. 117–45.

McLanahan, S.S. and Sandefur, G. (1994) *Growing Up With a Single Parent*, Cambridge, MA: Harvard University Press.

Miller, D.T. (1977) 'Altruism and threat to a belief in a just world', *Journal of Experimental Social Psychology*, 13: 113–24.

Piaget, J. (1932) *Le Judgement Moral Chez L'enfant*, Alcan: Paris.

Piaget, J (1952) *The Origins of Intelligence in Children*, New York: International Universities Press.

42   H. Sallay and C. Dalbert

Richey, H.W. and Richey, M.H. (1978) 'Attribution in the classroom: How just is the just world?', *Psychology in the Schools*, 15: 216–22.

Ross, H.S., Filyer, R.E., Lollis, S.P., Perlman, M. and Martin, J.L. (1994) 'Administering justice in the family', *Journal of Family Psychology*, 8: 254–73.

Rubin, Z. and Peplau, A. (1973) 'Belief in a just world and reactions to another's lot: A study of participants in a national draft lottery', *Journal of Social Issues*, 29: 73–93.

Runyin, N. and Jackson, P.L. (1988) 'Divorce: Its impact on children', *Perspectives in Psychiatric Care*, 24: 243–54.

Sallay, H. and Dalbert, C. (2002) 'Women's perception of parenting: A German–Hungarian comparison', *Applied Psychology in Hungary*, 3–4: 55–65.

Sallay, H. and Münnich, Á. (1999) 'Családi nevelési attitûdök percepciója és self-fejlõdéssel való összefüggbései' [Relations between the perception of child rearing practices and self-development], *Magyar Pedagógia*, 2: 157–75.

Schlegel, A. and Barry, H. (1991) *Adolescence: An Anthropological Inquiry*, New York: Free Press.

Sherwood, W.J. and Siegel, J.P. (1989) 'Marital disruption and physical illness: The impact of divorce and spouse death on illness', *Journal of Traumatic Stress*, 2: 555–62.

Simmons, C.H. and Lerner, M.J. (1968) 'Altruism as a search for justice', *Journal of Personality and Social Psychology*, 9: 157–75.

Stephan, C.W. and Holahan, C.K. (1982) 'The influence of status and sex-typing on assessments of occupational outcome', *Sex Roles*, 8: 823–33.

4 Transmission of the belief in a just world in the family

Ute Schönpflug and Ludwig Bilz

Introduction

The development of the belief in a just world

The just-world hypothesis first developed by Lerner (1965) has stimulated much research in the realm of social orientations. Only ten years later Rubin and Peplau (1975) developed a scale to measure the belief in a just world (BJW) as an attitudinal continuum extending between two poles of total acceptance and total rejection of the notion that the world is a just place. They analyse the development of the BJW from three perspectives. From a cultural point of view that conveys the view that children in Western societies grow up with the explicit message (in fairy tales, in Christian and Jewish religion) that this world is a just place. This BJW has motivational implications for the developing child. Children will begin a 'personal contract' (Rubin and Peplau, 1975: 74) with themselves that enables them to invest in long-term activities. The basis of this contract to postpone gratification or reinforcements is a growing BJW. From a cognitive developmental point of view Piaget's concept of *immanent justice* (1965) is a precursor of this general BJW. There is evidence (Medinnus, 1959; Weisz, 1980) that the tendency to attribute meaning to non-causal contingent events and their interpretation as either positively or negatively reinforcing decreases with age. In addition, it will be shaped by personal experiences of injustice (Rubin and Peplau, 1975) or by the increasing insight into chance governing the coincidences of many events (Dalbert, 2001). Dalbert assumes that in the secondary school age a transformation takes place of the 'belief in immanent justice' into the more mature BJW. The BJW may thus compensate for the unpleasant experiences of a world dominated by chance.

Furnham (1993) observed BJW in twelve societies all over the world. Nearly 1700 psychology students from 12 countries completed the Rubin and Peplau (1975) Belief in a Just World Scale. The scale has two components: belief in a just world and belief in an unjust world. There were predictable differences with regard to societies in both components. Both

44   *U. Schönpflug and L. Bilz*

rank-ordered just world and unjust world scores correlated significantly and positively with Hofstede's (1984) cultural dimension of power-distance, whereas rank ordered unjust world scores correlated negatively with individualism. A stable hierarchy in a society in which persons have their positions is associated with believing in a just world. Individualism is also associated with an increase in BJW and, consequently, in countries with a high level of individualism (e.g. the USA) BJW is also relatively high.

The transmission of the belief in a just world in the family

The BJW exhibits individual differences that have to be analysed. Dalbert (1999, 2001) investigated whether factors other than those associated with cognitive development impact on the development of the BJW. Thus, she looked into familial socialisation strategies and their influence on the emerging BJW. In accordance with Grusec and Goodnow's (1994) sociali-sation model, Dalbert found that observational learning rather than explicit instruction could be a mechanism for the transmission of the BJW in the family.

In a study including 105 'intact' families (child, mother, father; average age of children $M = 11.6$ years) Dalbert (2001; see also Dalbert and Radant in this volume) investigated the direct similarity between parents' and children's BJW as well as the moderating effect of family climate on the intensity of the similarity of the belief in a just world in the family. No *direct* association between parental and filial BJW was found. The BJW of the children correlated neither with father's nor with mother's BJW. Dalbert concluded that the BJW is not transmitted directly, i.e. via direct instruction by the parents.

The *indirect effect* of the family climate on the similarity of the BJW in parents and children was tested by means of regression analyses, including moderators. The results revealed a positive and significant relationship between child's and father's BJW when fathers described the family climate as emotional (a harmonious family life, low control, no inconsistent parenting strategies). However, as this effect was not observed when children reported their family's climate to be harmonious, Dalbert does not generalise the moderating impact of family climate on parent–child similarity. But there were some hints in her research that supported the moderating role of family climate in the formation of similarity: in the study cited above and in an additional retrospective study with 247 female students a positive correlation was observed between personal BJW and an emotionally positive family climate.

In an additional retrospective research, Sallay and Dalbert (2001; see also Sallay and Dalbert in this volume) examined whether the BJW was dependent on the educational strategies utilised by parents of intact famil-ies. Subjects were 217 students who were asked to recall their parents' edu-cational strategies. In their regression analyses an inconsistent educational

Transmission of the BJW in the family 45

style was a predictor of a low general belief in a just world. Dalbert and Radant's research does not support the assumption of a direct link of transmission of the BJW from parental to filial generation. There is some evidence, however, that characteristics of the parental educational style (consistency, conformity) and of family climate (emotionality, fairness) influence children's degree of their BJW.

The transmission process and the role of transmission mechanisms

This study aims at exploring the role of transmission mechanisms (Schönpflug, 2001a, b) that enhance transmission of the BJW from generation to generation within a given culture. Cultural reproduction is essentially a question of transmission, the passing on of beliefs, norms and other information from individual to individual or from generation to generation. The roots of thinking about cultural transmission as opposed to genetic transmission are located in biology. The biologist Cavalli-Sforza (1993; Cavalli-Sforza and Feldman, 1981) wrote a seminal book on the specific phenomena related to cultural as opposed to biological transmission. The term 'cultural' applies to traits that are acquired by any process of non-genetic transmission, whether by imprinting, conditioning, observation and imitation or as a result of direct teaching. Cavalli-Sforza (1993) pointed out that genetic transmission might not be the only source for parent–offspring biological similarity. Social orientations, skills and accumulated knowledge are also similar in parent–offspring dyads and – as far as the scientific insights of today hold – are not tied to genes. Hence, other mechanisms of transmission must be found in order to explain this kind of social or psychological similarity between successive generations.

Boyd and Richerson (1985) understand culture as being transmitted from one generation to the next via teaching and imitation of knowledge, of values and of other factors that influence behaviour. Some findings suggest that vertical (parent–offspring) as opposed to horizontal (peer) transmission serves the function of spreading less primitive cultural units, and that horizontally transmitted traits are advantageous in rapidly changing, spatially heterogeneous environments. Evolutionary intergenerational thinking extends this thinking by looking at investments in progeny over more than one subsequent generation.

Sociologists look at transmission issues from a cultural capital point of view. Recent work by Brinton (1988) suggested that education and family make up a conjoint system of human development. She sees this system as having a social-institutional dimension and a familial dimension of exchanges and investments. Bourdieu's (1984) notion of cultural capital suggests a general description of what is transmitted. Families and schools work in concert to ensure the educational advantages of some groups, while the disadvantaged position of other groups remains. A conjoint

46   *U. Schönpflug and L. Bilz*

system of cultural capital transmission requires us to consider the complex relationships between families, school types, educational experiences, and educational outcomes (e.g. Persell *et al.*, 1992). Nauck (2001) emphasises that the transmission of cultural capital is a special process when it takes place in a culture contact situation. In addition, sociological analyses are aware that the results of the intergenerational transmission have to be separated from societal changes. Parents and offspring similarity is influenced to a certain extent by the 'zeitgeist' of the historic epoch they are living in as well as by transmission processes (Boehnke, 2001).

This study is predominantly interested in variables that affect the extent and selectivity of transmission, e.g. the 'transmission mechanisms' (Schönpflug, 2001a, b). Rudy and Grusec (2001) point to the interaction of cultural context with the effectiveness of transmission mechanisms: authoritarian parenting is an ineffective transmission mechanism in individualistic cultures, but enhances transmission in a collective culture, as it is associated with parental warmth.

The carriers of transmission

Different social systems or cultures weigh various possible transmitters or models in the transmission process differentially: mother, father, teacher, peers differ in their importance for the cultural transmission of certain behaviours or traits. Concordance among transmitters with reference to the transmitted contents ensures the greatest transmission effects. Knafo and Schwartz (2001) demonstrated that the similarity between successive generations of migrants is less than that of the families already in the receiving society, due in part to perceived inconsistencies and uncertainty of orientation of the transmitting parents. Ter Bogt *et al.* (2001) demonstrated that the recipient of the transmission, the offspring generation, has a potent selective filter enhancing transmission from the parent generation, i.e. being a non-youth-centrist or adult-oriented generation. These attitudes may be corroborated by acceptance of parents as models. Different cultural contexts provide (a) different model(s) or favour (b) one particular model for copying.

The contents of transmission

Important theoretical approaches to cultural transmission (Boyd and Richerson, 1985; Cavalli-Sforza and Feldman, 1981; Cavalli-Sforza, 1993) offer evidence that the various 'channels' or directions of transmission (vertical, horizontal and oblique) transport different transmission contents. The vertical transmission from parent to child includes traits such as: personality traits, cognitive development, attitudes, attainments of educational and occupational status, upward/downward mobility, patterns of socialisation, sex-role conceptions, sexual activity, attitudes toward feminism, political beliefs and activities, religious beliefs, dietary habits and legal and illegal drug abuse, phobias, self-esteem, language and linguistic usage. Horizontally (via peers) and obliquely channels (via adults other than parents) transmit traits which include attitudes, career and social mobility, aspirations, sex-role and sexual behaviour, adolescent behaviour, aggressive behaviour, altruistic behaviour, morals, social values, conformity, language and dialect, technological innovations, clothing fashions, consumer behaviour, children's games, rituals, stories and rhymes. As may be learned from these lists many traits are transmitted in either way. Other traits follow a dual inheritance model, i.e. genetic and cultural transmission: handedness, cerebral dominance, intelligence and possibly religious and political beliefs (Laland, 1993).

The role of transmission mechanisms

Research findings from the transmission of values, beliefs and lifestyles frequently show little direct transmission. Also, in these domains only low similarity between parents and children was found with analyses including direct paths (Kohn, 1983). The search for factors mediating or moderating the similarity proved to be more successful: the search for transmission mechanisms or moderators of transmission (e.g. Rohan and Zanna, 1996; Schönpflug, 2001b) provided evidence for effective interventions in the transmission process; 'transmission mechanisms' are characteristics of parents and children, the family or their social contexts that enhance transmission. If the BJW is a possible content of intergenerational transmission then the same transmission mechanisms as found for values, beliefs and lifestyles may be operating in this transmission process.

Two further factors that may play a decisive role in socialisation models are acceptance of parents as models of behaviour and professional adaptation to a discontinuously changing societal context. In the theoretical approach of Grusec and Goodnow (1994) the acceptance and the correct perception of parental messages are basic for the efficiency of educational strategies. Darling and Steinberg (1993) determined openness for parental influence as a crucial transmission mechanism. Discontinuous societal contexts are given through migration to another country or transformation of societal structures. Not only do children adapt more rapidly to new contexts than their parents, also, parents may be less motivated to transmit their social orientations, as they feel insecure in their orientations. They may feel that their orientations are inadequate for the changing context.

Developmental perspective on transmission

The effects of transmission mechanisms may be confounded with developmental phenomena, namely the existence of biologically founded 'critical

48   *U. Schönpflug and L. Bilz*

periods', such as are known, for example, in the acquisition of the pronunciation of a language. But there probably exist a host of other age-dependent sensitivities in acquiring specific behaviours or cognitions via transmission. The developmental task of becoming an autonomous person predominates in adolescence. In this stage, transmission attempts from the side of the parents may be less effective than at other times because of high resistance on the children's side during this developmental period.

Furthermore, the mode of transmission may be age-specific because of normative developmental transitions in the socio-cultural context: obligatory full-day schooling, for instance, implies that children are among their peers for long hours during the day. This is a favourable condition for horizontal (peer-to-child) and oblique (non-parent-to-child) transmission and a less favourable one for vertical transmission (parent-to-child).

Hypotheses

This study tries to add some new aspects to the body of research on transmission. It aims at clarifying the role of three transmission mechanisms for the transmission of the BJW: acceptance of parents as models, concordance of parental beliefs in a just world and adaptation to the labour force in the changing society of the reunified Germany. Based on previous research findings we hypothesise that (a) acceptance of parents as models enhances the transmission of the BJW from parents to children. As already known since Bandura's social learning theory of observational learning, models with high authority and credibility are more accepted by learners than models lacking those features (Bandura, 1969). If parents have socially desirable features such as good education and good placement in the societal structure they are more likely to influence their children successfully. The acceptance of the BJW by children from their parents may be associated with a general acceptance of parents as models of behaviour.

According to Cavalli-Sforza and Feldman (1981), similarity of attitudes, beliefs or values in parents leads to a greater transmission rate. Analysing social science data they were able to demonstrate that the transmission of religious and political attitudes from mother and father to children was enhanced when parents had similar strong attitudes. Parents with discordant attitudes or attitudes of low intensity were less efficient transmitters. A second aim of this study was to confirm the finding that concordance in parental attitudes enhances transmission with regard to the BJW: (b) parental concordance in positive affirmative BJW enhances the transmission of the BJW from parents to their children.

A third transmission mechanism was included that was expected to enhance transmission of the BJW, i.e. the experience of one's own adaptation to the labour market after the reunification of the country. The level of the BJW and its transmission may be low in such unstable social states as

Transmission of the BJW in the family 49

existed after the reunification of Germany. In line with previous research (Phalet and Schönpflug, 2001; Knafo and Schwartz, 2001) with immigrant families discontinuity in the social context is expected to reduce the motivation of the parents for transmission and also the openness of the children to accept transmission efforts, hence less transmission should take place and consequently less similarity should be observed. The third hypothesis is formulated for the third transmission mechanism, the parental adaptation to the labour market in a discontinuously changing society. It may be expected that (c) the positivity of the parental experience of their own adaptation to the labour market is a transmission mechanism that increases transmission of the BJW from parent to child. Success on the labour market is a highly desirable feature. The parents' social status is associated with being placed in the labour market of the societal context. Successful parents have thus higher probability to be accepted as models by their children, and may thus be more successful transmitters of their social orientations. In addition, they may feel that their social orientations are adequate and develop greater motivation to transmit them as compared to less successfully adapting parents. These hypotheses were tested in an East German social context, twelve years after the reunification of Germany.

Method

Samples

The investigation was part of the cross-cultural project 'Transmission of values in immigrant and German families'. Data collection took place from June to December 2000 in the city of Halle (Saale) in East Germany and adjacent regions. In total, 289 families with complete questionnaire sets (child, mother, father) were analysed in the study. The main data were collected in five secondary or middle and six high schools in grades nine and ten. The school tracks differ with regard to the level of education they offer: the secondary or middle school starts at age 12 and finishes at age 16, the high school starts at age 12 and finishes at age 19 with an exam that serves as an entrance qualification to university education. The sample of school students with complete families amounted to 212 students (33.1 per cent male and 65.8 per cent female students), 201 had no missing parts in the questionnaire. The average age of the school students' mothers was 42.2 years ($SD = 5.8$), that of the fathers was 44.4 years ($SD = 6.9$). The adolescents were between 14 and 17 years old ($M = 15.3$ years, $SD = 0.84$) from grades 9 and 10, corresponding to the 9th and 10th years of schooling. Additionally, a college students sample was recruited that included $n = 88$ with complete family data. Most of them were psychology students (35.2 per cent male, 64.8 per cent female; average age $M = 21.1$, $SD = 2.6$) of the Martin Luther University of Halle-Wittenberg

50   *U. Schönpflug and L. Bilz*

and their parents. The age ranges were 19 ($n = 31$), 20–21 ($n = 24$) and 22–24 years ($n = 33$).

Procedure

The adolescents were contacted in their schools. Those students who wanted to participate were grouped together in a separate room during school hours. They completed a structured questionnaire of 20 pages in about 60 to 90 minutes under the supervision of two researchers. After the session, the researchers handed each student an envelope containing two complementary questionnaires for the parents. The students were asked to give the envelope to their parents. After completion, the two parental questionnaires with their family code number were enclosed in the envelope and brought back to school, where the researchers collected them.

Measures

Belief in a just world

The questionnaire included the General Belief in a Just World Scale (Dalbert, Montada and Schmitt, 1987). The scale consists of six items (e.g. 'I think basically the world is a just place') of the Likert type with six response activities ranging from 1 ('not true at all') to 6 ('very true') – values from 2 to 5 had no value label. Internal consistency was Alpha = 0.76 for the adolescent group, for their fathers Alpha = 0.84 and for their mothers Alpha = 0.77. The corresponding values for the young adult group was Alpha = 0.77 for the students, Alpha = 0.78 for their fathers, and Alpha = 0.77 for their mothers.

Acceptance of parents as models

An eight-item scale to measure the acceptance of parents as models was developed by Bilz (2001; sample item 'In many respects my parents are a model for me'). A principal component analysis with a one-factor constraint identified one factor explaining 40.39 per cent of the variance. The scale yielded an Alpha of 0.78 for the adolescent sample and an Alpha of 0.82 for the college sample. The scale measures to what extent parents are accepted by their children as models for attitudes, behaviour and lifestyle. The scale had four response possibilities ranging from 1 ('describes it very poorly') to 4 ('describes it very well').

Adaptation to the labour market after reunification of Germany

One question concerning the experience of one's own placement on the labour market after reunification as compared to before was included in both parents' questionnaires. Twelve years after reunification each parent was asked: 'Is your present job better, equal to or worse as compared to the time before the reunification of Germany?' Responses could be given by choosing between three answers: 1 ('worse'), 2 ('equal') and 3 ('better').

Results

Intensity of belief in a just world in different groups

A single analysis for all subsamples (adolescent school samples, college sample) was not possible, as age and subsample were confounded. Therefore, a four-factor analysis of variance based on the adolescent subsamples with repeated measurements was performed. It included father's, mother's and child's BJW as the within-subject factor family role, age of child (15, 16 years of age), school track (secondary or high school) and gender as three between-subject factors. Only the main effect of family role was significant ($F(1,195) = 5.71$, $p < 0.05$), indicating that the BJW of the children exceeded that of their parents: $M = 2.81$, $SD = 0.95$ for the adolescents, $M = 2.38$, $SD = 0.92$ for their fathers, and $M = 2.27$, $SD = 0.84$ for their mothers, respectively. The post-hoc mean comparisons (t-tests) for dependent samples yielded the following t-values: father–mother $t = 1.72$, $p < 0.05$, father–child $t = -5.82$, $p < 0.001$, mother–child $t = -8.23$, $p < 0.001$. There were no significant interactions.

For the college students sample a similar analysis of variance was performed on the basis of the three age groups (19 years, 20–21 years, 22–24 years) and gender as two between-subject factors and family roles as the within-subject factor. Again the analysis of variance resulted in a significant family role effect ($F(1,80) = 12.18$, $p < 0.001$), but in addition there were two significant interactions: family role × gender ($F(1,88) = 4.04$, $p < 0.05$) and family role × age group ($F(1,88) = 3.05$, $p < 0.05$). The corresponding means are depicted in Figures 4.1 and 4.2.

Figure 4.1 shows the gender distribution of the ratings of BJW for the three family roles. Male college students' mothers and fathers held a higher BJW than female students' parents. But female students themselves held higher BJW than the male students. Post-hoc single-mean comparisons for the family roles in the male and female samples were not significant. Figure 4.2 shows the mean BJW of the three family roles in the three age groups. Although the means for the three family roles showed a decreasing trend with increasing age, only in the youngest age group did the means of the family role pairs differ significantly from each other as t-tests for dependent samples revealed: father–mother difference $t = 2.12$, $p < 0.05$, father–child difference $t = 2.15$, $p < 0.05$.

Finally, a direct age comparison of the high school students group and the college students group was performed. The higher-level school sample was selected to control for educational level, as in Germany the students can proceed to a university degree only with a high school degree. In this

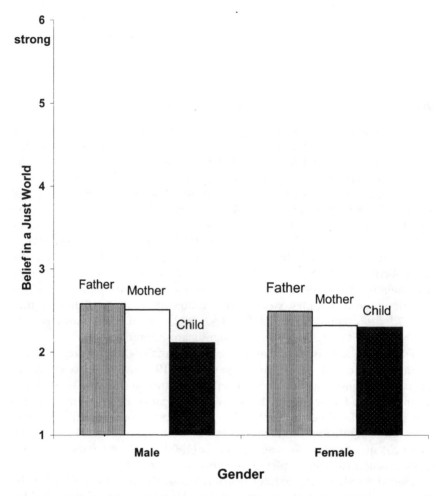

Figure 4.1 Female and male students' own and their parents' belief in a just world (college students sample).

analysis of variance the two between-subject factors were age group (college students vs. high school students) and gender, the within-subject factor was again family role. The analysis yielded a significant family role main effect ($F(1,197) = 7.12$, $p<0.01$; $M=2.42$, $SD=0.92$ for fathers, $M=2.27$, $SD=0.80$ for mothers, and $M=2.49$, $SD=0.88$ for the child); and a significant family role × age group interaction ($F(1,197) = 19.40$, $p<0.001$). The corresponding values for the school students were $M=2.33$, $SD=0.90$ for the fathers, $M=2.17$, $SD=0.77$ for the mothers, and $M=2.69$, $SD=0.88$ for the child; the corresponding values for the students were: $M=2.51$, $SD=0.94$ for the fathers, $M=2.36$, $SD=0.83$ for the mothers, and $M=2.28$, $SD=0.87$ for the child.

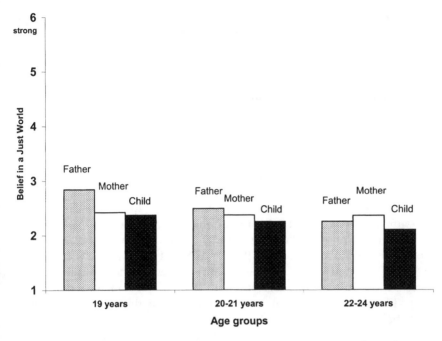

Figure 4.2 Belief in a just world of father, mother and child as dependent on child's age (college students sample).

To summarise these results. We learn from these analyses that the children's level of BJW surpassed that of their parents in the school students' sample, but not in the college students' sample. Fathers of college students held the highest BJW. Within this sample this held only true for the fathers of 19-year-old students. The levels of BJW were closer between the two parents than those between parent and child. The level of BJW in the family, above all that of the children, was higher when children went to a lower-level school track as compared to a higher-level school type. In addition, the older the children, the less they believed in a just world. Only in the college students sample was there a gender effect: the family roles revealed higher levels of beliefs in families with male students as compared to female students. However, the daughters held higher BJW than the sons. Otherwise, in the school students' sample and in the college students' sample there was no significant gender effect for children.

Concordance of parental belief in a just world as transmission mechanism

In accordance with Cavalli-Sforza and Feldman (1981), the means of the scale values of mothers, fathers and their child were subtracted from their respective scale values (mother: $M = 2.19$, father: $M = 2.37$, adolescent child: $M = 2.62$) for the school students sample. Positive resultant values represented high BJW (H) and negative resultant values represented low BJW (h). The rows in Table 4.1 represent the four possible combinations of the parental BJW (H × H, h × h, H × h, h × H). For each of the parental combinations the level of the child's BJW is given in the same dichotomised form (H or h) and, in addition, the mean value of the child with parents in any of the four groups. The concordant combinations (H × H or h × h) were more frequent ($n = 124$) than the discordant ones (H × h or h × H) ($n = 68$).

In support of our hypothesis (b) the child's BJW depended on the concordance of the parental attitudes: in the H × H group there was a majority of children with a BJW of more than average intensity (H = 35 vs. h = 17) and in the h × h group children with lower intensity prevail (h = 45 vs. H = 27). Parents with discordant attitudes were not as frequent as parents with concordant attitudes, and their offspring was as likely to hold intensive as well as low BJW: for H × h: H = 12 and h = 19 and for h × H: h = 18 and H = 19. No significance test was made for the frequency distribution; instead the corresponding means were analysed (see Table 4.1). To test for significant mean differences of the child's intensity of BJW between the four groups, a one-way analysis of variance was performed with both parents' concordance of BJW (H × H, h × h, H × h, h × H) as independent and the child's BJW as the dependent variable. The effect of concordance of parental attitudes was significant ($F(3,188) = 6.28$, $p < 0.001$). A post-hoc Scheffé test ($p < 0.05$) yielded a significant mean difference between the child's BJW in the H × H compared to the other three groups. Thus, children for whom both parents believed strongly in a just world also hold a significantly stronger BJW than children of the other three groups. Hypothesis (b) is thus corroborated.

Table 4.1 Child's belief in a just world as dependent on parental concordance of their belief in a just world

Parental BJW	Child's BJW				
Father × Mother	H	h	M	SD	n
H × H[a]	35	17	3.08	0.92	52
h × h[b]	27	45	2.41	0.90	72
H × h	12	19	2.49	0.97	31
h × H	18	19	2.50	0.83	37

Notes
a high BJW.
b low BJW.

Transmission of the BJW in the family 55

Belief in a just world and adaptation to a discontinuous social context

The intensity of the experience of a discontinuously changing context in the East of Germany after the reunification with West Germany resulted in different levels of BJW, as the corresponding two analysis of variance – run with the school students sample of 201 children and their parents – showed. The analysis of variance included either fathers' evaluation of their job adaptation or mothers' with three levels (worse than, equal to or better than before the reunification), the three samples (secondary, high school and college), family role and gender as between-subject factors with age as a covariate. The evaluation factor for fathers resulted in a significant main effect ($F(2,250) = 4.82$, $p<0.01$). The corresponding means were $M=2.25$, $SD=0.83$; $M=2.38$, $SD=0.87$; $M=2.58$, $SD=0.93$ for worse, no change or better, respectively. The means revealed that averaged over all three family roles the fathers' evaluation of his job adaptation as worse, no change or better compared to before the reunification of Germany had an influence on the BJW of all three family members: the increasing positive evaluation of the father led to an increasing BJW for all three family members. There were no other significant effects involving fathers' evaluation of job as a factor. Mothers' evaluation of job adaptation after the reunion of the two German states also had a main effect ($F(2,244) = 4.65$, $p<0.01$). The corresponding means for worse, no change or better averaged over father, mother and the child's BJW were: $M=2.36$, $SD=0.93$; $M=2.47$, $SD=0.87$ and $M=2.59$, $SD=0.82$, respectively. For mothers' adaptation to the job situation after the reunion, there was, in addition, a significant influence of family role in interaction with mother's evaluation ($F(1,244) = 5.63$, $p<0.001$). The effect was based on mothers' differential reaction to the experience after the reunification concerning their job adaptation: $M=2.08$, $SD=0.82$ for mothers' own BJW when they thought that their job situation was worse than before the reunification, $M=2.37$, $SD=0.88$ when they thought there was no change, and $M=2.47$, $SD=0.83$ when they thought it was better. Again the post-hoc Scheffé tests revealed that the worse and the better condition differed significantly in their means. This was not found for the child's or the father's BJW. For mothers' evaluation, there was also a significant interaction of evaluation $\times$ gender $\times$ group ($F(4,244) = 2.80$, $p<0.05$). As post-hoc Scheffé tests revealed, this effect was only due to a reversal of the usual increasing pattern in mothers' own BJW as a reaction to their evaluation of their job experience for mothers of male secondary school students. The means were $M=1.81$, $SD=0.83$ for worse, $M=2.50$, $SD=0.89$ for better and $M=2.77$, $SD=0.91$ for no change. Only the means for 'worse' and 'equal' differed significantly for mothers' own BJW.

56   *U. Schönpflug and L. Bilz*

Adaptation to a discontinuous social context and acceptance of parents as models as moderator of transmission

Direct transmission of the BJW will be analysed by means of moderated regression of the child's BJW on the parental BJW. According to Larson and Almeida (1999) the beta-weights were interpreted as transmission coefficients. A multiple regression analysis allows us to partial out the effect of other variables that may influence the size of the transmission coefficient. Thus, variables that are known to influence the transmission coefficient in the case of the BJW transmission, e.g. age, gender and school track, were introduced as controlling variables into the multiple regression. Moreover, acceptance of the parents (AP) and adaptation to the labour market (AL) were introduced as moderators of the direct transmission of the BJW in separated regression analyses.

In the first analyses, acceptance of the parents (AP) was introduced as a moderator. In stepwise multiple regressions for fathers and mothers separately, in the first step the impact of BJW, acceptance of parents (AP), age of child, gender of child and group (two school tracks and college) were introduced, whereas in the second step acceptance of the parents as moderator of the influence of the parents' BJW (BJW × AP) was tested. Due to the high correlation of the AP variable with the interaction term BJW × AP, AP was trichotomised and in this transformed way was also introduced into the interaction term. This measure reduced the multicollinearity problem to an acceptable extent. Table 4.2 shows the results of two multiple regressions including the child's BJW as criterion and mother's (column 3) or father's BJW (column 1) as the source of the direct transmission.

The results indicate direct transmission from both parents to their child: $beta = 0.17$ for fathers and $beta = 0.13$ for mothers, both coefficients significant at $p < 0.05$. But these transmission effects were moderated by acceptance of parents for both parents: $beta = 0.15$ for fathers and $beta = 0.14$ for mothers (both $p < 0.05$). The R^2 changes of 0.01 for the gain of variance explained by the interaction term were small, however, for both mother and father analyses. Except for the group factor ($beta = -0.25$ for fathers and $beta = -0.24$ for mothers, both $p < 0.001$) no other main effect was significant. The overall R^2 for both analyses was also low. The child's BJW was only explained to the extent of 11 to 14 per cent by the predictors included in the analyses, including the control variables.

We may conclude from the results of these first transmission analyses that there is direct transmission of BJW from both parents separately on the child's BJW when controlled for acceptance of parents and the child's age, gender and school track and when parental BJW is moderated by children's acceptance of their parents. The father's impact seems to be somewhat stronger than the mother's. Acceptance of parents may thus be understood as one of the many 'transmission mechanisms' found in other transmission research (e.g. Phalet and Schönpflug, 2001; Schönpflug, 2001b).

Table 4.2 Multiple regressions of the child's belief in a just world (BJW) on father's and mother's belief in a just world: Direct transmission coefficients (beta of BJW) and moderated transmission coefficients (beta BJW × AP or BJW × AL)

	Child's BJW			
	Father		Mother	
Main effects				
Parents' BJW	0.17*	0.11	0.13*	0.23*
Acceptance of the parent (AP)	0.05	–	0.04	–
Adaptation to the labour market (AL)		−0.06	–	0.02
Age	−0.02	−0.04	−0.09	−0.10
Gender[a]	−0.07	−0.06	−0.06	−0.06
Group[b]	−0.25***	−0.26***	−0.24***	−0.24**
R^2	0.13	0.13	0.10	0.10
Interaction effects				
BJW × AP	0.15*	–	0.14*	–
BJW × AL	–	0.19*	–	−0.02
R^2	0.14	0.14	0.11	0.10
R^2-change	0.01	0.01	0.01	0.00

Notes
* $p < 0.05$.
** $p < 0.01$.
*** $p < 0.001$.
a 1 = male; 2 = female.
b 1 = secondary school; 2 = high school; 3 = college.

The second transmission mechanism tested was adaptation to the labour market after the reunification of Germany. Again, two multiple regression analyses similar to those described above were performed for mother and father separately, with adaptation to the labour market (AL) included as moderator. Mothers' BJW had a direct impact on their child's BJW (*beta* = 0.23, $p < 0.001$), but revealed no moderated transmission as indicated by the insignificant interaction effect (*beta* = −0.02). Evaluation of own adaptation to the labour market, age and gender of the child had no significant main effects for mothers. School track of the child was significant (*beta* = −0.24, $p < 0.001$) revealing that the higher the educational level the lower the child's BJW.

For fathers no significant direct transmission coefficient was found (*beta* = 0.11, $p > 0.05$), but there was a significant interaction term (*beta* = 0.19, $p < 0.05$) indicating that fathers transmitted their BJW more effectively when they positively evaluated their adaptation to the labour market after the reunification of Germany. The interaction only added one per cent explanatory power to that of the variable pool (13 per cent). The group factor school track was also significant in the analysis of the fathers (*beta* = −0.26, $p < 0.001$).

58   *U. Schönpflug and L. Bilz*

These results support the hypothesis (a) stating that the acceptance of parents as models on the side of the children is a transmission mechanism for both fathers and mothers. They also corroborate partly hypothesis (c) that adaptation to the labour market after the reunification is a moderator in the transmission process of the BJW. However, parental adaptation to the labour market is an effective enhancing moderator for fathers only. Mothers revealed only a direct transmission effect in the corresponding analysis.

Discussion

This study aimed at clarifying whether there is any transmission of the social orientation of the BJW from parent to child in the social context of a socio-politically discontinuous environment, and what kind of transmission mechanisms may be identified. Vertical transmission from parent to child guarantees intergenerational continuity and prevents intergenerational gaps. Intergenerational gaps may be deleterious to the handing down of cultural wisdom, including social orientations, and skills. In addition, this study looked at the effects of three transmission mechanisms: at 'acceptance of parents as models', at 'concordance in level of BJW between both parents' and at 'parents' adaptation to the labour market' in the transformation process after the reunification of Germany.

The basic question of the transmission of the BJW from either parent to child may be answered positively. In all three subsamples – secondary school, high school and college students – analysed together in this study there were significant transmission coefficients for fathers' and mothers' BJW, either in a non-moderated way (for mothers when adaptation to the labour market was included as moderator) or when moderated (for fathers when adaptation to the labour market was the moderator) or when moderated and non-moderated transmission occurred together (for mothers and fathers when acceptance of parents was included as a moderator). In general, we may conclude that the BJW is transmitted intergenerationally within the family even in the discontinuous social context that occurred in East Germany with reunification. Although the previous political system based on communism and socialism had failed to fulfil the people's needs, parents believed in a just world and wanted to communicate to their children their own beliefs. The sizes of the transmission coefficients are comparable to those obtained with other contents of transmission in other samples (e.g. Kohn, 1983; Rohan and Zanna, 1996; Schönpflug, 2001a, b; Whitbeck and Gecas, 1988).

However, Dalbert and Radant (in this volume) did not find any correlation between parents' and their children's BJW. A possible reason for their finding of no transmission of the BJW in the family may be the age of the children included in their study. The children in their sample have an average age of 11 years, whereas our students in the school samples are

Transmission of the BJW in the family 59

15 to 16 years old: as we find significant transmission coefficients we may conclude that the transmission process seems to get more effective with the age of the children. When analysed separately the transmission coefficient increased in our samples from mid-adolescence to young adulthood. This has to be interpreted, however, in the light of the finding that as children grow older they approach their parents' scepticism with regard to justice in this world. If no strategies or efforts on the parents' side may be identified that make clear that the similarity between parents and children is the result of these strategies and efforts, then the similarity may also be seen as the outcome of cognitive development of the adolescent children into adulthood: cognitive development at this stage adapts to the experience that chance and meaningless contiguities may be the 'cause' of events experienced.

Aboud (1988) concluded from a review of antecedent conditions of similarity between parents and children that there is little parental influence when children are very young; the influence increases, however, with increasing age of the children. Aboud declares that the understanding and internalisation of social attitudes functions in late childhood and early adolescence. In addition, the data collected within the scope of this study reveal an age effect when the school sample is compared to the college sample. The comparison of only the high-school students' sample with the college sample provides a fair ground for concluding an age effect in the increasing effectiveness of transmission of the BJW. Why should transmission be more intense in families of college students? As adolescence is a period of individuation and autonomy, both these tendencies may result in less acceptance of parental influences. In young adulthood these features have stabilised, and, in addition, college students may feel closer to their parents because their parents usually support them emotionally and economically at an age when their peers are already earning their own living.

One important new result of this study is the balanced position of the two parents in the transmission process of the BJW. Both analyses of the father as transmitter showed moderator effects, those of the mother just in the case of acceptance of parents as moderator. On the other hand, for fathers there seems to be no direct transmission effect, when evaluation of their adaptation after the reunification of Germany was introduced as the moderator. We may only speculate about the father's influence in the transmission process: the social and economic opportunities of complete families in Germany still depend more on the fathers' resources and the concomitant attitudes and social orientations than on the mothers'. If the father holds a more resourceful position his concomitant BJW will be more convincing to the child than the mother's, because conventional thinking of the social context supports this. Indeed, our mean differences show that fathers who evaluated their adaptation to the socio-economic context after the reunification of Germany positively also revealed higher

60   *U. Schönpflug and L. Bilz*

BJW. The father's positive evaluation of his own socio-economic status also had a significant effect on the child's level of BJW. This was not observed for the mother's evaluation. No matter how positive she evaluated her own position in the labour market after reunification as compared to before, the child held an indiscriminately high level of BJW. Consequently, in the transmission analysis we found no moderator effect for her evaluation.

There is no dominance of the father in the transmission process of the BJW when parental BJW is moderated by the child's acceptance of parents. According to the analyses for the two samples of school students and the college students together the moderating effect of acceptance of parents as models balances the transmission effect between parents, whereas the moderating effect of adaptation to the labour market after reunification polarises the differential effect of direct transmission for both father and mother. However, the interactions only explained one per cent additional variance as compared to the group of main effects examined in the first step of the multiple regressions.

The hypothesis that concordance in intensity of parental BJW is a favourable antecedent condition for transmission of a feature is corroborated. Concordance of strong but not a weak belief in both parents leads to strongly believing children. When one parent held strong and the other weak beliefs, or when both parents held a weak belief, the children revealed a lower BJW, as the analysis of the mean levels of child's BJW showed. Cavalli-Sforza and Feldman's (1981; Cavalli-Sforza, 1993) main idea about cultural transmission of social orientations thus seems to be valid when other contents of transmission than those included in Cavalli-Sforza's analyses are examined. The level of BJW in the various subsamples indicates that the BJW might be understood as a sign of lack of cognitive sophistication: younger persons and persons with lower education hold stronger beliefs in a just world. These results are in line with Dalbert's (2001) findings. She interprets them as indicating decline of BJW with growing cognitive maturity and insights into the randomness of this world. On the other hand, successful people like those that have adapted to the labour market in insecure times show stronger BJW. Further analyses should clarify whether an unproblematic feeling of global self-worth or self-efficacy rather than lack of sophistication is a feature of younger and less educated persons and whether global self-worth or self-efficacy is associated with BJW (see e.g. Correia and Vala in this volume).

To conclude, this study provides evidence that age and educational level, but not gender, when other factors are partialled, determine the formation of the BJW. Children's acceptance of their parents as models, the parents' positive evaluation of their adaptation to socio-economic context and their concordance in attitudes with their marital partner are efficient transmission mechanisms. In addition, this study was able to demonstrate that fathers contribute to their child's BJW moderated by

Transmission of the BJW in the family 61

both factors, acceptance of parents as models and adaptation to the labour market, whereas mothers' transmission is moderated by the child's acceptance of parents as models but not by her self-rated adaptation to the labour market after the reunification of Germany.

Transmission is a process and as such is dependent on time. The paradigm chosen here with its cross-sectional measurements does not allow causal interpretations in the strict sense of the notion of causality. The idea of transmission as used here is one of explained variance of a criterion, the child's BJW, by a predictor, the parent's BJW with other plausible predictors partialled. We assume, however, that mechanisms of transmission like explicit or implicit influence attempts on the part of the parent and selective filter mechanisms for acceptance on the part of the child interact to result in parent–child similarity. Exact specification of the mechanisms involved and their enhancement through what kind of transmission mechanisms are still issues to be studied. According to Grusec and Goodnow (1994), one antecedent condition for the child's internalisation of parental features is the child's correct perception of these features. Furthermore, other models than the parents, as e.g. 'forerunners' (Bengtson and Troll, 1978) or outstanding adult persons of a society (oblique transmission) and peer models (horizontal transmission) and their influence on the child with regard to various transmitted content areas and in various contexts should be examined.

The bi-directional influence in the transmission process has been stressed by Kuczynski et al. (1997) and earlier by Bengtson and Troll (1978). In line with their thinking children also transmit to their parents. An extension of this research in this direction is highly desirable and will certainly reveal an important developmental dimension.

References

Aboud, F. (1988) *Children and Prejudice*, Cambridge, MA: Basil Blackwell.

Bandura, A. (1969) 'Social learning theory of the identificatory process', in Goslin, D.A. (ed.), *Handbook of Socialization Theory and Research*, Chicago: Rand McNally.

Bengtson, V. and Troll, L. (1978) 'Youth and their parents: Feedback and intergenerational influence in socialization', in Lerner, R.M. and Spanier, G.B. (eds), *Child Influence on Marital and Family Interaction: A Life Span Perspective*, New York: Academic Press.

Bilz, L. (2001) *Wertetransmission in Familien mit Kindern im Jugendalter*, Unpublished Diploma Thesis, Halle (Saale): Martin Luther University.

Boehnke, K. (2001) 'Parent–offspring value transmission in a societal context: Suggestions for a utopian research design – with empirical underpinnings', *Journal of Cross-Cultural Psychology*, 32: 230–41.

Bourdieu, P. (1984) *Distinction: A Social Critique of the Judgment of Taste*, Cambridge, MA: Harvard University Press.

Boyd, R. and Richerson, P.J. (1985) *Culture and the Evolutionary Process*, Chicago: University of Chicago Press.

62   U. Schönpflug and L. Bilz

Brinton, M.C. (1988) 'The social-institutional bases of gender stratification: Japan as an illustrative case', *American Journal of Sociology*, 94: 300–34.

Cavalli-Sforza, L.L. (1993) 'How are values transmitted?', in Hechter, M., Nadd, L. and Michail, R.E. (eds.), *The Origins of Values. Part III: Biological Perspectives*, New York: Aldine de Gruyter.

Cavalli-Sforza, L.L. and Feldman, M.W. (1981) *Cultural Transmission and Evolution: A Quantitative Approach*, Princeton, NJ: Princeton University Press.

Dalbert, C. (1999) 'The world is more just for me than generally: About the Personal Belief in a Just World Scale's validity', *Social Justice Research*, 12: 79–98.

Dalbert, C. (2001) *The Justice Motive as a Personal Resource: Dealing with Challenges and Critical Life Events*, New York: Kluwer Academic/Plenum Publishers.

Dalbert, C., Montada, L. and Schmitt, M. (1987) 'Glaube an eine gerechte Welt als Motiv: Validierungskorrelate zweier Skalen', *Psychologische Beiträge*, 29: 596–615.

Darling, N. and Steinberg, L. (1993) 'Parenting style as context: An integrative model', *Psychological Bulletin*, 113: 487–96.

Furnham, A. (1993) 'Just world beliefs in twelve societies', *The Journal of Social Psychology*, 133: 317–29.

Grusec, J.E. and Goodnow, J.J. (1994) 'Impact of parental discipline methods on the child's internalization of values: A reconceptualization of current points of view', *Developmental Psychology*, 30: 4–19.

Hofstede, G. (1984) *Culture's Consequences*, London: Sage.

Knafo, A. and Schwartz, S.H. (2001) 'Value socialization in families of Israeli-born and Soviet-born adolescents in Israel', *Journal of Cross-Cultural Psychology*, 32: 213–28.

Kohn, M.L. (1983) 'On the transmission of values in the family: A preliminary formulation', *Research in Sociology of Education and Socialization*, 4: 1–12.

Kuczynski, L., Marshall, S. and Schell, K. (1997) 'Value socialization in a bidirectional context', in Kuczynski, L. and Grusec, J.E. (eds), *Parenting and Children's Internalization of Values*, New York: John Wiley.

Laland, K.N. (1993) 'The mathematical modelling of human culture and its implications for psychology and the human sciences', *British Journal of Psychology*, 84: 145–69.

Larson, R.W. and Almeida, D.M. (1999) 'Emotional transmission in the daily lives of families: A new paradigm for studying family process', *Journal of Marriage and the Family*, 61: 5–20.

Lerner, M. (1965) 'Evaluation of performance as a function of performer's reward and attractiveness', *Journal of Personality and Social Psychology*, 1: 355–60.

Medinnus, G.R. (1959) 'Immanent justice in children: A review of the literature and additional data', *Journal of Genetic Psychology*, 94: 253–62.

Nauck, B. (2001) 'Intercultural contact and intergenerational transmission in immigrant families', *Journal of Cross-Cultural Psychology*, 32: 150–73.

Persell, C.H., Catsambis, S. and Cookson, P.W. (1992) 'Family background, school type, and college attendance: A conjoint system of cultural capital transmission', *Journal of Research on Adolescence*, 2: 1–23.

Phalet, K. and Schönpflug, U. (2001) 'Intergenerational transmission of collectivism and achievement values in two acculturation contexts: The case of Turkish families in Germany and Turkish and Moroccan families in the Netherlands', *Journal of Cross-Cultural Psychology*, 32: 186–201.

Piaget, J. (1965) *The Moral Judgment of the Child*, New York: Free Press.

Transmission of the BJW in the family 63

Rohan, M.J. and Zanna, M.P. (1996) 'Value transmission in families', in Seligman, C., Olson, J.M. and Zanna, M.P. (eds.), *The Psychology of Values: The Ontario Symposium. Vol. 8*, Hillsdale: Lawrence Erlbaum.

Rubin, Z. and Peplau, L.A. (1975) 'Who believes in a just world?', *Journal of Social Issues*, 31: 65–89.

Rudy, D. and Grusec, J.E. (2001) 'Correlates of authoritarian parenting in individualist and collectivist cultures and implications for understanding the transmission of values', *Journal of Cross-Cultural Psychology*, 32: 202–12.

Sallay, H. and Dalbert, C. (2001) 'The development of world beliefs in relation to parental education: The impact of being raised in an one-parent or an intact family', Xth European Conference on Developmental Psychology, Uppsala, Sweden.

Schönpflug, U. (2001a) 'Perspectives on cultural transmission. Introduction: The special issue', *Journal of Cross-Cultural Psychology*, 32: 131–4.

Schönpflug, U. (2001b) 'Intergenerational transmission of values: The role of transmission belts', *Journal of Cross-Cultural Psychology*, 32: 174–85.

Ter Bogt, T.E.M., Meeus, W.H.J., Raaijmakers, Q.A.W. and Vollebergh, W.A.M. (2001) 'Youth centrism and the formation of political orientations in adolescence and young adulthood', *Journal of Cross-Cultural Psychology*, 32: 229–40.

Weisz, J.R. (1980) 'Developmental change in perceived control: Recognizing noncontingency in the laboratory and perceiving it in the world', *Developmental Psychology*, 16: 385–90.

Whitbeck, L.B. and Gecas, V. (1988). 'Value attributions and value transmission between parents and children', *Journal of Marriage and the Family*, 50: 829–40.

5 Transformation of the justice motive?

Belief in a just world and its correlates in different age groups

Jürgen Maes and Manfred Schmitt

This chapter refers to two lines of just world research that might be perceived as contradictory. On the one hand, belief in a just world (BJW) is regarded as a resource that is helpful in providing personal well-being, promoting trust and confidence and enabling engagement in long-term activities. On the other hand, there is a tradition of portraying BJW as part of a rather conservative socio-political ideology connected with the maintenance of prejudice and excluding victims and the socially underprivileged. Both might be true, and they might be differentially true in different stages of life. We will investigate this by comparing the correlates of justice beliefs in different age groups using data from the research project 'Justice as a problem within reunified Germany' in which appraisals of quality of life were measured along with an extensive set of personality variables.

Two lines of just world research

While in the beginning just world research was dominated by attempts to explain reactions towards victims and victimisation (e.g. Lerner, 1970), researchers in the last decade have focused on the adaptive functions of just world beliefs (e.g. Dalbert, 2001, for an extensive review of this research). Within this line of research, Lerner's original assumptions (Lerner, 1977) found support: BJW serves as a buffer against stress and protects mental health, it nurtures the feeling of being treated fairly by others and thus helps individuals to build up trust in other people and society, it enables investments in long-term goals, and it provides a conceptual framework which helps to interpret the events of one's personal life in a meaningful way and thus to find meaning in life. Just these vital functions form the motivational force of BJW according to Lerner's original conception. In order to be able to survive in a complex social world, people depend on their belief in justice. Without it they would lack a powerful resource of trust, optimism and meaning; therefore, they are not willing to give it up when confronted with contradictory evidence and try to maintain their original belief in justice by nearly any means.

BJW in different age groups   65

A different line of research portrays belief in a just world as part of a commonly shared socio-political ideology that includes conservatism, adherence to traditional values, identification with high-status groups and even proneness to prejudice (Lazarus, 2002). In this view, BJW is not the expression of a justice motive but a means of system justification (Jost and Burgess, 2000). There is a large amount of empirical evidence for this connection. Early in the history of just world research, Rubin and Peplau (1975) reported positive correlations between BJW and positive attitudes towards political organisations and the government. High-scorers uttered more conservative attitudes and had a more positive attitude towards President Nixon at the time when his impeachment was discussed. Additionally, a negative correlation with political activism was found. Connors and Heaven (1987) found BJW to be correlated with a preference of right-wing political parties and with a position on the right of the left–right continuum. Similarly, Wagstaff (1983) as well as Wagstaff and Quirk (1983) reported that voters of the Conservative Party in England and Scotland had higher BJW scores. Comparable results were obtained by Furnham and Gunter (1984) for British voters, Smith and Green (1984) for American voters, and Dalbert *et al.* (1987) for German voters.

Rubin and Peplau (1975) also supposed a connection with authoritarianism because authoritarian people admire the powerful in society and just world believers devalue the weak. They obtained a considerable correlation with the F-scale of Adorno *et al.* (1950). Connors and Heaven (1987) also observed a positive correlation within a sample of students from Australia. Comparably, Finamore and Carlson (1987), as well as Mohr and Luscri (1995), found BJW to be associated with punitive criminal justice attitudes. Using the German just world scale (Dalbert *et al.*, 1987), Dalbert (1992) found correlations between just world belief and authoritarianism for German students and also for Spanish teachers. In general, BJW is associated with viewing underprivileged groups as responsible for their situation (e.g. Furnham and Procter, 1989; Montada, 1992; Montada and Schneider, 1989), with opposing socialism and libertarianism, and with believing in a non-interventionist economy (Rim, 1983). In a recent study by Campbell *et al.* (2001) BJW was associated with dispositional attributions for poverty. Maes *et al.* (2000) found that, contrary to their predictions, even different variants of BJW, which had been found to work quite differently in many ways, were equally linked to indicators of political conservatism.

Dittmar and Dickinson (1993: 259) resume: 'It may be argued that all these sets of beliefs and social attitudes are related in a coherent and consistent fashion: they all support the status quo and are more characteristic of a generally right-wing political orientation than a left-wing one.' In their own study, 45 per cent of the overall variance in just world scores was accounted for by political beliefs; moreover, their subjects were able to predict consensually another person's just world beliefs only on the basis

66   *J. Maes and M. Schmitt*

of a political label (position on the left–right continuum), independently of their own political orientation. These results led them to consider whether just world beliefs stem from societal influence rather than from personal needs. They doubt the motivational origin of BJW and offer a social-constructionist approach as an alternative explanation: 'Thus, just world beliefs are seen as part of the socially shared knowledge to which children are exposed and consequently have at their disposal to make sense of their social environment [...], lay theories, which can be viewed as a quasi-autonomous "thinking environment" which predates and informs individual thought (but which would not exist if it was not constantly reproduced/transformed in social interchanges)' (1993: 260).

Thus, there is empirical evidence for both: the function of BJW as a resource for well-being and action-orientation, and the connection of BJW with conservatism and right-wing positions. However, there is no plausible reason why there should be a necessary link between the functions of beliefs in justice and a conservative world-view. On the contrary, it is known from research on political movements (e.g. Rucht and Roth, 1999) that especially young people and adolescents share an idealistic view of the world and of mankind and that justice is a central element of this idealistic world-view. Often, young people assume that they are living in a world that is consistent with their ideals, and if they detect discrepancies they will, at least for a short period, be motivated to protest against these discrepancies and to engage in pro-social commitments to make the world a little bit more consistent with their moral view. However, it is also a fact known from research on political movements (Rucht and Roth, 1999) that subsequent disillusionment may result and, thus, ideals may fade away. Krettenauer (1998) described a new form of moral individualism in adolescence, which allows moral options and solidarity independent from traditional affiliations. As a result of these considerations, we expect different patterns of BJW in different age groups. We expect belief in a just world to be correlated with indicators of an idealistic and moral view of the world in adolescence but not in adult groups. We expect the traditionally found connections of BJW with indicators of a conservative political orientation only in the adult groups but not for adolescents.

Patterns of just world beliefs in different age groups

We will test these assumptions using data from the German research project 'Justice as a problem within reunified Germany' in which beliefs in a just world were measured along with a large set of appraisals of life quality and personality measures as part of a longitudinal survey on the psychological consequences of the German unification. First, we will describe our sample and then present the correlations of justice beliefs with indicators of well-being, indicators of an idealistic world-view and indicators of a right-wing political orientation.

Sample

In order to maximise the demographic heterogeneity and representativeness of our sample, participants were recruited on the basis of a geographical division of Germany into 18 cells (East/West × North/Middle/ South × Large towns/Medium-sized towns/Small towns). The facets are fully crossed. Two communities were chosen from each of the 18 cells. Registration offices of two communities in each cell provided random samples from the population of all inhabitants between 15 and 75 years of age. Additional respondents were randomly drawn from electronic telephone directories. In all, 2531 participants returned questionnaires at the first measurement occasion. The proportion of males was 58 per cent in East Germany and 61 per cent in West Germany. The sample is representative according to many, but not all, demographic variables. Men and participants with higher education are most severely overrepresented. A detailed description of the sample is available on the Internet (Schmal *et al.* 1996). Most data presented here are from the first round of data collection in spring 1996. Questionnaires were sent by mail and answered anonymously. The scales for measuring the constructs of the current analysis were embedded in a large set of approximately 3000 items. These items were divided into five questionnaire booklets that were mailed to participants on a monthly basis.

Justice beliefs in different age groups

Within this research project, we assessed four forms of belief in a just world: (a) general belief in a just world (measured with the scale of Dalbert *et al.*, 1987), (b) general belief in an unjust world, as well as (c) belief in immanent justice and (d) belief in ultimate justice as two distinguishable variants of just world beliefs (Schmitt and Maes, 1998; Maes and Schmitt, 1999). Belief in immanent justice characterises a conception of justice according to which nearly everything that happens is seen as an expression of justice as the inherent principle upon which the world is based; this is very similar to a form of justice belief that Piaget (1932) observed in little children. Belief in ultimate justice characterises a conception of justice according to which people can tolerate current injustice, but expect every injustice to be resolved and compensated for at some point in the future (Maes, 1998b). More information about these two forms of justice beliefs is provided by Maes and Kals (this volume). All scales range from 0 ('do not agree at all') to 5 ('do agree totally'). The internal consistency is $\alpha = 0.72$ for immanent justice (6 items, e.g. 'Misfortune is the just punishment for a bad character'), $\alpha = 0.90$ for ultimate justice (12 items, e.g. 'Those who have suffered will be compensated one day', $\alpha = 0.75$ for belief in an unjust world (6 items, e.g. 'Many people suffer an unjust fate'), and $\alpha = 0.72$ for general belief in a just world

(6 items, e.g. 'By and large, the world is a just place'). In order to get sizeable subgroups we considered only four different age groups: 14–25-year-olds ($N = 231$, 9.2 per cent of our sample), 26–45-year-olds ($N = 901$, 35.7 per cent of our sample), 46–65-year-olds ($N = 1023$, 40.6 per cent of our sample), and over-65s ($N = 366$, 14.5 per cent of our sample). We would have preferred to form a separate group of 14–20-year-olds, but this group would be considerably smaller than all the other groups, and the highest N available would be $N = 101$ (4 per cent of our sample).

Figure 5.1 depicts the mean values of the four justice beliefs in the four subgroups. It had been shown earlier with a sample of 11–19-year-old school students (Maes, 1998a) that beliefs in immanent and ultimate justice markedly decrease with age; now it seems that this trend is continued in the adult age ranges. General BJW is slightly decreasing in young and middle adulthood whereas it is slightly increasing again in the older age groups. A comparable age curve was observed by Dalbert (2001). Except for belief in an unjust world, we found significant differences for the three justice beliefs. Scheffé tests ($p < 0.05$) revealed that for belief in ultimate justice, the youngest group ($M_1 = 1.63$, $SD_1 = 1.04$) was significantly different from all other groups ($M_2 = 1.22$, $SD_2 = 0.96$; $M_3 = 1.15$, $SD_3 = 0.91$; $M_4 = 1.24$, $SD_4 = 0.98$). Comparable differences were found for immanent justice: group 1 ($M_1 = 1.74$, $SD_1 = 1.03$) differed significantly from all other groups ($M_2 = 1.43$, $SD_2 = 1.01$; $M_3 = 1.33$,

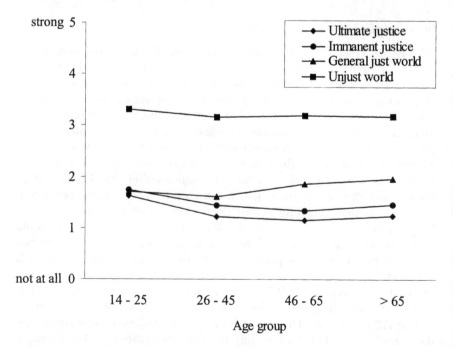

Figure 5.1 Justice beliefs in four different age groups.

$SD_3 = 1.04$; $M_4 = 1.46$, $SD_4 = 1.13$). Concerning general belief in a just world, group 2 ($M_2 = 1.61$, $SD_2 = 0.87$) differed significantly from group 3 ($M_3 = 1.86$, $SD_3 = 0.94$) and group 4 ($M_4 = 1.96$, $SD_4 = 0.95$), and group 1 ($M_1 = 1.70$, $SD_1 = 0.95$) differed significantly from group 4. The mean values for belief in an unjust world were: $M_1 = 3.31$, $SD_1 = 0.91$; $M_2 = 3.16$, $SD_2 = 1.01$; $M_3 = 3.19$, $SD_3 = 1.04$; $M_4 = 3.17$, $SD_4 = 1.10$. We will now turn to the correlational patterns of BJW within the four age groups. In that, we will only analyse general BJW and belief in ultimate justice, which has been found to be more suited as a resource than immanent justice (Maes and Schmitt, 1999; Maes and Kals, this volume).

Justice beliefs and well-being

First, we will look at the resource hypothesis again. We tested this hypothesis using several indicators of mental health and positive attitudes towards one's work. We expected positive correlations of the two justice beliefs with these indicators for all age groups. Well-being and mental health were measured with a modified German version of the Beck Depression Inventory (Schmitt and Maes, 2000; $\alpha = 0.90$, 20 items, e.g. 'I feel sad'), a German version of the Rosenberg Self-Esteem Scale (RSS; Rosenberg, 1965; $\alpha = 0.84$, 10 items, e.g. 'Considering everything, I am satisfied with myself'), and the subscale 'Mental Health' of the Trier Personality Questionnaire (TPQ-MH; Becker, 1989; $\alpha = 0.90$, 19 items, e.g. 'I am feeling full of drive and energy'). Identification with one's work is a new scale (Seiler et al., 1998) measuring the tendency to identify with one's work and to find joy and fulfilment in it ($\alpha = 0.87$, 6 items, e.g. 'It is not comprehensible not to identify with one's job'). Approving work as a way to a good life (single item) and approving economising and saving money ($\alpha = 0.75$, 4 items, e.g. 'If you win a lot of money you should save it up for the future instead of spending it') emerged as dimensions from a German work-ethic scale (Maes and Schmitt, 2001).

Depression was only slightly related to the two justice scales but in the expected direction for general BJW (Table 5.1). The more subjects believed in justice, the less they felt depressed. This correlation was the highest in the age group that ranged from 46 to 65. Belief in ultimate justice was also slightly but positively related to depression. We do not interpret this correlation to mean that belief in ultimate justice leads to depression, but rather that when depressed, people seek consolation in referring to their belief in ultimate justice, which in turn promises compensation for suffering and hardship. Self-esteem was only slightly related to beliefs in justice for the younger age groups, but considerably so for the over-65 group. Mental health showed the expected positive relationship to justice beliefs for almost every age group. Mental health indicates current well-being in the present situation whereas self-esteem includes a reflection and reviewing of many experiences in life. This might explain why self-esteem, in contrast to

70   *J. Maes and M. Schmitt*

Table 5.1 Correlations of justice beliefs with indicators of subjective well-being and
mental health

Variable	Age group	Variables	
		GBJW	BULT
Depression	14–25	−0.09	0.09
	26–45	−0.06**	0.13**
	46–65	−0.19**	0.02
	>65	−0.07	0.10*
Self-esteem	14–25	0.03	0.14**
	26–45	−0.00	0.14**
	46–65	0.08**	0.09**
	>65	0.29**	0.30**
Mental health	14–25	0.18**	−0.02
	26–45	0.10**	0.09**
	46–65	0.29**	0.15**
	>65	0.25**	0.16**
Identification with work	14–25	0.27**	0.23**
	26–45	0.17**	0.13**
	46–65	0.16**	0.12**
	>65	0.21**	0.18**
Economising, saving money	14–25	0.18**	0.28**
	26–45	0.17**	0.20**
	46–65	0.07*	0.16**
	>65	0.19**	0.25**
Working for a good life	14–25	0.22**	0.16*
	26–45	0.01	0.03
	46–65	0.03	0.05
	>65	0.02	−0.04

Notes
GBJW = General belief in a just world; BULT = Belief in ultimate justice.
* $p < 0.05$.
** $p < 0.01$.

mental health, is only related to justice beliefs in the oldest age group. In
old age, BJW might be used to evaluate one's own life and to integrate
experiences in a meaningful way, whereas in youth it is more important to
find trust in one's own future and to engage in long-term activities. This
should prove true for the variables concerning work and profession.
Indeed, identification with one's work was associated with justice beliefs in
all age groups, but was highest for the youngest group. Support for
economising and saving money was associated with justice beliefs in all age
groups. Finally, working for a good life was only associated with justice
beliefs in the youngest group, those starting their professional lives. Presumably, this creates good motivation to engage in professional life.

BJW in different age groups 71

Justice beliefs and idealistic world-views

In accordance with the work on social movements (Rucht and Roth, 1999) and in contrast to research portraying BJW simply as part of a right-wing ideology, we expected justice beliefs to be associated with indicators of idealistic world-views particularly in the youngest group. To test this assumption, we gathered several indicators of idealistic or moral world-views: Machiavellianism is a tendency to use other people for one's own purposes and the conviction that a purpose justifies any means. This tendency is opposed to moral convictions; it was measured with a short form of the German Machiavellianism scale by Henning and Six (1977). Alpha for this scale is $\alpha = 0.85$ (seven items, e.g. 'It is not so important how you win but that you win'). Self-transcendent values according to Schwartz (1992) are also known to be indicators of a moral view of the world ($\alpha = 0.65$, four items, e.g. 'justice and peace', 'benevolence and altruism'). The other indicators of a moral world-view listed in Table 5.2 are single-item measures. We asked our subjects for the social groups they would most identify with. Informative for our purposes is the identification with the German nation, and in contrast, the identification with humanity, which might be regarded as an indicator of moral individualism according to Krettenauer (1998). We also asked our subjects for their opinion about central human motives as central parts of their conception of the world: what are the central aims of human striving? Informative for our purposes are two items: 'striving for possession' as an indicator of a materialistic world-view, and 'striving for justice' as an indicator of an idealistic world-view.

The results are shown in Table 5.2. Machiavellianism was not associated with justice beliefs in the youngest group whereas it was positively related to justice beliefs in adulthood and old age. Self-transcendent values were not at all related to justice beliefs in the older age groups but they were considerably related to belief in ultimate justice in the 14–25-year-old group. The identification with the German nation showed a clear picture, as did identification with humanity. The identification with the German nation was significantly related to justice beliefs in the adult groups, whereas this relation was missing for the youngest age group. Identification with humanity was related positively to justice beliefs within the youngest and oldest groups, and the highest correlation was observed for ultimate justice in the youngest age group. The more people believed in justice, the more they assumed that other people's behaviour is motivated by their striving for justice, and this assumption was more pronounced in the young group and more for belief in ultimate justice. The assumption of possession as a central motive showed a different picture: this assumption was related positively to justice beliefs in the older groups whereas it was negatively related to justice beliefs in the youngest group (although these correlations were not significant).

72 *J. Maes and M. Schmitt*

Table 5.2 Correlations of justice beliefs with indicators of an idealistic world-view

Variable	Age group	Variables	
		GBJW	BULT
Machiavellianism	14–25	−0.04	−0.08
	26–45	0.02	0.07*
	46–65	0.12**	0.18**
	>65	0.20**	0.23**
Self-transcendent values	14–25	0.06	0.28**
	26–45	0.01	0.04
	46–65	0.03	0.02
	>65	0.00	0.03
Identification German nation	14–25	0.09	0.04
	26–45	0.21**	0.13**
	46–65	0.27**	0.20**
	>65	0.21**	0.20**
Identification Humanity	14–25	0.10	0.25**
	26–45	−0.05	0.05
	46–65	0.02	0.04
	>65	0.12*	0.13*
World-view: striving for justice	14–25	0.12	0.23**
	26–45	0.07*	0.14**
	46–65	0.03	0.07*
	>65	0.13*	0.15**
World-view: striving for possession	14–25	−0.03	−0.15
	26–45	0.09*	0.02
	46–65	0.08*	0.06*
	>65	0.10*	0.17**

Notes
GBJW = General belief in a just world; BULT = Belief in ultimate justice.
* $p < 0.05$.
** $p < 0.01$.

Justice beliefs and socio-political orientations

Finally, we will turn to the correlational patterns of justice beliefs with indicators of political conservatism and a right-wing ideology. The large amount of research literature that confirms a close connection between BJW and a conservative socio-political ideology led us to expect positive correlations of both variants of BJW with such indicators. But, according to our considerations we did not expect such a close connection in youth and young adulthood. To test this hypothesis, we used a questionnaire that allowed us to measure a large set of basic socio-political attitudes, among them conservatism, fascism, socialism, economic liberalism, environmentalism and authoritarianism (Maes, 2001). The conservatism scale includes 12 items (e.g. 'Many modern ideas destroy our cultural heritage'), the fascism scale includes 16 items (e.g. 'Even if it is not acceptable to say it aloud today, a people that does not look after the purity of its genetic make-up will perish'), the socialism scale includes 8 items (e.g. 'As long as some people exploit others there will not be a peaceful world'), the economic liberalism scale includes 8 items (e.g. 'Only a free market guarantees progress which is for the benefit of all'), the environmental scale includes 12 items (e.g. 'Without the preservation of nature all other political aims are senseless'), and the authoritarianism scale includes 9 items (e.g. 'Every human being has a need for submission to a true authority'). All of these scales are very homogeneous $(0.74 < \alpha < 0.91)$ and rather stable over a two-year period (1996–8): $0.70 < r_{96/98} < 0.84$.

The results are depicted in Table 5.3. Conservatism, which includes an

Table 5.3 Correlations of justice beliefs with indicators of socio-political orientation

Variable	Age group	Variables	
		GBJW	BULT
Conservatism	14–25	0.15*	0.30**
	26–45	0.12**	0.20**
	46–65	0.08**	0.17**
	>65	0.18**	0.23**
Fascism	14–25	0.04	0.05
	26–45	0.16**	0.24**
	46–65	0.21**	0.31**
	>65	0.21**	0.39**
Socialism	14–25	0.14*	0.21**
	26–45	−0.09*	0.03
	46–65	−0.07*	−0.01
	>65	0.01	0.07
Economic liberalism	14–25	0.14*	−0.02
	26–45	0.23**	0.15**
	46–65	0.35**	0.25**
	>65	0.28**	0.32**
Environmentalism	14–25	0.04	0.22**
	26–45	−0.10**	0.15**
	46–65	−0.05	0.06*
	>65	0.05	0.16*
Authoritarianism	14–25	0.01	−0.02
	26–45	0.10**	0.21**
	46–65	0.23**	0.27**
	>65	0.28**	0.37**

Notes
GBJW = General belief in a just world; BULT = Belief in ultimate justice.
* $p < 0.05$.
** $p < 0.01$.

74 *J. Maes and M. Schmitt*

approval of law-and-order politics, a sceptical view of modern times and a preference for evolutionary rather than revolutionary societal changes was moderately associated with the two justice beliefs. Fascism was not related at all to the two justice beliefs in the youngest age group, but was significantly related to the two justice beliefs in all other groups. Moreover, it was more strongly related to the belief in ultimate justice compared to the general BJW. The highest correlation was observed for fascism and belief in ultimate justice in the over-65 group. It seems that the correlations increase constantly with age. Socialism was not at all or only slightly negatively related to justice beliefs in the older groups whereas it was significantly and positively related to the two justice beliefs in the youngest group. Economic liberalism, which includes an approval of non-interventionist politics and a strict demand for a free market was significantly related to the justice beliefs for all groups older than 25 years while such a clear association was missing in the youngest group. Concerning environmentalism, differences between general BJW and belief in ultimate justice emerged. While environmentalism was not at all or only slightly negatively related to general BJW, there were positive correlations for the belief in ultimate justice, the strongest being for the young subgroup. Since environmentalism includes caring for a preservation of the world and our natural surroundings for future generations, it is not surprising that it was more related to the more future-oriented form of just world belief. Finally, a very clear pattern emerged for authoritarianism. Here, we observed a constant increase in the correlations with age. Authoritarianism was not at all related to the two justice beliefs in the youngest subgroup while the significant positive correlations increased continuously in the older groups. In sum, these data confirm the traditionally found connections between BJW and indicators of political conservatism, but only for the groups older than 25 years. For the adolescents and young adults in our sample a rather different and sometimes opposite pattern emerged.

Conclusion

With reference to the just-world resource literature, our data may provide some additional evidence that justice beliefs may have beneficial functions in supporting mental health and action-orientation. However, this is differentially true for different dimensions of mental health in different age groups. Only the subscale mental health from the personality questionnaire of Becker (1989) correlated comparably with BJW in all age groups, whereas self-esteem (see also Correia and Vala, in this volume) was linked only to justice beliefs in the adult groups and especially in the over-65 group. This can be understood if one considers that the mental health scale measures subjects' mental condition in the present situation (like feeling full of energy and drive, feeling able to cope with difficulties, feeling responsible for one's own luck, being in a good mood, being in a

BJW in different age groups 75

good physical and mental condition) whereas the notion of self-esteem requires a reflection and continuous evaluation of one's feelings and experiences. It seems that in youth self-esteem is rather independent from BJW whereas in old age a clear connection between both becomes visible. Given that humans have a need to perceive their lives in a consistent fashion (Schmitt, 1990), they may more and more review and summarise their personal experiences in a consistent way and make it congruent with their fundamental beliefs like BJW. The possible ways to explain and cope with failure, lack of success, breakdowns and unfulfilled dreams change and diminish over the life-span. In youth, one may wait for the next opportunity, expect to have further chances or console oneself by expecting a just compensation at another time. In old age, some of these possibilities fade away; in order not to despair one may adopt a religious perspective and expect compensation in another life or find justice in one's review of life by convincing oneself that one deserved one's fate or that the failure had good aspects. Generally, in youth, belief in a just world seems to be more action-oriented whereas in old age it is more associated with the evaluation of one's life and the integration of one's experiences in one conceptual frame. The action-orientation of BJW in youth became visible in the correlations with the maxim of working for a good life, which appeared only in the young group, and the identification with one's work, which correlated higher with justice beliefs in the young compared to the other groups.

Moreover, we found consistent correlational patterns of just world beliefs with several indicators of idealistic world-views and several indicators of a conservative socio-political ideology. Dimensions of idealistic world-views were associated with justice beliefs almost exclusively in the young group, whereas indicators of conservative attitudes correlated significantly with justice beliefs only in the older groups and were not at all or even negatively connected to justice beliefs in the young group. Though the strength of the correlations was moderate, they all point in the same direction: BJW is not just the adoption of a commonly available socio-political ideology, at least not in adolescence and young adulthood. Instead, our data suggest that there is a change in the differential meaning of BJW in different age groups. There are two possible explanations for these findings. One is that they reflect developmental change, the other is that they merely reflect changing historical trends in society. The developmental explanation refers to psychological processes when growing older, whereas the zeitgeist explanation refers to different societal and ideological influences in the time when the older groups grew up. Adopting the zeitgeist explanation, one might argue that the correlations of justice beliefs with fascism as well as with authoritarianism are due to a greater acceptance of fascist and authoritarian ideologies during adolescence of the older age cohorts. But, this should only be true for those over 65 in 1996, and not for the cohorts of the 46–65-year-olds and even

76   *J. Maes and M. Schmitt*

the 26–45-year-olds, for whom similar correlations were found. Thus, we are more prone to accept the developmental explanation. One story our data might tell is that BJW is a manifestation of personal needs and derives from basic motivations in youth and is shaped and changed so that later on it becomes more and more congruent with societal ideologies in adult life. The critical period seems to be the time when the young adults start their professional lives, when they are getting more and more involved in societal institutions and professional networks and are adopting more and more public roles and positions. In this period, we observe (a) a signific-ant decrease in justice beliefs, which appears as a continuation of a decrease in justice beliefs that was observed for 11–19-year-old school pupils (Maes, 1998a), and (b) some reshaping and transformations of justice beliefs, which become visible in the contrasting correlational pat-terns. Interestingly, we observed that justice beliefs were again associated with an identification with humanity and with viewing the striving for justice as a central human motive when subjects are released from the bonds of professional life in the over-65 group.

Beyond such interpretations, our data are informative for a fundamen-tal question of just world research: the question of the origins of BJW. Dittmar and Dickinson (1993) opposed two theoretical explanations for the inculcation of just-world beliefs in individuals: the individual-motive explanation and the social-learning approach. According to the first approach, the need to believe in a just world is a universal, intrapsychic motive; according to the latter, just world beliefs stem from societal influ-ence rather than from personal needs. Lerner had already considered both possibilities: on the one hand, he offered a lot of arguments as to why BJW can be regarded as an expression of a justice motive (Lerner, 1977); on the other hand, he also took societal influences into account. When considering the connection between BJW and the Protestant work ethic, Lerner (1980: 150–1) wrote: 'Although we may be stretching it a bit, the correlation with the Protestant Ethic measures may imply that there is a strong social learning component in the development of BJW. People adopt the belief as a function of their being socialized into the dominant cultural ethic.'

We also think that there is no necessary contradiction between the two positions. We have no doubts that both exist: individual motives as well as socio-political ideologies. There is no reason to question that individual motives may influence political behaviour and the adoption of socio-political ideologies. Furthermore, there is no reason to question that socio-political ideologies may influence behaviour and even the manifesta-tion and development of motives. Instead of continuing endless discus-sions regarding whether just world beliefs are caused by socio-political ideologies or vice versa, research should rather aim at investigating the complex interrelations and mutual influences. In doing so, it is important to note that there is not only one motive but several motives and that

BJW in different age groups 77

there is not only one socio-political ideology commonly available, but presumably several. Research on the interrelations of individual motives and socio-political ideologies may, for example, try to answer which combination of individual motives decides which of several commonly available ideologies is adopted. Or, it may try to clarify how individuals deal with discrepancies between individual motives and prevailing socio-political ideologies. Individual motives may harmonise or clash with socio-political ideologies encountered in social life; if the latter is the case, individuals will oppose or try to accommodate to the contradicting views. These processes are worth studying.

In doing so, it is necessary to have a clear conception of the motives involved. Here, we encounter a typical shortcoming of many studies on BJW. Even researchers who assume a possible motivational basis for BJW often tend to trace back justice beliefs to other motives than justice, such as a need for security or a need for a controllable world. Dittmar and Dickinson (1993), for example, consider the possibility that a basic need for a stable and controllable world gives rise to both variations in BJW and political orientation. This point of view stands in a long tradition in the social sciences, and even in justice psychology, to regard justice merely as a derived motive, which serves other more fundamental needs (Montada, 1998b). Rational choice theories consider self-interest as the only effective human motive. According to this view, social actors observe rules of justice only because they guarantee a maximum profit for all participants of a social exchange. However, there is a large body of evidence, both theoretical and empirical, that justice is a primordial motive, an end in itself and a moral imperative (Montada, 1998b). In science as well as in everyday life, the impact of justice motives is often underestimated whereas the impact of self-interest is seriously overestimated (Kals *et al.*, 2001).

At this point, the work of Miller and Ratner (1996, 1998) becomes important. In a set of studies by Miller and Ratner (1998), for instance, subjects overestimated the influence of self-interest even if their own actual behaviour was apparently not governed by self-interest. Miller and Ratner (1996) reveal self-interest not as a social fact but rather as a modern myth. However, this myth has severe consequences and a considerable power on subjects' world-views and their own behaviour. According to Miller (1999), self-interest is not only the central element of a dominant cultural world-view in Western society but has meanwhile become a social norm which prescribes the adequate way to behave and to describe one's own and other people's behaviour. This norm influences people's actions and opinions as well as the accounts they give for their actions and opinions: subjects normalise behaviour congruent with self-interest and pathologise behaviour incongruent with self-interest, they experience discomfort and fear social isolation when they take actions incongruent with self-interest, and they justify their behaviour in terms of self-interest. In a recent study by Ratner and Miller (2001) subjects predicted that they would be evaluated negatively were they to take action on behalf of a cause in which they had no stake. The norm of self-interest leads people to act and speak as though they care more about their material self-interest than they really do.

This line of research may shed new light on our data. Apparently, the correlational patterns in the adolescent and young adult group were more consistent with the notion of a justice motive while the correlational patterns in the older age groups were more consistent with the adoption of a conservative socio-political ideology. According to the reasoning of Miller and Ratner (1996), adults may feel forced to harmonise their behaviour and the accounts for their own behaviour with the current myth of self-interest. Typical self-interests like power, possession and material desires are classically linked to political conservatism. Authors who explained BJW by the socialisation of a political ideology usually thought of primary socialisation in childhood and early youth. Our data give rise to the supposition that a transformation of just world beliefs may rather be a result of secondary socialisation and may happen later with growing into social institutions and public roles. The experienced culture in adolescence may be different from the experienced culture in adult life. It might be that only professional life is governed by the myth of self-interest and its normative influences, while the influences experienced in childhood and youth are more conducive to a culture of justice. Justice and understanding, for example, are usually among the widely shared goals of education in kindergarten, in school and in the family. This may encourage young people to develop justice motives independently from available conservative world-views. If this reasoning is true and such a difference between the adolescent world and the adult world really exists, then growing into adult life might be perceived as a shock and initiate the processes of normative accommodation described by Miller and Ratner (1996). This stepwise process of reconciling one's justice needs with prevailing societal ideologies might be responsible for the ambiguous nature of BJW, which has already been called a hybrid of the justice motive and self-interest (Montada, 1998a).

This is one story our data might tell. However, we did not assess the variables which might help to understand and explain the supposed process of a slow transmission of just world beliefs. What we clearly need are more studies that describe in a more detailed fashion, and on a micro-social level all factors in the adolescents' and the young adults' world which might affect the shaping and development of justice motives as well as the adoption of socio-political world views. This is not the only question that is left for future research. For example, we discussed developmental and zeitgeist explanations for the differences we observed between the age groups. Of course, it is plausible to assume that both may account separately for the patterns we found. In order to clarify this, we would need

BJW in different age groups 79

long-term longitudinal studies which seldom if ever exist. Finally, we should aim to understand the psychological meaning of the decrease in justice beliefs that were found for school pupils (Maes, 1998a) and the continued decrease in the young adulthood group that we reported here. Does this decline in justice beliefs reflect disappointment in view of violated justice motives, accommodation to social norms, or just veridical perception? Furthermore, what are the consequences of this decline? Recently, Furnham (2003) made a prognosis of the survival of just world research for many years to come. We hope that a large part of that future research will be on the development and the variability of just world beliefs during the lifespan, and on the process of permanent interactions between individual needs for justice and social constructions of justice.

Acknowledgements

This research was supported by a grant of the Deutsche Forschungsgemeinschaft granted to the second author (Schm1092/1-1; Schm1092/1-2; Schm1092/1-3)

References

Adorno, T.W., Frenkel-Brunswick, E., Levinson, D.J. and Sanford, R.N. (1950) *The Authoritarian Personality*, New York: Harper.

Becker, P. (1989) *Trierer Persönlichkeitsfragebogen (TPF)* [The Trier personality questionnaire], Göttingen: Hogrefe.

Campbell, D., Carr, S. and MacLachlan, M. (2001) 'Attributing "third world poverty" in Australia and Malawi', *Journal of Applied Social Psychology*, 31: 409–30.

Connors, J. and Heaven, P.C. (1987) 'Authoritarianism and just world beliefs', *Journal of Social Psychology*, 127: 345–6.

Dalbert, C. (1992) 'Der Glaube an die gerechte Welt: Differenzierung und Validierung eines Konstrukts' [The belief in a just world: Differentiation and validation of a construct], *Zeitschrift für Sozialpsychologie*, 23: 268–76.

Dalbert, C. (2001) *The Justice Motive as a Personal Resource: Dealing with Challenges and Critical Life Events*, New York: Kluwer Academic/Plenum Publishers.

Dalbert, C., Montada, L. and Schmitt, M. (1987) 'Glaube an eine gerechte Welt als Motiv: Validierungskorrelate zweier Skalen' [Belief in a just world as a motive: Correlations for the validation of two scales], *Psychologische Beiträge*, 29: 596–615.

Dittmar, H. and Dickinson, J. (1993) 'The perceived relationship between the belief in a just world and sociopolitical ideology', *Social Justice Research*, 6: 257–72.

Finamore, F. and Carlson, J.M. (1987) 'Religiosity, belief in a just world and crime control attitudes', *Psychological Reports*, 61: 135–8.

Furnham, A. (2003) 'Belief in a just world: Research progress over the past decade', *Personality and Individual Differences*, 34: 795–817.

Furnham, A. and Gunter, B. (1984) 'Just world beliefs and attitudes towards the poor', *British Journal of Social Psychology*, 23: 265–9.

Furnham, A. and Procter, E. (1989) 'Belief in a just world: Review and critique of the individual difference literature', *British Journal of Social Psychology*, 28: 365–84.

80   J. Maes and M. Schmitt

Henning, H.-J. and Six, B. (1977) 'Konstruktion einer Machiavellismus-Skala' [Construction of a machiavellianism scale], *Zeitschrift für Sozialpsychologie*, 8: 185–98.

Jost, J.T. and Burgess, D. (2000) 'Attitudinal ambivalence and the conflict between group and system justification motives in low status groups', *Personality and Social Psychology Bulletin*, 26: 293–305.

Kals, E., Maes, J. and Becker, R. (2001) 'The overestimated impact of self-interest and the underestimated impact of justice motives', *Trames – Journal of the Humanities and Social Sciences*, 5: 269–87.

Krettenauer, T. (1998) *Gerechtigkeit als Solidarität – Entwicklungsbedingungen Sozialen Engagements im Jugendalter* [Justice as solidarity – developmental conditions of prosocial commitments in youth], Weinheim: Deutscher Studien Verlag.

Lazarus, E.D. (2002) 'The role of culture, ideology, and causal attributions in prejudice', *Dissertation Abstracts International*, 62 (10-B): 4840.

Lerner, M.J. (1970) 'The desire for justice and reactions to victims', in Macaulay, J. and Berkowitz, L. (eds), *Altruism and Helping Behavior*, New York: Academic Press.

Lerner, M.J. (1977) 'The justice motive in social behavior. Some hypotheses as to its origins and forms', *Journal of Personality*, 45: 1–52.

Lerner, M.J. (1980) *The Belief in a Just World. A Fundamental Delusion*, New York: Plenum Press.

Maes, J. (1998a) 'Geht es in der Schule gerecht zu? – Überzeugungen der Schülerinnen und Schüler und deren Folgen' [Is school life just? – Pupils' convictions and their consequences], in Kaiser, A. and Kaiser, R. (eds), *Entwicklung und Erprobung von Modellen der Begabtenförderung am Gymnasium mit Verkürzung der Schulzeit. Abschlussuntersuchung in der Gymnasialen Oberstufe (MSS)*, Mainz: von Hase and Koehler.

Maes, J. (1998b) 'Immanent justice and ultimate justice – two ways of believing in justice', in Montada, L. and Lerner, M.J. (eds), *Responses to Victimizations and Belief in a Just World*, New York: Plenum Press.

Maes, J. (2001) 'Solidarität – eine Frage der Persönlichkeit? Das Beispiel der Solidarität Westdeutscher mit Ostdeutschen' [Solidarity – a question of personality? The example of West German solidarity towards East Germans], in Bierhoff, H.-W. and Fetchenhauer, D. (eds), *Solidarität. Konflikt, Umwelt und Dritte Welt*, Opladen: Leske and Budrich.

Maes, J. and Schmitt, M. (1999) 'More on ultimate and immanent justice: Results from the research project "Justice as a problem within reunified Germany"', *Social Justice Research*, 12: 65–78.

Maes, J. and Schmitt, M. (2001) 'Protestantische-Ethik-Skala (PES): Messeigenschaften und Konstruktvalidität' [Protestant ethics: Measuring properties and construct validity], *Berichte aus der Arbeitsgruppe 'Verantwortung, Gerechtigkeit, Moral'*, No. 146, Trier: Universität Trier, Fachbereich I – Psychologie. Online, available at: http://www.uni-trier.de/uni/fb1/psychologie/gip/beri146.pdf (accessed 20 May 2003).

Maes, J., Schmitt, M. and Seiler, U. (2000) 'Politischer Konservatismus und der Glaube an Gerechtigkeit' [Political conservatism and the belief in justice], *Zeitschrift für Politische Psychologie*, 8: 39–53.

Miller, D.T. (1999) 'The norm of self-interest', *American Psychologist*, 54: 1053–60.

Miller, D.T. and Ratner, R.K. (1996) 'The power of the myth of self-interest', in Montada, L. and Lerner, M.J. (eds), *Current Societal Issues About Justice*, New York: Plenum Press.

BJW in different age groups 81

Miller, D.T. and Ratner, R.K. (1998) 'The disparity between the actual and the assumed power of self-interest', *Journal of Personality and Social Psychology*, 74: 53–62.

Mohr, P.B. and Luscri, G. (1995) 'Blame and punishment. Attitudes to juvenile and criminal offending', *Psychological Reports*, 77: 1091–6.

Montada, L. (1992) 'Attribution of responsibility for losses and perceived injustice', in Montada, L., Filipp, S.-H. and Lerner, M.J. (eds), *Life Crises and the Experience of Loss in Adulthood*, Hillsdale, NJ: Lawrence Erlbaum.

Montada, L. (1998a) 'Belief in a just world: A hybrid of justice motive and self-interest?', in Montada, L. and Lerner, M.J. (eds), *Responses to Victimizations and Belief in a Just World*, New York: Plenum Press.

Montada, L. (1998b) 'Justice: Just a rational choice?', *Social Justice Research*, 12: 81–101.

Montada, L. and Schneider, A. (1989) 'Justice and emotional reactions to the disadvantaged', *Social Justice Research*, 3: 313–44.

Piaget, J. (1932) *Le Jugement Moral Chez L'enfant* [Moral judgement in the child], Paris: Alcan.

Ratner, R.K. and Miller, D.T. (2001) 'The norm of self-interest and its effects on social action', *Journal of Personality and Social Psychology*, 81: 5–16.

Rim, Y. (1983) 'Belief in a just world, personality, and social attitudes', *Personality and Individual Differences*, 4: 707–8.

Rosenberg, M. (1965) *Society and the Adolescent Self-image*, Princeton, NJ: Princeton University Press.

Rubin, Z. and Peplau, L.A. (1975) 'Who believes in a just world?', *Journal of Social Issues*, 31: 65–89.

Rucht, D. and Roth, R. (eds) (1999) *Jugendkulturen, Politik und Protest* [Youth cultures, politics and protest], Opladen: Leske and Budrich.

Schmal, A., Maes, J. and Schmitt, M. (1996). 'Gerechtigkeit als innerdeutsches Problem: Untersuchungsplan und Stichprobe' [Justice as a problem within Germany: Research design and sample], *Berichte aus der Arbeitsgruppe 'Verantwortung, Gerechtigkeit, Moral'*, No. 97), Trier: Universität Trier, Fachbereich I – Psychologie. Online, available at: http://www.uni-trier.de/uni/fb1/psychologie/gip/beri96.pdf (accessed 20 May 2003).

Schmitt, M. (1990) *Konsistenz als Persönlichkeitseigenschaft? Moderatorvariablen in der Persönlichkeits- und Einstellungsforschung* [Consistency as a personality trait? Moderator variables in personality and attitude research], Berlin: Springer.

Schmitt, M. and Maes, J. (1998) 'Perceived injustice in unified Germany and mental health', *Social Justice Research*, 11: 59–78.

Schmitt, M. and Maes, J. (2000) 'Vorschlag zur Vereinfachung des Beck-Depressions-Inventars (BDI)' [Proposal for a simplification of the Beck Depression Inventory], *Diagnostica*, 46: 38–46.

Schwartz, S.H. (1992) 'Universals in the content and structure of values: Theoretical advances and empirical tests in 20 countries', in Zanna, M. (ed.), *Advances in Experimental Social Psychology*, vol. 25, San Diego, CA: Academic Press.

Seiler, U., Schmitt, M. and Maes, J. (1998) 'Gerechtigkeit als innerdeutsches Problem: Analyse der Meßeigenschaften von Meßinstrumenten für Kernvariablen des Lebensbereichs Arbeit und Beruf' [Justice as a problem within Germany: Analysis of measuring properties for core variables in the domain of work and professional life], *Berichte aus der Arbeitsgruppe 'Verantwortung,*

82   *J. Maes and M. Schmitt*

Gerechtigkeit, Moral', No. 116, Trier: Universität Trier, Fachbereich I – Psychologie. Online, available at: http://www.uni-trier.de/uni/fb1/psychologie/gip/beri116.pdf (accessed 20 May 2003).

Smith, K.B. and Green, D.N. (1984) 'Individual correlates of the belief in a just world', *Psychological Reports*, 54: 435–8.

Wagstaff, G.F. (1983) 'Correlates of the just world in Britain', *Journal of Social Psychology*, 121: 145–6.

Wagstaff, G.F. and Quirk, M.A. (1983) 'Attitudes to sex-roles, political conservatism and belief in a just world', *Psychological Reports*, 52: 813–14.

Part II

The belief in a just world as a resource for mental health and coping in adolescence

6 Belief in a just world, subjective well-being and trust of young adults

Isabel Correia and Jorge Vala

Developmental psychologists (Levinson, 1978; Vaillant, 1977) highlight the numerous challenges that adolescents and young adults face as they become more autonomous and independent in this stage of life. They leave their parents' home, choose and take up an occupation, make plans for the future and learn their constraints, and establish a home and a family of their own. These challenges can be very distressing, and young adults need psychosocial resources to cope with them. In this chapter, we will show that the belief in a just world (BJW) may be positively associated with the ability to cope with these tasks in a way that sustains mental health.

BJW and mental health

The belief-in-a-just-world theory (Lerner, 1980) states that the BJW, according to which all of us get what we deserve, is a fundamental delusion that enables the feeling of invulnerability to persist, even when people are confronted with injustice. According to Lerner, 'People want to and have to believe they live in a just world so that they can go about their daily lives with a sense of trust, hope, and confidence in their future' (1980: 14). The BJW is therefore hypothesised to have the adaptive function of instilling people with confidence and giving meaning to events, which is especially important when people face new tasks. Indeed, there is empirical evidence for associations between BJW and several dimensions of mental health (see Dalbert, 2001, for a review). Moreover, Dalbert (2001) has identified three main functions of the BJW that mediate the effect of BJW on mental health. The first function is to dispose individuals to behave fairly: high believers in a just world will be motivated to achieve their goals by just means. By acting fairly, they respect the terms of the personal contract, which gives them the assurance of being fairly rewarded. Moreover, behaviour congruent with the justice motive will lead to better mental health. The second function of the BJW is to enhance trust in others and in the fairness of one's fate. This has several adaptive consequences because it gives individuals the confidence (a) to invest in

86   I. Correia and J. Vala

long term goals, (b) to trust others, whom they expect to treat them fairly, and (c) that the tasks they perform will be fairly rewarded and are within their ability to cope, thus prompting better performance in achievement tasks. The third function of the BJW is to provide a framework that helps individuals to interpret their life in a way that preserves the BJW – by restoring justice either psychologically (for example, minimising the injustice) or behaviourally (for example, claiming compensation). This is especially important for innocent victims.

Studies relating BJW and mental health have developed along two lines: with samples of victimised individuals and of non-victimised individuals. As far as victimised individuals are concerned, the data seem to support the hypothesis that BJW is positively associated with victims' mental health. There is some evidence of this, for example, in the cases of mothers of disabled children (Dalbert, 1998) and unemployed workers (Cubela, 2000; Dalbert, 1998; Montada, 1998). Moreover, Hafer and Correy (1999) have shown that when high just world believers face a negative outcome, they make more internal attributions and fewer external attributions than low just-world believers. The authors also found that these attributions lead strong believers in a just world to perceive the negative outcome as less unjust, and to have more positive and fewer negative emotions. Seen in terms of Dalbert's (2001) three functions of the BJW, the relationship between BJW and mental health would be mediated by an interpretation of the event that preserves the victim's BJW.

Another set of studies, to which this study belongs, has examined the relationship between BJW and the mental health of non-victimised individuals facing day-to-day challenges. As we will show, the empirical evidence firmly supports the association between BJW and mental health. According to Dalbert (2001), this association is mediated by trust in others and in the fairness of one's fate. In this chapter, we will present three studies that provide additional evidence for the association between BJW and the mental health of non-victimised young adults. In Studies 1 and 2, we will show that BJW is positively associated with several indicators of mental health in two samples of young adults. In Study 3, in a sample of young adults taken from a representative sample of the Portuguese population, we will show that BJW is associated with trust. Before presenting these studies, we will give an overview of the literature on the relationship between BJW and the constructs considered in the studies.

BJW and life satisfaction

Satisfaction with life is conceptualised as the cognitive component of subjective well-being (Diener *et al.*, 1985). Research has shown that satisfaction with life is positively correlated with another dimension of well-being, namely self-esteem, and negatively correlated with neuroticism (Johnston *et al.*, 1995). Dalbert (1998, 1999) and Dalbert *et al.*, (2001)

BJW, subjective well-being and trust 87

obtained significant positive correlations between BJW and satisfaction with life in several samples of university students. Dalbert and Maes (2002) found significant positive correlations between BJW and satisfaction with life, satisfaction with school experience, and school performance in a sample of 1000 5th to 12th grade pupils. Moreover, Dalbert and Katona-Sallay (1996) found a positive correlation between BJW and satisfaction with life up to the point of the assessment. Lipkus *et al.* (1996) showed that several BJW scales are positively correlated with satisfaction with life, and Cubela (2000) confirmed this positive association. Finally, in two samples of couples, Lipkus and Bissonnette (1996) verified that BJW predicted matrimonial satisfaction and a low frequency of conflicts in older couples. For younger couples, the tendency was in the same direction, but was not significant.

BJW and self-esteem

Baumeister (1998) defines self-esteem as the degree to which an individual evaluates him- or herself positively. Self-esteem seems to be associated with psychological well-being, whether the individual finds him- or herself in a favourable or an adverse situation (e.g. Taylor and Brown, 1988). Therefore, self-esteem is considered a personal resource that reduces the impact of negative events in life. Self-esteem is also negatively correlated with depression (Tennen and Affleck, 1993) and with social anxiety (Leary and Kowalski, 1995). Few studies have analysed the correlation between BJW and self-esteem, and the results reported for four different samples are rather diverse: Feather (1991) found correlations of between 0.10 and 0.23; Dalbert (1992a, cited by Dalbert, 2001) reported a correlation of 0.19 between the two constructs, and Dalbert (1999) obtained a correlation of 0.31. Further studies may help to improve our understanding of this relationship.

BJW and interpersonal and institutional trust

As we have already mentioned, one of the functions of the BJW is to enhance trust in others and in the fairness of one's fate (Dalbert, 2001). Several studies have shown a relationship between BJW and both interpersonal and institutional trust. Peplau and Tyler (1975, cited by Rubin and Peplau, 1975) found a positive relationship between scores on the BJW scale and the tendency for higher trust in politicians, a more positive evaluation of political measures, the evaluation of the *status quo* as desirable, and political and economical conservatism. They also found positive correlations between BJW and attitudes to political organisations and government. Therefore, Rubin and Peplau (1975) underline that the BJW may lead to an uncritical acceptance of authority. In three experiments, Zuckerman and Gerbasi (1977) showed that, compared with those low in

88   *I. Correia and J. Vala*

BJW, people high in BJW showed more trust in an experimental scenario in the field of social psychology, were more likely to believe a promise made to them, and placed more trust in the actions of the government. Along the same lines, Fink and Guttenplan (1975, cited by Rubin and Peplau, 1975) obtained a strong positive correlation between the BJW and interpersonal trust (Rotter, 1967), specifically institutional trust, trust in the honesty of the others, and trust that the others will not take advantage of the individual. Recently, Bègue (2002) also found a strong correlation between BJW and interpersonal trust. Finally, in a sample of young couples, Lipkus and Bissonnette (1996) showed that the higher the BJW, the higher the trust in the spouse. In sum, all of these studies substantiate the association between BJW and trust in several domains.

BJW and perception of injustice

The definition of BJW as 'the belief that people get what they deserve or, conversely, deserve what they get' (Lerner and Simmons, 1966: 204) means a belief in a world in which justice prevails. Dalbert (2001) showed that one of the functions of the BJW is to provide a framework helping people to interpret life in a way that maintains justice: for example, by perceiving the unjust event as fair and thus restoring justice psychologically. In fact, the empirical evidence seems to support the hypothesis of a positive association between BJW and justice perceptions. In two samples of married couples (Lipkus and Bissonnette, 1996, 1998) and in a sample of dating couples (Lipkus and Bissonnette, 1998), BJW was more strongly associated with the tendency to respond constructively to potentially aggressive behaviour on the part of the partner. One of the reasons for this is that participants with a higher BJW perceive less injustice in the way they are treated by their partner. Furthermore, Finamore and Carlstone (1987) noticed that BJW was associated with the opinion that the police make few mistakes and with a negative attitude towards individuals sentenced for crimes.

Clayton (1992) confronted her subjects with a list of 18 unjust situations and found that people high in BJW tended to evaluate the situations as fairer than people low in BJW did. Dalbert and Yamauchi (1994) showed that participants high in BJW regarded the situation of a disadvantaged group as fairer. Cubela (2000) showed that Croatian employees with a high BJW perceived fewer injustices in the workplace than participants with a low BJW.

BJW and locus of control

According to Rotter (1966), perceived control is defined as a generalised expectancy of internal as opposed to external control of reinforcement and involves a causal analysis of success and failure: (a) if an event is perceived as resulting from the action of another person or forces external to the individual such as luck or fate, then the individual has a belief in external control; (b) if, however, an event is perceived as resulting from the behaviour or characteristics of the individual, then the individual has a belief in internal control. A belief in the opportunity to determine one's own destiny is important when it comes to coping with stress; for instance, in the recovery of patients hospitalised in intensive care units (see Lefcourt, 1982, for a review of the literature).

The relationship between the constructs locus of control and BJW has been described at two levels: the theoretical level and the empirical level. At the theoretical level, the concept of control over one's own life and environment seems central to the two concepts (Furnham and Procter, 1992). Indeed, it is common to both BJW and locus of internal control that bad luck is not the sole cause of bad things (Montada, 1994). Schmitt (1998) notes that some correlation between BJW and the need for control is to be expected because, under certain conditions, justice may imply control (we know what to do to obtain a certain result) and control may imply justice (we can implement justice), and both serve the basic need for security and well-being. However, as Lerner (1980) points out, justice may be dispensed by an omnipotent force. Maes (1994) argues that high BJW and locus of internal control are not theoretically identical: internal control does not imply fair decisions, nor does it prevent the occurrence of injustices. Maes concludes that BJW involves finding meaning in an event, while the belief in the locus of internal control is centred on attributing greater importance to individual actions.

According to Lerner (1980), BJW as measured on the Rubin and Peplau scale differs significantly from the locus of control, despite the relationships between the two concepts. In an analysis of Rotter's (1966) locus of control scale, Collins (1974) found four factors, one of which was BJW. Other authors replicated this result (Zuckerman and Gerbasi, 1977). However, as mentioned by Zuckerman and Gerbasi (1977), it was not possible to find a locus of control factor in Rubin and Peplau's (1975) BJW scale. Maes (1994) tried to compare the explanatory validity of the theory of BJW and of the hypothesis of defensive attribution in order to explain secondary victimisation – the additional victimisation inflicted by observers who blame or devalue a victim (Brickman et al., 1982). Maes's study supports the independence of the two constructs, although it does confirm that both contribute to the assignment of responsibility and to blaming the victim in the case of cancer patients.

On the empirical level, several studies have obtained correlations between BJW and the locus of control. Most of the empirical studies have found positive correlations between BJW and locus of internal control (see Table 6.1). However, the findings of Steensma et al. (1994) clearly contradict the rest of the empirical evidence. The reasons for this contradiction are still unexplained. In sum, BJW and locus of control seem to be

90   I. Correia and J. Vala

Table 6.1 Correlations between BJW and internal locus of control in different studies

Bierhoff *et al.* (1991)	0.17
Clayton (1992)	0.38
Furnham and Karani (1985)	0.27
Rubin and Peplau (1973)	0.44
Steensma *et al.* (1994)	−0.48
Zuckerman and Gerbasi (1977)	0.20

distinct constructs, despite the positive correlation between BJW and internal locus of control. Dalbert (2001) suggests that an internal locus of control may mediate the relationship between BJW and achievement, because high believers in a just world tend to attribute their results to their own actions (good things happen to good people), and attributing outcomes to one's ability and effort (internal locus of control) promotes better performance in achievement tasks.

BJW and optimism

Lerner titled his 1980 book *Belief in a Just World: A Fundamental Delusion*, indicating that individuals have an illusory belief that people are always fairly rewarded and that good things happen to good people while bad things happen to bad people. Optimism, like BJW, is a positive illusion about the world, the illusion that the world will be benevolent towards the individual, irrespective of his or her actions (good things will happen). However, as Dalbert (2001) showed, BJW and optimism are two relatively independent dimensions, both of which affect mental health in different ways: BJW is a coping resource that helps victims to overcome an unjust fate; optimism is merely a positive illusion associated with good mental health, but is not a resource helping individuals to cope with victimisation.

According to Sheier and Carver (1985), an optimistic orientation reflects the generalised expectation that good things will happen. Sheier and Carver (1987) reviewed the literature that evidenced a positive relationship between optimism (measured in different ways) and physical well-being (as determined by various symptoms like recovery from heart surgery), self-esteem and locus of internal control. They also obtained negative correlations between optimism and depression, and between optimism and perceived stress.

If BJW motivates people to behave fairly, and behaving according to the terms of the personal contract leads individuals to expect that they will be fairly rewarded, one would expect BJW to be positively associated with optimism – both in everyday activities and when individuals face serious risks. Indeed, empirical evidence supports this association. The first study that found BJW to be empirically associated with optimism was conducted by Lerner (1978): both BJW and optimism were aggregated on the same factor. Lambert *et al.* (1998) found a negative, although not significant, correlation between BJW and the estimated probability of threatening events such as dying in a flood, being hit by a tornado, being involved in a plane hijack, dying of hepatitis, dying of leukaemia and contracting AIDS. These correlations were stronger and more significant for authoritarian individuals who experience the environment in a more threatening way. Lambert *et al.* (1998) explain this result by proposing that the BJW can provide a buffer against the perception of risk for those high in authoritarianism. For those low in authoritarianism, no such buffer is necessary because there is no perception of personal invulnerability to risks. These results are in line with the findings of Maes (1998), which indicated that the higher the BJW, the higher the estimated probability of finding meaning in a serious disease (cancer) and of maturing during the process, the greater the individual's confidence in being able to cope with such a serious disease should he or she contract it, and the higher the feeling of personal invulnerability to that disease. However, when individuals imagined that they had the disease, the higher their BJW, the more likely they were to accept it. Chasteen *et al.* (1996, cited by Lambert *et al.*, 1998) found that individuals high in BJW were more optimistic about the changes and difficulties associated with getting older than those low in BJW.

The empirical evidence reviewed so far supports the hypothesis that the BJW may be associated with young adults' ability to cope with autonomy-related challenges. In particular, we expected BJW to be positively associated with optimism, mental health (self-esteem, satisfaction with life and happiness), locus of internal control, trust and perceptions of social justice.

Study 1

In Study 1, we explore the association of BJW with satisfaction with life, self-esteem, optimism and locus of control, as well as the intercorrelations between the other variables. To our knowledge, this is the first time that all of these constructs have been taken into account simultaneously. We predict positive associations between BJW and satisfaction with life, optimism, internal locus of control and self-esteem.

Participants and procedure

The participants in this study were 252 second-year psychology undergraduates aged between 19 and 25 years ($M = 21.30$, $SD = 1.67$); 204 (81 per cent) were female and 48 (19 per cent) male. During lesson time, participants were invited to participate in a research project studying the properties of some scales and the relationship between several constructs. The time required to complete the questionnaire was around 25 minutes.

92   *I. Correia and J. Vala*

At the end of the study participants were thanked for taking part and were debriefed.

Measures

We measured the *BJW* with a Portuguese version of the General Belief in a Just World Scale (GBJW) devised by Dalbert *et al.*, (1987). The scale consists of six items (Alpha = 0.60), and responses were given on a 7-point scale from 1 ('completely disagree') to 7 ('completely agree') rather than on the original 6-point scale. We measured *self-esteem* with Rosenberg's (1965) 10-item self-esteem scale (Alpha = 0.80). Responses were given on a 4-point scale from 1 ('completely disagree') to 4 ('completely agree'). *Satisfaction with life* was measured with the Satisfaction with Life Scale designed by Diener *et al.* (1985; Alpha = 0.82). Responses to its five items were given on a 7-point scale from 1 ('completely disagree') to 7 ('completely agree'). High means on all of these scales indicate strong endorsement of the construct. *Optimism* was assessed with the eight items of the Life Orientation Test (Sheier and Carver, 1985; Alpha = 0.71) measuring dispositional optimism. Responses were given on a 5-point scale from 1 ('completely disagree') to 5 ('completely agree'). Four items were recoded so that the higher the scale mean, the higher the level of optimism. *Locus of control* was measured with Rotter's (1966) locus of control scale (KR-20 = 0.71). Answers indicating an internal locus of control were coded as 1, those indicating an external locus of control as 0, and the scores for all the items were summed. The higher the score, the higher the locus of internal control. To prevent systematic influences of the response to some scales on the responses to other scales, the order of the scales was randomised for each participant.

Results

Correlations between the variables are given in Table 6.2. As expected, BJW is strongly associated with satisfaction with life, and moderately associated with optimism. This result is in line with the findings of authors such as Maes (1998), Lambert *et al.* (1998), and Dalbert (1998, 1999). BJW is also significantly associated with self-esteem, although the relationship is weak. As mentioned above, few studies have explored this association, and there are discrepancies in the results obtained. We believe this relationship should be further explored. Finally, BJW is also associated with locus of control, although not very strongly. This is consistent with most of the studies which have found a positive relationship between these two measures. Furthermore, all correlations between optimism, satisfaction with life, and locus of control are significant.

To explore the existence of a direct link between BJW and the two mental health dimensions, satisfaction with life and self-esteem, we con-

BJW, subjective well-being and trust 93

Table 6.2 Study 1: Correlations between belief in a just world, internal locus of control, optimism, satisfaction with life and self-esteem

	BJW	LC	Opt	SL	Self-esteem
Belief in a just world (BJW)	–	0.14*	0.19**	0.33***	0.13*
Internal locus of control (LC)	–	–	0.33***	0.14*	0.20**
Optimism (Opt)	–	–	–	0.39***	0.54***
Satisfaction with life (SL)	–	–	–	–	0.40***

Notes
* $p < 0.05$.
** $p < 0.01$.
*** $p < 0.001$.

ducted multiple regression analyses for each mental health dimension separately. In both analyses, optimism and locus of internal control were entered in the first step and BJW was entered in the second step, thus controlling for the effects of optimism and locus of control on mental health (Table 6.3). The results show a direct link between BJW and satisfaction with life when controlling for optimism and locus of internal control; however, there was no such relation between BJW and self-esteem. Moreover, optimism, but not internal locus of control, predicted self-esteem and satisfaction with life. Overall, the results of Study 1 revealed that BJW and satisfaction with life were uniquely associated, and that this held even when controlling for optimism and locus of control. No such unique relationship was observed for BJW and self-esteem.

Table 6.3 Study 1: Regression from satisfaction with life and self-esteem on optimism, locus of control and belief in a just world

Variables	Self-esteem			Satisfaction with life		
	R^2	Beta	t	R^2	Beta	t
Step 1						
Optimism	0.30	0.55	9.06***	0.14	0.33	5.30***
Internal locus of control	0.30	0.03	0.42	0.14	0.01	0.13
Step 2						
BJW	0.30	0.03	0.45	0.22	0.28	4.78***

Notes
* $p < 0.05$.
** $p < 0.01$.
*** $p < 0.001$.

94   *I. Correia and J. Vala*

Study 2

Study 2 was an exact replication of Study 1, except that the locus of control was not included. The participants in this study were 186 undergraduate students aged between 18 and 25 years (M =19.83, SD= 1.36); 122 (65.8 per cent) were female and 64 (34.2 per cent) male. With the exception of locus of control, the same measures were applied as in Study 1: General Belief in a Just World Scale: Alpha = 0.72; Self-esteem Scale: Alpha = 0.86; Satisfaction with Life Scale: Alpha = 0.80; Life Orientation Test: Alpha = 0.78. Responses to all items were given on 6-point scales ranging from 1 ('completely disagree') to 6 ('completely agree').

Results

Correlations between the variables are given in Table 6.4. As expected, BJW was positively correlated with satisfaction with life, self-esteem and optimism. These results are in line with the findings of Study 1.

To explore the relationship between BJW and the two mental health dimensions, satisfaction with life and self-esteem, we ran multiple regression analyses for each mental health dimension separately, controlling for the effects of optimism (Table 6.5). In both analyses, optimism was entered in the first step and BJW was entered in the second step. As in Study 1, the results reveal a direct link between BJW and satisfaction with life when controlling for optimism; however, there is no such relation between BJW and self-esteem.

Study 3

In Study 3 we analysed the correlations between BJW and subjective well-being, trust and perceptions of social justice in a sample of young adults taken from a representative sample of the Portuguese population. This study is based on the results of a national survey forming part of the European Values Survey (Halman, 2001). The national survey, called Social

Table 6.4 Study 2: Correlations between belief in a just world, optimism, satisfaction with life and self-esteem

	BJW	*Opt*	*SL*	*Self-esteem*
Belief in a just world (BJW)	–	0.21**	0.35***	0.19**
Optimism (Opt)	–	–	0.55***	0.66***
Satisfaction with life (SL)	–	–	—	0.58***

Notes
* $p<0.05$.
** $p<0.01$.
*** $p<0.001$.

BJW, subjective well-being and trust 95

Table 6.5 Study 2: Multiple regression analysis with optimism and belief in a just world as predictors and satisfaction with life and self-esteem as criteria

Variables	Self-esteem			Satisfaction with life		
	R^2	Beta	t	R^2	Beta	t
Step 1 Optimism	0.43	0.66	11.67***	0.30	0.55	8.80***
Step 2 BJW	0.44	0.07	1.23	0.36	0.24	3.86***

Notes
* $p<0.05$.
** $p<0.01$.
*** $p<0.001$.

Attitudes of the Portuguese People 1999, is coordinated internationally by the European Values Foundation and in Portugal by Manuel Villaverde Cabral and Jorge Vala, who are both at the Institute of Social Sciences of the University of Lisbon. The questionnaire implemented in this national survey included measures of BJW, subjective well-being, trust and perceptions of social justice. We expect higher BJW to be associated with higher subjective well-being, institutional trust and perceptions of social justice.

Sample

The total sample consisted of 1000 individuals aged 18 or over, living in places in Portugal with 10 or more houses. These individuals constitute a random representative sample of the Portuguese population, based on the data of the 1991 Census. The data were collected between October and December 1999 and included 100 sampling points. The participants were interviewed in their homes using a structured questionnaire. This took approximately one hour. For Study 3, we analysed the answers given by all individuals aged between 18 and 25. Thus, the sample for this study consists of 142 young adults (63 male and 79 female) with a mean age of 21.43 years ($SD = 2.31$). This sample is not representative, but because the original sample was selected at random it is heterogeneous, giving the results greater external validity.

Questionnaires

Belief in a just world was measured with the six items of the GBJW scale devised by Dalbert *et al.* (1987; Alpha = 0.70). Responses were given on a 5-point scale from 1 ('completely disagree') to 5 ('completely agree'). The facet of subjective well-being covered was *happiness*, which was measured using the question 'Considering all the aspects of your life, would you say

96   *I. Correia and J. Vala*

that you are ...', with response categories ranging from 1 ('not happy at all') to 4 ('very happy'). *Interpersonal trust* was measured with the following question: 'In general, do you think that most people can be trusted or, on the contrary, do you think that it is necessary to be very careful?' Participants were required to choose between the alternatives 0 ('It is necessary to be very careful') and 1 ('Most other people are to be trusted'). To evaluate *institutional trust*, participants were asked to indicate the degree of trust they feel in each of the following institutions: the church, the armed forces, the educational system, the press, the trade unions, the police, parliament, the civil service, the social security system, the European Union, NATO, the United Nations (UN), the health care system, the justice system and major companies, on 4-point scales from 1 ('none') to 4 ('a great deal'). Responses to these questions were averaged to form an institutional trust measure (Alpha = 0.88). The perception of social justice was measured in terms of the perception of respect for human rights in Portugal assessed by the question 'In your opinion, what is the level of *respect for human rights* in Portugal?' on a 4-point scale from 1 ('no respect at all') to 4 ('a lot of respect').

Results

The results show that BJW is positively correlated with institutional trust only (Table 6.6). The more the young adults endorsed the belief that the world is, by and large, a just place, the more they trusted institutions such as the police or the educational system.

Discussion

Young adulthood is a stage of life in which people have to mobilise social and psychological resources in order to face the new challenges associated

Table 6.6 Study 3: Correlations between belief in a just world, happiness, interpersonal trust, institutional trust and perceptions of social justice

	BJW	Happiness	Interpersonal trust	Institutional trust	Respect for human rights
BJW	–	0.12	0.08	0.19*	0.12
Happiness	–	–	0.09	0.17	0.15
Interpersonal trust	–	–	–	0.09	0.04
Institutional trust	–	–	–	–	0.11
Respect for human rights	–	–	–	–	–

Notes
* $p < 0.05$.
** $p < 0.01$.
*** $p < 0.001$.

BJW, subjective well-being and trust 97

with their increasing independence. BJW seems to be one of these resources. In particular, BJW is associated with life satisfaction. Moreover, in Studies 1 and 2, we also found that this relation is a unique one when controlling for optimism and internal locus of control. The more the young adults believed in a general just world, the more satisfied they were with their life. This result is in line with the empirical evidence gathered to date. However, BJW and self-esteem did not prove to be uniquely associated, although a reliable and validated self-esteem measure was used. It is our opinion that future studies should explore the relationship between BJW and self-esteem in more depth.

The positive association between BJW and locus of internal control is in line with most of the empirical evidence. Nevertheless, as shown in Table 6.1, the correlations between these constructs that have been obtained to date vary greatly. This supports the notion that BJW and locus of control are distinct constructs, and that the relationship between them may vary across subjects or conditions. More studies are needed to clarify this association.

BJW was positively associated with institutional trust. This result is in line with the findings of other studies (e.g. Peplau and Tyler, cited by Rubin and Peplau, 1975; Zuckerman and Gerbasi, 1977). The expected positive association between BJW and interpersonal trust was not found, however. This result contradicts the findings of Fink and Guttenplan (1975, cited by Rubin and Peplau, 1975), Lipkus and Bissonnette (1996) and Zuckerman and Gerbasi (1977). Likewise, the expected positive association between BJW and the perception of social justice was not confirmed, thus contradicting the results of Lipkus and Bissonnette (1996, 1998), Finamore and Carlstone (1987), Clayton (1992), Dalbert and Yamauchi (1994) and Cubela (2000).

In sum, the studies presented in this chapter support the assumption that young adults who believe in a just world have better mental health in terms of life satisfaction, and that they thus have better social and psychological resources helping them to cope with developmental tasks than individuals who do not believe in a just world. Is this a simple association or does it reflect causality? BJW theory assumes that it is the BJW that leads to better mental health. However, most evidence of the relationship between BJW and the psychological constructs with which it is associated, particularly those related to psychological well-being, is correlational, and thus does not permit conclusions to be drawn about the direction of the association between BJW and mental health (Dalbert and Maes, 2002). In fact, although BJW theory hypothesises a causal relationship between BJW and mental health, studies on mood and processing of information seem to suggest that it is the heuristic processing of information present when people are in a better mood that leads to a lower perception of injustice and consequently to the preservation of the BJW. In fact, according to the mood-as-information approach (Schwarz, 1990; Schwarz and Clore, 1983,

98   *I. Correia and J. Vala*

1988), a positive mood may serve as a signal that everything is all right, meaning that the motivation for effortful information processing is reduced, and the information is processed more heuristically than systematically. This is an avenue for future research in which experimental studies will play an important role. At this stage of research, we can only take note of the positive association between BJW and mental health.

Acknowledgements

This chapter is part of a larger research programme that was partially supported by two grants from the *Fundação para Ciência e Tecnologia* (PRAXIS/PSI/12091/1998 and POCTI/PSI/12091/1998 Programmes). Study 3 is based on the results of an annual national attitude survey 'Atitudes Sociais dos Portugueses' coordinated by M. Villaverde Cabral and J. Vala.

References

Baumeister, R.F. (1998) 'The self', in Gilbert, D.T., Fiske, S.T. and Lindzey, G. (eds), *The Handbook of Social Psychology*, New York: McGraw-Hill.

Bègue, L. (2002) 'Beliefs in justice and faith in people: Just world, religiosity and interpersonal trust', *Personality and Individual Differences*, 32: 375–82.

Bierhoff, H.W. (1991) 'Evidence for the altruistic personality from data on accident research', *Journal of Personality*, 59: 263–80.

Brickman, P., Rabinowitz, V.C., Karuza, J., Coates, D., Cohen, E. and Kidder, L. (1982), 'Models of helping and coping', *American Psychologist*, 37: 368–84.

Clayton, S.D. (1992) 'The experience of injustice: Some characteristics and correlates', *Social Justice Research*, 5: 71–91.

Collins, B.E. (1974) 'Four components of the Rotter internal–external scale: Belief in a difficult world, a just world, a predictable world and a politically responsive world', *Journal of Personality and Social Psychology*, 29: 381–91.

Cubela, V. (2000) *Relationship Between Belief in a Just World and Well-being in Employed and Unemployed in Croatia,* paper presented at the 7th Biennial Conference of the European Association for Research in Adolescence, Jena, Germany, June.

Dalbert, C. (1998) 'Belief in a just world, well-being, and coping with an unjust fate', in Montada, L. and Lerner, M.J. (eds), *Responses to Victimizations and Belief in a Just World,* New York: Plenum Press.

Dalbert, C. (1999) 'The world is more just for me than generally: About the Personal Belief in a Just World Scale's validity', *Social Justice Research*, 12: 79–98.

Dalbert, C. (2001) *The Justice Motive as a Personal Resource. Dealing with Challenges and Critical Life Events,* New York: Plenum Press.

Dalbert, C. and Katona-Sallay, H. (1996) 'The "belief in a just world" construct in Hungary', *Journal of Cross-Cultural Psychology*, 27: 293–314.

Dalbert, C. and Maes, J. (2002) 'Belief in a just world as a personal resource in school', in Ross, M. and Miller, D.T. (eds), *The Justice Motive in Everyday Life,* Cambridge: Cambridge University Press.

Dalbert, C. and Yamauchi, L.A. (1994) 'Belief in a just world and attitudes towards immigrants and foreign workers: A cultural comparison between Hawaii and Germany', *Journal of Applied Social Psychology*, 24: 1612–26.

Dalbert, C., Lipkus, I.M., Sallay, H. and Goch, I. (2001) 'A just and an unjust world: Structure and validity of different world beliefs', *Personality and Individual Differences*, 30: 561–77.

Dalbert, C., Montada, L. and Schmitt, M. (1987) 'Glaube an eine gerechte Welt als Motiv: Validierungskorrelate zweier Skalen', *Psychologische Beiträge*, 29: 596–615.

Diener, E., Emmons, R.A., Larson, R.J. and Griffin, S. (1985) 'The satisfaction with life scale', *Journal of Personality Assessment*, 49: 71–6.

Feather, N.T. (1991) 'Human values, global self-esteem and belief in a just world', *Journal of Personality*, 59: 83–107.

Finamore, F. and Carlstone, J. (1987) 'Religiosity, belief in a just world and crime control attitudes', *Psychological Reports*, 61, 135–8.

Furnham, A. and Karani, R. (1985) 'A cross-cultural study of attitudes to women, just world and locus of control beliefs, *Psychologia*, 28: 11–20.

Furnham, A. and Procter, E. (1992) 'Sphere-specific just world beliefs and attitudes to AIDS', *Human Relations*, 45: 265–80.

Hafer, C.L. and Correy, B.L. (1999) 'Mediators of the relation between beliefs in a just world and emotional responses to negative outcomes', *Social Justice Research*, 12: 189–202.

Halman, L. (2001) *The European Values Study: A Third Wave*, Tilburg: WORC, Tilburg University.

Johnston, M., Wright, S. and Weinman, J. (1995) *Measures in Health Psychology: A User's Portfolio*, Windsor, Berkshire: NFER-Nelson.

Lambert, A.J., Burroughs, T. and Chasteen, A.L. (1998) 'Belief in a just world and right-wing authoritarianism as moderators of perceived risk', in Montada, L. and Lerner, M.J. (eds), *Responses to Victimizations and Belief in a Just World*, New York: Plenum Press.

Leary, M.R. and Kowalski, R. (1995) *Social Anxiety*, New York: Guilford.

Lefcourt, H.M. (1982) *Locus of Control: Current Trends in Theory and Research*, Hillsdale, NJ: Lawrence Erlbaum.

Lerner, M.J. (1978) '"Belief in a just world" versus the "authoritarianism" syndrome . . . but nobody liked the Indians', *Ethnicity*, 5: 229–37.

Lerner, M.J. (1980) *Belief in a Just World: A Fundamental Delusion*, New York: Plenum Press.

Lerner, M.J. and Simmons, C.H. (1966) 'The observer's reaction to the "innocent victim": Compassion or rejection?', *Journal of Personality and Social Psychology*, 4: 203–10.

Levinson, D. (1978) *The Seasons of a Man's Life*, New York: Knopf.

Lipkus, I.M. and Bissonnette, V.L. (1996) 'Relations among belief in a just world, willingness to accommodate and marital well being', *Personality and Social Psychology Bulletin*, 22: 1043–56.

Lipkus, I.M. and Bissonnette, V.L. (1998) 'The belief in a just world and willingness to accommodate among married and dating couples', in Montada, L. and Lerner, M.J. (eds), *Responses to Victimizations and Belief in a Just World*, New York: Plenum Press.

Lipkus, I.M., Dalbert, C. and Siegler, I.C. (1996) 'The importance of distinguishing the belief in a just world for self versus for others: Implications for psychological well-being', *Personality and Social Psychology Bulletin*, 22: 666–77.

100   I. Correia and J. Vala

Maes, J. (1994) 'Blaming the victim: Belief in control or belief in justice?' *Social Justice Research*, 7: 69–90.

Maes, J. (1998) 'Immanent justice and ultimate justice: Two ways of believing in justice', in Montada, L. and Lerner, M.J. (eds), *Responses to Victimizations and Belief in a Just World*, New York: Plenum Press.

Montada, L. (1994) 'Injustice in harm and loss', *Social Justice Research*, 7: 5–28.

Montada, L. (1998) 'Belief in a just world: A hybrid of justice motive and self-interest?', in Montada, L. and Lerner, M.J. (eds), *Responses to Victimizations and Belief in a Just World*, New York: Plenum Press.

Rosenberg, M. (1965) *Society and the Adolescent Self-image*, Princeton, NJ: Princeton University Press.

Rotter, J.B. (1966) 'Generalized expectancies for internal versus external control of reinforcement', *Psychological Monographs*, 80: 1–28.

Rotter, J.B. (1967) 'A new scale for the measurement of interpersonal trust', *Journal of Personality*, 35: 651–65.

Rubin, Z. and Peplau, L.A. (1973) 'Belief in a just world and reactions to another's lot: a study of participants in the National Draft Lottery', *Journal of Social Issues*, 29: 73–93.

Rubin, Z. and Peplau, L.A. (1975) 'Who believes in a just world?' *Journal of Social Issues*, 31: 65–89.

Schmitt, M.J. (1998) 'Methodological strategies in research to validate measures of belief in a just world', in Montada, L. and Lerner, M.J. (eds), *Responses to Victimizations and Belief in a Just World*, New York: Plenum Press.

Schwarz, N. (1990) 'Feelings as information: Informational and motivational functions of affective states', in Sorrentino, R. and Higgins, E.T. (eds), *Handbook of Motivation and Cognition: Foundations of Social Behavior*, New York: Guilford.

Schwarz, N. and Clore, G. (1983) 'Mood, misattribution, and judgments of well-being: Informative but directive functions of affective states', *Journal of Personality and Social Psychology*, 45: 513–23.

Schwarz, N. and Clore, G. (1988) 'How do I feel about it? The informative function of affective states', in Fiedler, K. and Forgas, J.P. (eds), *Affect, Cognition and Social Behavior*, Göttingen: Hogrefe.

Sheier, M.F. and Carver, C.S. (1985) 'Optimism, coping and health: Assessment and implications of generalized outcome expectancies', *Health Psychology*, 4: 219–47.

Sheier, M.F. and Carver, C.S. (1987) 'Dispositional optimism and physical well-being: The influence of generalized outcome expectancies on health', *Journal of Personality*, 55: 169–210.

Steensma, H., den Hartigh, E. and Lucardie, E. (1994) 'Social categories, just world belief, locus of control and causal attributions of occupational accidents', *Social Justice Research*, 7: 281–99.

Taylor, S.E. and Brown, G. (1988) 'Illusion and well-being: A social psychological perspective on mental health', *Psychological Bulletin*, 103: 193–210.

Tennen, H. and Affleck, G. (1993) 'The puzzles of self-esteem: A clinical perspective', in Baumeister, R. (ed.), *Self-esteem: The Puzzle of Low Self-regard*, New York: Plenum Press.

Vaillant, G.E. (1977) *Adaptation to Life*, Boston: Little, Brown.

Zuckerman, M. and Gerbasi, K.C. (1977) 'Belief in internal control or belief in a just world: The use and misuse of the I-E scale in prediction of attitudes and behavior', *Journal of Personality*, 45: 356–78.

7 Belief in a just world, personality and well-being of adolescents

Claudia Dalbert and Jozef Dzuka

Introduction

The belief in a just world (BJW) is a stable personality characteristic that evolves as a concomitant of cognitive development. Children assume that the world is governed by justice, and that justice emanates from events and occurrences themselves. They do not see random events as arbitrary, but instead infer causality. As predicted by just world theory, the tendency to assume causality in random events is most pronounced when either positive outcomes follow good motives or negative outcomes follow bad motives (Jose, 1990). Young children's belief in immanent justice (Piaget, 1932/1997) can be classified as a cognitively immature reaction, and a strong belief in immanent justice is typical of children younger than 7 or 8 years of age. As they grow older, children learn that a great deal of what happens in the world actually occurs at random, that evil is sometimes rewarded and that people do not always get what they deserve. They seem to cope with this knowledge by attempting to restore justice in the world. Apparently similar reactions can be observed for older children, adolescents and even adults. A significant difference in the behavioural patterns of different age groups has been found in previous studies, however. Third-graders (children in their third year of schooling) and older respondents are aware of the randomness of events. Despite this knowledge, they defend their BJW by constructing contingency in random events whenever possible. They do so by reconstructing justice in the world, e.g. by declaring random fates to be self-inflicted or deserved. Indeed, the firmer the BJW, the more pronounced this type of reaction. Thus, the development of a belief in a just world – as opposed to a belief in immanent justice – can be interpreted as a consequence of cognitive maturity.

During adolescence a differentiation of two different just-world beliefs can be observed: on the one hand, the belief in a personal just world in which one is usually treated fairly, and on the other, the belief in a general just world in which people in general get what they deserve. This differentiation into two types of belief is clearly apparent among

102   *C. Dalbert and J. Dzuka*

fifth-graders, at least (see Dalbert and Radant in this volume). The strength of both beliefs also seems to decrease over adolescence and young adulthood (Dalbert, 2001). Both developmental changes – differentiation and decline – can be interpreted as consequences of growing cognitive maturity. The more cognitively mature the individual, the more pronounced the decline in general BJW. However, the sharper the decline in general BJW, the less pronounced the decrease in personal BJW, such that a weak general BJW can be seen as compensated by a stronger personal BJW. This enables adolescents to cope with difficult developmental tasks.

Growing cognitive maturity undermines teenagers' belief that the world is a generally just place. This implies the loss of an important personal resource which would have enabled them to develop their own philosophy of life, invest in long-term goals and perform better. In this sense, the decline in general BJW implies a significant developmental loss. The compensation of this loss by a less pronounced decline in personal BJW endows cognitively mature adolescents with a strong BJW, an important personal resource for their further development. Overall, then, adolescence is a critical period in the establishment of just world beliefs. It is during this stage of life that the belief in a general just world is established and differentiated from the belief in a personal just world. Thus, adolescents can fall back on their personal belief in a just world as a resource while coping with the developmental tasks of this phase of life.

One important function of the belief in a just world, and particularly the belief in a personally just world, is its potential to protect mental health. In two questionnaire studies we, thus, tested the impact of BJW on mental health – described in terms of subjective well-being – during adolescence. In particular, we were interested in exploring the complex relationship of BJW and global personality dimensions – namely neuroticism and extraversion – with subjective well-being.

BJW and mental health

The relationships between BJW and several dimensions of mental health have been examined frequently. On the one hand, BJW serves as a buffer protecting mental health when individuals are under threat of being treated unfairly (e.g. Dalbert, 2002) or are coping with critical life-events (e.g. Agrawal and Dalal, 1993; Brown and Grover, 1998; Bulman and Wortman, 1977; Lerner and Somers, 1992). In such conditions, BJW acts as a buffer shielding the individuals' self-esteem and life satisfaction and decreasing their feelings of anger. It seems that BJW sustains mental health by facilitating the assimilation of unfairness – more specifically, by minimising experienced unfairness and self-blaming and preventing self-focused rumination. People high in BJW seem less likely to feel that they are victims of discrimination (Lipkus and Siegler, 1993). They tend to

BJW, personality and well-being 103

blame themselves for their fate being – at least partly – self-inflicted (Hafer and Correy, 1999), to play down the perpetrator's actions as being unintentional (Dalbert, 2002) and, as a consequence, to minimise experienced unfairness (Dalbert, 1996). Moreover, those high in BJW are less likely to ruminate about themselves (Dalbert, 1997), which would lead to an increase in anger (Rusting and Nolen-Hoeksema, 1998).

On the other hand, BJW helps subjects to cope with their daily activities. It increases trust in others and confidence in achieving one's goals (see Dette *et al.* in this volume), it enhances performance (Tomaka and Blascovich, 1994), and it promotes fairness (Dalbert, 1999; Hafer, 2000). As such, BJW and mental health usually also exhibit an adaptive relationship in non-victim samples (e.g. Dalbert, 1998). Individuals with a strong BJW are more satisfied with their life, exhibit a more positive mood, are less likely to be depressive, and show a higher level of self-esteem. However, the relationship between BJW and mental health is stronger in victim samples than in non-victim samples; it is strongest when mental health is described in terms of life satisfaction, and often weaker when negative mood states are examined (for a review see Dalbert, 2001). Studies differentiating between the two dimensions of BJW have found that personal BJW is more strongly correlated with well-being than general BJW (Lipkus *et al.*, 1996; Dalbert, 1999). As yet, however, no such studies have been conducted with adolescent samples. Thus, our aim was to examine the relationship between BJW and mental health – measured in terms of well-being – in adolescence, and to test the hypothesis that this relationship is stronger for the personal than for the general BJW.

BJW and personality

Personality is structured hierarchically (e.g. Cantor, 1990; Epstein, 1990; Eysenck, 1947). According to established personality theories, a personality is represented by its behaviour and dispositions, which are organised in a hierarchical way. The higher the hierarchical level, the more stable the entities are assumed to be (e.g. Vaidya *et al.*, 2002). Manifestations in a specific situation are located on the lowest level. Habitual behaviour – behaviour which reoccurs under similar conditions – can be found on a higher level. For example, individuals may habitually react to an injustice by trying to re-establish justice. The theory of BJW offers a further explanation for this response, namely, that these people are motivated to believe that the world is governed by justice and, as a consequence, to try to defend this belief by (re-)establishing justice. Thus, personality traits found on a higher level of personality may predispose individuals to engage in behaviours that become habitual, and the belief in a just world may be interpreted as such a personality factor. If BJW is a personality factor, it should be constant over time and specific situations. Dalbert (2001) summarised findings evidencing that BJW is a stable construct, and

104   *C. Dalbert and J. Dzuka*

that it indeed remains stable over time and across situations. An even higher level of personality is defined by constellations of traits that can be summed up in global personality dimensions, namely extraversion and neuroticism. Eysenck (1982) characterised extraversion by activity and sociability, and neuroticism by unpredictability and over-sensitivity. In our view, BJW is a personality trait that influences a person's reactions to justice-relevant situations and impacts on their well-being. Habitual positive well-being involves frequent satisfying and joyful experiences, accompanied by infrequent experiences of unpleasant emotions (Diener *et al.*, 1997). Thus, habitual subjective well-being should not be seen as a trait, but as a habitual response that can be influenced by personality traits such as BJW.

There is some evidence to suggest that BJW as a personality trait is correlated with the global personality dimensions. Heaven and Connors (1988) and Rim (1983) observed a negative correlation between BJW and neuroticism. Furthermore, women who score low on BJW have been found to be more introverted (Heaven and Connors, 1988). However, Rim (1983) found no such relationship. Lipkus *et al.* (1996) found a positive relationship between general BJW and extraversion. The same held for the personal belief in a just world, which also correlated negatively with neuroticism. However, Wolfradt and Dalbert (2003) observed no such relationships between general BJW and neuroticism or extraversion. Finally, in a sample of Slovakian students, Dzuka and Dalbert (2002) revealed a negative relationship between personal, but not general, BJW and neuroticism but not extraversion. In sum, empirical findings indicate a negative relationship between personal BJW and neuroticism, in particular.

Personality and well-being

Research into the relationship between broad personality dimensions and well-being has revealed that extraversion correlates positively with the frequency of positive affect, and neuroticism with the frequency of negative affect (Costa and McCrae, 1980; Emmons and Diener, 1986; Larsen and Ketelaar, 1991; Meyer and Shack, 1989; Watson and Clark, 1984). According to Costa and McCrae (1980: 673), 'Extraversion ... predisposes individuals toward positive affect, whereas neuroticism ... predisposes individuals toward negative affect.' Thus, the question arises of whether the adaptive relationship between (personal) BJW and well-being may be caused by neuroticism, which is negatively correlated with (personal) BJW on the one hand and with subjective well-being on the other.

However, Schwenkmezger (1991) argued that this simple correlational approach fails to do justice to the complex character of the relationship between personality and subjective well-being. For example, Hotard *et al.* (1989) showed that social relations only affect the subjective well-being of introverted individuals, and not that of their extraverted counterparts.

BJW, personality and well-being 105

Consequently, McFatter (1994: 577) summed up the relationship between personality – in particular extraversion (E) and neuroticism (N) – and subjective well-being – in terms of positive (PA) and negative (NA) affect – by stating that 'the common claim that extraversion is related to measures of PA but not NA, whereas neuroticism is related to measures of NA but not PA, is probably misleading. Although the claim may be true for simple zero-order correlations that describe only relations of marginal distributions, it does not accurately reflect how E and N are jointly related to PA and NA.' Possible interactions may well explain why Costa and McCrae's findings (1980) could not be replicated consistently (for a meta-analysis, see DeNeve and Cooper, 1998). Potential moderators of the relationship between personality and well-being also have to be taken into account. Diener and Fujita (1995) differentiate between three kinds of moderators: material, social and personal resources. We consider BJW to be a personal resource that not only makes an individual contribution to explaining well-being, above and beyond that of global personality dimensions (Lipkus *et al.*, 1996), but that may also moderate the personality's impact on well-being.

Two questionnaire studies with adolescents were conducted to test the following hypotheses: (a) BJW should correlate positively with subjective well-being. (b) This should hold even when controlling for global personality dimensions, namely extraversion and neuroticism, and (c) the relationship should be stronger for the personal than for the general BJW. Further, we aimed to explore possible interactions between personality and BJW in explaining subjective well-being. Finally, Study 1 was carried out cross-culturally in order to differentiate between global and culture-specific effects.

Study 1

In Study 1, $N = 178$ Slovakian adolescents (103 females and 75 males) with a mean age of 16.84 years ($SD = 1.16$; ranging between 15 and 20 years) and $N = 203$ German adolescents (105 females and 98 males) with a mean age of 17.10 years ($SD = 1.00$; ranging between 16 and 20 years) participated; both samples were drawn from university-track secondary schools. Just world beliefs were measured with the 6-item General Belief in a Just World Scale (Dalbert *et al.*, 1987; Slovakian sample: Alpha = 0.57; German sample: Alpha = 0.68) and the 7-item Personal Belief in a Just World Scale (Dalbert, 1999; Alpha = 0.76/0.85). Extraversion (Alpha = 0.78/0.74) and neuroticism (Alpha = 0.73/0.82) were measured using the respective scales of the Freiburg Personality Inventory (Fahrenberg *et al.*, 1978), each consisting of 7 items. The cognitive dimension of subjective well-being was measured with the 7-item General Satisfaction with Life Scale (Alpha = 0.78/0.89; Dalbert *et al.*, 1984), and the emotional dimension with two subscales of the Subjective Emotional Habitual Well-Being Scale

Table 7.1 Correlations in Study 1

	1	2	3	4	5	6	7	8
1 Gender	–	0.05	0.15*	-0.07	0.10	0.18**	0.20**	0.18**
2 Extraversion	-0.04	–	-0.21**	0.15*	0.17*	0.38**	0.41**	-0.22**
3 Neuroticism	0.03	-0.09	–	-0.26**	-0.27**	-0.44**	-0.34**	0.54**
4 General BJW	-0.04	-0.02	-0.13	–	0.33**	0.17*	0.17*	-0.10
5 Personal BJW	-0.07	0.11	-0.18*	0.39**	–	0.61**	0.41**	-0.30**
6 Life satisfaction	0.09	0.39**	-0.20**	0.18*	0.46**	–	0.64**	-0.34**
7 Positive affect	0.07	0.38**	-0.19**	-0.00	0.18*	0.49**	–	-0.27**
8 Negative affect	0.20**	-0.22**	0.55**	-0.08	-0.22**	-0.23**	-0.30**	–

Notes

The correlations of the German sample ($N=203$) are shown above the diagonal, the correlations of the Slovakian sample ($N=178$) below the diagonal.

* $p<0.05$.

** $p<0.01$.

BJW, personality and well-being 107

(Dzuka and Dalbert, 2002): positive affect (Alpha = 0.67/0.73) and negative affect (Alpha = 0.69/0.70), the first consisting of 4 items and the second of 6 items. All items were rated on 6-point rating scales, with 6 indicating a strong construct. Means were used as scale values.

The correlations between personality, BJWs and well-being are presented separately for both samples in Table 7.1. In the German sample, both BJWs correlated positively with extraversion and negatively with neuroticism. In the Slovakian sample, there was only a significant negative correlation between neuroticism and personal BJW. In the German sample, all four personality variables showed the expected correlations with the three well-being dimensions, with the exception of general BJW with negative affect. In the Slovakian sample, the same was true, with the exception of general BJW with positive and negative affect.

Multiple regressions were run for each well-being dimension and each sample separately in order to test whether BJWs could make an independent contribution to explaining well-being, above and beyond gender and the two global personality dimensions, and to explore whether the BJWs could moderate the impact of the global personality dimensions on well-being. In each multiple regression, gender was entered in the first step, extraversion and neuroticism were entered stepwise in the second block, the BJWs were entered stepwise in the third block, and the four interaction terms of both BJWs with the two global personality dimensions were entered stepwise in the final block. Interaction terms which were not significant and main effects which were neither part of an interaction nor revealing a significant main effect were deleted from the regression equation. Results are depicted in Table 7.2.

In the Slovakian sample, life satisfaction was predicted by extraversion, personal BJW and the interaction of general BJW with extraversion, explaining a total of 35 per cent of the variance. The more extraverted they were, and the more they believed in a personal just world, the more satisfied Slovakian adolescents were with their life. Furthermore, the more they believed in a general just world, the higher their life satisfaction – though this held only for those who were not extraverted ($M - SD = 2.12$; $b = 0.16$) as opposed to those who were highly extraverted ($M + SD = 3.30$; $b = -0.12$). In the German sample, life satisfaction was also predicted by extraversion and personal BJW, as well as by gender, neuroticism, the interaction of personal BJW with extraversion and the interaction of general BJW with neuroticism, explaining a total of 59 per cent of the variance. The more extraverted and the less neurotic they were, the more satisfied the German adolescents were with their life. Moreover, the more they believed in a personal just world, the more satisfied they were with their life. The latter was especially true of those who were less extraverted ($M - SD = 2.25$; $b = 0.66$) compared to those who were highly extraverted ($M + SD = 3.34$; $b = 0.33$). Likewise, the more they believed in a general just world, the more satisfied they were with their life. However, this was

108   C. Dalbert and J. Dzuka

Table 7.2 Well-being on gender, extraversion, neuroticism, general and personal BJW and the interactions of both BJWs with both personality dimensions in Study 1 (multiple regression; accepted models; $p < 0.05$)

Predictor	R	R^2	b	t	p
Slovakian sample					
Life satisfaction ($F_{total} = 23.130$; $df = 4/173$; $p < 0.001$)					
Extraversion	0.39	0.15[c]	1.23	–	–
Personal BJW	0.57	0.33[c]	0.39	6.07	0.000
General BJW	0.57	0.33	0.67	–	–
General BJW × Extraversion	0.59	0.35[c]	−0.24	−2.44	0.016
			−0.77		
Positive Affect ($F_{total} = 18.143$; $df = 2/175$; $p < 0.001$)					
Extraversion	0.38	0.15[c]	0.40	5.33	0.000
Neuroticism	0.41	0.17[b]	−0.17	−2.34	0.021
			3.18		
Negative Affect ($F_{total} = 32.404$; $df = 3/174$; $p < 0.001$)					
Gender	0.20	0.04[c]	0.21	2.91	0.004
Neuroticism	0.58	0.33[c]	0.52	8.64	0.000
Extraversion	0.60	0.36[c]	−0.17	−2.69	0.008
			1.76		
German sample					
Life satisfaction ($F_{total} = 40.492$; $df = 7/195$; $p < 0.001$)					
Gender	0.18	0.03[b]	0.26	3.13	0.002
Neuroticism	0.50	0.25[c]	−1.03	–	–
Extraversion	0.57	0.33[c]	1.57	–	–
Personal BJW	0.73	0.53[c]	1.33	–	–
General BJW	0.73	0.53	−0.69	–	–
Personal BJW × Extraversion	0.75	0.57[c]	−0.30	−0.90	0.000
General BJW × Neuroticism	0.77	0.59[c]	0.23	3.42	0.001
			0.93		
Positive Affect ($F_{total} = 27.247$; $df = 4/198$; $p < 0.001$)					
Gender	0.20	0.04[b]	0.25	3.18	0.002
Extraversion	0.45	0.21[c]	0.39	5.34	0.000
Neuroticism	0.54	0.29[c]	−0.21	−3.73	0.000
Personal BJW	0.60	0.36[c]	0.23	4.48	0.000
			2.71		
Negative Affect ($F_{total} = 33.569$; $df = 3/199$; $p < 0.001$)					
Gender	0.18	0.03[b]	0.17	2.27	0.025
Neuroticism	0.55	0.31[c]	0.41	7.73	0.000
Personal BJW	0.58	0.34[c]	−0.15	−3.07	0.002
			2.31		

Notes
a $p < 0.05$.
b $p < 0.01$.
c $p < 0.001$.
Gender was coded: 1 = female, 0 = male.

BJW, personality and well-being 109

only true of those who were neurotic ($M + SD = 3.40$; $b = 0.09$), as opposed to those who were not neurotic ($M - SD = 1.94$; $b = -0.24$). Finally, female German students were more satisfied with their life than their male counterparts.

In the Slovakian sample, positive affect was predicted by extraversion and neuroticism. The same was true of the German sample, but gender and personal BJW also predicted positive affect here. The more extraverted and the less neurotic the adolescents were, the more positive affect they experienced. Furthermore, German females and German adolescents with a strong belief in a personal just world experienced more positive affect.

In the Slovakian sample, negative affect was predicted by gender, neuroticism and extraversion. The same was true of the German sample, but with personal BJW rather than extraversion predicting negative affect. The more neurotic the adolescents were, the less extraverted the Slovakian students were, and the less the German adolescents believed in a personal BJW, the more they experienced negative affect. Furthermore, females experienced more negative affect than males.

Taken collectively, in both samples all three well-being dimensions were predicted by at least one of the global personality dimensions (extraversion, neuroticism) in the expected way. In addition, the personal but not the general BJW exhibited a positive impact on well-being when controlling for global personality dimensions, particularly in the German sample. The more the German adolescents believed that events in their life were essentially just, the more satisfied they were with their life, the more often they experienced positive affect, and the less often they experienced negative affect. In the Slovakian sample, only life satisfaction was predicted by the personal BJW. The data thus support our first three hypotheses. Another aim of our first study was to test for possible interactions between the global personality dimensions and the BJWs. Interaction effects were found in both samples, predicting life satisfaction only. The three interactions may be summarised as indicating that BJWs become especially important when adolescents are in particular need of a buffer because their global personality structure does not add to their life satisfaction. Finally, gender effects were more pronounced in the German than in the Slovakian sample. However, it seems that female students tend to produce higher values in all well-being dimensions, both positive and negative.

Study 2

The interaction effects between BJW and global personality dimensions in predicting life satisfaction were a particularly interesting outcome of the first study. We therefore ran a replication study with another sample of Slovakian adolescents in order to confirm this effect. $N = 201$ Slovakian

110   *C. Dalbert and J. Dzuka*

adolescents (101 females and 100 males) with a mixed educational background and a mean age of 16.32 years ($SD = 1.40$; ranging from 14 to 20 years) participated in Study 2, which was an exact replication of Study 1. Correlations are given in Table 7.3, and the results of the multiple regression analyses are shown in Table 7.4. Again, personal BJW correlated more strongly than general BJW with both global personality dimensions

Table 7.3 Correlations in Study 2

	1	2	3	4	5	6	7	8
1 Gender	–	0.04	0.02	0.07	0.18**	0.10	0.32**	0.15*
2 Extraversion	–	–	0.00	0.15*	0.21**	0.33**	0.30**	−0.08
3 Neuroticism	–	–	–	0.03	−0.14*	−0.16*	−0.29**	0.46**
4 General BJW	–	–	–	–	0.58**	0.33**	0.21**	−0.01
5 Personal BJW	–	–	–	–	–	0.50**	0.31**	−0.14*
6 Life Satisfaction	–	–	–	–	–	–	0.40**	−0.26**
7 Positive Affect	–	–	–	–	–	–	–	−0.13
8 Negative Affect	–	–	–	–	–	–	–	–

Notes
Slovakian sample ($N = 201$).
* $p < 0.05$.
** $p < 0.01$.

Table 7.4 Well-being on gender, extraversion, neuroticism, general and personal BJW and the interactions of both BJWs with both personality dimensions in Study 2 (Slovakian sample; multiple regression; accepted models; $p < 0.05$)

Predictor	R	R²	b	t	p
Life satisfaction ($F_{total} = 42.483$; $df = 2/198$; $p < 0.001$)					
Extraversion	0.33	0.11ᶜ	0.35	3.86	0.000
Personal BJW	0.55	0.30ᶜ	0.42	7.40	0.000
			1.72		
Positive Affect ($F_{total} = 21.241$; $df = 4/196$; $p < 0.001$)					
Gender	0.32	0.10ᶜ	0.48	4.67	0.000
Neuroticism	0.44	0.19ᶜ	−0.36	−4.55	0.000
Extraversion	0.53	0.28ᶜ	0.41	4.20	0.000
Personal BJW	0.55	0.30ᶜ	0.17	2.75	0.007
			2.78		
Negative Affect ($F_{total} = 30.096$; $df = 2/198$; $p < 0.001$)					
Gender	0.15	0.02ᵃ	0.20	2.28	0.024
Neuroticism	0.48	0.23ᶜ	0.49	7.36	0.000
			1.18		

Notes
a $p < 0.05$.
b $p < 0.01$.
c $p < 0.001$.
Gender was coded: 1 = female, 0 = male.

in the expected direction. All four personality dimensions revealed the expected correlations with the three well-being dimensions. Life satisfaction was again predicted by extraversion and personal BJW. However, no interaction effects were observed. The more extraverted they were and the more they believed in a personal just world, the more satisfied the Slovakian adolescents were with their life. Positive affect was again predicted by neuroticism and extraversion, but additionally by gender and personal BJW. The latter mirrors the findings for the German sample. The less neurotic and the more extraverted they were, and the more strongly they endorsed the personal BJW, the more positive affect the Slovakian adolescents experienced. Young Slovakian females revealed more positive affect, but also more negative affect. This had also been observed in Study 1. Apart from gender, negative affect was again predicted by neuroticism, but not by extraversion. The more neurotic the Slovakian students were, the more they experienced negative affect.

In sum, Study 2 replicated five of the six main effects for the four personality dimensions. Additionally, personal BJW showed a main effect on positive affect, which was only the case for the German sample in Study 1. The gender effect that female students revealed higher values on both positive and negative affect scales was replicated and extended. However, the interaction effect between general BJW and extraversion was not confirmed in Study 2.

Discussion

The relationships between four personality dimensions – the two global personality dimensions, extraversion and neuroticism, and both just world beliefs – and three dimensions of habitual subjective well-being were explored in three samples of adolescents from Slovakia and Germany. Starting with the relationships between the BJWs and the two global personality dimensions, it can be summarised that relationships were stronger for the personal than for the general BJW, and that the relationship between personal BJW and neuroticism was stronger than that between personal BJW and extraversion. This result mirrors previous research (Dzuka and Dalbert, 2002; Heaven and Connors, 1988; Lipkus *et al.*, 1996; Rim, 1983). We have argued that personality is hierarchically structured, and that neuroticism is a more global and stable personality dimension than personal BJW. From a developmental perspective, the consistent negative relationship between personal BJW and neuroticism raises the question of whether the degree of neuroticism is a causal determinant in the development of personal BJW. Future developmental studies should include neuroticism as well as parenting (Dalbert and Radant, in this volume) and specific life circumstances such as growing up with both parents or just one parent (Sallay and Dalbert, in this volume) in order to disentangle the independent contributions of neuroticism,

112   *C. Dalbert and J. Dzuka*

parenting and life circumstances in fostering the development of a personal belief in a just world.

The consistent negative relationship between neuroticism and personal BJW has concrete implications for the prediction of subjective well-being – namely, that it is important to control for global personality in terms of neuroticism when testing the independent contribution that personal BJW makes to buffering subjective well-being. This necessity is confirmed by the finding that, as expected, the personal BJW played a more important role than the general BJW in predicting subjective well-being. Five out of nine correlations between general BJW and well-being were significant. However, general BJW did not show any significant main effect in explaining subjective well-being, and only contributed to two significant interactions. We will return to this point below. Personal BJW correlated with the three habitual well-being dimensions in all three samples. However, when controlling for the global personality dimensions the picture changed, with personal BJW only making an independent contribution in six of the nine multiple regression tests of the relationship between personal BJW and well-being. Personal BJW independently and consistently contributed to explaining life satisfaction, and predicted positive affect twice. However, it was only in the German sample that personal BJW also impacted on negative affect.

Thus, the question arises of whether the impact of personal BJW on well-being is more typical for German adolescents than for Slovakian adolescents. We have no hypothesis to explain why this should be the case. This culturally different pattern of results needs to be replicated before it can be interpreted in theoretical terms.

Comparison of the three well-being dimensions showed that the relationship between personal BJW and life satisfaction was the most consistent, followed by positive affect. Negative affect was unrelated to personal BJW, with one exception. This pattern of results mirrors observations within adult samples (Dalbert, 1998). Thus, we can conclude that BJW is most typically related to the positive, rather than the negative aspects of well-being, including the cognitive dimension of life satisfaction in particular, but also the emotional dimension as depicted by the positive affect scale. This relationship can be interpreted as reflecting the BJW's character as a basic and illusionary schema about the world. BJW fosters the tendency to deny complex injustices that cannot be readdressed, whether these injustices are experienced (e.g. Hafer and Correy, 1999; Lipkus and Siegler, 1993) or observed (Montada et al., 1986). Moreover, it prompts individuals to deny discrimination against their own group more strongly than discrimination against other groups (Dalbert and Yamauchi, 1994). As such, the notion of justice within one's social world is more a positive illusion than a reflection of reality, and this positive illusion seems to foster a positive outlook (Lerner, 1978), thus enhancing well-being.

Our results provide a certain amount of evidence to support the notion that beliefs in a just world become especially important for adolescents whose well-being, in terms of life satisfaction, for example, is not enhanced by their global personality dimensions, especially those low on extraversion. Belief in a just world proved to be a protective resource enhancing the life satisfaction of the introverted adolescents in our sample. This is consistent with the assumption that BJW works as a buffer, particularly for those in need of such protection (Dalbert, 2001). Up to now, the buffering effect of the BJW has been explored by comparing victim and non-victim groups, for example, and showing that BJW is more important in explaining the well-being of victims than of non-victims. In the light of the present results, one might add that not only victims of an unjust fate are in need of a buffer. Deficits in the global personality structure may also necessitate this kind of protective shield. However, our interaction results are very preliminary. The interactions were only observed for life satisfaction, and not for either of the other well-being dimensions, and only in two of the three samples. Moreover, in one case, there was an interaction between extraversion and personal BJW; in another case, an interaction emerged between general BJW and extraversion. Although the interactions operate in the expected direction, more studies are needed to decide whether this is a systematic or a random pattern.

Conclusion

The results of our studies unambiguously indicate that the belief in a personal just world – i.e. that events in one's own life are generally just – is negatively correlated with neuroticism. Neurotic adolescents tend to have a weak belief in a personal just world. However, personal BJW was positively correlated with positive well-being, measured in terms of life satisfaction and positive affect, even when controlling for the impact of neuroticism (and extraversion) on well-being. Thus, the personal BJW seems to have a unique impact on subjective well-being. Further studies should explore how this adaptive impact is mediated, and whether it is most beneficial for introverted adolescents. Additionally, the effects of neuroticism in shaping the development of just world beliefs are in need of closer examination.

Acknowledgements

Studies were supported by grant VEGA: 1/9190/02, awarded to the second author.

114   C. Dalbert and J. Dzuka

References

Agrawal, M. and Dalal, A.K. (1993) 'Beliefs about the world and recovery from myocardial infarction', *The Journal of Social Psychology*, 133: 385–94.

Brown, J. and Grover, J. (1998) 'The role of moderating variables between stressor exposure and being distressed in a sample of serving police officers', *Personality and Individual Differences*, 24: 181–5.

Bulman, R.J. and Wortman, C.B. (1977) 'Attributions of blame and coping in the "real world": Severe accident victims react to their lot', *Journal of Personality and Social Psychology*, 35: 351–63.

Cantor, N. (1990) 'From thought to behavior: "Having" and "doing" in the study of personality and cognition', *American Psychologist*, 45: 735–50.

Costa, P.T. Jr. and McCrae, R.R. (1980) 'Influence of extraversion and neuroticism on subjective well-being: Happy and unhappy people', *Journal of Personality and Social Psychology*, 38: 668–78.

Dalbert, C. (1996) *Über den Umgang mit Ungerechtigkeit. Eine psychologische Analyse* [Dealing with injustice. A psychological analysis], Bern: Huber.

Dalbert, C. (1997) 'Coping with an unjust fate: The case of structural unemployment', *Social Justice Research*, 10: 175–89.

Dalbert, C. (1998) 'Belief in a just world, well-being, and coping with a unjust fate', in Montada, L. and Lerner, M.J. (eds), *Responses to Victimizations and Belief in a Just World* (pp. 87–105). New York: Plenum Press.

Dalbert, C. (1999) 'The world is more just for me than generally: About the Personal Belief in a Just World Scale's validity', *Social Justice Research*, 12: 79–98.

Dalbert, C. (2001) *The Justice Motive as a Personal Resource. Dealing with Challenges and Critical Life Events*, New York: Kluwer Academic/Plenum Publishers.

Dalbert, C. (2002) 'Beliefs in a just world as a buffer against anger', *Social Justice Research*, 15: 123–45.

Dalbert, C. and Yamauchi, L. (1994) 'Belief in a just world and attitudes toward immigrants and foreign workers: A cultural comparison between Hawaii and Germany', *Journal of Applied Social Psychology*, 24: 1612–26.

Dalbert, C., Montada, L. and Schmitt, M. (1987) 'Glaube an eine gerechte Welt als Motiv: Validierungskorrelate zweier Skalen', *Psychologische Beiträge*, 29: 596–615.

Dalbert, C., Montada, L., Schmitt, M. and Schneider, A. (1984) *Existentielle Schuld: Ergebnisse der Item- und Skalenanalysen* (= Berichte aus der Arbeitsgruppe 'Verantwortung, Gerechtigkeit, Moral' No. 24). Universität Trier FB I – Psychologie.

DeNeve, K.M. and Cooper, H. (1998) 'The happy personality: A meta-analysis of 137 personality traits and well-being', *Psychological Bulletin*, 124: 197–229.

Diener, E. and Fujita, F. (1995) 'Resources, personal strivings, and subjective well-being: A nomothetic and idiographic approach', *Journal of Personality and Social Psychology*, 68: 926–35.

Diener, E., Suh, E. and Oishi, S. (1997) 'Recent findings on subjective well-being', *Indian Journal of Clinical Psychology*, 24: 25–41.

Dzuka, J. and Dalbert, C. (2002) 'Vývoj a overenie validity Škál emocionálnej habituálnej subjektívnej pohody (SEHP)' [Development and validation of the Emotional Habitual Subjective Well-being Scale (EHWS)], *Československá Psychologie*, 46: 234–50.

Emmons, R.A. and Diener, E. (1986) 'Influence of impulsivity and sociability on subjective well-being', *Journal of Personality and Social Psychology*, 50: 1211–15.

BJW, personality and well-being 115

Epstein, S. (1990) 'Cognitive-experiential self-theory', in Pervin, L.A. (ed.), *Handbook of Personality. Theory and Research*, New York: Guilford Press.

Eysenck, H.J. (1947) *Dimensions of Personality*, London: Routledge and Kegan Paul.

Eysenck, H.J. (1982) *Personality, Genetics, and Behavior*, New York: Springer-Verlag.

Fahrenberg, J., Selg, H. and Hampel, R. (1978) *Das Freiburger Persönlichkeitsinventar FPI* [The Freiburg Personality Inventory], Manuel, 3rd edition, Göttingen: Hogrefe.

Hafer, C.L. (2000) 'Investment in long-term goals and commitment to just means drive the need to believe in a just world', *Personality and Social Psychology Bulletin*, 26: 1059–73.

Hafer, C.L. and Correy, B.L. (1999) 'Mediators of the relation of beliefs in a just world and emotional responses to negative outcomes', *Social Justice Research*, 12: 189–204.

Heaven, P.C. and Connors, J. (1988) 'Personality, gender, and "just world" belief', *Australian Journal of Psychology*, 40: 261–6.

Hotard, S.R., McFatter, R.M., McWhirter, R.M. and Stegall, M.E. (1989) 'Interactive effects of extraversion, neuroticism, and social relationships on subjective well-being', *Journal of Personality and Social Psychology*, 57: 321–31.

Jose, P.E. (1990) 'Just-world-reasoning in children's immanent justice judgements', *Child Development*, 61: 1024–33.

Larsen, R. and Ketelaar, T. (1991) 'Personality and susceptibility to positive and negative emotional states', *Journal of Personality and Social Psychology*, 61: 132–40.

Lerner, M.J. (1978) '"Belief in a just world" versus the "authoritarianism" syndrome . . . but nobody liked the Indians', *Ethnicity*, 5: 229–37.

Lerner, M.J. and Somers, D.G. (1992) 'Employees' reactions to an anticipated plant closure: The influence of positive illusions', in Montada, L. and Filipp, S.H. (eds), *Life Crises and Experiences of Loss in Adulthood*, Hillsdale, NJ: Lawrence Erlbaum Associates.

Lipkus, I.M. and Siegler, I.C. (1993) 'The belief in a just world and perceptions of discrimination', *Journal of Psychology*, 127: 465–74.

Lipkus, I.M., Dalbert, C. and Siegler, I.C. (1996) 'The importance of distinguishing the belief in a just world for self versus for others: Implications for psychological well-being', *Personality and Social Psychology Bulletin*, 22: 666–77.

McFatter, R.M. (1994) 'Interactions in predicting mood from extraversion and neuroticism', *Journal of Personality and Social Psychology*, 66: 570–8.

Meyer, G.J. and Shack, J.R. (1989) 'Structural convergence of mood and personality: Evidence for old and new directions', *Journal of Personality and Social Psychology*, 57: 691–706.

Montada, L., Schmitt, M. and Dalbert, C. (1986) 'Thinking about justice and dealing with one's own privileges: A study of existential guilt', in Bierhoff, H.W., Cohen, R. and Greenberg, J. (eds), *Justice in Social Relations*, New York: Plenum Press.

Piaget, J. (1932/1997) *The Moral Judgment of the Child*, Glencoe, IL: Free Press.

Rim, Y. (1983) 'Belief in a just world, personality and social attitudes', *Personality and Individual Differences*, 4: 707–8.

Rusting, C.L. and Nolen-Hocksema, S. (1998) 'Regulating responses to anger: Effects of rumination and distraction on angry mood', *Journal of Personality and Social Psychology*, 74: 790–803.

116   C. Dalbert and J. Dzuka

Schwenkmezger, P. (1991) 'Persönlichkeit und Wohlbefinden', in Abele, A. and Becker, P. (eds), *Wohlbefinden. Theorie – Empirie – Diagnostik*, Weinheim: Juventa.

Tomaka, J. and Blascovich, J. (1994) 'Effects of justice beliefs on cognitive, psychological, and behavioral responses to potential stress', *Journal of Personality and Social Psychology*, 67: 732–40.

Vaidya, J.G., Gray, E.K., Haig, J. and Watson, D. (2002) 'On the temporal stability of personality: Evidence for differential stability and the role of life experiences', *Journal of Personality and Social Psychology*, 83: 1469–84.

Watson, D. and Clark, L.A. (1984) 'Negative affectivity: The disposition to experience aversive emotional states', *Psychological Bulletin*, 96: 465–90.

Wolfradt, U. and Dalbert, C. (2003) 'Personality, values, and belief in a just world', *Personality and Individual Differences*, 35: 1911–18.

8 The implications and functions of just and unjust experiences in school

Claudia Dalbert

Adolescents spend a huge amount of their time at school, in an environment that can be seen as one of the most important socialisation settings of adolescence. The aim of schooling is not only for students to acquire knowledge and develop successful learning skills and related competencies. The school context and the educational practices experienced in school should also have a positive impact on students' personality development, strengthening their achievement motivation, enhancing their strategies for coping with stressful tasks and supporting the development of social responsibility. As such, the success of schooling cannot be measured in terms of grades and a successful school career alone. Social and achievement-related personality dimensions and mental health should also be taken into account. To understand the functions of just and unjust experiences in school, we also need to take a broader look at the gains and losses associated with (un)fairness experiences in school. The following research review will (a) outline the implications of just and unjust experiences in school, (b) highlight how these experiences are shaped by the belief in a just world (BJW) and (c) describe the consequences of the BJW and (un)just experiences in school for a successful school career and personality development.

The implications of (un)just experiences in school

Students and teachers alike are concerned with justice in school. Students want to be treated fairly by others, and regard fairness as one of the most important characteristics of a good teacher (Hofer *et al.*, 1986). Teachers describe themselves as justice-minded, reporting that they try to treat their students fairly and strive for fairness when making important decisions such as grading, or when reproving students or distributing privileges (Kanders, 2000). Nevertheless, students often complain about being treated unfairly by their teachers. Studies in different cultures have revealed similar pictures of what students throughout the world experience as just and unjust in school.

Fan and Chan (1999) asked Chinese secondary-school students to give

118   *Claudia Dalbert*

an example of a just and of an unjust event. The 450 just and 656 unjust events provided by the 680 participants were then content-analysed. About two-thirds of the events were assigned to the four or five most frequently mentioned categories (reported by 9 to 25 per cent of the sample), showing that the content of (un)fair experiences in school is widely shared within student populations. Forty-seven per cent of the fair events were related to distributive justice in terms of fair punishment (e.g. punishment for undesirable behaviour), fair assessment of performance (e.g. general comments on the assessment system) and fair rewards (e.g. similar reward for similar performance). At the same time, 34 per cent of the unfair events related to unfair punishment (e.g. different punishment for the same behaviour) and unfair assessment (e.g. different results for the same performance). Upholding justice (e.g. open praise for honest behaviour, no accusations made before evidence had been sought) was a frequently mentioned category, accounting for 9.5 per cent of the fair events reported, while unjustified accusations (e.g. being falsely accused of talking in class) accounted for 13.6 per cent of the unfair events mentioned. Additionally, 14.4 and 19.0 per cent of the fair and unfair events respectively involved examples of fair (e.g. helping) and unfair interpersonal treatment (e.g. favouritism). Male school students reported unjust punishments and accusations more often than females, but were less concerned about interpersonal treatment. The events were also classified according to the procedural rule operating. Four procedural rules were most often described as differentiating between just and unjust events: consistency (e.g. consistent with promises or across individuals), bias-suppression (e.g. no bias according to gender), representativeness (e.g. listened to explanation) and accuracy (e.g. sought facts, no offenders allowed to escape).

Israelashvili (1997) asked 1st-, 7th- and 9th-year children in Israel to give an example of unjust treatment during school time. About 56 per cent of the students experienced feelings of injustice at school. The experiences reported most often related to distribution of goods (19.2 per cent), arbitrariness of official figures (19.1 per cent), punishment (17.8 per cent) and unfriendly and aggressive treatment (14.9 per cent). Male students reported more examples relating to punishment and grading, whereas females gave more examples of lack concerning recognition.

Distributive justice of grading

Grades not only reflect performance as assessed by ability tests. Parental schooling, ethnicity and other factors also seem to impact on the actual grades received (Jasso and Resh, 2002). Moreover, descriptions of just and unjust experiences in the school setting most often relate to grading issues, thus illustrating concerns about distributive justice. The justice of distributions can be assessed in terms of the discrepancy between the

Just and unjust school experiences   119

actual distribution and the distributive norms which should be applied in a given situation. The three most prominent norms (e.g. Schwinger, 1980) are the equity principle, according to which goods should be distributed in proportion to input, the equality principle, which stipulates equal outcomes for equal achievements, and the need principle, which specifies that goods or rewards should be distributed in line with the needs of the recipient. To learn more about the distributive justice of grading, a pilot study was run in which school students were presented with a short vignette describing two students who had attained equal points in a dictation in their native language (German). Participants were then asked to decide which grades the students should be given by rating three options on a scale from 1 ('very unfair') to 6 ('very fair'). The response options represented the equality principle ('Both should receive the same grade'), the need principle ('The student who needs a better grade to move up to the next year should receive a better grade') and the equity principle ('The student who made more of an effort should receive the better grade').

The sample consisted of $N = 898$ secondary students from years 7 to 9 in Germany. Of these, $n = 187$ students (103 male, 84 female) attended low-level secondary schools (*Hauptschulen*); $n = 443$ students (193 male, 250 female) attended mid-level secondary schools (*Realschulen*); and $n = 268$ students (104 male, 164 female) attended high-level secondary schools (*Gymnasien*). The students' ages ranged between 12 and 18 years ($M = 14.1$). A four-way interaction with distributive norm as a three-level within-subject factor (equity, equality, need), type of school (low-, mid-, high-level secondary school) and grade level (7, 8, 9) as three-level between-subjects factors, and gender as a two-level between-subject factor revealed a significant ($p < 0.001$) main effect for norm and two significant two-way interactions: norm by gender and norm by school. *A posteriori* tests showed that all students endorsed the equality principle most strongly ($M = 5.61$, $SD = 0.96$), and felt that two students with equal points should be given the same grade. Endorsements of the equity ($M = 2.22$, $SD = 1.41$) and the need principles ($M = 2.56$; $SD = 1.56$) were much weaker. Moreover, only the equality principle was rated above the scale midpoint and thus evaluated as a fair distribution principle, whereas both other principles were rated below the scale midpoint and thus as unfair. However, this main effect was qualified by the type of school attended. Students from low-level schools endorsed the equality principle ($M = 5.36$, $SD = 1.26$) less strongly than their counterparts from mid-level ($M = 5.71$, $SD = 0.82$) or high-level schools ($M = 5.67$, $SD = 0.82$). In contrast, students from low-level schools ($M = 2.59$, $SD = 1.53$) showed more of a preference for the equity principle, and thus for grading practices that take effort into account, than those from mid-level ($M = 2.09$, $SD = 1.29$) or high-level schools ($M = 2.10$, $SD = 1.39$). Male and female students differed only in their rating of the need principle, with males seeing it as less

120　　*Claudia Dalbert*

unjust ($M=2.76$, $SD=1.69$) than females ($M=2.38$, $SD=1.40$). Moreover, the preference for the equality principle correlated negatively with the preference for the equity ($r=-0.34$, $p<0.001$) or the need principle ($r=-0.12$, $p<0.001$), the two of which correlated positively ($r=0.33$, $p<0.001$). This pattern of results indicates that there is a fundamental difference between the justice principle that equal achievements should result in equal grades on the one hand, and principles differentiating between equal achievements for specific reasons (need or effort).

Overall, the results of the German study mirror the observations made in Hong Kong and Israel. School students want grades to be given according to the equality principle, with the same results earning the same grades. The German study also compared this equality principle with other distributive norms, in particular the equity principle, which stipulates that student effort should also impact on grading. What is seen as a just distribution of grades differs depending on the type of school. Students attending low-level secondary schools in Germany tend to be low-achievers from a weak social background (Deutsches PISA-Konsortium, 2001). Compared to their counterparts from mid- or high-level schools, these students perceived the equality principle as less just, and grading schemes that take effort into account as more just. These preliminary results of a direct comparison of different distribution principles for grading may be interpreted as indicating that more disadvantaged students feel that inputs other than achievement should affect the grades they are assigned. In particular, they feel that effort should – at least under specific circumstances – raise the grade allocated. However, another interpretation is also possible. It is well documented that preferences for different distribution norms differ depending on the type of relationship (Schmitt and Montada, 1982; Schwinger, 1980). The contrasting preferences within the different types of schools may thus reflect a different quality of the relationship between students and teachers. Students from mid- and high-level secondary schools may understand the relationship with their teachers as more of a working relationship, while students from low-level schools may interpret it as more of a caring relationship in which teachers may deviate from strict equality if this is to the students' benefit. However, these preliminary results should be interpreted with caution. Replications are needed. Moreover, future studies should consider school subjects other than the native language and assess student–teacher relationships directly.

Summary

In sum, when asked to describe fair and unfair events in school, a majority of students refer to teachers' distributive behaviour. Grading, in particular, is a key topic here, and students feel that equal achievement should result in equal grades. However, lower-achieving students from a weaker

Just and unjust school experiences 121

social background seem more likely to regard effort as an input that teachers should also take into account while grading. Interpersonal treatment by teachers was the students' second major justice concern. Being treated with trust reflects one's standing in the group (Lind and Tyler, 1988) and thus provides feedback on whether one is valued by the group. Male and female students did not differ much in their general justice judgements concerning grades received or teacher behaviour in general (Dalbert and Stöber, 2003). However, there is a clear gender difference as regards content. Male students worried more about distributive justice (i.e. grading, punishment), while females were more concerned about interpersonal treatment (i.e. being treated with respect). This gender difference may be caused by teachers' reacting differently to male and female students. Alternatively, it may occur because male adolescents tend to have more problems with discipline and aggression than female adolescents, who are typically struggling to bolster their impaired self-esteem during puberty. With respect to procedural fairness, the students evaluated equal and sincere treatment, in which the accused are given a voice, to be fair procedure. Most importantly, results clearly show that unfairness experiences in schools are far from rare.

BJW and (un)just experiences in school

The belief in a just world endows individuals with the confidence that they will be treated fairly by others and will not fall victim to an unforeseeable disaster. Individuals high in BJW are able to place more trust in others (Zuckerman and Gerbasi, 1977) and reveal more dyadic trust in times of need (Dalbert, 2001a), for example. This has adaptive consequences. Being confronted with an injustice, either observed or experienced, threatens the belief that justice prevails in the world. Individuals high in BJW therefore try to restore justice either in reality or psychologically. Thus, one function of the BJW is to provide a framework helping individuals to interpret the events of their personal life in a meaningful way. When individuals high in BJW experience an unfairness that cannot be resolved in reality, they usually try to assimilate this experience to their BJW. This holds not only for observers of an unfairness (for a review, see Lerner and Miller, 1978), but for persons facing an unfairness themselves (e.g. Comer and Laird, 1975; Bulman and Wortman, 1977). A key way of assimilating unfairness to one's BJW is by playing down the unfairness. In samples as different as unemployed blue-collar workers and mothers of a disabled child, Dalbert (1996) found that individuals high in BJW evaluated their fate less as unfair than those low in BJW. Lipkus and Siegler (1993) found that old and middle-aged adults high in BJW felt less discriminated against in several respects than adults low in BJW. Hafer and Correy (1999) found that high-BJW university students were more likely to feel fairly treated than their low-BJW counterparts. In sum,

122   *Claudia Dalbert*

research outside the school setting indicates that BJW increases perceived fairness.

School studies have shown that teacher fairness consists in more than giving fair grades. Students evaluate a large variety of teacher behaviour in terms of justice. In our studies, we therefore differentiated between the perceived fairness of the grades received and overall teacher fairness. Students were asked to rate their grades in the native language (German), English and mathematics on a scale from 1 ('very unfair') to 6 ('very fair'). In our initial studies, students also assessed teacher fairness using a single additional rating of teacher behaviour towards them. We have since developed a reliable Just School Climate Scale (Dalbert and Stöber, 2002) consisting of 10 items describing just and unjust teacher behaviour (e.g. 'My teachers generally treat me fairly'; 'My teachers often behave unfairly toward me', reverse coded). Because of the generality, this scale, which relates to the general behaviour of all teachers a student has dealings with – rather than the specific behaviour of a single teacher, as is the case for the justice ratings of grades – we take it as a measure of a just school climate. The scale has a retest correlation of $r = 0.65$ over a period of about 6 months, thus indicating some stability in the perceived justice of teacher behaviour (Dalbert and Stöber, 2002).

In several studies we investigated the relationship between BJW, the perceived justice of grades and perceived teacher justice. The BJW was measured with the Personal Belief in a Just World Scale (Dalbert, 1999), which taps the students' belief that events in their life are usually fair. We observed similar results in samples from different types of German secondary schools and covering grade levels (years) 5 to 12 (Dalbert, 2000, 2001b; Dalbert and Maes, 2002; Dalbert and Stöber, 2003). On average, justice of grades and teacher justice shared about 10 per cent of their variance. Unsurprisingly, both correlated with the grades received: the better the grades, the more just the perception of the grades and of the teachers' general behaviour. However, both justice ratings correlated with BJW as well, even when controlling for the grades received. The more the students believed in a personally just world, the more they perceived their grades and their teachers' behaviour towards them as just. These relationships between the two justice ratings on the one hand and grades and BJW on the other were not moderated by gender, type of school or grade level. In other words, these relationships held for male and female students from all secondary-school grade levels and types of secondary school. A reliable difference was observed between the justice of grades and teacher justice. The grades allocated had more of an impact on the perceived justice of grades than on perceived teacher justice, whereas BJW had more of an effect on teacher justice than on justice of grades. This was true whether teacher fairness was assessed with the single item or with the Just School Climate Scale. Overall, these results confirm that BJW strengthens justice perceptions in school, and suggest that the more general the justice rating, the more this is the case.

The assimilation process outlined above can be seen as mediated by different cognitive reactions: playing down the perpetrator's actions as being unintentional (Dalbert, 2002) and avoiding self-focused rumination (Dalbert, 1997), for example. A typical reaction which mediates the BJW's impact on justice judgements is to rationalise the observed or experienced unfairness as being at least partly self-inflicted (Comer and Laird, 1975; Karuza and Carey, 1984; Kiecolt-Glaser and Williams, 1987). In a study with university students, Hafer and Correy (1999) found that high-BJW subjects were more likely to make internal attributions and less likely to make external attributions of their negative outcomes, thus inhibiting feelings of unfairness. In a study with about 1000 German secondary school students, Dalbert and Maes (2002) found a positive relationship between BJW and internal attributions. Students high in school-specific belief in a just world (sample item, 'All in all, life is very just in school') were more likely to attribute their achievements to internal, unstable causes such as their own effort, careful completion of homework assignments and use of effective learning strategies (e.g. knowing how to memorise things), and were less likely to attribute their achievements to external causes such as chance or their teachers (e.g. teacher competence).

In school-specific justice ratings, the justice of grades should be differentiated from overall teacher justice, which covers more than the fair allocation of grades. Overall, the results of school studies lend support to the assumption that a high belief in a just world enhances both kinds of justice ratings. The more school-goers believe in a just world – for example, that injustice is the exception rather than the rule in their life or, more specifically, that school is usually a just place – the more they tend to assimilate experienced unfairness to their BJW. This assimilation process can be shaped by different cognitions. Attributions are often used in this process and are of particular importance in school. Results provide evidence to support the hypothesis that school students high in BJW tend to attribute their achievements to unstable, internal causes such as their own behaviour, and seem to avoid external attributions. This attribution pattern can be seen as mediating the BJW's impact on the justice ratings. Outcomes caused by one's own behaviour are not perceived as unjust.

Consequences of the BJW and (un)just experiences in school

Whether or not students feel treated fairly in school is of central importance to their school career. In the following, I will argue that BJW in general and school-specific (un)fairness experiences in particular can affect students' legal socialisation, their feelings of empowerment, their achievement motivation and achievement and, finally, their well-being.

124   *Claudia Dalbert*

Legal socialisation

One important developmental task of adolescence is to develop a positive attitude towards institutional authorities such as the school, the police and the law. Adolescents have to learn that institutions and the persons representing them are legitimate and that this legitimacy is defined by institutional rules which are laid down by the legal system and which limit individual behaviour. This seems to be an important precondition for developing an intrinsic motivation to obey the law and institutional rules (Tyler, 1984). School is one of the first institutions with which children come into close contact, and where they can gain some understanding of institutional authorities. Emler *et al.* (1987) revealed that children aged between 7 and 11 have already gained an intuitive understanding of the formal constraints of teacher behaviour, of the hierarchical character of institutional authority, and of the separation of institutional duties and personal preferences. During adolescence, young people need to develop a personal attitude towards institutional authorities. In two samples of adolescents aged between 12 and 17 years, Emler and Reicher (1987) measured attitudes towards institutional authorities, namely the school, the police and the law, and they inspected this attitude and its relationship to self-reported behavioural non-compliance. There were noticeable differences in the adolescents' attitudes towards institutional authorities, with female students consistently exhibiting a more positive attitude than males. Moreover, it seems that adolescents adopt an attitude towards institutional authorities as such, rather than separate positions towards each form of authority. Young males on average reported more behavioural non-compliance – including breaching school rules or the legal code – than their female counterparts. However, a consistent negative correlation between attitude and behaviour was found for both sexes. The more negative their attitude towards the institutional authorities, the greater the degree of self-reported behavioural non-compliance.

Tyler (1990) has argued that the more positive the perception of procedural justice, the more affirmative the perception of institutional authorities and their legitimacy. The most visible institutional role in school is likely to be that of the teacher. The perceived justice of the teachers' behaviour may impact on attitudes towards the school authorities. The more students perceive their teachers' behaviour as just, the more positive their attitude to the school authorities is likely to be. Following Tyler (1990), perceptions of procedural justice should be particularly relevant in bolstering the legitimacy of the school authorities. Moreover, justice experiences within school and the legitimacy granted to the school authorities can be expected to shape student attitudes towards institutional authorities outside the school. Thus, mediated by the attitudes to the school authorities, justice experiences in school may

Just and unjust school experiences 125

be important for developing a positive attitude to other institutional authorities.

To my knowledge, Gouveia-Pereira *et al.* (2004) were the first to link research on legal socialisation and justice psychology. They conducted a study with 448 school students aged from 15 to 18 years. Three dimensions of school-related justice perceptions were assessed. Procedural justice covers procedural rules such as accuracy, consistency, neutrality and representativeness – the dimensions most frequently mentioned by the students in Fan and Chan's study (1999). Justice of grades reflects different distributive justice norms in the context of grading. A third dimension describes the equal treatment of students by their teachers. The perceived legitimacy of the school authorities was assessed separately from that of institutional authorities outside school, in particular the law, judicial authorities such as judges, and the police.

Procedural justice and equal treatment by teachers – but not distributive justice – explained unique variance in the legitimacy of the school authorities. The more the students felt equally treated by their teachers, and the stronger their perception of procedural fairness, the more positive their attitude towards the school authorities. All three justice dimensions correlated positively with the legitimacy of institutional authorities outside school, even when taking the perceived legitimacy of the school authorities into account. The more the school context was perceived as being just, and the more positive the attitudes towards the school authorities, the more positive the students' attitudes towards institutional authorities outside school.

In sum, this line of research lends support to the notion that fairness experiences in school are a crucial factor in the development of positive attitudes towards the school authorities, which in turn foster a positive attitude towards other institutional authorities. Furthermore, the BJW promotes justice perceptions in school where grades or general teacher behaviour are concerned. It is therefore reasonable to assume that the BJW – at least mediated by justice perceptions – will foster the development of positive attitudes towards institutional authorities, which in turn seem to promote behaviour compliant with legal and institutional rules.

The BJW is indicative of the personal contract and the obligation to behave fairly, and thus to engage in rule-compliant behaviour. Studies have shown that university students high in BJW are more motivated to attain their goals by just means (Hafer, 2000). Only university students with a strong BJW censured their own unjust behaviour by a decrease in self-esteem (Dalbert, 1999). Young male prisoners who strongly endorsed the BJW engaged in more rule-compliant behaviour during imprisonment (Otto and Dalbert, in this volume). This is in line with the results of experiments (Dalbert, 2002) indicating that individuals high in BJW are better able to cope with anger-evoking situations. The ability to control one's anger is an important competency which can prevent aggressive behaviour

126   *Claudia Dalbert*

during adolescence (Wilson *et al.*, 2003) and can thus be expected to increase rule-compliant behaviour. However, all previous studies on the BJW and rule-compliant behaviour have been conducted outside school. Nevertheless, it is reasonable to assume that this relationship will hold in the school context as well, but that it may be mediated by justice perceptions and a positive attitude towards the school authorities.

Empowerment

One aim of education should be to empower students and to strengthen their belief in having control over their lives. Experiences of injustice, or even exposure to the unjust treatment of others, may decrease feelings of control and increase feelings of powerlessness. In contrast, the BJW can strengthen the feeling of being in control of one's life and able to steer one's life course successfully. I will highlight two particular dimensions of empowerment: self-efficacy and the belief in successful goal attainment. BJW can be expected to have a positive impact on both, thanks to two functions of the BJW.

First, the BJW provides people with a framework that helps them to interpret events in their life in a meaningful way. Individuals with a strong BJW are more likely to attribute events in their life to internal factors, and thus to perceive them as fair. Second, the BJW promotes trust in fairness. Individuals high in BJW place more trust in others (Zuckerman and Gerbasi, 1977). In achievement situations, they expect their efforts to be fairly rewarded, and assume that the tasks set will be fair, i.e., within their capabilities (Tomaka and Blascovich, 1994). School students high in BJW are thus more likely to attribute their achievements to internal factors (Dalbert and Maes, 2002) and to evaluate their grades and their teachers' behaviour towards them as being more fair (e.g. Dalbert and Stöber, 2003). Accordingly, I expect BJW to promote school students' feelings of self-efficacy (Bandura, 1977). The stronger their BJW, the more students should believe that they can cope with school-related demands (school-related self-efficacy) and social demands (social self-efficacy).

There is preliminary evidence to support this hypothesis. Dette *et al.* (in this volume) found a positive correlation between social self-efficacy and the general and personal BJW in a sample of German secondary-school students. The stronger their BJW, the better the students felt able to cope with social demands such as making new friends in a new class or apologising for misbehaviour (Satow and Mittag, 1999). In another school study with 350 students from high-level German secondary schools (*Gymnasien*), a positive correlation was found between personal BJW and school-related self-efficacy (Dalbert, 2001b). Students with a strong BJW felt better able to cope with school-related challenges such as learning something new or difficult, or to compensate for being absent due to illness (Jerusalem and Satow, 1999). Overall, these preliminary results support the hypothesis

Just and unjust school experiences 127

that the BJW – and presumably justice experiences in school – promote self-efficacy beliefs in various respects. There is much evidence to show that self-efficacy is conducive to a successful school career (for a review see Dalbert and Stöber, in press).

A second aspect of empowering school students is to support their beliefs in being able to attain their personal goals in life. Individuals high in BJW are able to place more trust in others, thus boosting their confidence in their own future. People high in BJW are more likely to invest in their future because they are confident that their investments will be fairly rewarded (Hafer, 2000). Dette *et al.* (in this volume) conducted a thorough analysis of the relationship between BJW and the belief in successful goal attainment, and found that BJW showed a unique impact on the belief in being able to attain one's social or vocational goals, the two goal domains most often mentioned by adolescents asked about their hopes and fears (e.g. Nurmi *et al.*, 1994). In the same vein, young prisoners with a strong BJW are more likely to believe that they can attain their personal goals (Otto and Dalbert, in this volume). Furthermore, expected goal success can be seen as a critical predictor of goal investments (e.g. Brunstein, 1993), which may indeed lead to successful goal attainment. In sum, the BJW increases confidence in one's future and in attaining one's goals – experiences of justice should further reinforce these beliefs – and expected goal success can be seen as a crucial precondition for coping with the developmental tasks faced during adolescence and young adulthood.

Achievement

A strong academic achievement motivation is a precondition for achievement in school. Research on achievement motivation (Heckhausen, 1989) has consistently shown that pride in one's own performance and confidence in future success encourage investments in future achievement, while fear of failure often undermines achievement. As described above, BJW fosters unstable, internal attributions of school achievement, and internal attributions are especially important for future achievement behaviour. An internal attribution enables the successful achiever to feel proud of his or her accomplishments, and confident of being equally successful in the future (Heckhausen, 1989; Rheinberg, 1995). This, in turn, strengthens the achievement motivation. For the unsuccessful achiever, in contrast, attribution to unstable causes such as chance or effort increases optimism about future achievements. However, only internal attribution to unstable causes can provide the unsuccessful achiever with insights into how to improve his or her future performance. This process, along with the enhancement of school-related self-efficacy (see above), should lead to stronger achievement motivation and a moderate aspiration level. It has been shown that a moderate aspiration level is most conducive to

128   *Claudia Dalbert*

successful task-related behaviour, with a low aspiration level leading to diminished effort, and a high aspiration level prompting conflicts.

BJW fosters the assumption of being treated fairly, as well as attributions to internal, unstable causes, and school-related self-efficacy. As such, BJW should be positively correlated with positive academic motivation and other favourable achievement conditions such as pride in one's achievement, confidence in future success, and a medium aspiration level. In a study with about 1000 German secondary school students, Dalbert and Maes (2002) showed that students high in school-specific BJW revealed more pride in their own achievements (e.g. 'I am proud of my achievements in school'), more confidence in future success (e.g. 'I am confident that my next class test will be good') and a moderate aspiration level (e.g. 'I try to get results a little bit better than the last ones'). In a study with about 350 German secondary-school students, Dalbert (2001b) observed a positive relationship between BJW and academic motivation (e.g. 'I do my homework as well as possible') and identification with the school (e.g. 'I am proud of my school'). Moreover, teacher fairness – but not the fairness of grades – showed additional effects on academic motivation and identification with the school. Taken collectively, the more school students believed in a just world and the more they felt fairly treated by their teachers, the better their academic motivation, the more confidence they showed in their success, the prouder they were of their efforts, the more likely they were to demonstrate a moderate aspiration level, and the more positive their attitude towards school. Overall, students high in BJW showed a better motivational orientation towards school achievement than students low in BJW.

Achievement motivation should be seen as a process (Heckhausen, 1989) that increasingly stabilises an adaptive or a maladaptive orientation towards achievement. Empirical findings support the notion that a strong BJW fosters a positive motivational orientation towards achievement. As such, we would expect high just-world believers to outperform low just-world believers. To my knowledge, Tomaka and Blascovich (1994) were the first to test for the expected positive relationship between BJW and achievement. They presented their subjects with two laboratory tasks. Subjects high in BJW outperformed subjects low in BJW on both tasks, thus lending support to the hypothesis that school students high in BJW should score higher on achievement tasks. Studies (Dalbert, 2000, 2002; Dalbert and Stöber, 2003) have repeatedly found a small, but significant, positive relationship between BJW and grades received. The more the school students believed in a just world, the better the grades they received. This is evidence to support the hypothesised adaptive relationship between BJW and achievement in school, and the BJW's impact on achievement may be mediated by a positive motivational orientation towards school.

However, caution should be taken in interpreting these data, which are

Just and unjust school experiences 129

all cross-sectional in nature. Good grades and BJW may both foster a positive motivational orientation towards achievement. What looks like an adaptive effect of the BJW on achievement may turn out to be an effect of prior achievement only. Longitudinal studies are needed to disentangle the effects of prior achievement, BJW and motivational orientation on school achievement.

Distress

High just-world believers are expected to be better able to cope with daily challenges, as well as with critical life-events. BJW makes people confident in being treated fairly by others, thus enabling them to invest in their future and to deal with their environment as though it were stable. Additionally, the BJW provides a conceptual framework that helps individuals to interpret the events of their personal life in a meaningful way. As a consequence, high just-world believers are better able to cope with unjust events and to sustain their well-being when confronted with unfairness. Finally, the BJW is indicative of the obligation to behave fairly and thus promotes rule-compliant behaviour. High just-world believers are thus less likely to get into trouble than low just-world believers. These three functions of the BJW should result in greater well-being among high just-world believers than among low just-world believers.

The hypothesis of a positive relationship between BJW and well-being has been tested numerous times. Dalbert (2001a) provides a review of this relationship for victims of critical life-events (see also Dalbert on unemployment, in this volume) and concludes that the BJW acts as a buffer, protecting their mental health and well-being. However, this adaptive relationship is mediated by the victim's coping efforts, and under specific circumstances BJW may in fact promote maladaptive coping reactions which do not protect well-being.

A positive relationship between BJW and well-being can also be observed in the general population (for a review see Dalbert 2001a), but this relationship is often weaker than that observed within victim samples (Dalbert, 1998). Closer examination of this relationship has revealed that BJW is especially helpful in anger-evoking situations (Dalbert, 2002). BJW is regarded as a buffer helping the victims of unfairness to cope with this experience, and anger is the most typical emotion in response to unfairness (Scherer, 1997; Smith and Ellsworth, 1985). Thus, BJW should protect mental health and well-being particularly in anger-evoking situations (provided that these situations are unfair, which will often be the case). The adaptive effect of BJW on mental health in anger-evoking situations seems to be mediated by at least three reactions. Individuals high in BJW can be expected to play down the unfairness of an anger-evoking situation and thus feel better about it. They can further be expected to justify the unfairness they experience as being self-inflicted and, in consequence,

130   *Claudia Dalbert*

to be less angry about it. Finally, they can be expected to avoid self-focused rumination, and this is likely to protect their mental health and buffer feelings of anger (Rusting and Nolen-Hoeksema, 1998). In sum, the BJW's function as a buffer was expected to be particularly salient in anger situations, leading to reduced anger and protecting mental health. In two experiments, Dalbert (2002) showed that in an anger-evoking situation, participants high in BJW were less angry than participants low in BJW and that they suffered no decrease in self-esteem, whereas those low in BJW reported increased feelings of anger and decreased self-esteem. We can thus conclude that individuals high in BJW are better able to cope with anger-evoking situations and consequently display higher levels of well-being.

There are no less than four reasons to expect a positive relationship between BJW and well-being in samples of school students as well. First, students high in BJW have a positive motivational orientation towards achievement in school. They expect to be treated fairly, show a stronger academic motivation and are more confident of success. This should result in fewer feelings of threat and stress in achievement situations and more feelings of a fair challenge. In Tomaka and Blascovich's laboratory study (1994), participants high in BJW showed a significantly lower degree of threat appraisal on both experimental tasks. In general, they rated the tasks to be more of a challenge than a threat (i.e. they perceived the threat to be within their perceived ability to cope). In contrast, subjects low in BJW felt threatened by the tasks (i.e. they perceived the threat to exceed their perceived ability to cope). After completing the tasks, and consistent with their threat appraisals, subjects high in BJW reported experiencing less stress than subjects low in BJW. Furthermore, the autonomic reactivity of the subjects was consistent with their self-reports. Hafer and Correy (1999) found that high-BJW students were more likely to make internal attributions and less likely to make external attributions of their negative outcomes, thus leading to reduced feelings of unfairness which, in turn, led to fewer negative emotions. Although conducted with university students, both studies support the hypothesis that a high BJW will lessen distress in achievement situations and thus enhance the well-being of school students.

Second, feelings of being treated unjustly lead to distress and negative emotions, particularly anger. A strong BJW increases the likelihood of reducing observed or experienced unfairness, which should in turn lead to enhanced well-being. Evidence for the expected positive relationship between BJW and justice perceptions in school, namely fairness of grades and teacher fairness, is described above. A positive relationship between BJW and well-being in school can thus also be expected, because BJW promotes justice perceptions in school, and these justice perceptions mediate the BJW's impact on distress and well-being in school.

Third, BJW should promote a positive attitude towards the school author-

Just and unjust school experiences 131

ities and encourage rule-compliant behaviour. High just-world believers should get into less trouble in school, which can again be expected to limit distress and increase well-being in school. Finally, a strong BJW and experiences of justice seem to empower school students, and to increase their self-efficacy and their confidence in successful goal attainment. Teaching these kinds of life skills was an important part of a school-based intervention programme shown to prevent adolescent depression (Spencer *et al.*, 2003), thus lending further empirical support to the hypothesised positive relationship between BJW and well-being.

In sum, there are several reasons to expect a positive relationship between BJW and well-being in school. Several school studies with German secondary-school students have confirmed the expected positive relationship between BJW and distress in school (Dalbert and Maes, 2002). A school-specific BJW is associated with less perceived pressure to achieve, less test anxiety, less aversion to school, less vegetative dystonia, less shyness, less introversion and fewer depressive moods. Maes and Kals (2002, and in this volume) differentiate between the belief in immanent justice and the belief in compensating or ultimate justice, and show that the adaptive relationship between BJW and well-being in school is most typical of the belief in ultimate justice. Further studies have compared the impact of BJW and school-specific justice perceptions on well-being (Dalbert, 2000; Dalbert and Maes, 2002; Dalbert and Stöber, 2003) and revealed that the effect of BJW on well-being is partly mediated by teacher fairness. However, BJW is still as important as teacher fairness in explaining distress in school. Note that neither the grades received nor the perceived fairness of these grades explains a unique amount of variance in distress when controlling for BJW and teacher fairness (Dalbert and Stöber, 2003). School students with a strong BJW and those who perceived their teachers as treating them fairly experienced school as less stressful than those with a weak BJW and those who felt that they were treated unjustly by their teachers. It was this general trust in justice – rather than receiving poor or unfair grades – that explained distress in school.

Conclusion

School students often observe or experience unjust events in school. A majority of students refer to the distributive behaviour of teachers when describing fair and unfair events in school. Grading, in particular, is a key topic, and students feel that equal achievements should be rewarded by equal grades. Moreover, all students want to be treated with interpersonal respect and in accordance with a procedure that is consistent, unbiased and accurate. There are also some differences within the student population. Lower-achieving students from a weaker social background seem more likely to view effort as an input that teachers should take into account when allocating grades. Male students were more worried about

132 *Claudia Dalbert*

distributive justice (i.e. grading, accusation), while females were more concerned about interpersonal treatment (i.e. being treated with respect).

Both the general belief that events in one's life are just and school-specific experiences of (un)fairness impact on various domains of the school career and development during adolescence. The stronger the BJW and the more justice is experienced in school, the more successful the legal socialisation of school students, the stronger their empowerment, the better their achievement record, and the less distressed they feel in school. Overall, injustice in school has been shown to have detrimental effects on important aspects of adolescent development. Therefore, we should invest in making school a fairer place than is obviously the case today. Teachers should take their students' justice concerns seriously and start to communicate with their students about (un)just experiences in school, with the aim of jointly improving the situation. This seems to be a promising way of enhancing the school career and development during adolescence.

References

Bandura, A. (1977) 'Self-efficacy: Toward a unifying theory of behavioral change', *Psychological Review*, 84: 191–215.

Brunstein, J.C. (1993) 'Personal goals and subjective well-being: A longitudinal study', *Journal of Personality and Social Psychology*, 65: 1061–70.

Bulman, R.J. and Wortman, C.B. (1977) 'Attributions of blame and coping in the "real world": Severe accident victims react to their lot', *Journal of Personality and Social Psychology*, 35: 351–63.

Comer, R. and Laird, J.D. (1975) 'Choosing to suffer as a consequence of expecting to suffer: Why do people do it?', *Journal of Personality and Social Psychology*, 32: 92–101.

Dalbert, C. (1996) *Über den Umgang mit Ungerechtigkeit. Eine psychologische Analyse* [Dealing with injustice. A psychological analysis], Bern: Huber.

Dalbert, C. (1997) 'Coping with an unjust fate: The case of structural unemployment', *Social Justice Research*, 10: 175–89.

Dalbert, C. (1998) 'Belief in a just world, well-being, and coping with a unjust fate', in Montada, L. and Lerner, M.J. (eds), *Responses to Victimizations and Belief in a Just World*, New York: Kluwer Academic/Plenum Publishers.

Dalbert, C. (1999) 'The world is more just for me than generally: About the Personal Belief in a Just World Scale's validity', *Social Justice Research*, 12: 79–98.

Dalbert, C. (2000) 'Gerechtigkeitskognitionen in der Schule' [Justice cognitions in school], in Dalbert, C. and Brunner, E.J. (eds), *Handlungsleitende Kognitionen in der pädagogischen Praxis*, Hohengehren: Schneider.

Dalbert, C. (2001a) *The Justice Motive as a Personal Resource: Dealing with Challenges and Critical Life Events*, New York: Plenum Press.

Dalbert, C. (2001b) *'Justice Concerns in School'*, Talk given at the University of Michigan at Ann Arbor, MI, USA, October.

Dalbert, C. (2002) 'Beliefs in a just world as a buffer against anger', *Social Justice Research*, 15: 123–45.

Dalbert, C. and Maes, J. (2002) 'Belief in a just world as personal resource in

Just and unjust school experiences 133

school', in Ross, M. and Miller, D.T. (eds), *The Justice Motive in Everyday Life*, Cambridge: Cambridge University Press.

Dalbert, C. and Stöber, J. (2002) 'Gerechtes Schulklima' [Just school climate], in J. Stöber, *Skalendokumentation zum Projekt 'Persönliche Ziele von SchülerInnen in Sachsen-Anhalt'* (Hallesche Berichte zur Pädagogischen Psychologie No. 3), Halle (Saale): Martin-Luther-Universität Halle-Wittenberg, Institut für Pädagogik.

Dalbert, C. and Stöber, J. (2003) *'Predictors and Consequences of (Un-)just Experiences at School'*, unpublished manuscript, Martin Luther University, Halle-Wittenberg,

Dalbert, C. and Stöber, J. (in press). 'Forschung zur Schülerpersönlichkeit' [Research on school students' personality], in Helsper, W. and Böhme, J. (eds), *Handbuch der Schulforschung*, Opladen: Leske and Budrich.

Deutsches PISA-Konsortium (eds) (2001) PISA 2000. *Basiskompetenzen von Schülerinnen und Schülern im internationalen Vergleich* [Basis competencies of school students in an international comparison], Opladen: Leske and Budrich.

Emler, N. and Reicher, S. (1987) 'Orientations to institutional authority in adolescence', *Journal of Moral Education*, 16: 108–16.

Emler, N., Ohana, J. and Moscovici, S. (1987) 'Children's belief about institutional roles. A cross-national study of representations of the teacher's role', *British Journal of Educational Psychology*, 57: 26–37.

Fan, R.M. and Chan, S.C.N. (1999) 'Students' perceptions of just and unjust experiences in school', *Educational and Child Psychology*, 16: 32–50.

Gouveia-Pereira, M., Vala, J., Palmonari, A. and Rubini, M. (2004) 'School experience, relational justice and legitimization of institutional authorities', *European Journal of Psychology of Education*, in press.

Hafer, C.L. (2000) 'Investment in long-term goals and commitment to just means drive the need to believe in a just world', *Personality and Social Psychology Bulletin*, 26: 1059–73.

Hafer, C.L. and Correy, B.L. (1999) 'Mediators of the relation of beliefs in a just world and emotional responses to negative outcomes', *Social Justice Research*, 12: 189–204.

Heckhausen, H. (1989) *'Motivation und Handeln'* [Motivation and action], Berlin: Springer.

Hofer, M., Pekrun, R. and Zielinski, W. (1986) 'Die Psychologie des Lerners' [The psychology of the learner], in Weidenmann, B., Krapp, A., Hofer, M., Huber, G.L. and Mandl, H. (eds), *Pädagogische Psychologie*, Weinheim: Psychologie Verlags Union.

Israelashvili, M. (1997) 'Situational determinants of school students' feeling of injustice', *Elementary School Guidance and Counseling*, 31: 283–92.

Jasso, G. and Resh, N. (2002) 'Exploring the sense of justice about grades', *European Sociological Review*, 18: 333–51.

Jerusalem, J. and Satow, L. (1999) 'Schulbezogene Selbswirksamkeitserwartung (WIRKSCHUL)' [School-related self-efficacy], in Schwarzer, R. and Jerusalem, M. (eds), *Skalen zur Erfassung von Lehrer- und Schülermerkmalen: Dokumentation der psychometrischen Verfahren im Rahmen der Wissenschaftlichen Begleitung des Modellversuchs Selbstwirksame Schulen*, Berlin: Freie Universität Berlin und Humboldt-Universität zu Berlin.

Kanders, M. (2000) *Das Bild der Schule aus der Sicht der Schüler und Lehrer II* [The image of school from the perspective of students and teachers II], Dortmund: IFS-Verlag.

134 Claudia Dalbert

Karuza, J., Jr. and Carey, T.O. (1984) 'Relative preference and adaptiveness of behavioral blame for observers of rape victims', *Journal of Personality*, 52: 249–60.

Kiecolt-Glaser, J.K. and Williams, D.A. (1987) 'Self-blame, compliance, and distress among burn patients', *Journal of Personality and Social Psychology*, 53: 187–93.

Lerner, M.J. and Miller, D.T. (1978) 'Just world research and the attribution process: Looking back and ahead', *Psychological Bulletin*, 85: 1030–51.

Lind, E.A. and Tyler, T.R. (1988) *The Social Psychology of Procedural Justice*, New York: Plenum Press.

Lipkus, I.M. and Siegler, I.C. (1993) 'The belief in a just world and perceptions of discrimination', *Journal of Psychology*, 127: 465–74.

Maes, J. and Kals, E. (2002) 'Justice beliefs in school: Distinguishing ultimate and immanent justice', *Social Justice Research*, 15: 227–44.

Nurmi, J.-E., Poole, M.E. and Kalakoski, V. (1994) 'Age differences in adolescent future-oriented goals, concerns, and related temporal extension in different sociocultural contexts', *Journal of Youth and Adolescence*, 23: 471–87.

Rheinberg, F. (1995) *Motivation*, Stuttgart: Kohlhammer.

Rusting, C.L. and Nolen-Hocksema, S. (1998) 'Regulating responses to anger: Effects of rumination and distraction on angry mood', *Journal of Personality and Social Psychology*, 74: 790–803.

Satow, L. and Mittag, W. (1999) 'Selbswirksamkeitserwartung im Umgang mit sozialen Anforderungen (WIRKSOZ)' [Self-efficacy in dealing with social demands], in Schwarzer, R. and Jerusalem, M. (eds), *Skalen zur Erfassung von Lehrer- und Schülermerkmalen: Dokumentation der psychometrischen Verfahren im Rahmen der Wissenschaftlichen Begleitung des Modellversuchs Selbstwirksame Schulen*, Berlin: Freie Universität Berlin und Humboldt-Universität zu Berlin.

Scherer, K.R. (1997) 'The role of culture in emotion-antecedent appraisal', *Journal of Personality and Social Psychology*, 73: 902–22.

Schmitt, M. and Montada, L. (1982) 'Determinanten erlebter Gerechtigkeit', *Zeitschrift für Sozialpsychologie*, 13: 32–44.

Schwinger, T. (1980) 'Gerechte Güter-Verteilung: Entscheidungen zwischen drei Prinzipien' [Just distribution of goods: Decision between three principles], in Mikula, G. (ed.), *Gerechtigkeit und soziale Interaktion*, Göttingen: Hogrefe.

Smith, C.A. and Ellsworth, P.C. (1985) 'Patterns of cognitive appraisal in emotion', *Journal of Personality and Social Psychology*, 48: 813–38.

Spencer, S.H., Sheffield, J.K. and Donovan, C.L. (2003) 'Preventing adolescent depression: An evaluation of the problem solving for life program', *Journal of Clinical and Consulting Psychology*, 71: 3–13.

Tomaka, J. and Blascovich, J. (1994) 'Effects of justice beliefs on cognitive, psychological, and behavioral responses to potential stress', *Journal of Personality and Social Psychology*, 67: 732–40.

Tyler, T.R. (1984) 'The role of perceived injustice in defendant's evaluations of their courtroom experience', *Law and Society Review*, 18: 51–74.

Tyler, T.R. (1990) *Why People Obey the Law*, Princeton, NJ: Yale University Press.

Wilson, A.J., Lipsey, M.W. and Derzon, J.H. (2003) 'The effects of school-based intervention programs on aggressive behavior: A meta-analysis', *Journal of Clinical and Consulting Psychology*, 71: 136–49.

Zuckerman, M. and Gerbasi, K.C. (1977) 'Belief in a just world and trust', *Journal of Research in Personality*, 11: 306–17.

9 Two facets of the belief in a just world and achievement behaviour at school

Jürgen Maes and Elisabeth Kals

This chapter focuses on the role of justice beliefs, namely belief in immanent justice and belief in ultimate justice, in understanding learning processes at school. It is divided into four sections. First, the importance of just world theory for educational psychology and for the understanding of learning and achievement is outlined. Then, the concepts of immanent justice and ultimate justice are introduced, and their difference in meaning is illustrated. Previous findings on the differential meaning of the two facets for school students are summarised, including the importance of the two facets for students' well-being and first insights into the socialisation of ultimate and immanent justice. Finally, new findings are added which aim to clarify the role of the two facets in the learning process and in achievement situations.

The importance of just world theory for educational psychology and for the understanding of the learning student

In its first 30 years, just world research has mainly portrayed belief in a just world (BJW) as an antisocial trait related to the derogation of innocent victims and the denial of help (e.g. Furnham and Procter, 1989; Maes, 1998a). This pattern was studied in experimental (Lerner and Miller, 1978; Lerner *et al.*, 1976) as well as in self-report research (Montada and Schneider, 1989, 1991; Montada, 1991, 1992). Only in recent years have studies begun to show how individual BJW functions as a resource in everyday life, enabling individuals to deal with stress and develop action orientations (e.g. Tomaka and Blascovich, 1994; Dalbert, 1998, 2001; Hafer and Correy, 1999). This shift in just world research is completely consistent with Lerner's original theory. According to his justice motive theory (Lerner, 1977), it is precisely the fact that people are strongly reliant on BJW for developing long-term reality orientations that constitutes its motivational force. Lerner (1977) described the BJW as an essential human motive: in order to be able to survive in a complex social world, people depend on their belief in justice. It enables them to invest

136   J. Maes and E. Kals

time and energy in future-oriented activities, to build up trust in fellow people and social institutions, and to find meaning in the events of life. Therefore, people assume that they live in a world where everybody gets what he or she deserves and deserves what he or she gets. Because of its crucial functions, people are willing to defend and maintain their BJW, even if they are confronted with obvious injustices in everyday life. They do so by trying to restore justice and helping victims, but if this is not possible – because there was no opportunity to do so, because help would have been too costly, or because well-meant efforts have failed – they will restore justice cognitively by means of perceptual distortions and delusions. They try to convince themselves that nothing bad has really happened, that there was a point to the injustice, or that the victim did not deserve any better. Thus, Lerner's original conception combines statements on the functions and on the effects of BJW.

Since it was so important to understand and explain the 'blaming the victim' phenomenon (Ryan, 1971), the first 30 years of just world research focused almost exclusively on possible consequences of BJW like admiring social winners (Lerner, 1965) and rejecting social losers (Lerner and Simmons, 1966). The essential functions of BJW described by Lerner – without which BJW would not gain the status of a motive – were, however, widely neglected by succeeding researchers. Investigators were more interested in *how* people defend and maintain their BJW, and not so much in *why* they do it. It is only in the past decade that research has increasingly turned to the functions of BJW. Hafer (2000) directly tested the assumption that BJW is important in planning future activities. In her experiment, subjects who had been primed to think of their long-term goals in university devalued an innocent victim more than subjects who had focused on a neutral topic. Recently, BJW has increasingly been perceived as a coping resource in everyday life and as a buffer against stress (for a review: Dalbert, 2001). Hafer and Correy (1999) reported that students high in BJW tend to attribute negative results to internal rather than external factors and experience less subjective stress. Dalbert (1997, 1998) showed that BJW can help people to cope with critical life-events such as unemployment. In a laboratory study conducted by Tomaka and Blascovich (1994), subjects had to solve arithmetic tasks. Those high in BJW perceived the stressful situation more favourably, considering it as being more of a challenge than a threat (this was also reflected in their autonomic reactions), and performed better than subjects low in BJW. Interestingly enough, this change in the research perspective has corresponded to a shift in the social evaluation of the just world phenomenon. When research concentrated on effects such as victim derogation, BJW had extremely negative connotations, and was categorised as an antisocial trait. Since studies have begun to point to the BJW's function as a resource in everyday activities, however, it has had increasingly positive connotations.

Astonishingly, although the functions of BJW are particularly relevant to processes of learning and instruction in school and continued education, educational psychologists have largely overlooked the just world phenomenon (Maes, 1999). Each learning process requires the individual to delay the gratification of short-term desires in favour of long-term investments of time and energy. This would not be reasonable without a fundamental faith in justice. Learning to delay gratification (Mischel, 1974) is a basic component of the socialisation process in Western societies, and is closely connected to the development of conceptions of justice. Lerner (1977) describes the acquisition of this ability in analogy to Freud's development from the pleasure to the reality principle, and proposes the concept of a 'personal contract'. According to the terms of this contract, the growing child commits themself to postponing immediate needs dictated by the pleasure principle, and in return is assured of being rewarded for long-term investments later on. In other words, the individual agrees to behave in a certain way on condition that certain positive consequences, to which they will then be entitled, will result. Thus, the personal contract contains the individual's conceptions of what he or she can expect from others, and of what he or she deserves.

The individual takes on certain obligations (e.g. to learn, to acquire competence and qualifications) in order to obtain certain entitlements. Once the personal contract is developed, the individual's behaviour acquires a new motivational basis – the person will no longer try to get what they desire, but what they deserve. In order to be able to function in a complex environment, the individual has to rely on the 'agreements' of the personal contract being valid and being observed by all relevant social partners. Everyday observations of injustice and breaches of the rules threaten the validity of the personal contract. If an individual witnesses that a member of his or her own group does not get what he or she deserves, this will jeopardise the personal contract. In a series of experiments, Lerner and his colleagues were able to show that even primary-school children oriented their behaviour toward conceptions of deserving and entitlement, and not toward their own desires (Lerner, 1974; Long and Lerner, 1974; Braband and Lerner, 1975). The child's experiences in school may validate their personal contract or cast doubt on their validity. Therefore, the experience of injustice is not only a temporary stressor, but can threaten painstakingly developed reality orientations and make pupils wonder whether learning is actually worth their while. Conversely, positive experiences can reinforce the personal contract and encourage further investments in learning and achievement.

Until recently, the just world phenomenon had not been investigated in the school context. Dalbert and Maes (2002) presented data from different school studies and were essentially able to confirm their hypothesis that BJW can serve as a resource that enables achievement behaviour and protects pupils' mental health in school. School-specific BJW proved to be correlated with well-being and motivation, whereas school-specific belief

138   *J. Maes and E. Kals*

in an unjust world coincided with stress and reduced well-being. BJW seemed to support the perception of a fair school climate, increase well-being and motivation, and create a good learning environment. BJW and perceived fairness proved to be a better predictor of stress than did grades.

The different meanings of immanent justice and ultimate justice

All these results were obtained with scales that refer very globally to the prevalence of justice in the world (Dalbert *et al.*, 1987), in one's own life (Dalbert, 1999) or in school (Maes, 1996b). Recent studies, however, have shown that it is possible to distinguish between variants of BJW that have differential effects. For example, belief in immanent justice, according to which nearly everything that happens is an expression of justice as the inherent principle the world is based upon, can be differentiated from belief in ultimate justice, according to which people can tolerate current injustice, but expect every injustice to be resolved and compensated at some point in the future (Maes, 1998d). As Piaget (1932) noted, people may believe in immanent justice as an inherent principle that governs the course of the world. If this principle is valid, a person's success will be indicative of his or her exceptional moral virtue, and a person's failure, of his or her vice and moral misdemeanour. On the other hand, people may believe in ultimate justice, and assume that although injustices may occur in the world, all of them will be compensated in the long run. This tendency is derived from certain religious doctrines, in which consolation for the present injustice on Earth is provided through the promise of higher justice – perhaps in another world or within a larger time frame. Thus, ultimate justice implies a less unquestioned and more open perception of given situations, as it admits that situations may be ambivalent and ambiguous. Both variants can be traced far back to the roots of Judaeo-Christian culture; consequently, the Bible provides numerous examples of each type of belief (Maes, 1998d).

Again, this distinction is completely in accordance with Lerner's initial assumptions. Lerner (1980) has explicitly pointed out that victim derogation is not the only strategy used to maintain one's belief in a just world. Other strategies might be the construction of different worlds (of which only those relevant for the observer must be just) or the adoption of different time perspectives. Even the early experiment conducted by Lerner and Simmons (1966) demonstrates different ways to maintain one's belief in a just world. Their subjects did, indeed, devalue an 'innocent victim' who received electric shocks in a 'pretended learning experiment' but only if they believed that injustice would continue to exist in the next experimental session. If, on the other hand, they were told that the victim would be rewarded in the next session (and justice would be restored in this way), they would not devalue that person any more. Thus, Lerner and Simmons introduced the expectation of future justice as a situational variable. In situations which imply the restoration of justice in the near future, observers' reactions differ from situations which do not imply any salient hint that justice will be restored soon. Since behaviour is not only influenced by situational determinants, situations may be conceived differently by subjects, there may be biases and habits to filter situational features differently. Some people may fundamentally expect a just compensation in the future, other people don't share this opinion. Therefore, the expectation of future justice can be introduced as a dispositional variable.

The validity of this distinction was worked out for the first time in a study on cancer (Maes, 1998d). It was found that beliefs in immanent and ultimate justice differentiated significantly with respect to the direction or strength of their relationship to other belief systems (e.g. control beliefs, freedom beliefs), and also to other cognitive, emotional and behavioural indices, including the judgement's harshness levied upon victims, illness-related emotions, behaviour toward victims and health behaviour. The frequently reported connection between BJW and derogation of victims holds only for belief in immanent justice (BIJ), whereas belief in ultimate justice (BUJ) coincides with more favourable views of victims. Only immanent justice was correlated with accusations, blame, and acceptance of sanctions against victims, whereas ultimate justice showed absolutely no correlation or even negative correlations. On the other hand, belief in ultimate justice showed clear positive relationships with adaptive processes such as the ability to find meaning in severe illness, optimism and confidence in coping with severe illness. It appeared that the expectation that justice will be restored in the long run increased the willingness to contribute to such a compensation, and even to behave in a more health-oriented manner and to avoid risky behaviour (Maes, 1998d).

Meanwhile, the importance of this distinction has been demonstrated in the areas of health and illness (Maes, 1998d), pro-social commitments (Maes, 1998b), and politics (Maes and Schmitt, 1999; Maes et al., 2000). In the political arena, differences were found in the willingness to take on responsibility (higher for BUJ), and in the preference for certain principles for distributive justice (Deutsch, 1975). Only BIJ correlated with a preference for the equity principle, whereas BUJ correlated with a preference for the equality and need principles (Maes and Schmitt, 1999).

What we already know about the two facets of BJW in the school context

Is the differentiation between immanent and ultimate justice of any significance in the school context? The results of recent research favour the differentiation. In the following, we will summarise what is known so far about the role of the two variants for school pupils. Maes and Kals

140   J. Maes and E. Kals

(2002) reported data from a study in which items tapping immanent and ultimate justice beliefs were implemented in a school-specific just world questionnaire and assessed as part of a large canon of variables.

A school-specific questionnaire for the assessment of immanent and ultimate justice

The scales for BIJ and BUJ were derived from a factor-analytic examination of a school-specific 21-item just world questionnaire (Maes, 1998c). The BUJ scale contains 5 items (examples: 'If somebody is treated unjustly in school, he will usually be compensated in some way', 'If there is any injustice in school, it will be compensated at some point', $\alpha = 0.69$). The BIJ scale contains 6 items ('Those who don't succeed in school don't deserve any better', 'If you are a good person, you're sure to do well in school', $\alpha = 0.74$). The inter-correlation of the scales for school-specific BIJ and BUJ is $r = 0.34$. For reasons of conceptual validation, Maes and Kals (2002) investigated the correlations of the two facets with future expectations for 'good' and 'bad' pupils and the assumed significance of scholastic achievement for later life (whether 'good' or 'bad' pupils would perform well or badly in their adult life). Those believing in immanent justice were found to assume that good achievements are deserved, and a guarantee that the person will be rewarded accordingly in later life. Similarly they expected a bad life as a punishment for bad pupils ($r = 0.43$). They were less inclined to infer a good future for bad pupils. For those believing in ultimate justice bad results in school may be undeserved and may be compensated later on in life. Thus, pupils high in ultimate justice felt no need to predict future failure for 'bad' students and were found to believe that even 'bad' pupils may succeed in adult life.

The two facets and well-being

In order to test the resource hypothesis (Dalbert, 2001), Maes and Kals (2002) used five indicators of subjective well-being: school anxiety, fear of other people, stress, aversion to school and euphoria. Here, it became very clear that it is crucial to differentiate between the two facets, and that not every facet of just world belief has positive effects on personal well-being. Only a low aversion to school was related to both facets. Apart from that, ultimate justice seemed to be more suited as a resource than immanent justice did. BUJ was associated with less stress and with more euphoria. BIJ, on the other hand, was connected to more school anxiety, more fear of others (parents, teachers, peers) and less euphoria. These results are quite plausible in that one might have objective reasons for fear and anxiety if each school outcome is regarded not only as a temporary event, but as an indicator of one's moral virtue. In case of misfortune or failure, BIJ can imply serious problems for low-achievers, including self-reproaches and reduced self-esteem (e.g. Beradt, 1981; Bettelheim, 1943; Comer and Laird, 1975; Montada, 1994, 1995). For pupils believing in ultimate justice, such temporary events are more ambiguous, might have different meanings, and do not necessarily reveal anything about the person. One can turn to the positive side and rely on ultimate justice as a personal resource.

The socialisation of the two facets

Thus far, rather little research has been conducted into the development, stabilisation and destabilisation of just world beliefs. Maes and Kals (2002) considered the possible socialisation of just world beliefs by studying their connections to perceived parental education styles and teachers' behaviour. They did not find any differences between the perceived parenting behaviour of mothers and fathers. But, friendly and supportive behaviour of both parents seemed to favour BUJ, whereas strict parenting behaviour seemed to strengthen BIJ. This appears plausible: immanent justice implies a moral view of the world, governed by principles that are compatible with strict parenting styles. On the other hand, the ability to tolerate ambiguities and maintain a positive attitude toward the future, even in the case of negative experiences, is more likely to be fostered by friendly and supportive parenting styles. One may, however, question the direction of the effect. It might just as well be the reverse: pupils' belief in ultimate or immanent justice might lead them to see their parents' behaviour in a different light. The same is true of the patterns that emerged for the two facets and pupils' experience of their teachers and their lessons. The considerable correlations that emerged between BUJ and the experience of competent teachers and interesting lessons can be interpreted in different ways: either competent teachers and good instruction are able to shape school children's justice beliefs, or pupils' BUJ enables them to interpret their school experiences in a favourable way, so that they are able to make the best of the opportunities available at school and create a positive learning environment.

The two facets of BJW in achievement situations

So far, it makes sense to distinguish immanent and ultimate justice as two facets of BJW in school. But, do they also have differential effects in concrete learning situations when pupils are confronted with tasks, when they set their aspiration level, when they appraise their chance to solve the task, when they search for the causes of success and failure? Dalbert and Maes (2002) found that BJW seemed to promote internal variable attributions, moderate aspiration levels and confidence in success, and thus created favourable preconditions for achieving behaviour. Will this hold for both facets of BJW, or will BUJ once again prove to be more suited as a resource in achievement situations?

142   J. Maes and E. Kals

Sample

In order to clarify this, we use the same scales and the same data set that Maes and Kals (2002) used. Subjects were 1274 pupils from five grammar schools in Rhineland-Palatinate (Germany) who participated in the pilot reform project 'Development and testing of different models for nurturing the gifted in grammar schools with a shortened school period' (for more details, see Kaiser *et al.*, 1994; Dalbert and Maes, 2002). Essentially, the study entailed a complete assessment of the selected class levels in the five participating schools, but participation rates were reduced due to lack of parental consent and illness on the day of assessment (Kaiser and Seiler, 1998). The overall participation rate was 64.3 per cent of the pupils who might have been recruited under optimal conditions. Age ranged from 11 to 21, with 50 per cent in the 13–16 age group (11: 29; 12: 104; 13: 195; 14: 187; 15: 243; 16: 204; 17: 155; 18: 101, 19: 31; 20: 5; 21: 1); 50.8 per cent of the participants were male.

Instruments and method

Existing instruments, theoretical aspects and qualitative prior tests were taken into account in the development of new instruments. Furthermore, the instruments were developed in a permanent discussion process with teachers from the participating schools, and representatives of the ministry, the pupils and their parents (see Maes, 1996a). All scales were obtained from factor analyses (main component analysis with varimax rotation) and examined using standard methods of item and scale analysis. If not stated otherwise, scales range from 0 ('do not agree at all') to 5 ('completely agree'). All scales used have satisfying Alphas ($0.65 < \alpha < 0.87$).

In the following, we will present the correlational patterns of the two facets with different indicators of learning styles and achievement motivation. Some of our hypotheses were derived from psychological theories on achievement motivation (Heckhausen, 1989), some are more explorative. As mentioned before, the two scales for BIJ and BUJ are positively inter-correlated ($r = 0.34$). Therefore, we will not only present the bivariate correlations of the two variants with third variables, but also the first-order partial correlations calculated by partialling out the contribution of the other just world facet to the correlation with the respective third variable. In the tables, we will also present a statistical comparison of the bivariate correlations to show whether the differences between correlations are significant; error probability was set at five per cent. A formula by Olkin (1967) was applied in the calculations.

The two facets, in relation to learning aims and aspiration levels

From achievement motivation theory (Heckhausen, 1989) it is known that a moderate aspiration level is most conducive to successful task-related behaviour, with a low aspiration level producing diminished effort and a high aspiration level producing conflicts (as long as you cannot always be sure to live up to your high expectations). Dalbert and Maes (2002) showed that BJW is positively correlated with favourable achievement conditions such as a medium aspiration level. A high aspiration level, which is known to be ambiguous, correlated with both belief in a just and an unjust world. In the present study, we expected a medium aspiration level to be related more to BUJ and, since achievement indicates moral virtue, a high aspiration level to be more clearly related to BIJ. In addition, we revealed the correlations with the three general aims of learning: receiving praise, attaining good grades and learning with joy.

As predicted, only BIJ was related to a high aspiration level (three items, e.g. 'I want to be the best') whereas the positive bivariate correlation of BUJ faded away when BIJ was controlled for (Table 9.1). A medium aspiration level (three items, e.g. 'I want grades a little bit better than previous ones') which is regarded as a favourable precondition for learning went along with BUJ, but was negatively related to BIJ. Both the

Table 9.1 Partial correlational analysis: two BJW facets with pupil's aims in learning and aspiration levels ($1169 < N < 1187$)

Variable	Correlation[2]	Variables		Comparison of correlations[1]	
		Immanent justice	Ultimate justice	z_{emp}	z_{crit}
Receive praise	bivariate	0.16**	0.10**	1.82	–
	partial	0.13**	0.05	–	–
Enjoy learning	bivariate	−0.13**	−0.02	3.31	>1.96
	partial	−0.13**	0.03	–	–
Good grades	bivariate	0.18**	0.07*	3.34	>1.96
	partial	0.18**	0.01	–	–
High aspiration level	bivariate	0.25**	0.12**	4.03	>1.96
	partial	0.22**	0.04	–	–
Medium aspiration level	bivariate	−0.09**	0.06*	4.56	>1.96
	partial	−0.11**	0.10**	–	–

Notes
1 An error level of 5 per cent was set for the comparisons of correlations; this results in a critical z-value of 1.96.
2 partial: 'immanent justice' and 'ultimate justice' discarded respectively.
* $p < 0.05$.
** $p < 0.01$.

144   *J. Maes and E. Kals*

positive and the negative correlations increased when the respective other facet was partialled out. Similarly, pupils high in BUJ and high in BIJ differed in their general learning aims (Table 9.1). Only BIJ correlated with receiving praise (three items, e.g. 'to be praised by my teachers') and attaining good grades (two items, e.g. 'to get good grades') as learning aims. These correlations did not change when BUJ was partialled out. On the other hand, slight positive correlations of BUJ with these learning aims vanished when BIJ was discarded. Only BIJ was related negatively to having fun (three items, e.g. 'to experience interesting things') as a learning aim, whereas BUJ appeared completely unrelated to this aim.

The two facets and achievement-oriented emotions

Dalbert and Maes (2002) found BJW to be related to achievement-oriented emotions like pride (positively) and fear of failure (negatively). In the present study we looked at the correlations to fear of disgrace (four items, e.g. 'I fear that I might disgrace myself with my answers') and pride in achievement (five items, e.g. 'I am proud to know the right answers during the lessons'). We expected both facets to be associated with pride but only BIJ to be associated with fear of disgrace. Indeed, both were related to pride in one's achievement, but BIJ considerably higher than BUJ (Table 9.2). On the other hand, BIJ was also correlated with fear of disgrace, whereas the positive correlation of BUJ vanished when BIJ was partialled out.

Table 9.2 Partial correlational analysis: two BJW facets with achievement-oriented emotions ($1227 < N < 1343$)

Variable	Correlation[2]	Variables		Comparison of correlations[1]	
		Immanent justice	Ultimate justice	z_{emp}	z_{crit}
Fear of disgrace	bivariate	0.19**	0.11**	2.49	>1.96
	partial	0.16**	0.05	–	–
Pride in achievement	bivariate	0.27**	0.20**	2.23	>1.96
	partial	0.22**	0.12**	–	–

Notes
1 An error level of 5 per cent was set for the comparisons of correlations; this results in a critical z-value of 1.96.
2 partial: 'immanent justice' and 'ultimate justice' discarded respectively.
* $p < 0.05$.
** $p < 0.01$.

The two facets and self-ascribed capabilities and learning styles

For explorative reason we correlated BUJ and BIJ also with trait-like preconditions of learning: memory (eight items, e.g. 'My memory for numbers/stories/pictures is rather bad/rather good'), capacity of concentration (four items, e.g. 'I am able to concentrate during the lessons'), proneness to give up soon (three items, e.g. 'I will give up soon if I do not find the answer immediately'), proneness to make every effort when confronted with difficult tasks (five items, e.g. 'If I do not find the answer immediately I will stick at the task until I know the answer'), and curiosity (nine items, e.g. 'I am curious about how strange countries look/how the world will look in 500 years'). All these capabilities were measured via self-ascription. Since memory, concentration and making every effort in resolving a task imply longer time periods and therefore require a greater long-term confidence in justice, we expected them to be more closely related to BUJ. The same is true for curiosity since curiosity reflects a strong interest in the future and openness to the unknown. Results (Table 9.3) show that pupils believing in ultimate justice believed themselves to have a better memory, a better concentration and the capacity of making every effort when confronted with difficult tasks. Pupils high in BIJ, on the other hand, believed that they were more prone to give up quickly when

Table 9.3 Partial correlational analysis: two BJW facets with self-ascribed capacities and learning styles $(1180 < N < 1256)$

Variable	Correlation[2]	Variables		Comparison of correlations[1]	
		Immanent justice	Ultimate justice	z_{emp}	z_{crit}
Memory	bivariate	−0.12**	0.02	4.34	>1.96
	partial	−0.13**	0.06*	–	–
Concentration	bivariate	0.07*	0.15**	2.49	>1.96
	partial	0.02	0.13**	–	–
Giving up soon	bivariate	0.14**	0.03	3.41	>1.96
	partial	0.14**	−0.02	–	–
Making every effort	bivariate	0.07*	0.16**	2.80	>1.96
	partial	0.01	0.15**		
Curiosity	bivariate	−0.04	0.08**	3.64	>1.96
	partial	−0.08**	0.11**	–	–

Notes
1 An error level of 5 per cent was set for the comparisons of correlations; this results in a critical z-value of 1.96.
2 partial: 'immanent justice' and 'ultimate justice' discarded respectively.
* $p < 0.05$.
** $p < 0.01$.

146   *J. Maes and E. Kals*

confronted with difficult tasks. Finally, BUJ went along with more curiosity while BIJ was negatively related to curiosity. These correlations increased when the respective other facet was controlled for.

The two facets and attributions for success and failure

The perceived causes of success and failure have a decisive influence on achievement behaviour, and BJW should foster achievement by promoting internal attributions. Dalbert and Maes (2002) showed that BJW was most consistently correlated with the attributions to internal variable causes of success and failure. Overall, pupils high in BJW were most likely to explain their own success and failure in school by their own efforts, their home-work and their applied learning strategies, whereas pupils high in belief in an unjust world in the Dalbert and Maes (2002) study tended to explain their school achievements more by external forces like chance, class climate or their teachers. Concerning our differentiation between ulti-mate and immanent justice we expected more favourable attributions of success and failure for BUJ. Attributions for success and failure were measured in three different ways in our questionnaire: with one sub-questionnaire on general causes for success and failure ('What does it depend on whether somebody has success in school or not?'), and two specific sub-questionnaires on one's own success and failure ('How do you explain your own success?', 'How do you explain your own failure?'). Following these introductory questions, a comprehensive list of possible causes for success and failure was offered to the participants.

As predicted, BUJ was slightly related to favourable attributions of success and failure such as own efforts (nine items, e.g. 'whether you are prepared to make every effort') and applying learning strategies (five items, e.g. 'whether you know how to memorise items best') whereas BIJ was negatively related to these explanations (Table 9.4). This pattern was stable whether general explanations or explanations for one's own results were given. Only BIJ was related to the external attribution to teachers (four items, e.g. 'whether your teachers like you'), whereas the initial positive correlation of BUJ disappeared when BIJ was discarded. The same was true for the attribution of one's own success to stable abilities (two items, e.g. 'because I am so gifted'). Both facets were associated with reli-gious attributions (three items, e.g. 'whether God means well for you') and moral explanations (in the case of success: five items, e.g. 'because I was honest and did good deeds'; in the case of failure: six items, e.g. 'because I was naughty and committed bad deeds'). The correlation with the attribution to God's will was the only one where we did not find the slightest difference between the two variants. Another moral explanation, behaving well and being good, as an explanation for success and failure, was correlated with both variants as well but was significantly stronger with BIJ. In the case of their own success, both facets were associated with

BJW and school achievement behaviour 147

Table 9.4 Partial correlational analysis: two BJW facets with attributions for success and failure ($739 < N < 1122$)

Variable	Correlation[2]	Variables		Comparison of correlations[1]	
		Immanent justice	Ultimate justice	z_{emp}	z_{crit}
General					
Own efforts	bivariate	−0.06	0.03	2.18	>1.96
	partial	−0.07*	0.07*	–	–
Learning strategies	bivariate	−0.09*	0.04	3.16	>1.96
	partial	−0.11**	0.07*	–	–
Teachers	bivariate	0.22**	0.12**	2.47	>1.96
	partial	0.19**	0.05	–	–
Religious attribution:	bivariate	0.23**	0.23**	0.00	–
God's will	partial	0.17**	0.17**	–	–
Behaving well	bivariate	0.29**	0.18**	2.77	>1.96
	partial	0.25**	0.09**	–	–
Own Success					
Moral explanations	bivariate	0.23**	0.26**	0.91	–
	partial	0.16**	0.19**	–	–
Work and effort	bivariate	0.02	0.11**	2.64	>1.96
	partial	−0.02	0.11**	–	–
Stable abilities	bivariate	0.21**	0.09**	3.57	>1.96
	partial	0.19**	0.02	–	–
Own failure					
Moral explanations	bivariate	0.30**	0.15**	4.55	>1.96
	partial	0.27**	0.06	–	–
Work and effort	bivariate	−0.07*	0.04	3.22	>1.96
	partial	−0.09**	0.07*	–	–

Notes
1 An error level of 5 per cent was set for the comparisons of correlations; this results in a critical *z*-value of 1.96.
2 partial: 'immanent justice' and 'ultimate justice' discarded respectively.
* $p < 0.05$.
** $p < 0.01$.

giving moral explanations (like being a good/bad person, committing or omitting good deeds, helping or not helping other pupils). But, in the case of their own failure only BIJ was – even stronger than in the case of success – associated with moral explanations, whereas the positive correlation of BUJ vanished when BIJ was partialled out.

148   *J. Maes and E. Kals*

The two facets and life satisfaction

Finally, we will turn to pupils' overall evaluations of their experiences in school. Our questionnaire yielded three dimensions: satisfaction with own achievements (four items, e.g. 'I am satisfied with my performance'), with one's school (three items, e.g. 'I am satisfied with the quality standards at my school'), and with one's private life (three items, e.g. 'I am satisfied with my friendships'). BUJ showed positive correlations to all of these three dimensions (Table 9.5). Only, for satisfaction with own achievements could no significant difference be found. For satisfaction with one's school, the correlation of BUJ was significantly higher than for BIJ. Concerning satisfaction with one's private life, BIJ even showed a negative correlation, whereas BUJ was positively related. Both correlations increased when the respective other facet was discarded.

Conclusion

The correlations of the two facets with variables representing the learning process and achievement-related behaviour can be regarded as another test of the resource hypothesis. Dalbert and Maes (2002) regarded BJW as a resource for learning because they found favourable attributions for success and failure and favourable aspiration-level settings associated with BJW. As for well-being, it appears now that BUJ is more suitable to be used as a resource than BIJ is. Regardless of what happens, BUJ may create favourable circumstances for the individual: under positive circumstances

Table 9.5 Partial correlational analysis: two BJW facets with life satisfaction ($1230 < N < 1247$)

Variable	Correlation[2]	Variables		Comparison of correlations[1]	
		Immanent justice	Ultimate justice	z_{emp}	z_{crit}
Satisfaction with own achievement	bivariate	0.13**	0.16**	0.93	–
	partial	0.07**	0.13**	–	–
Satisfaction with school	bivariate	0.14**	0.26**	3.80	>1.96
	partial	0.06*	0.23**	–	–
Satisfaction with private life	bivariate	−0.02	0.13**	4.64	>1.96
	partial	−0.07*	0.15**	–	–

Notes
1 An error level of 5 per cent was set for the comparisons of correlations; this results in a critical *z*-value of 1.96.
2 partial: 'immanent justice' and 'ultimate justice' discarded respectively.
* $p < 0.05$.
** $p < 0.01$.

BJW and school achievement behaviour   149

it may provide satisfaction and self-esteem, under severe circumstances it may enable coping and adaptation. Moreover, it is related to internal variable attributions and medium aspiration level settings which are known to encourage and favour achievement behaviour. The role of BIJ is much more ambiguous: it can only be regarded as a resource for pupils with constantly good learning results. They might be able to afford attributions to internally stable causes and high aspiration-level settings. Since they regard their results as indicative for their moral virtue they cannot acquiesce in medium aspiration levels. Only the fulfilment of high aspiration levels is suited to showing that they are morally good persons. For high believers in immanent justice with varying or bad learning results such high aspiration levels are suited to producing conflicts and generating vicious circles. The same is true for their attributions: if they give moral explanations and infer their own wickedness from their failure this might result in maladaptive self-reproach and ruminating thoughts. Success and failure are not only regarded as a result of learning and achieving but also as indicators of one's moral virtue. This might also explain why BIJ goes along with pride in one's achievements as well as with fear of disgrace. Pupils high in BIJ have more reasons to fear failure because in their eyes this failure might irrevocably reveal that they are not good persons.

Within this line of argumentation, it also seems clear that only BIJ was associated with receiving praise and attaining good grades as fundamental aims of learning pupils, because for them receiving praise and attaining good grades is tantamount to a confirmation of their good character and moral virtue. Missing praise and bad grades might result in serious problems caused by permanent moral self-reproach. Having fun and learning with joy have no place in this strict view of the learning process and its results. In this respect, it is not surprising that BIJ was negatively related to satisfaction with one's private life whereas BUJ was positively related to any dimension of life satisfaction we measured. Moreover, this is in line with the patterns that Maes and Kals (2002) found for several other indicators of subjective well-being.

Striking are the relations we found between the two facets and self-ascribed capacities and capabilities such as memory, concentration, preparedness to make every effort and proneness to give up quickly when confronted with a difficult task. It is not yet clear whether these correlations reflect real connections to these capabilities or only differences in the pupils' self-concept. Further research should clarify whether these correlations stand when objective measures of memory, concentration or the other abilities are employed. If they do, this would powerfully substantiate the status of BUJ as a resource in the learning process.

References

Beradt, C. (1981) *Das Dritte Reich des Traums* [The Third Reich in dreams], Frankfurt: Suhrkamp.

Bettelheim, B. (1943) 'Individual and mass behavior in extreme situations', *Journal of Abnormal and Social Psychology*, 38: 417–52.

Braband, J. and Lerner, M.J. (1975) 'A little time and effort – who deserves what from whom?', *Personality and Social Psychology Bulletin*, 1: 177–81.

Comer, R. and Laird, P.C. (1975) 'Choosing to suffer as a consequence of expecting to suffer: Why do people do it?', *Journal of Personality and Social Psychology*, 32: 92–101.

Dalbert, C. (1997) 'Coping with an unjust fate: The case of structural unemployment', *Social Justice Research*, 2: 175–89.

Dalbert, C. (1998) 'Belief in a just world, well-being, and coping with an unjust fate', in Montada, L. and Lerner, M.J. (eds), *Responses to Victimizations and Belief in a Just World*, New York: Plenum Press.

Dalbert, C. (1999) 'The world is more just for me than generally: About the Personal Belief in a Just World Scale's validity', *Social Justice Research*, 12: 79–97.

Dalbert, C. (2001) *The Justice Motive as a Personal Resource: Dealing with Challenges and Critical Life Events*, New York: Kluwer Academic/Plenum Publishers.

Dalbert, C. and Maes, J. (2002) 'Belief in a just word as a personal resource in school' in Ross, M. and Miller, D.T. (eds), *The Justice Motive in Everyday Life*, New York: Cambridge University Press.

Dalbert, C., Montada, L. and Schmitt, M. (1987) 'Glaube an eine gerechte Welt als Motiv: Validierungskorrelate zweier Skalen' [Belief in a just world as a motive: Correlations for the validation of two scales], *Psychologische Beiträge*, 29: 596–615.

Deutsch, M. (1975) 'Equity, equality, and need: What determines which values will be used as the basis of distribution justice?', *Journal of Social Issues*, 31: 137–49.

Furnham, A. and Procter, E. (1989) 'Belief in a just world: Review and critique of the individual difference literature', *British Journal of Social Psychology*, 28: 365–84.

Hafer, C.L. (2000) 'Investment in long-term goals and commitment to just means drive the need to believe in a just world', *Personality and Social Psychology Bulletin*, 26: 1059–73.

Hafer, C.L. and Correy, B.L. (1999) 'Mediators of the relation of beliefs in a just world and emotional responses to negative outcomes', *Social Justice Research*, 12: 189–204.

Heckhausen, H. (1989) *Motivation und Handeln* [Motivation and action], Berlin: Springer.

Kaiser, A., Lüken, A., Maes, J. and Winkels, R. (1994) 'Schulzeitverkürzung – auf der Suche nach dem bildungspolitischen Kompromiss' [On shortening the school period – searching for a compromise in educational politics], *Grundlagen der Weiterbildung – Zeitschrift für Weiterbildung und Bildungspolitik im In- und Ausland*, 5: 219–23.

Kaiser, R. and Seiler, U. (1998) 'Beschreibung der Stichproben' [Description of the samples], in A. Kaiser and R. Kaiser (eds), *Entwicklung und Erprobung von Modellen der Begabtenförderung am Gymnasium mit Verkürzung der Schulzeit. Abschlussuntersuchung in der Gymnasialen Oberstufe (MSS)*, Mainz: Von Hase and Koehler.

Lerner, M.J. (1965) 'Evaluation of performance as a function of performer's reward and attractiveness', *Journal of Personality and Social Psychology*, 1: 355–60.

Lerner, M.J. (1974) 'The justice motive: "Equity" and "parity" among children', *Journal of Personality and Social Psychology*, 29: 539–50.

Lerner, M.J. (1977) 'The justice motive in social behavior. Some hypotheses as to its origins and forms', *Journal of Personality*, 45: 1–52.

Lerner, M.J. (1980) *The Belief in a Just World. A Fundamental Delusion*, New York: Plenum Press.

Lerner, M.J. and Miller, D.T. (1978) 'Just world research and the attribution process: Looking back and ahead', *Psychological Bulletin*, 85: 1030–51.

Lerner, M.J. and Simmons, C.H. (1966) 'The observer's reaction to the "innocent victim": Compassion or rejection?', *Journal of Personality and Social Psychology*, 4: 203–10.

Lerner, M.J., Miller, D.T. and Holmes, J.G. (1976) 'Deserving and the emergence of forms of justice', in Berkowitz, L. (ed.), *Advances in Experimental Social Psychology*, Vol. 9, New York: Academic Press.

Long, G.T. and Lerner, M.J. (1974) 'Deserving, the "personal contract" and altruistic behavior by children', *Journal of Personality and Social Psychology*, 29: 551–6.

Maes, J. (1996a) 'FEES – Die Fragebögen zur Erfassung der Einstellung zum Schulversuch' [FEES – The questionnaires for the assessment of attitudes towards the school model], in Ministerium für Bildung, Wissenschaft und Weiterbildung Rheinland-Pfalz (ed), *Entwicklung und Erprobung von Modellen der Begabtenförderung am Gymnasium mit Verkürzung der Schulzeit. Abschlußbericht*, Mainz: Von Hase and Koehler.

Maes, J. (1996b) 'Nicht-kognitive Persönlichkeitsmerkmale' [Non-cognitive personality traits], in Ministerium für Bildung, Wissenschaft und Weiterbildung Rheinland-Pfalz (ed.), *Entwicklung und Erprobung von Modellen der Begabtenförderung am Gymnasium mit Verkürzung der Schulzeit. Abschlußbericht*, Mainz: Von Hase and Koehler.

Maes, J. (1998a) 'Eight stages in the development of research on the construct of belief in a just world?', in Montada, L. and Lerner, M.J. (eds), *Responses to Victimizations and Belief in a Just World*, New York: Plenum Press.

Maes, J. (1998b) 'Existentielle Schuld und Verantwortung für den Aufbau an ostdeutschen Hochschulen' [Existential guilt and responsibility for the development of East German universities], in Reichle, B. and Schmitt, M. (eds), *Verantwortung, Gerechtigkeit und Moral. Zum psychologischen Verständnis ethischer Aspekte im menschlichen Verhalten*, Weinheim: Juventa.

Maes, J. (1998c) 'Geht es in der Schule gerecht zu? – Überzeugungen der Schülerinnen und Schüler und deren Folgen' [Is school life just? – Pupils' convictions and their consequences], in Kaiser, A. and Kaiser, R. (eds) *Entwicklung und Erprobung von Modellen der Begabtenförderung am Gymnasium mit Verkürzung der Schulzeit. Abschlussuntersuchung in der Gymnasialen Oberstufe (MSS)*, Mainz: Von Hase and Koehler.

Maes, J. (1998d) 'Immanent justice and ultimate justice – two ways of believing in justice', in Montada, L. and Lerner, M.J. (eds), *Responses to Victimizations and Belief in a Just World*, New York: Plenum Press.

Maes, J. (1999) 'Gerechtigkeitsempfinden und Lernen. Der Glaube an eine gerechte Welt im Kontext von Schule und Weiterbildung' [The sense of justice and learning. Belief in a just world in the context of school and continued education], *Grundlagen der Weiterbildung. Zeitschrift für Weiterbildung und Bildungspolitik im In- und Ausland*, 10: 55–8.

152 J. Maes and E. Kals

Maes, J. and Kals, E. (2002) 'Justice beliefs in school: Distinguishing ultimate and immanent justice', *Social Justice Research*, 15: 227–44.

Maes, J. and Schmitt, M. (1999) 'More on ultimate and immanent justice: Results from the research project "Justice as a problem within reunified Germany"', *Social Justice Research*, 12: 65–78.

Maes, J., Schmitt, M. and Seiler, U. (2000) 'Politischer Konservatismus und der Glaube an Gerechtigkeit' [Political conservatism and the belief in justice], *Zeitschrift für Politische Psychologie*, 8: 39–53.

Mischel, W. (1974) 'Processes in delay of gratification', in Berkowitz, L. (ed.) *Advances in Experimental Social Psychology*, Vol. 7, New York: Academic Press.

Montada, L. (1991) 'Life stress, injustice, and the question "Who is responsible?"', in H. Steensma and R. Vermunt (eds), *Social Justice in Human Relations*, Vol. 2, New York: Plenum Press.

Montada, L. (1992) 'Attribution of responsibility for losses and perceived injustice', in Montada, L., Filipp, S.-H. and Lerner, M.J. (eds), *Life Crises and the Experience of Loss in Adulthood*, Hillsdale, NJ: Lawrence Erlbaum.

Montada, L. (1994) 'Injustice in harm and loss', *Social Justice Research*, 7: 5–28.

Montada, L. (1995) 'Bewältigung von Ungerechtigkeiten in erlittenen Verlusten' [Coping with injustices in losses], *Report Psychologie*, 2: 14–26.

Montada, L. and Schneider, A. (1989) 'Justice and emotional reactions to the disadvantaged', *Social Justice Research*, 3: 313–44.

Montada, L. and Schneider, A. (1991) 'Justice and prosocial commitments', in Montada, L. and Bierhoff, H.W. (eds), *Altruism in Social Systems*, Toronto: Hogrefe.

Olkin, I. (1967) 'Correlations revisited', in Stanley, J.C. (ed.), *Improving Experimental Design and Statistical Analysis*, Chicago: Rand McNally.

Piaget, J. (1932) *Le Jugement Moral Chez L'enfant* [Moral judgement in the child], Paris: Alcan.

Ryan, W. (1971) *Blaming the Victim*, New York: Pantheon.

Tomaka, J. and Blascovich, J. (1994) 'Effects of justice beliefs on cognitive, psychological, and behavioral responses to potential stress', *Journal of Personality and Social Psychology*, 67: 732–40.

10 Belief in a just world as a resource for different types of young prisoners

Kathleen Otto and Claudia Dalbert

Adolescence is the period in life of heightened 'storm and stress', resulting in conflicts with parents and mood swings, as well as reckless, norm-breaking and antisocial risk behaviour, according to some psychologists, e.g. Arnett (1999). Young men are at particular risk of committing crimes as a means of testing a possible identity or in response to peer influences, for example (e.g. Dishion *et al.*, 1999; Vitaro *et al.*, 1997). Moffitt (1993) investigated the frequency and stability of criminal behaviour over the lifetime, and showed that approximately 95 per cent of all criminal acts are committed during adolescence. However, two groups of young male delinquents can be differentiated: 'adolescence-limited' and 'life-course-persistent' offenders. It would be helpful to learn more about the psychological conditions which can predict whether a delinquent adolescent becomes a life-course-persistent offender or desists from criminal behaviour after adolescence.

We would like to argue that the belief in a just world (BJW) can be one of the critical conditions determining whether or not adolescent criminality develops into a life-long criminal career. More specifically, offenders with a stronger personal BJW are expected to exhibit feelings and behaviour that should ease the rehabilitation process. As a first test of this hypothesis we ran a study with young offenders (Otto and Dalbert, 2004). All participants ($N = 66$) were young male prisoners from a German detention centre in Mecklenburg-West Pomerania. On average they were 20 years old, and the sentences they had received ranged from 6 months to about 140 months ($M = 30.9$, $SD = 25.45$). Their education level was low, with only 11 subjects having ten or more years of schooling. Eleven subjects were first-time offenders, and 42 were serving their first prison sentence. They had committed a total of 1343 recorded crimes including murder, manslaughter, physical violence and sex crimes. We studied the relationship between BJW and constructs expected to be especially relevant to predicting recidivism in this sample. The following eight variables were observed: the perceived justice of the sentence, the perceived justice of the trial, moral justification of the crime, feelings of guilt, anger expression style (especially anger-control, anger-out), the perceived prospects of

154   *K. Otto and C. Dalbert*

attaining personal goals after release and disciplinary problems occurring during imprisonment. The relevant data were collected by means of questionnaires and by reference to the prisoners' criminal records. In addition, the participants' personal (age, school education) and familial background (two objective variables assessing structural and emotional dysfunction of the family; two subjective variables describing the family climate) were assessed, and nine variables describing their criminal background (see below for details) were examined. Thus, the results reported hold when controlled for these three domains.

Just world research has identified at least three functions of the BJW (Dalbert, 2001): (a) it is indicative of a personal contract and the obligation to behave fairly, (b) it endows individuals with the confidence that they will be treated fairly by others and will not fall victim to an unforeseeable disaster, and (c) it provides a conceptual framework which helps individuals to interpret the events of their personal life in a meaningful way. These properties of the BJW describe the totality of the justice motive and explain a great variety of human behaviour. We assume that BJW also impacts on the feelings and behaviour of delinquent adolescents and young adults. Thus, just world theory may help us to understand the development of young prisoners and their prospects for rehabilitation.

BJW and criminality

These three functions of the BJW (Dalbert, 2001) can shed light on various aspects of criminality. BJW endows individuals with great trust in the fairness of the world, and this has several adaptive consequences. Individuals are motivated to defend their BJW whenever it is threatened. Being confronted with an injustice, either observed or experienced, threatens the belief that justice prevails in the world. Individuals high in BJW therefore try to restore justice either in reality or psychologically. When they experience unfairness they do not believe can be resolved in reality, they try to assimilate this experience to their BJW. In short, BJW provides a framework helping individuals to interpret the events of their personal life in a meaningful way. This can be done by justifying the experienced unfairness as being at least partly self-inflicted (Bulman and Wortman, 1977; Comer and Laird, 1975; Lupfer *et al.*, 1998), by playing down the unfairness (Dalbert, 1996; Lipkus and Siegler, 1993) and by avoiding self-focused rumination (Dalbert, 1997). The assimilation of unfairness to one's BJW is often highly adaptive – enhancing well-being (e.g. Hafer and Correy, 1999) and reducing feelings of anger (Dalbert, 2002).

In sum, the belief in a just world provides a conceptual framework that helps individuals to interpret the events of their personal life in a meaningful way. The prisoners' perceptions of their trial and the sentence passed should therefore be affected by their BJW. There is no doubt that it is important for offenders to feel that they were treated fairly during the legal proceedings and that the punishment imposed (here, a prison sentence) corresponds to the crime committed. On the basis of findings from just world research, strong just-world believers can be expected to perceive both their trial and their sentence as more just than weak believers. As a consequence, they can be expected to experience more feelings of guilt and to be less likely to justify or excuse their offence. Taken collectively, perceiving the trial and sentence as just may be the decisive factor allowing offenders to accept their sentence and develop an intrinsic motivation to obey the law in the future (Haller *et al.* 1995; Tyler, 1984). Furthermore, the offender's belief in a personal just world may be an essential condition for the development of such an intrinsic motivation.

BJW was measured with the Personal Belief in a Just World Scale (Dalbert, 1999). Multiple regression analyses were run to test the relationship between BJW and the outcome variables (Otto and Dalbert, 2004) – in this case, the fairness judgements concerning the sentence and the trial. The fewer offences the prisoners had committed, and the stronger their belief in a personal just world, the more they tended to believe that their sentence was basically just. Additionally, personal BJW played the main role in predicting the perceived justice of the trial. Prisoners who had fewer previous convictions and who endorsed the belief in a personal just world more strongly reported the trial to have been fairer. Contrary to expectations, the personal BJW did not contribute directly to explaining feelings of guilt, though the two variables did display a significant correlation in the expected direction ($r = 0.29$, $p < 0.05$). Instead, the effect of personal BJW on feelings of guilt was mediated by the perceived justice of the trial. The more the young offenders perceived their trial as just, the more guilty they felt. Also contrary to expectations, moral justification of the crime – although negatively correlated with guilt feelings – was unrelated to the BJW. Younger prisoners, and those who had already been in prison for a longer period, showed a stronger tendency to morally justify or excuse the crime they had committed.

BJW is regarded as a buffer helping victims of unfairness to cope with their experiences. The most typical emotion in response to unfairness is anger (e.g. Smith and Ellsworth, 1985). Strong just-world believers can thus be expected to be better able to cope with feelings of anger. Experiments have shown that high just-world believers experience less anger and that their self-esteem is less impaired by anger-evoking situations than is the case for weak believers (Dalbert, 2002). Individuals high in BJW not only experience anger less often, but are less likely to express their anger with overt verbal (e.g. insults, sarcasm) or physical behaviour (e.g. slamming doors, throwing objects). In addition, high just-world believers may be more likely to curb and control their angry feelings. Thus, high just-world believers can be expected to report more anger-control and less

156   K. Otto and C. Dalbert

anger-out than weak believers. In a student sample, Dalbert (2002) reported a negative relationship between BJW and anger-out and a positive relationship between BJW and anger-control, thus confirming the expected relationships. This buffering effect on anger expression style (Schwenkmezger et al., 1992; Spielberger, 1988) was also found for the young prisoners, with personal BJW emerging to be the only meaningful predictor of anger-control and anger-out. The more the prisoners believed that the world is fair to them personally, the more they tended to control their feelings of anger, and the less likely they were to express their anger in overt behaviour. In sum, our study confirmed that the BJW functions as an interpretative framework, thus enhancing fairness judgements. This can in turn be expected to increase feelings of guilt and reduce moral justification – and to lessen anger and maladaptive anger expression styles, which could be supported in the study with just one exception: moral justification. We return to this below.

Second, the belief in a just world endows individuals with the confidence that they will be treated fairly by others and will not fall victim to unforeseeable disasters. This is the personal contract: I am obliged to behave fairly and, as a result, I am able to trust in a just world. Thus, individuals high in BJW are able to place more trust in others. They are less suspicious of others (Zuckerman and Gerbasi, 1977), less cynical about the prosocial behaviour of others (Furnham, 1995), and expect to be treated fairly by others – by being confronted only with fair tasks, for example (Tomaka and Blascovich, 1994). This trust in fairness has several consequences. People high in BJW are more likely to invest in their future because they are confident that their investments will be fairly rewarded. This includes goal-directed behaviour such as investment in long-term goals (Hafer, 2000) and unspecific investments in times of need – for example, prosocial behaviour with the aim of ensuring a positive outcome for oneself when this is most needed (Zuckerman, 1975). Moreover, individuals high in BJW feel less threatened and less distressed by the demands of others, because they are confident that they will be treated fairly (Tomaka and Blascovich, 1994). Consequently, it is hypothesised that strong believers in a just world will be more confident of achieving their personal goals after release from prison than weak believers. The young prisoners were asked to describe five personal goals they wanted to achieve in life. These goals included going unpunished in future, getting rich, coming off drugs, getting married, starting a family, and starting an occupational training programme. Prisoners were then asked to rate each goal according to its prospects of success. The response options here were $1 = 0$ per cent, $2 = 20$ per cent, $3 = 40$ per cent, $4 = 60$ per cent, $5 = 80$ per cent, and $6 = 100$ per cent probability of attaining the desired goal. On average, the adolescents thought they had a good chance of success in their personal goals ($M = 5.01$). Apart from the frequency of offences in their criminal career, the personal BJW played a significant role in pre-

BJW as a resource for young prisoners   157

dicting the perceived attainability of personal life goals. The fewer offences the prisoners had committed thus far, and the more they endorsed the personal BJW, the more confident they were that they would succeed in achieving their personal goals.

Third, the belief in a just world is indicative of the obligation to behave fairly. In a just world, a positive future is not the gift of a benevolent world, but a reward for the individual's behaviour and character. Consequently, individuals high in BJW try to behave fairly. The more they believe in a just-world, the more compelled they feel to strive for justice themselves. Thus, BJW is indicative of a personal contract (Lerner, 1977), the terms of which oblige the individual to behave fairly. Consequently, fairness is a more salient self-concept dimension for high just-world believers than for low just-world believers (Tanaka, 1999). High just-world believers are more likely to help accident victims (Bierhoff et al., 1991) and patients they perceive as blameless (DePalma et al., 1999). Likewise, West Germans high in BJW are more likely to show solidarity with East Germans (Schmitt, 1998). BJW has been shown to be one of the important correlates of social responsibility as a trait (Bierhoff, 1994), and to be significantly related to the commitment to just means (Hafer, 2000). However, even individuals high in BJW may sometimes behave unfairly. Such motive-incongruent behaviour clearly constitutes a violation of the personal contract and is censured by, for example, a decrease in self-esteem (Dalbert, 1999). In sum, the commitment to this personal contract leads the individual to strive for justice in his or her own actions and, as a consequence, to trust in being treated fairly by others. This should also exert an influence on offenders. Because the BJW motivates individuals to behave fairly, prisoners with strong beliefs in a just world should be more likely to conform to the demands of the penal system and less likely to violate prison rules. Thus, prisoners with a particularly strong belief in a just world can be expected to experience fewer disciplinary problems during their term of imprisonment. The number of disciplinary problems recorded by the prison authorities was ascertained from the prisoners' criminal files. On average, two disciplinary problems were recorded for each prisoner. However, there was a great deal of variation within the sample ($SD = 3$). As expected, BJW explained a significant amount of the variance in disciplinary problems, in addition to the amount already explained by the length of the prison sentence and conviction for sex crimes. Longer prison sentences, convictions for sex crimes and a weaker personal BJW were associated with a higher frequency of disciplinary problems in prison.

The power of the personal BJW compared to other variables traditionally used to predict the cognitive, emotional and behavioural outcomes of offenders (personal and familial background, criminal career) is illustrated by the total effects shown in Table 10.1. A total effect is the sum of a variable's direct effect and its indirect effects. For each significant

158   K. Otto and C. Dalbert

Table 10.1 Total effects of personal and familial background, criminal career and personal belief in a just world on justice judgements and outcome variables

	Personal background	Familial background	Criminal career	Personal BJW
Justice of sentence	–	–	−0.30	0.30
Justice of trial	–	–	−0.32	0.48
Moral justification	−0.30	–	0.35	–
Feelings of guilt	–	–	−0.14	0.22
Anger-control	–	–	–	0.48
Anger-out	–	–	–	−0.28
Prospects of success in personal goals	–	–	−0.32	0.26
Disciplinary problems	–	–	0.61	−0.27

Note
With the exception of disciplinary problems, which are reported in terms of the number of offences against prison rules (ranging from 0 to 13), all scale values ranged from 1 to 6, with 6 indicating a strong endorsement of the construct.

predictor, the total effects for each of the eight dependent measures were determined separately. The total effects of variables belonging to each predictor set (personal or familial background, criminal career) were then aggregated to form an overall measure of the total effect of the predictor set. As shown by Table 10.1, none of the predictor sets were better able to explain the perceived justice of the sentence and the trial, feelings of guilt, anger-control and anger-out than the personal BJW of the young prisoners. The criminal career was a better predictor of the perceived prospects of attaining personal goals and of disciplinary problems, though personal BJW had a high total effect on both variables. Moral justification was the only outcome variable that was not predicted by personal BJW.

BJW as buffer for all prisoners or only for some?

This pattern of results clearly supports the hypothesis that BJW is an important buffer helping young prisoners to cope with their experiences on several dimensions, and which may thus enhance their chances of rehabilitation after release. However, the observed relationships may hold only for some delinquents, and not for others. To gain a better understanding of the impact of the personal BJW among different types of young offenders, interactions between BJW and properties of the criminal career were tested with respect to the eight outcome variables. This was done by means of moderated multiple regression analyses (see Saunders, 1956), with the eight outcome variables being regressed onto the personal BJW, the criminal career and the interaction term of the two (= the product). Additionally, we controlled for the main effects observed in the linear analyses reported above. The participants' criminal careers were

BJW as a resource for young prisoners 159

described by nine pieces of information drawn from their criminal records: age at first crime and age at first conviction in years, detention (0 = first custodial sentence; 1 = one or more previous custodial sentences), violent crimes (0 = no violent crimes; 1 = one or more violent crimes), sex crimes (0 = no sex crimes; 1 = one or more sex crimes), number of previous convictions, number of offences in criminal career, number of days already spent in prison and length of prison sentence in days. Nine moderated regression analyses – testing the interaction of BJW with each of the nine aspects of the criminal background – were conducted for each outcome variable. Because the high number of tests increases the possibility of significance errors, and given the exploratory nature of the analyses, the results should be interpreted with caution. Because of the small sample size, the significance level was increased to $p = 0.10$. The results of the significant moderated regressions are presented in Table 10.2.

As shown by Table 10.2, our interaction analyses revealed that a significant interaction between personal BJW and detention predicted the perceived justice of the trial above and beyond the linear effect of previous convictions. This interaction explained a further 4 per cent of the variance in the perceived justice of the trial in addition to the 10 per cent already explained by previous convictions and the 22 per cent explained by personal BJW. The implication of the interaction is shown in Figure 10.1, which shows regression lines for offenders serving their first custodial sentence as well as for those serving their second or third custodial sentence. The number of previous convictions was fixed at its mean ($M = 2.14$). The more the prisoners endorsed the belief in a personal just world, the more they reported their trial to have been fair. This was especially true for those who were imprisoned for the first time ($n = 42$; $b = 0.83$) compared to those who had been imprisoned before ($b = 0.02$). Those prisoners who were incarcerated for the first time and who revealed a strong personal BJW gave their trial the highest fairness ratings. Those who either did not believe in a personal just world or who had already been incarcerated several times rated their trial to have been significantly less just.

In the main effect analysis described above, moral justification was unexpectedly found to be independent of BJW, but related to the age of the offenders and the time they had already spent in prison. The younger prisoners were more likely to justify or excuse their crime. This result may indicate that moral justification is typical of morally immature individuals. Indeed, the results of a meta-analysis have shown that the moral reasoning of juvenile delinquents (aged 11 to 17 years) is lower than that of non-delinquents of the same age group (Nelson *et al.*, 1990). Furthermore, our interaction analyses revealed a significant interaction between BJW and time in prison that explained 5 per cent of the variance in moral justification – in addition to the 7 per cent already explained by the prisoner's age

160   K. Otto and C. Dalbert

Table 10.2 Regression models for justice of trial, moral justification, feelings of guilt, anger-control, anger-out and prospects of success in personal goals (accepted models; $p < 0.10$)

Predictor	R	R^2	b	t	p
Justice of trial ($F_{total} = 8.874$; $df = 4/61$; $p < 0.001$)					
Previous convictions	0.31	0.10[b]	−0.27	−2.46	0.017
Detention	0.33	0.11	2.15	−	−
Personal BJW	0.57	0.33[c]	0.83	−	−
Detention × Personal BJW	0.61	0.37[+]	−0.63	−1.98	0.052
			1.22		
Moral justification ($F_{total} = 4.839$; $df = 4/61$; $p = 0.002$)					
Age	0.26	0.07[a]	−0.19	−2.80	0.007
Time in prison	0.44	0.19[b]	−0.001	−	−
Personal BJW	0.44	0.19	−0.29	−	−
Time in prison × Personal BJW	0.49	0.24[+]	0.0009	1.98	0.052
			8.01		
Feelings of guilt ($F_{total} = 6.577$; $df = 4/61$; $p < 0.001$)					
Justice of trial	0.45	0.20[c]	0.30	2.87	0.006
Age at first conviction	0.48	0.23	−0.51	−	−
Personal BJW	0.48	0.23	−2.63	−	−
Age at first conviction × Personal BJW	0.55	0.30[a]	0.17	2.43	0.018
			9.95		
Anger-control ($F_{total} = 8.944$; $df = 3/62$; $p < 0.001$)					
Offences in criminal career	0.07	0.01	0.07	−	−
Personal BJW	0.51	0.25[c]	0.88	−	−
Offences in criminal career × Personal BJW	0.55	0.30[a]	−0.02	−2.06	0.043
			0.65		
Anger-out ($F_{total} = 5.535$; $df = 3/62$; $p = 0.002$)					
Criminal acts of violence	0.25	0.06	3.49	−	−
Personal BJW	0.36	0.13[a]	0.29	−	−
Criminal acts of violence × Personal BJW	0.46	0.21[a]	−0.74	−2.55	0.013
			1.99		
Prospects of success in personal goals ($F_{total} = 7.569$; $df = 3/62$; $p < 0.001$)					
Offences in criminal career	0.36	0.13[b]	−0.09	−	−
Personal BJW	0.44	0.20[a]	−0.31	−	−
Offences in criminal career × Personal BJW	0.61	0.37[c]	0.02	3.68	0.081
			6.54		

Notes
+ $p < 0.10$.
a $p < 0.05$.
b $p < 0.01$.
c $p < 0.001$.

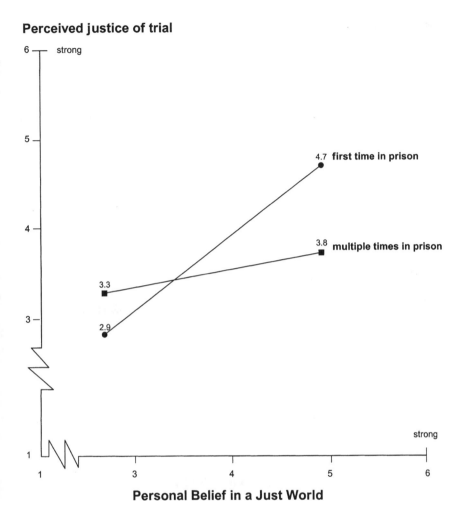

Figure 10.1 Change in the perceived justice of the trial as a function of personal belief in a just world and detention.

and the 12 per cent explained by time in prison. The implications of this interaction are illustrated in Figure 10.2, which shows regression lines for short-term ($M - SD = 2.19$ days) and long-term prisoners ($M + SD = 509.17$ days), while the age of the prisoners was fixed at its mean ($M = 19.8$). The adolescents who had already been in prison longer were likely to morally justify their crime, and BJW was not important in predicting moral justification among these long-term prisoners ($b = 0.17$). The same did not hold for short-term prisoners, who were less likely to morally justify their crime. Furthermore, the more the short-term prisoners believed in a personal just world, the less likely they were to engage in

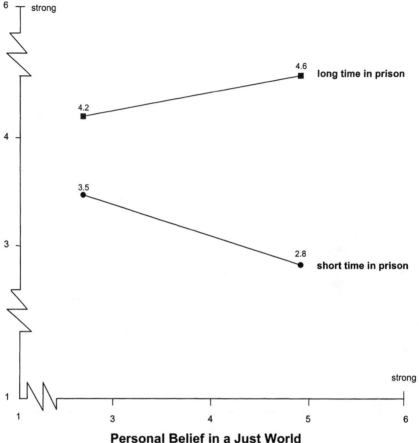

Figure 10.2 Change in moral justification as a function of personal belief in a just world and time in prison.

moral justification of their crime ($b = -0.29$). In sum, BJW serves as a buffer only for those adolescents who were at an early stage of their prison term; a strong BJW prevents these offenders from seeking moral justification for their crimes. It may be that offenders adapt to the norms of the inmate social system during the period of imprisonment, leading them to justify their criminal career by denying responsibility for the crimes they committed, condemning the legal system, or appealing to higher loyalties (Sykes and Matza, 1957), and that this process cannot be prevented by BJW.

Feelings of guilt were negatively correlated with moral justification and were predicted by the perceived justice of the trial. In addition, our analyses revealed a significant interaction between BJW and age at first conviction. This interaction explained 10 per cent of the variance in feelings of guilt in addition to the 20 per cent already explained by the justice of the trial. The relevance of the personal BJW for feelings of guilt is illustrated in Figure 10.3. The perceived justice of the trial was fixed at its mean ($M = 3.72$). The later in life the adolescents were convicted the first time ($b = 0.52$), the more important the BJW. The more the adolescents who were convicted later ($M = 18.54$ years old) believed in a personal just world, the more guilt they felt concerning their crime. For those not convicted until late adolescence, BJW impacted on their guilt feelings even

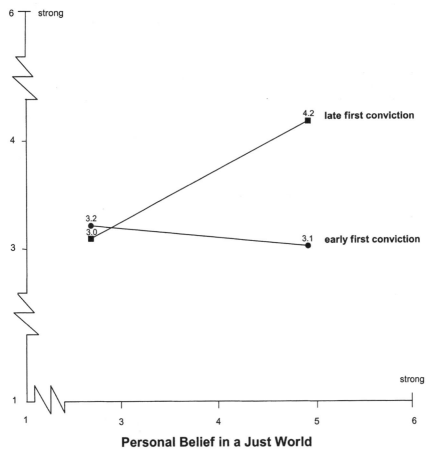

Figure 10.3 Change in feelings of guilt as a function of personal belief in a just world and age at first conviction.

164   K. Otto and C. Dalbert

when they felt that their trial had not been fair. For these offenders, the personal contract, with its obligation to behave fairly, seems to function in its own right, and any breach of the contract is censured by guilt feelings. For those convicted for the first time early in adolescence ($M = 15.18$ years old), BJW did not predict guilt feelings ($b = -0.05$). Thus, adolescents who did not believe in a personal just world and/or who were first convicted in early adolescence, tended not to reveal feelings of guilt. In fact, their guilt feelings were dependent only on the perceived justice of the trial.

As described above, the personal BJW was the only significant predictor explaining anger-control and anger-out. The moderated regression analyses revealed two significant interactions. Anger-control was explained by the interaction of the number of offences in the criminal career and BJW, whereas anger-out was predicted by the interaction of violent crimes and BJW. The former interaction explained 5 per cent of the variance in anger-control in addition to the 24 per cent already explained by personal BJW. The latter interaction explained 8 per cent of the variance in anger-out in addition to the 7 per cent explained by personal BJW. Thus, the personal BJW functions as a buffer for all prisoners in that it helps to control their feelings of anger (see Figure 10.4). However, this effect was much stronger for prisoners with fewer previous offences ($b = 0.75$) than for those with more offences in their criminal career ($b = 0.19$). Additionally, BJW reduced the probability of anger-out (see Figure 10.5). The more the prisoners who had already conducted a violent crime ($n = 47$) believed in a personal just world, the less likely they were to display anger-out behaviour ($b = -0.45$). In contrast, BJW was not important in explaining the anger-out behaviour of those who had not yet conducted a violent crime ($b = 0.29$). Put another way, for those offenders with a strong personal BJW, whether or not they had ever committed a violent crime was not a crucial factor – their BJW seems to protect them from anger-out behaviour. However, the likelihood that the prisoners low in BJW will display outburst behaviour differs strongly, dependent on their criminal career. Weak believers who had already committed violent crimes revealed a strong tendency to anger-out behaviour. It can be assumed that anger-out is particularly closely connected to certain kinds of violent crimes, such as physical violence or damage to property. It can thus be hypothesised that prisoners with a weak BJW and a record of criminal violence will not be well protected from committing future crimes that may be associated with outbursts of rage.

Both the frequency of offences in the criminal career and the personal BJW significantly predicted the perceived prospect of success in personal goals. Additionally, the moderated multiple regression analyses revealed a significant interaction between the number of offences in the criminal career and BJW. In addition to the two main effects, which explained a

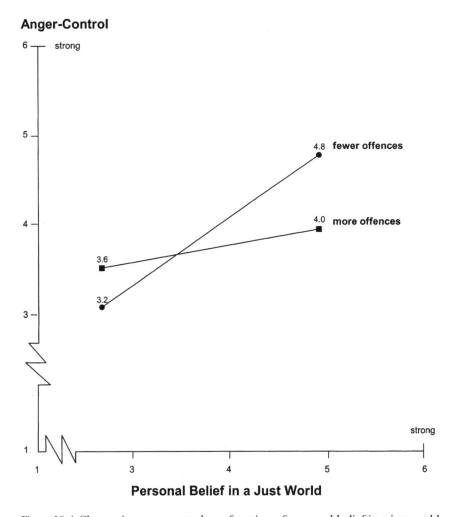

Figure 10.4 Change in anger-control as a function of personal belief in a just world and the number of offences in the criminal career.

total of 20 per cent of the variance in the perceived prospect of success in personal goals, the interaction term explained a further 17 per cent of the variance. As illustrated in Figure 10.6, BJW was less important in predicting prisoners' confidence in being able to achieve their goals among adolescents with a relatively low number of offences ($M = 6.34$ offences; $b = -0.18$) than among those with a relatively high number of offences ($M = 34.32$ offences; $b = 0.38$). The more the recurrent offenders believed in a personal just world, the stronger their belief that they would succeed in their personal goals. Weak just-world believers with a high number of offences were less sure about attaining their personal goals. It is

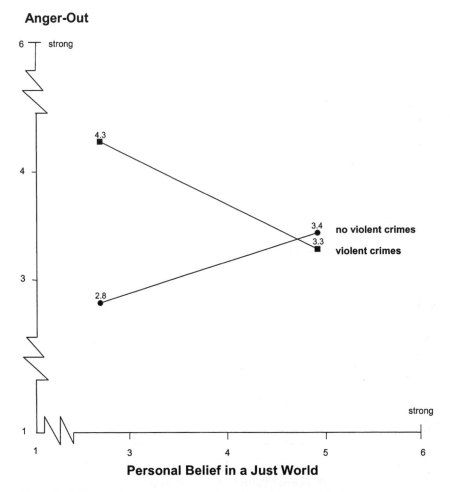

Figure 10.5 Change in anger-out as a function of personal belief in a just world and violent crimes.

well known that the expected goal success can be seen as a critical predictor for goal investments (e.g. Brunstein, 1993). We would like to argue that investments in personal goals could be a critical condition for rehabilitation after release from prison. Low just-world believers with a high number of offences thus seem to be at the highest risk of relapsing and committing further crimes rather than investing in their personal goals.

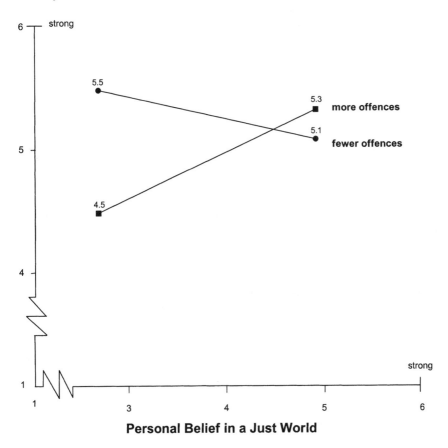

Figure 10.6 Change in prospects of success in personal goals as a function of personal belief in a just world and the number of offences in the criminal career.

Discussion

The results of our study unambiguously support the hypothesis that the belief in a personal just world is an important resource for young prisoners. As predicted by the justice motive theory, BJW impacted on all eight outcome variables observed in our study. Indeed, the personal BJW emerged as the most important variable in predicting the feelings and behaviour of the young prisoners. For most dependent variables, personal BJW was just as important as – or even more important than – features of the criminal career. Age, school education and objective or subjective

168   *K. Otto and C. Dalbert*

features of the familial background did not explain any of the observed outcome variables at all.

The young prisoners' moral attitudes emerged as strongly dependent on their belief that, overall, events in their personal life are just. The stronger this belief, the more they perceived their sentence and their trial to be just and, in consequence, the more guilt they felt about their crime. However, high just world believers only perceived their trial to be just if this was their first time in prison. For those who had already been imprisoned several times, BJW had no impact on the perception of the trial's fairness. Furthermore, for those offenders convicted of their first crime early in life, the probability of guilt feelings was low and was not moderated by BJW. The amount of guilt felt by those convicted later in life depended on their BJW: the more they believed in a just world, the stronger their feelings of guilt. Furthermore, the stronger the young offenders' belief in a just world, the less likely they were to deny moral responsibility for their crime. However, the latter held only for those young offenders who had not yet been in prison for long. The longer they had been incarcerated, the more likely they were to justify their crime, and this held independent of their BJW. Moreover, the length of imprisonment was the only one of the nine characteristics of the criminal career that was significantly related to BJW. The longer the young offenders had been in the detention centre, the weaker their BJW.

Overall, the belief in a personal just world seems to increase the perceived fairness of one's sentence and, even more importantly, the perception of procedural fairness in one's trial. Moreover, it intensifies feelings of guilt. These results can be interpreted as indicating that the personal BJW helps to establish an internal motivation to obey the law in the future, which may prevent further criminal acts. However, this seems to hold only for those young prisoners with a less serious criminal career (i.e. those who were either in prison for the first time or first convicted later in adolescence). Moffitt (1993) made a distinction between temporary and persistent antisocial behaviour. There is a good chance that those prisoners with a longer criminal record, i.e. who were younger when first convicted and who have committed more offences, will embark on a life-course-persistent criminal career. Those who did not fall foul of the law until later in adolescence have a good chance of remaining adolescence-limited offenders. BJW seems to be a critical resource for the future development of this group.

Our analysis provides us with additional insights into the preconditions of violent crime. Prisoners who tend to express their anger by outburst behaviour may be seen as most likely to engage in violent criminal behaviour. This holds particularly for those with a weak belief in a personal just world. Although BJW was shown to strengthen anger-control, this was again especially true of prisoners with a less serious criminal career, in particular, for those who had committed fewer offences in their criminal career.

Imprisonment itself seems to have a negative impact on the young prisoners' moral attitudes. Not only does the time spent in prison seem to weaken the personal BJW, the longer the term of imprisonment, the less the personal BJW is able to prevent the prisoners from morally justifying their criminal behaviour. The length of imprisonment as well as previous custodial sentences is an appropriate indicator of the imprisonment process. Following Hepburn and Stratton (1977), incarceration is characterised by the loss of personal property and autonomy, the deprivation of goods and services, the isolation and boredom entailed by confinement, the restrictions of movement and heterosexual behaviour, and the proximity to known and dangerous criminals. The longer the prisoners are exposed to the effects of the penal system, the weaker the effect of their BJW and, partly in consequence, the weaker their chances of rehabilitation. Not only do their moral attitudes suffer, the likelihood of disciplinary problems and outburst behaviour increases, and their confidence in being able to attain personal goals is shattered. These results are in line with findings of Kraus (1993), who summarised that, in the very best case, the punishments of the criminal justice system have no effects on the further development of offenders, but that in the worst case they in fact lead to an increase in criminal behaviour after release from prison. This indicates that imprisonment is not the best developmental intervention for adolescents and young adults.

Clearly, our results should be interpreted with caution. The study is cross-sectional in nature, meaning that no causal conclusions can be drawn. The results may be affected by the prisoners' tendency to answer in a socially desirable way. The covariance may be overestimated because personality factors that may underlie both BJW and the outcome variables were not controlled for. The sample size is small and a high number of statistical tests were conducted. Thus, the probability of false conclusions is inflated. Nevertheless, BJW was the single variable found to be correlated with all outcome variables – including objective data about the number of disciplinary problems during the term of imprisonment. Moreover, this result held even when controlled for numerous variables describing the personal and familial background and the criminal career of the young prisoners. Therefore, we would like to conclude that the personal belief in a just world helps to establish an internal motivation to obey the law in the future, especially for those offenders with a less serious criminal career on the one hand, and fewer prison experiences on the other.

References

Arnett, J.J. (1999) 'Adolescent storm and stress, reconsidered', *American Psychologist*, 54: 317–26.

Bierhoff, H.W. (1994) 'Verantwortung und altruistische Persönlichkeit' [Responsibility and altruistic personality] *Zeitschrift für Sozialpsychologie*, 25: 217–26.

170   K. Otto and C. Dalbert

Bierhoff, H.W., Klein, R. and Kramp, P. (1991) 'Evidence for the altruistic personality from data on accident research', *Journal of Personality*, 59: 263–80.

Brunstein, J.C. (1993) 'Personal goals and subjective well-being: A longitudinal study', *Journal of Personality and Social Psychology*, 65: 1061–70.

Bulman, R.J. and Wortman, C.B. (1977) 'Attributions of blame and coping in the "real world": Severe accident victims react to their lot', *Journal of Personality and Social Psychology*, 35: 351–63.

Comer, R. and Laird, J.D. (1975) 'Choosing to suffer as a consequence of expecting to suffer: Why do people do it?', *Journal of Personality and Social Psychology*, 32: 92–101.

Dalbert, C. (1996) *Über den Umgang mit Ungerechtigkeit. Eine psychologische Analyse*, Bern: Huber.

Dalbert, C. (1997) 'Coping with an unjust fate: The case of structural unemployment' *Social Justice Research*, 10: 175–89.

Dalbert, C. (1999) 'The world is more just for me than generally: About the Personal Belief in a Just World Scale's validity', *Social Justice Research*, 12: 79–98.

Dalbert, C. (2001) *The Justice Motive as a Personal Resource: Dealing with Challenges and Critical Life Events*, New York: Kluwer Academic/Plenum Publishers.

Dalbert, C. (2002) 'Beliefs in a just world as a buffer against anger', *Social Justice Research*, 15: 123–45.

DePalma, M., Madey, S.F., Tillman, T.C. and Wheeler, J. (1999) 'Perceived patient responsibility and belief in a just world affect helping', *Basic and Applied Psychology*, 21: 131–7.

Dishion, T.J., McCord, J. and Poulin, F. (1999) 'When interventions harm: Peer groups and problem behavior', *American Psychologist*, 54: 755–64.

Furnham, A. (1995) 'The just world, charitable giving and attitudes to disability', *Personality and Individual Differences*, 19: 577–83.

Hafer, C.L. (2000) 'Investment in long-term goals and commitment to just means drive the need to believe in a just world', *Personality and Social Psychology Bulletin*, 26: 1059–73.

Hafer, C.L. and Correy, B.L. (1999) 'Mediators of the relation between beliefs in a just world and emotional responses to negative outcomes', *Social Justice Research*, 12: 189–204.

Haller, V., Machura, S. and Bierhoff, H.W. (1995) 'Urteil und Verfahrensgerechtigkeit aus der Perspektive jugendlicher Strafgefangener' [Sentence and procedural justice in the view of adolescent prisoners], in Bierbauer, G., Gottwald, W. and Birnbreier-Stahlberger, B. (eds), *Verfahrensgerechtigkeit*, Cologne: Verlag Dr. Otto Schmidt.

Hepburn, J.R. and Stratton, J.R. (1977) 'Total institutions and inmate self-esteem', *British Journal of Criminology*, 17: 237–49.

Kraus, L. (1993) 'Empirische Untersuchung krimineller Karrieren anhand von Hell- und Dunkelfelddaten' [Empirical study of criminal careers using registered and not registered data], *Monatszeitschrift für Kriminologie und Strafrechtsreform*, 76: 256–68.

Lerner, M.J. (1977) 'The justice motive: Some hypotheses as to its origins and forms', *Journal of Personality*, 45: 1–52.

Lipkus, I.M. and Siegler, I.C. (1993) 'The belief in a just world and perceptions of discrimination', *Journal of Psychology*, 127: 465–74.

Lupfer, M.B., Doan, K. and Houston, D.A. (1998) 'Explaining unfair and fair outcomes: The therapeutic value of attributional analysis', *British Journal of Social Psychology*, 37: 495–511.

Moffitt, T.E. (1993) 'Adolescence-limited and life-course-persistent antisocial behavior: A developmental taxonomy', *Psychological Review*, 100: 674–701.

Nelson, J.R., Smith, D.J. and Dodd, J. (1990) 'The moral reasoning of juvenile delinquents: A meta-analysis', *Journal of Abnormal Child Psychology*, 18: 231–9.

Otto, K. and Dalbert, C. (2004) '*Belief in a Just World and its Functions for Young Prisoners*', Manuscript submitted for publication.

Saunders, D.R. (1956) 'Moderator variables in prediction', *Educational and Psychological Measurement*, 16: 209–22.

Schmitt, M. (1998) 'Gerechtigkeit und Solidarität im wiedervereinigten Deutschland' [Justice, and solidarity in the reunited Germany], in Reichle, B. and Schmitt, M. (eds), *Verantwortung, Gerechtigkeit und Moral. Zum Psychologischen Verständnis Ethischer Aspekte im Menschlichen Verhalten*, Weinheim: Juventa.

Schwenkmezger, P., Hodapp, V. and Spielberger, C.D. (1992) *Das State-Trait-Ärgerausdrucks-Inventar STAXI: Handbuch* [The State-Trait Anger Expression Inventory], Bern: Huber.

Smith, C.A. and Ellsworth, P.C. (1985) 'Patterns of cognitive appraisal in emotion', *Journal of Personality and Social Psychology*, 48: 813–38.

Spielberger, C.D. (1988) *State-trait Anger Expression Inventory: Professional Manual*, Odessa, FL: Psychological Assessment Resources.

Sykes, G. and Matza, D. (1957) 'Techniques of neutralization: A theory of delinquency', *American Sociological Review*, 22: 664–70.

Tanaka, K. (1999) 'Judgments of fairness by just world believers', *Journal of Social Psychology*, 139: 631–8.

Tomaka, J. and Blascovich, J. (1994) 'Effects of justice beliefs on cognitive appraisals of and subjective, physiological, and behavioral responses to potential stress', *Journal of Personality and Social Psychology*, 67: 732–40.

Tyler, T.R. (1984) 'The role of perceived injustice in defendants' evaluations of their courtroom experience', *Law and Society Review*, 18: 51–74.

Vitaro, F., Tremblay, R.E., Kerr, M., Pagani, L. and Bukowski, W.M. (1997) 'Disruptiveness, friends' characteristics, and delinquency in early adolescence: A test of two competing models of development', *Child Development*, 68: 676–89.

Zuckerman, M. (1975) 'Belief in a just world and altruistic behavior', *Journal of Personality and Social Psychology*, 31: 972–6.

Zuckerman, M. and Gerbasi, K.C. (1977) 'Belief in a just world and trust', *Journal of Research in Personality*, 11: 306–17.

Part III

Belief in a just world and career development

11 Belief in a just world as a resource for unemployed young adults

Claudia Dalbert

Health and early unemployment

Unemployment has increased over the past decade and is now a chronic problem in most European societies, particularly in East Germany since unification and in the countries of Central Europe since the transformation of their political systems (e.g. Frese, 1994). The psychological consequences of unemployment are well known: it is a prime risk factor for mental and physical health. Unemployed individuals are very likely to become depressed, and the longer the period of unemployment the greater is the psychological distress (Häfner, 1990). Many school leavers looking for their first job have to contend with unemployment and job insecurity. The mental health of unemployed adolescents and young adults is weaker than that of their employed peers (e.g. Axelsson and Ejlertsson, 2002), and those with poor mental health are in turn less likely to find a job (Taris, 2002). However, school leavers who accept a job for which they are overqualified may experience detrimental health effects similar to those reported by their unemployed peers (O'Brien and Feather, 1990).

Today's employment arrangements are rather complex. Creed and Reynolds (2001) compared the psychological distress and deprivation of young adults aged 16 to 26 years who were unemployed with no access to any paid work or with access to some casual work with those who were either unemployed, but with access to regular part-time or casual work, or in full-time employment. Young unemployed adults with sporadic access to casual work revealed more psychological distress and were more deprived, economically and experientially ('Most of my days are pretty unstructured'), than those with regular access to casual work at least. These results show that unemployment not only impairs mental health and threatens young adults with manifest problems such as financial worries, but also confronts them with latent problems such as a lack of time structure (Jahoda, 1982). The significance of time structure for the mental health of young employed adults was underpinned by a study by Martella and Maass (2000). The life satisfaction of unemployed adults

176   *Claudia Dalbert*

aged from 19 to 31 years was significantly associated with the existence of a fixed time structure, even when controlling for extraversion and subjective income. The loss of time structure as a result of unemployment and the increase in harmful behaviour such as smoking and drinking excessively (Kieselbach, 1995) is assumed to mediate the impact of early unemployment on various health indicators.

There is doubtless a significant relationship between employment status on the one hand and health and deprivation on the other, even for young adults just entering the job market. However, the question remains of whether this pattern mirrors selection into unemployment – meaning that unemployed individuals already exhibited problems such as unfavourable health behaviour before becoming unemployed – or whether it reflects a socialisation process triggered by early unemployment – meaning that problems such as unhealthy behaviour develop as a result of exposure to unemployment. Hammarström and Janlert (2002) conducted a longitudinal study with 14-year follow-up on 16-year-old school leavers entering the workforce. They monitored smoking, alcohol abuse, somatic symptoms and psychological symptoms. For most of the students, a selection effect was observed – that is, their behaviour and symptoms were crucial in determining their career development immediately after leaving school. Nevertheless, even after controlling for this initial health status, early unemployment was significantly associated with unfavourable health behaviour and symptoms at age 30.

In sum, early unemployment seems to have a significant impact on later development. Young adults leaving school have to make the difficult transition from the education system to the workforce. Coping with this transition is an important developmental task, the outcome of which is decisive for their development. Those who succeed in entering the labour force can expect their future career to develop positively, and to enjoy better future health. Those who fail are likely to suffer from impaired health and the lack of psychological supports such as a fixed time structure. Apart from doubts about their future employment prospects, they will face difficulties with respect to other developmental tasks such as becoming economically and psychologically independent of their parents and starting a family of their own.

BJW and mental health during unemployment

Falling victim to unemployment implies suffering an unjust fate, a fate that is highly aversive but not self-inflicted. Unfairness seems to be a central theme for unemployed individuals. Indeed, study participants who are unemployed or threatened by the possibility of losing their job rate their fate as significantly more unfair than victims of other fates such as giving birth to a premature or disabled child (Dalbert, 1997). Moreover, young adults (particularly young men) applying for their first job consider

BJW as a resource for young unemployed   177

unemployment to be a stigmatic situation (Kulik, 2001). Although unemployed individuals often evaluate their fate as unfair, justice theories have rarely been applied to psychological unemployment research (Kieselbach, 1995). The feeling of being treated unfairly constitutes a serious threat to mental health and psychological functioning (Dalbert, 2001), and the psychological outcomes of unemployment may be caused in part by this feeling of unfairness. Individuals cope differently with experienced unfairness, and investigating coping from a justice-psychological perspective – more specifically, a just world perspective – may deepen our understanding of the psychological consequences of unemployment. This chapter will thus review previous studies on BJW, mental health and emotion-focused coping with unemployment. Additionally, further hypotheses about the possible functions of the BJW for problem-focused coping with early unemployment – getting a first job or re-entering employment – will be proposed, supported by studies conducted outside the field of unemployment. Three other chapters in this book (12–14) provide further empirical evidence of the importance of the BJW for career development.

According to Lerner's (1965, 1980) just world hypothesis, people are motivated to believe that the world is basically a fair place where people get what they deserve and deserve what they get. Consequently, the belief in a just world (BJW) serves different adaptive functions, and people try to protect this belief when they are confronted with injustice. Several experimental and correlational studies have provided evidence to support the assumption that people protect their BJW, both when they observe unfairness done to others (for a review, see Dalbert, 1996; Furnham and Procter, 1989; Lerner and Miller, 1978) and when they suffer unfairness themselves (Bulman and Wortman, 1977; Comer and Laird, 1975; for a review, see Furnham, 2003). Unemployed individuals usually regard their joblessness as an extremely unfair loss experience (Dalbert, 1997). Thus, they should be motivated to protect their BJW, and the BJW should serve as a buffer shielding their mental health. Individuals high in BJW will be more likely to assimilate the experienced unfairness to their BJW and, in so doing, maintain their mental health.

Meanwhile, a high number of studies have confirmed the hypothesised positive relationship between the BJW and various dimensions of mental health for both victim and non-victim groups (for a review, see Dalbert, 2001). Some of the available victim studies were conducted with samples of unemployed individuals or workers threatened by unemployment. In a questionnaire study of workers facing unemployment due to the closure of a plant, Lerner and Somers (1992) found a positive relationship between two broad factors: well-being and personal beliefs including BJW, and concluded that workers high in BJW were better off. A contrasting effect was observed by Benson and Ritter (1990), who found unemployed adults high in BJW to be more depressed. In a study conducted in East Germany, Dalbert (1993) compared the relationship between BJW and mental health

178   *Claudia Dalbert*

in a non-victim group (East German female students) and a victim group (East German women unemployed or threatened by job insecurity). The study revealed that women high in BJW were more satisfied with their life, showed a better mood level, and exhibited more positive and less negative moods at the time of the assessment. With the exception of negative mood, the relationships between BJW and mental health were the same for victims and non-victims. Negative mood only correlated significantly with BJW in the victim sample, but not in the non-victim sample. Note that the level of BJW itself did not vary between the two groups.

The first studies testing BJW as a resource for young adults entering the job market were conducted by Dzuka and Dalbert (2002) with young Slovakian adults aged 18 to 22 years. In two studies, they compared three groups of participants, namely young adults in short-term and long-term unemployment (up to 6 months vs. 11 months and more) and a control group (school students shortly before leaving school; university students), and explored the role of BJW as buffer for the unemployed participants' mental health (life satisfaction, personal worries, positive affect, negative affect, self-esteem). Following suggestions originating from earlier research (Furnham and Procter, 1989; Lerner and Miller, 1978), recent investigations have shown that it is necessary to distinguish the belief in a personal just world from the belief in a general just world (Dalbert, 1999; Lipkus *et al.*, 1996). The personal BJW reflects the belief that events in one's life are just; the general BJW reflects the belief that, basically, the world is a just place. It has been shown that both BJWs correlate significantly, and that individuals tend to endorse the belief in a personal just world more strongly than the belief in a general just world. Moreover, personal BJW seems to be more important in predicting mental health and well-being (Lipkus *et al.*, 1996; Dalbert, 1999).

As anticipated (Lipkus *et al.*, 1996; Dalbert, 1999), all participants in the studies by Dzuka and Dalbert (2002) endorsed the belief in a personal just world more strongly than the belief in a general just world, and the personal BJW proved to be more important in predicting mental health. The more the young adults endorsed the personal BJW, the more satisfied they were with their life, the more often they experienced positive affect and the better their self-esteem was. These adaptive relationships were consistently observed for all three groups, even when controlling for gender, subjective financial situation and further personality dimensions, namely social desirability, extraversion and neuroticism. However, the results for the negative mental health dimensions were mixed, with only general BJW playing a significant role. In Study 1, a positive (maladaptive) relationship between personal worries and BJW was found for those in long-term unemployment only. In Study 2, a negative (adaptive) relationship with negative affect was observed. Long-term unemployed young adults with a strong BJW experienced less negative affect than those with a weak general BJW.

With the exception of the negative mental health dimensions, both studies clearly support the hypothesis that the BJW – and in particular the personal BJW – buffers the mental health of young adults, whether they are preparing to enter the job market or are already faced with early unemployment. Moreover, the results of Study 1 (Dzuka and Dalbert, 2002) confirm that the meaning and impact of the BJW may change over time. Within the long-term unemployed group, personal and general BJW were not correlated, nor was there a significant difference in their means. A closer look at the general BJW showed that the items did not form a homogeneous scale within the long-term unemployed group. These results, in particular, raise the question of whether the BJW, and especially the general BJW, changes its meaning and impact with the length of unemployment. Individuals in long-term unemployment (here: ≥ 12 months) may find their BJW shattered by the enduring reality of their situation, and may respond by accommodating their BJW to their negative experiences. A similar pattern of results was not observed in Study 2, however.

Taken collectively, most previous studies have found an adaptive relationship between BJW and mental health. This adaptive relationship seems to be more pronounced for positive mental health dimensions such as life satisfaction, positive affect and self-esteem than for negative dimensions such as negative affect, depression or personal worries, and it seems to be more valid for the personal than for the general BJW. Most importantly, personal BJW has emerged as consistently and uniquely associated with positive mental health for young adults, even for those confronted with early unemployment. However, it is unclear whether this adaptive relationship also holds for those in long-term unemployment. This aspect, in particular, needs to be examined in more detail.

BJW and emotion-focused coping with unemployment

Overall, previous research seems to confirm that BJW buffers the mental health of unemployed individuals in general, and of school leavers entering the job market in particular. Moreover, it can be assumed that the BJW functions as an adaptive resource that helps individuals to cope with unemployment. Thus, coping efforts can be interpreted as mediating the BJW's impact on mental health. At least three coping reactions may have this effect, and are described below. BJW and ways of coping with unemployment were first investigated in a study with unemployed blue-collar workers in East Germany (e.g. Dalbert, 1997). Wherever possible, I will use empirical examples from this study with unemployed women to illustrate the point being made.

Compared with victims of other critical life events, unemployed respondents typically rate their joblessness as very unfair (Dalbert, 1997), and unfairness experiences are most typically accompanied by feelings of anger (Smith and Ellsworth, 1985). Respondents high in BJW aim to

180   *Claudia Dalbert*

reduce their experience of unfairness by *minimising self-experienced unfairness*. Old and middle-aged adults high in BJW are less likely to describe themselves as victims of several discriminations than adults low in BJW (Lipkus and Siegler, 1993). University students high in BJW are more likely to feel fairly treated than those low in BJW (Hafer and Correy, 1999). Most importantly, the more victims of strokes of fate believe in a just world, the more they tend to minimise the unfairness of this event – this also held for the unemployed workers (Dalbert, 1996). Thus, the BJW's adaptive effect on unemployed individuals' mental health may be mediated by their tendency to minimise the experienced unfairness. However, in the study with unemployed workers, the unfairness rating was not significantly correlated with any dimension of mental health (Dalbert, 1996).

BJW provides unemployed individuals with a conceptual framework which guides their interpretation of the event. One way to re-establish justice is to justify the experienced fate as being at least partly self-inflicted, because a self-inflicted misfortune is no longer unfair. Such *internal attributions* should protect the belief in a just world and enhance feelings of control over future life-events. Internal attributions can thus be interpreted as adaptive coping reactions. However, empirical results regarding the relationship between internal attribution and mental health are mixed (for a review, see Dalbert, 1996, 2001). Several studies have supported the hypothesis that BJW encourages victims to make internal attributions (e.g. Hafer and Correy, 1999; Kiecolt-Glaser and Williams, 1987). This has also been observed for unemployed individuals (Dalbert, 1996, 2001). Not surprisingly, the East German workers tended to attribute their unemployment largely to external forces such as political change. Only about 8 per cent of the women attributed their unemployment partly to their own behaviour. These behavioural attributions correlated significantly with the BJW, but not with any other variables. Women high in BJW were slightly more likely to see their own behaviour as having caused their unemployment in some way. Overall, however, behavioural attributions were rare and did not seem to be an important part of the coping process.

Unemployed individuals often find themselves in a state of despair, ruminating 'Why me?' and facing existential doubts. Brooding over the 'Why me?' question appears to be the opposite of the belief that the world is structured and just. Not being able to answer the 'Why me?' question can thus be assumed to present a serious threat to the BJW, which may explain why this question is maladaptive. It is well documented for various critical life-events other than unemployment that the question has a negative effect on mental and physical health (e.g. Bliesmeister *et al.*, 1992; Burgess and Holmstrom, 1979; Silver *et al.*, 1983; Rogner *et al.*, 1987; Witenberg *et al.*, 1983).

The 'Why me?' question can be expected to be especially distressing for unemployed individuals, because they are likely to have difficulties finding an answer. Making sense of the loss by, for example, reinterpreting the fate as self-inflicted is not a reasonable strategy for victims of structural unemployment. In such cases, there is usually a socially shared interpretation that external factors such as the factory management or political forces are responsible for job cuts. It can therefore be expected that individuals high in BJW will avoid the 'Why me?' question. This approach should be possible at the beginning of the period of unemployment, at least. However, facing existential doubts in form of the 'Why me?' question and, at the same time, feeling the need to believe in a just world can be expected to be very threatening to mental health.

The results of Dalbert's study (1996, 1997, 2001) underline the importance of the 'Why me?' question for unemployed individuals. The clear majority (81 per cent) of the unemployed women surveyed had indeed asked themselves this question, but only one-third had found an answer. Women who did not ask 'Why me?' endorsed the BJW more strongly than those who did. However, the relationship between the BJW and the 'Why me?' question was stronger for those who had been unemployed for six months or less. In sum, unemployed women high in BJW were found to avoid asking 'Why me?', especially in the first six months of unemployment. Finding an answer was independent of the BJW, however.

The consequences of BJW and coping strategies for mental health were analysed by means of moderated regression (Dalbert, 1997, 2001). Mental health was indicated by a depressive mood state (Hautzinger and Bailer, 1993; Radloff, 1977). The interactions between the BJW and asking the 'Why me?' question on the one hand and finding an answer on the other were both significant, and explained variance in depression in addition to the variance already explained by other variables, e.g. the length of unemployment. Finally, the interaction between the length of unemployment and finding an answer to the 'Why me?' question was also significant. Negative (adaptive) relationships between BJW and depression were observed for women who did not ask 'Why me?' in particular, as well as for those who had found an answer. In contrast, a positive (maladaptive) relationship between BJW and depression was observed for those who ruminated on the 'Why me?' question without coming to an answer. Additionally, the interaction between finding an answer and the length of unemployment revealed that being able to answer the 'Why me?' question was more protective for the long-term unemployed. Taken collectively, the BJW seems to protect those who do not ruminate on the 'Why me?' question and those who find an answer to this question from depressive symptoms, but to increase the likelihood of depressive symptoms among those facing existential doubts, i.e. those who ruminate on the 'Why me?' question while at the same time believing in a just world. Finally, finding an answer to the question seems to become more important, the longer the women are unemployed.

182   *Claudia Dalbert*

In sum, the BJW's adaptive effect on the unemployed women's mental health was mediated by the tendency of those high in BJW to avoid self-focused rumination. The more the blue-collar workers endorsed the BJW, the less likely they were to ruminate on the 'Why me?' question, and this was especially true for those who had been unemployed for less than seven months (Dalbert, 1997, 2001). The outcomes of rumination on the 'Why me?' question differed, depending on whether the questioner believed in a just world. Note that unemployed women low in BJW exhibited more variation in mental health than women high in BJW. This again demonstrates the buffering capacity of the BJW. While coping efforts could influence the unemployed women's mental health to a limited degree, BJW proved to have a far greater impact. It is crucial to be able to give meaning to one's life (Davis *et al.*, 1998), and BJW seems to be a major resource here. However, further coping studies need to test whether the BJW also impacts on the coping efforts of young adults facing early unemployment. The significant association between the BJW and the mental health of school leavers (Dzuka and Dalbert, 2002) is the first evidence to support this hypothesis.

BJW and problem-focused coping

Up to this point, the focus has been on emotion-focused coping. We now turn to problem-focused coping (Lazarus and Folkman, 1984), which is essential for dealing with unemployment (and other reversible fates). It would be a high price to pay for the preservation of mental health if unemployed individuals were not to actively look for a new job. To my knowledge, no studies have yet investigated the impact of BJW on problem-focused coping. However, there are good reasons to hypothesise that BJW should also promote problem-focused coping, i.e. efforts to find a new job or, in the case of school leavers, activities to obtain a first job.

Since BJW is a positive illusion, it may be suspected of fostering wishful thinking and passivity. Justice motive theory does not support such expectations, however. Questionnaire studies indicate that the BJW acts as a buffer encouraging problem orientation. People high in BJW have been found to be low in procrastination (Ferrari and Emmons, 1994), self-defeating behaviour (Schill *et al.*, 1992), wishful thinking and forgetfulness (Rim, 1986), but high in problem orientation and action planning (Rim, 1986). However, none of these studies involved victims coping with a stressful fate in general or unemployment in particular.

The study with unemployed workers described above (Dalbert, 1996, 1997) only touched briefly on this question. The unemployed blue-collar workers were asked whether they would be willing to change their occupation, a course of action which is still rather unusual in Germany. In a typical German occupational biography, the worker remains employed in their trained profession for the rest of their working life. The problem of between-profession mobility (BPM) hit the citizens of the former East Germany particularly hard, because many of their certified professions were uncommon or no longer required in the industries of the unified Germany. It thus seemed important to assess the unemployed women's BPM. A significant proportion of the women were willing to change their profession and were able to name concrete alternatives such as shop assistant, nursery-school teacher and the nursing professions. BPM showed no significant bivariate correlation with the dimensions of mental health, the BJW or the coping reactions mentioned. However, a multiple regression revealed that the interaction of the length of unemployment and BPM predicted depression, even when controlling for other factors such as emotion-focused coping (Dalbert, 1996). Thus, the women's BJW did not affect their BPM, but BPM emerged to be an important problem-focused coping reaction. With increasing length of unemployment, BPM seemed to become a problem-focused coping reaction, capable of decreasing depression. This first pattern of results indicates that BJW at least does not hinder problem-focused coping. Whether BJW actually promotes efforts to find a new job needs to be tested in future studies.

One function of the BJW is particularly relevant to understanding why it may support efforts to obtain a first job or to re-enter employment. BJW endows individuals with the confidence that they will be treated fairly by others and will not fall victim to an unforeseeable disaster. This is the personal contract: I am obliged to behave fairly and, as a result, I am able to trust in a just world (Lerner, 1977). Thus, individuals high in BJW are able to place more trust in others. They are less suspicious of others (Zuckerman and Gerbasi, 1977), less cynical about the prosocial behaviour of others (Furnham, 1995), and expect to be treated fairly by others – by being confronted only with fair tasks, for example (Tomaka and Blascovich, 1994). Overall, this trust in fairness has several consequences. People high in BJW are more likely to invest in their future because they are confident that their investments will be fairly rewarded. This includes goal-directed behaviour such as investment in long-term goals (Hafer, 2000). Moreover, individuals high in BJW feel less threatened and less distressed by the demands of others, because they are confident that they will be treated fairly (Tomaka and Blascovich, 1994). The impact of this function on unemployed individuals' problem-focused coping efforts has not yet been investigated. However, it can be hypothesised that the trust in being treated fairly by others should affect unemployed individuals' career development in several ways, and that the same should be true for young adults entering the job market.

First of all, BJW should increase investments in one's future employment opportunities – in the form of efforts to find a new job or applications for continued education or retraining, for example. The stronger the individuals' belief that they can successfully attain their personal goal of obtaining a new (or first) job, the more they will invest in goal

184   *Claudia Dalbert*

attainment, and the more persistent they will be (e.g. Brunstein, 1993). Dette *et al.* (in this volume) have shown that adolescent German school leavers with a strong BJW are confident that they will attain their vocational goals. Nevertheless, further studies are needed to test whether the BJW's adaptive impact on goal attainment can be generalised from expectations to actual investments, and whether it continues to hold when young people are actually confronted with unemployment. Second, after re-employment or when beginning their first job, employees have to convince their colleagues and their boss that they are good at their job in order to pass the trial period. In a laboratory study (Tomaka and Blascovich, 1994), subjects high in BJW experienced less threat, less stress and, most importantly, performed better than subjects low in BJW. This indicates that individuals high in BJW should be less stressed and more successful in achievement situations. Likewise, when starting a new or first job, individuals with a high BJW should feel less stressed and less threatened and should perform better during the trial period than those with a weak BJW.

Discussion

The overall pattern of results provides clear support for the assumption that a justice-psychological perspective may deepen our understanding of the psychological consequences of unemployment. Unemployed individuals typically evaluate their fate as extremely unfair, and coping with this unfairness is a challenge to them. In this chapter, studies indicating that the belief in a just world (BJW) is an adaptive resource in this coping process have been summarised. Unemployed individuals who believe in a just world seem to be more likely to protect their mental health. Unemployed individuals with a strong BJW – including school leavers facing early unemployment – reveal stronger self-esteem, are more satisfied with their life, show a better mood level and more often experience positive and less often negative affective states than their unemployed counterparts low in BJW. This adaptive impact on mental health seems to be mediated by individual coping efforts. Unemployed workers high in BJW are more likely to avoid the 'Why me?' question, thus averting depressive symptoms.

Note that the BJW's adaptive effect on mental health only seems to operate in the first six months or so of unemployment. If unemployed individuals are not successful in finding a new job during this time, another process seems to take effect. At this point, the BJW can no longer protect the individual from ruminating on the reasons for his or her unemployment. Unemployed individuals may still believe in a structured and just world, but their joblessness will make them start wondering whether the world really is a just place. These existential doubts could, in the long run, impair mental health. Moreover, unemployment may even-

BJW as a resource for young unemployed   185

tually shatter the belief in a just world itself. Individuals may start to accommodate their world beliefs to the enduring reality. Finding a satisfying answer to the search for meaning seems to be essential for individuals in long-term unemployment.

Thus far, studies on BJW and unemployment have centred on emotion-focused coping. Clearly, however, problem-focused coping in terms of finding new work is a central theme in the coping processes of unemployed individuals. Preliminary evidence suggests that BJW does not hinder problem-focused coping, but may rather increase investment in career development. Future studies should investigate the interrelationship between emotion- and problem-focused coping in more detail from a justice-psychological point of view. Other topics have as yet been completely neglected. Kokko *et al.* (2000) investigated selection into long-term unemployment. In particular, they followed individuals from the age of 8 to 36, and revealed a crucial factor at the age of 8 that predicted long-term unemployment during adulthood (between 27 and 36 years of age). Children who revealed low self-control of emotions, in particular aggression, at age 8 were significantly more likely to be unemployed for more than two years during adulthood. BJW has been shown to buffer against feelings of anger and to be negatively associated with an anger-expression style that makes outbursts of aggressive behaviour more likely (Dalbert, 2002). The individually varying BJW seems to begin developing around the age of 8 (Jose, 1990). Thus, the development of a strong BJW in childhood should be taken into account when examining early selection into long-term unemployment, because BJW enhances anger-control and reduces outburst behaviour which was shown to be selective for later unemployment.

Note that the evidence presented so far is correlational and cross-sectional, and that causal conclusions can only be hypothesised. Nevertheless, the correlational data were gathered in labour markets spanning East Germany, Slovakia and Canada, and results held even when controlling for concurrent factors such as the financial situation or global personality dimensions, hence giving the conclusions drawn some validity. Future research should take a longitudinal and multidimensional approach, thus allowing causal conclusions to be drawn.

Conclusion

Overall, the pattern of results indicates that a strong belief in a just world explains emotion-focused and, possibly, problem-focused coping and mental health during unemployment. A strong BJW enables unemployed individuals to sustain their mental health and to invest in their future. However, the longer the period of unemployment, the less they seem to be able to find meaning in their fate. These observations have implications for the psychological guidance of unemployed individuals. Future

186 *Claudia Dalbert*

investigations on the psychological consequences of unemployment should therefore take justice concerns into account. Furthermore, leaving school and applying for one's first job is a decisive point in individual development, with broad long-term consequences. Losing one's faith that the world is a just place where one can expect to be treated fairly may be one of the most serious psychological consequences faced by young adults confronted with long-term early unemployment.

References

Axelsson, L. and Ejlertsson, G. (2002) 'Self-reported health, self-esteem and social support among young unemployed people: a population-based study', *International Journal of Social Welfare*, 11: 111–19.

Benson, D.E. and Ritter, C. (1990) 'Belief in a just world, job loss, and depression', *Sociological Focus*, 23: 49–63.

Bliesmeister, J., Frey, D., Aschenbach, G. and Köller, O. (1992) 'Zum Zusammenhang zwischen psychosozialen Merkmalen und dem Gesundheitszustand HIV-Infizierter – eine interdisziplinäre Querschnittstudie' [About the relationship between psychosocial descriptors and the health state of HIV-infected – an interdisciplinary cross-sectional study], *Zeitschrift für Klinische Psychologie*, 21: 182–96.

Brunstein, J.C. (1993) 'Personal goals and subjective well-being: A longitudinal study', *Journal of Personality and Social Psychology*, 65: 1061–70.

Bulman, R.J. and Wortman, C.B. (1977) 'Attributions of blame and coping in the "real world": Severe accident victims react to their lot', *Journal of Personality and Social Psychology*, 35: 351–63.

Burgess, A.W. and Holmstrom, L.L. (1979) 'Adaptive strategies and recovery from rape', *American Journal of Psychiatry*, 136: 1278–82.

Comer, R. and Laird, J.D. (1975) 'Choosing to suffer as a consequence of expecting to suffer: Why do people do it?', *Journal of Personality and Social Psychology*, 32: 92–101.

Creed, P.A. and Reynolds, J. (2001) 'Economic deprivation, experiential deprivation and social loneliness in unemployed and employed youth', *Journal of Community and Applied Social Psychology*, 11: 167–78.

Dalbert, C. (1993) 'Gefährdung des Wohlbefindens durch Arbeitsplatzunsicherheit: Eine Analyse der Einflußfaktoren Selbstwert und Gerechte-Welt-Glaube' [Well-being threatened by job-insecurity: Analysing the effects of self-esteem and belief in a just world], *Zeitschrift für Gesundheitspsychologie*, 1: 235–53.

Dalbert, C. (1996) *Über den Umgang mit Ungerechtigkeit. Eine Psychologische Analyse* [Dealing with injustice. A psychological analysis], Bern: Huber.

Dalbert, C. (1997) 'Coping with an unjust fate: The case of structural unemployment', *Social Justice Research*, 10: 175–89.

Dalbert, C. (1999) 'The world is more just for me than generally: About the Personal Belief in a Just World Scale's validity', *Social Justice Research*, 12: 79–98.

Dalbert, C. (2001) *The Justice Motive as a Personal Resource: Dealing with Challenges and Critical Life Events*, New York: Kluwer Academic/Plenum Publishers.

Dalbert, C. (2002) 'Beliefs in a just world as a buffer against anger', *Social Justice Research*, 15: 123–45.

Davis, C.G., Nolen-Hoeksema, S. and Larson, J. (1998) 'Making sense of loss and

BJW as a resource for young unemployed 187

benefiting from the experience: Two construals of meaning', *Journal of Personality and Social Psychology*, 75: 561–74.

Dzuka, J. and Dalbert, C. (2002) 'Mental health and personality of Slovak unemployed adolescents: The impact of belief in a just world', *Journal of Applied Social Psychology*, 32: 732–57.

Ferrari, J.R. and Emmons, R.A. (1994) 'Procrastination as revenge: Do people report using delays as a strategy for vengeance?', *Personality and Individual Differences*, 17: 539–44.

Frese, M. (1994) 'Psychische Folgen von Arbeitslosigkeit in den fünf neuen Bundesländern: Ergebnisse einer Längsschnittstudie' [Psychological consequences of unemployment in the five new federal states], in Montada, L. (ed.), *Arbeitslosigkeit und Soziale Gerechtigkeit*, Frankfurt: Campus.

Furnham, A. (1995) 'The just world, charitable giving and attitudes to disability', *Personality and Individual Differences*, 19: 577–83.

Furnham, A. (2003) 'Belief in a just world: Research progress over the past decade', *Personality and Individual Differences*, 34: 795–817.

Furnham, A. and Procter, E. (1989) 'Belief in a just world: Review and critique of the individual difference literature', *British Journal of Social Psychology*, 28: 365–84.

Hafer, C.L. (2000) 'Investment in long-term goals and commitment to just means drive the need to believe in a just world', *Personality and Social Psychology Bulletin*, 26: 1059–73.

Hafer, C.L. and Correy, B.L. (1999) 'Mediators of the relation of beliefs in a just world and emotional responses to negative outcomes', *Social Justice Research*, 12: 189–204.

Häfner, H. (1990) 'Arbeitslosigkeit – Ursache von Krankheit und Sterberisiken' [Unemployment – cause of disease and mortality risks], *Zeitschrift für Klinische Psychologie*, 1: 1–17.

Hammarström, A. and Janlert, U. (2002) 'Early unemployment can contribute to adult health problems: Results from a longitudinal study of school leavers', *Journal of Epidemiology and Community Health*, 56: 624–30.

Hautzinger, M. and Bailer, M. (1993) *Allgemeine Depressionsskala (ADS)* [General Depression Scale], Weinheim: Beltz-Test.

Jahoda, M. (1982) *Employment and Unemployment. A Social-psychological Analysis*, Cambridge: Cambridge University Press.

Jose, P.E. (1990) 'Just-world-reasoning in children's immanent justice judgements', *Child Development*, 61: 1024–33.

Kiecolt-Glaser, J.K. and Williams, D.A. (1987) 'Self-blame, compliance, and distress among burn patients', *Journal of Personality and Social Psychology*, 53: 187–93.

Kieselbach, T. (1995) 'Arbeitslosigkeit und Ungerechtigkeitserleben: Perspektiven eines zukünftigen Umgangs mit beweglichen Transitionsprozessen' [Unemployment and experience of unfairness: perspectives for future dealing with transition processes], *Berichte aus dem Zentrum für Gerechtigkeitsforschung an der Universität Potsdam*, Vol. 2, Eröffnungssymposium.

Kokko, K., Pulkkinen, L. and Puustinen, M. (2000) 'Selection into long-term unemployment and its psychological consequences', *International Journal of Behavioural Development*, 24: 310–20.

Kulik, L. (2001) 'Assessing job search intensity and unemployment-related attitudes among young adults: Intergender differences', *Journal of Career Assessment*, 9: 153–67.

188   *Claudia Dalbert*

Lazarus, R.S. and Folkman, S. (1984) *Stress, Appraisal, and Coping*, New York: Springer.

Lerner, M.J. (1965) 'Evaluation of performance as a function of performer's reward and attractiveness', *Journal of Personality and Social Psychology*, 1: 355–60.

Lerner, M.J. (1977). 'The justice motive: Some hypotheses as to its origins and forms', *Journal of Personality*, 45: 1–52.

Lerner, M.J. (1980) *The Belief in a Just World: A Fundamental Delusion*, New York: Plenum.

Lerner, M.J. and Miller, D.T. (1978) 'Just world research and the attribution process: Looking back and ahead', *Psychological Bulletin*, 85: 1030–51.

Lerner, M.J. and Somers, D.G. (1992) 'Employees' reactions to an anticipated plant closure: The influence of positive illusions', in Montada, L. and Filipp, S.H. (eds), *Life Crises and Experiences of Loss in Adulthood*, Hillsdale, NJ: Lawrence Erlbaum Associates.

Lipkus, I.M. and Siegler, I.C. (1993) 'The belief in a just world and perceptions of discrimination', *Journal of Psychology*, 127: 465–74.

Lipkus, I.M., Dalbert, C. and Siegler, I.C. (1996) 'The importance of distinguishing the belief in a just world for self versus for others: Implications for psychological well-being', *Personality and Social Psychology Bulletin*, 22: 666–77.

Martella, D. and Maass, A. (2000) 'Unemployment and life satisfaction: The moderating role of time structure and collectivism', *Journal of Applied Social Psychology*, 30: 1095–108.

O'Brien, G.E. and Feather, N.T. (1990) 'The relative effects of unemployment and quality of employment on the affect, work values and personal control of adolescents', *Journal of Occupational Psychology*, 63: 151–65.

Radloff, L.S. (1977) 'The CES-D Scale: A self-report depression scale for research in the general population', *Applied Psychological Measurement*, 1: 385–401.

Rim, Y. (1986) 'Coping-Strategien, der Glaube an eine gerechte Welt, Konservatismus, Werteinstellungen und das Konfluenz-Modell' [Coping styles, belief in a just world, conservatism, value orientation, and the confluence model], *Schweizerische Zeitschrift für Psychologie*, 45: 17–27.

Rogner, O., Frey, D. and Havemann, D. (1987) 'Der Genesungsverlauf von Unfallpatienten aus kognitionspsychologischer Sicht' [The healing curve of accident patients from a cognitive-psychological perspective], *Zeitschrift für Klinische Psychologie*, 16: 11–28.

Schill, T., Beyler, J. and Morales, J. (1992) 'The role of just world belief and anger issues in self-defeating personality', *Psychological Reports*, 70: 595–8.

Silver, R.L., Boon, C. and Stones, M.H. (1983) 'Searching for meaning in misfortune, making sense of incest', *Journal of Social Issues*, 39: 81–102.

Smith, C.A. and Ellsworth, P.C. (1985) 'Patterns of cognitive appraisal in emotion', *Journal of Personality and Social Psychology*, 48: 813–38.

Taris, T.W. (2002) 'Unemployment and mental health: A longitudinal perspective', *International Journal of Stress Management*, 9: 43–57.

Tomaka, J. and Blascovich, J. (1994) 'Effects of justice beliefs on cognitive, psychological, and behavioral responses to potential stress', *Journal of Personality and Social Psychology*, 67: 732–40.

Witenberg, S.H., Blanchard, E.B., Suls, J., Tennen, H., McCoy, G. and McGoldrick, M.D. (1983) 'Perceptions of control and causality as predictors of compliance and coping in hemodialysis', *Basic and Applied Social Psychology*, 4: 319–36.

Zuckerman, M. and Gerbasi, K.C. (1977) 'Belief in a just world and trust', *Journal of Research in Personality*, 11: 306–17.

12 Belief in a just world and young adults' ways of coping with unemployment and the job search

Vera Cubela Adoric

Finding a worthwhile and satisfying job is one of the main developmental tasks of late adolescence and young adulthood. Unfortunately, this period of transition from school to work is hardly ever smooth. Although young people usually expect that it will take some time and some job search activity before they find a job, for some of them it turns into a fairly prolonged period characterised by repeated failures and even unfairness in the job search. To come to terms with such experiences and the anger and anxiety resulting from them, psychological resources are a real necessity. In this chapter the belief in a just world (BJW) is presented as a candidate for such a role.

In the first section, the empirical findings and theoretical considerations that are relevant to the BJW's relationship with the experience of unemployment are presented. As will be shown, previous research in this area has focused mainly on individuals who had a job but lost it for various reasons. It is questionable that these findings are also valid for unemployed young people with no job experience. Only Dzuka and Dalbert (2002) have as yet investigated young adults actually looking for their first job. Although they found no evidence for a decline in BJW endorsement with (length of) unemployment, some of their findings indicate that prolonged unemployment leads to changes in the functioning of this belief. It is not clear, however, if these are temporary or persistent changes, i.e. what happens to the BJW when the jobless spell lasts much longer than considered normal by most people?

This issue was examined in the study presented in the second section of this chapter. As will be shown, prolonged unemployment, and the various negative experiences entailed in the job search, are associated with weaker endorsement of the BJW. This does not imply, however, that the notion of a just world is rejected altogether. On the contrary, some results of this study suggest that the long-term unemployed feel a strong need to maintain the BJW. Based on the data obtained, several strategies that seem to serve such a function are proposed.

190　*Vera Cubela Adoric*

Previous research and theorising

The BJW reflects a schema of an ordered and meaningful world that contributes to one's sense of security, invulnerability and confidence that one's efforts will be rewarded in the future, and thus promotes long-term investments, coping with everyday stressors and more critical life-events and, consequently, psychological adjustment and well-being.

This basic assumption is supported by several sets of empirical findings. For example, BJW has been found to be associated with life satisfaction (e.g. Cubela *et al.*, 1999; Dalbert, 1998), a sense of coherence and dispositional optimism (e.g. Cubela and Ivanov, 2000), lower subjective likelihood of life-threatening events when these risks are acute (Lambert *et al.*, 1998) and appraisal of achievement demands as being within one's ability to cope (Dalbert and Maes, 2002; Tomaka and Blascovich, 1994). My recent survey of Croatian university students' expectations regarding their study and job prospects (Cubela Adoric, 2003) provides another set of results which is in line with this assumption. The more the students endorsed the personal BJW and the less they endorsed the belief in an *un*just world, the more confident they were that they would complete the current academic year and their degree as a whole successfully.

The answers the students provided to two open-ended questions are of more relevance to the subject of this chapter. Students were asked to estimate (a) how long they expected to be unemployed upon graduation, and (b) the average length of unemployment experienced by people with a similar qualification. The students expected to be unemployed for a shorter period of time than their peers, indicating that individuals tend to perceive their own employment prospects in a more positive (or less negative) light than those of other people. In addition, the more the students believed in a personal just world and the less they endorsed the belief in an unjust world, the shorter the unemployment period they expected for themselves. The fact that both world beliefs contributed to the prediction of expected unemployment duration is in line with previous findings indicating that the two are only partially related beliefs that can be reliably differentiated on the basis of their relationships with a sense of coherence and dispositional optimism and pessimism (Cubela and Ivanov, 2000). Note, however, that neither of the beliefs correlated significantly with estimations of the average length of peer unemployment or with the tendency to underestimate the length of one's own unemployment (as indicated by the difference between two estimations of unemployment length). That is, their association with predictions of the length of one's own unemployment has nothing in common with perceptions of the general length of unemployment or with the self-serving tendency in predicting one's own unemployment.

As these results show, the more confident one is that the world is generally an unjust place *and* the less confident one is of being treated fairly in this world, the longer the expected period of personal unemployment. Such a pessimistic view of one's world and job prospects does not necessarily mean that individuals who are less confident that a world is a just place are less likely to make the efforts required to find a job. Indeed, there is some evidence for just the opposite pattern. In a study with employed respondents who were about to lose their jobs, Lerner (2002) found a positive relationship between the BJW and efforts to find another job shortly after the employees were informed about the impending job loss. This turned into a negative relationship several weeks later, just before the workers actually lost their jobs. Especially among the less-qualified employees (who were at most risk of not finding another job), 'the less they believed in the justness of their world, the more upset and frightened they were, and the greater their efforts to find work' (Lerner, 1998: 160). This is in line with Hafer and Olson's (1998) findings that weak believers in a just world experience more discontent when confronted with an unjust outcome (such as a poor grade in school), and are more likely to take steps toward modifying an adverse situation (such as an unsatisfactory job situation) than strong believers in a just world.

This pattern of findings suggests that although the BJW may provide a person who is facing the possibility of unemployment with initial confidence and trust in the future, it is also potentially dysfunctional as, in the long run, it is associated with reduced job search activity and, therefore, poorer prospects of finding a job. It should be noted, however, that reduced job search activity is not necessarily a sign of demotivation. As argued by McFadyen and Thomas (1997), it may be a rational strategy of safeguarding one's psychological state in the face of persistent rejection. Indeed, the unemployed have to cope with great psychological distress stemming not only from their employment status, but also from the ensuing financial strain, the deprivation of the latent functions of work (including frustrated progression in establishing an occupational identity; Meeus *et al.*, 1997), the experience of repeated failure to find a job and the feeling of rejection (McFadyen and Thomas, 1997), as well as from the sense of personal injustice that arises when one's status is seen as a deprivation of one's inherent rights, including the right to have a job, to be treated fairly during the job search, and so on (Montada, 1996). Therefore, unemployed individuals are certainly in need of a resource that will help them to sustain their motivation for the job search and to come to terms with repeated failures and the ensuing negative emotions, anxiety and worries, and thus to attenuate the negative psychological consequences of unemployment, including its impact on one's view of the self and, especially in young people, on the development of the occupational identity.

Some studies suggest that the BJW can play a role in regulating one's cognitive and emotional response to unemployment and in maintaining

192   *Vera Cubela Adoric*

one's well-being and mental health – at least for the short-term unemployed. For example, Dalbert (1998) reported the findings of a study with a group of women who had lost their jobs. The BJW proved to protect these women, especially those who had been unemployed for less than half a year, from ruminating on the 'Why me?' question. Dalbert also found that this rumination moderates the BJW's relationship with depression, and an adaptive (i.e. negative) relation was found only for those not ruminating about their misfortune. For those who brooded on the 'Why me?' question, but had not yet found an answer, the reverse, positive relation was obtained. Moreover, a maladaptive relationship between BJW and well-being was found in a frequently cited study with unemployed individuals from Northern Ireland (Benson and Ritter, 1990). In addition to rumination, Dalbert also explored self-attribution of the job loss, and found a modest positive correlation with BJW, but not with depression. This pattern is in line with her assumption that the BJW fosters (unrealistic) causal self-attributions. Evidence for the assumed adaptiveness of these attributions in unemployed individuals has yet to be presented, however. Even when the unemployment rate is high or one perceives oneself as a victim of structural unemployment, one can still blame oneself for particular failures in the job search, if not for one's employment status in general. To my knowledge, the role of the BJW in coping with an unsuccessful job search has not been examined in previous research. Rejections perceived as unjust (e.g. the result of preferential treatment) should present an additional threat to BJW.

The results of the previously mentioned survey of Croatian students' job perspectives have another important implication. They clearly support previous notions that a period of unemployment after leaving school is in fact seen as a normative rather than an unexpected 'event' (e.g. Lackovic-Grgin, 2000). Specifically, the students predicted that they would personally experience unemployment for an average of about one year, whereas their average estimate for the general length of unemployment was about one-and-a-half years. The precise duration of the expected jobless spell is likely to be sensitive to the overall rate of unemployment, so one would probably find lower overall estimates of both types of joblessness in countries with lower unemployment rates than Croatia. Another noteworthy implication of this finding concerns the possible buffering effect that these expectations may have during the initial period of unemployment. Such an effect is evidenced by the finding that, unlike their 'older counterparts' (i.e. those who had had a job but lost it), unemployed school leavers, especially if jobless for a relatively short period of time, do not necessarily show a decline in mental health and well-being (e.g. Lackovic-Grgin, 2000; Meeus *et al.*, 1997). Similarly, Dzuka and Dalbert (2002) found no difference in the BJW level of adolescents in short- (i.e. 1–7 months) and long-term (i.e. 12–32 months) unemployment and of control subjects (secondary-school students). Before concluding that the endorsement of the BJW is not influenced by (length of) unemployment in young people, however, a replication of these findings is needed, with a larger sample and perhaps a wider range of unemployment durations.

It should also be noted that some of the other results reported by Dzuka and Dalbert suggest that the long-term unemployed may differ from the short-term unemployed or students and perhaps employed people with regard to BJW. In particular, they found that only students and the short-term unemployed endorsed the personal BJW more strongly than the general BJW, as is usually the case (Dalbert, 1999). The long-term unemployed endorsed both beliefs equally. Moreover, the general and personal BJWs were unrelated in this group. Together with the findings that the personal BJW was unrelated to life satisfaction in the long-term unemployed and that the general BJW was positively associated with actual worries in this group, these results suggest that long-term unemployment does not lead to changes in the level of the BJW, but to changes in its structure and/or function, presumably as a consequence of its accommodation to persistently adverse conditions (Dzuka and Dalbert, 2002).

One issue that still remains unclear is whether these changes reflect a permanent change, or just a temporary one accompanying the process of coping with unemployment. This issue is especially important with regard to the assumed adaptive importance of the BJW in the personal domain (Dalbert, 2001; Lipkus et al., 1996). As noted by Patton and Donohue (1998), people change during the experience of unemployment, and the initial optimism and hope is followed by periods that the stage theories of unemployment describe as exhaustion, pessimism, depression and anxiety, and finally by despair and futility or acceptance and resignation. The results of their study with a group of people who had been unemployed for over one year showed that strategies such as having a positive outlook and re-evaluating one's expectations are associated with the well-being of the long-term unemployed. According to McFadyen and Thomas (1997: 1470), 'a general distancing of oneself from work-related matters may be the means whereby stabilization of well being is achieved'. Meeus et al. (1997) argue that, as a result of failure in the work domain, the unemployed select comparison dimensions other than work to be important for their self-definition (e.g. interpersonal relations). This is reflected in an identity structure in which one's work identity status is of less importance for well-being than one's identity status in the other chosen domain.

The present study

The purpose of the present study was to broaden our understanding of the BJW's relationship with the experience of unemployment. Previous research findings, including those referring to the BJW in young people

194   *Vera Cubela Adoric*

looking for their first job, seem to converge towards the conclusion that unemployment does not produce a decline in the endorsement of the BJW. This is in line with the theory that the BJW is a fundamental belief that is fairly resistant to change. More empirical evidence is needed, however, before firm conclusions about the consequences of unemployment on the BJW can be drawn. One reason that this issue deserves further scrutiny is the observation that the negative psychological impact of unemployment only becomes apparent after a longer spell of joblessness (e.g. Dzuka and Dalbert, 2002; Lackovic-Grgin, 2000). Assuming that one's expectations with regard to the unemployment duration serve as a buffer against its negative impact, any decline in the BJW among the unemployed should become observable when the unemployment duration exceeds the expected jobless spell. For unemployed school leavers in Croatia, this critical point seems to be about one year after leaving school (Cubela Adoric, 2003).

In addition to the length of unemployment, other related factors have the potential to threaten the BJW. These include failures and unjust experiences in the job search. The BJW's relationship with these experiences has not been previously examined. It seems reasonable to expect that, with the accumulation of such negative events, especially if they are perceived as unfair, it becomes more difficult to sustain the belief in the justness of the world, and that at some subjectively critical point (e.g. high perceived frequency and/or seriousness of such events) the BJW accommodates to these experiences.

This negative relationship with the BJW can also be expected for experiences of injustice, because the BJW can influence the perception of unfairness. As shown by Hafer and Olson (1998), strong believers in a just world perceive less unfairness and, consequently, experience less intense negative emotions in response to unjust events, presumably because they use some of the strategies contributing to the maintenance of the just world schema and to neutralising the negative emotional consequences of such events. Dalbert (1998) proposed unrealistic self-blame as one of these strategies. In this study, I thus examine the relationship between self-blame and perceived unfairness and negative emotional responses to unjust events in the (un)employment context and, more importantly, the role of the BJW in these relations. Previous research suggests that significant bivariate relationships can be expected between these responses to unjust events and the endorsement of the BJW (Dalbert, 1998; Hafer and Olson, 1998). Inasmuch as self-blame reflects the reverse of the external attribution of injustice (which is one of the constitutive elements in Mikula's model of the experience of injustice; see Mikula, 1993), it should be negatively related to perceived unfairness and, consequently, to the intensity of the negative emotions. If, however, the self-blame of strong believers is in fact unrealistic and serves primarily to attenuate the negative emotional impact of the injustice, it should contribute to predicting the intensity of negative emotions independently of the perceived unfairness.

In sum, the hypotheses tested in this study were as follows: (a) long-term unemployed young adults believe less strongly in a just world than do their employed counterparts; (b) endorsement of the BJW in the unemployed is negatively associated with the length of unemployment and/or the frequency of failures in the job search; (c) endorsement of the BJW is negatively related to the frequency of unjust experiences in domains that are relevant to one's work status (e.g. in the job search for unemployed people and at the workplace for employed people); (d) the stronger one's BJW, the lower the perceived unfairness and the intensity of negative emotion in response to particular experiences of injustice, and the stronger the tendency towards self-blame; (e) the association between self-blame and the emotional response to the event is moderated by the BJW, and it is only for strong believers in a just world that self-blame predicts the negative emotional response to the event independently of the perceived unfairness.

These hypotheses were tested in a study conducted in the late spring of 1999, when the unemployment rate was about 19 per cent in Croatia as a whole, and about 27 per cent in the area of Zadar, where the study was carried out. According to the Employment Service's statistical report (local edition, No. 2, 1999), approximately 77 per cent of those officially registered unemployed had been out of work for at least six months, and about 25 per cent of them had had no job experience at all. The unemployed participants in this study represent 1 per cent of the overall number of registered unemployed in the Zadar area at the time, and 5 per cent of those who were continuously unemployed (i.e. had no previous job experience). They were not, however, representative of the unemployed population with regard to gender, age or education, since the only criterion for including an individual in the sample was that he or she had never had a job and had been continuously unemployed for at least one year. To obtain a more heterogeneous group with respect to unemployment duration than in some previous research (e.g. Dzuka and Dalbert, 2002), I set no upper limit for the length of unemployment. With regard to gender and education, the structure of this group was balanced, and matched the group of employed participants.

Method

Sample and procedure

One half of the sample consisted of 200 unemployed adults (100 females and 100 males) recruited with the aid of the local Employment Service. At the time of their participation in this study they had been unemployed for 8.5 years on average ($SD = 4.02$). Their mean age was 28.3 years

196   *Vera Cubela Adoric*

($SD = 3.37$), with men being older than women (29.2 vs. 27.5 years respectively, $t = 3.749$, $p < 0.01$). The mean length of unemployment was also higher in men than women (7.7 vs. 9.2 years respectively, $t = 2.638$, $p = 0.01$). After controlling for age, the gender difference in the length of unemployment was no longer significant ($F = 1.523$, $p = 0.22$). In response to an open-ended question about the number of unsuccessful job applications they had submitted up to the point of assessment, these participants reported between 0 (8 participants) and 65 (1 participant) applications. After examining the frequency distribution, it was decided to code these answers into four categories: less than 4 applications (36 per cent of participants), 4–9 applications (24 per cent of participants), 10–15 applications (21 per cent of participants) and 16 or more applications (16 per cent of participants). The remaining 3 per cent of participants did not answer this question.

The other half of the sample consisted of 100 males and 100 females who had a permanent job at the time of their participation in the study. They were contacted at their places of work and, among those who agreed to participate in this study, individuals who matched the unemployed participants in terms of marital status and educational level were contacted again for participation. The average length of employment in this group was 5.5 years ($SD = 3.83$), with the men being employed for about two years longer than the women (6.9 vs. 4.9 years, $t = 2.581$, $p = 0.01$). Their mean age was 29.3 years ($SD = 3.66$). Men were again older than women (30.1 vs. 28.6 years respectively, $t = 2.925$, $p < 0.01$). After controlling for age, the gender difference in the length of employment was no longer significant ($F = 0.980$, $p = 0.32$). There was no gender difference in the length of unemployment before finding a permanent job ($t = 0.290$, $p = 0.77$). The mean length of unemployment in this group was 4.6 years ($SD = 3.19$).

Both employed and unemployed subjects participated individually in the study. They were given a questionnaire that contained measures of the BJW, a one-item measure of the frequency of unjust experiences, and a series of items aimed to assess perceived unfairness, self-blame and discontent with respect to a particular experience of injustice.

Measures

The *belief in a just world* was assessed with Croatian versions of the six-item *General Belief in a Just World Scale* (Dalbert *et al.*, 1987; $alpha = 0.70$) and the seven-item *Personal Belief in a Just World Scale* (Dalbert, 1999; $alpha = 0.73$). The scales include positively worded items referring to the belief that one lives in a world that is generally or personally just (see Dalbert, 2000, 1999 for more details). Each item was rated on a six-point Likert-type scale ranging from 1 ('strongly disagree') to 6 ('strongly agree'). A participant's score on each measure was computed as the mean of his or her ratings on

BJW, unemployment and the job search 197

its individual items. Both scales have been successfully tested for validity and reliability in Croatian students and adults (Cubela Adoric, 2003; Cubela and Ivanov, 2000; Cubela *et al.*, 1999).

The frequency of unjust experiences was assessed using the following question: 'How often have you been unfairly treated when applying for a job (unemployed participants)/at your workplace (employed participants)?', to which participants answered by indicating one of the four following categories: 'never', 'rarely', 'often', 'regularly'. Thus, in this one-item measure unjust experiences were confined to unfair treatment and in a specific domain (rather than in general). Overall, 199 unemployed and 198 employed participants responded to this question. The frequency distribution for these responses was as follows: 75 'never', 69 'rarely', 44 'often' and 11 'regularly' (for unfair treatment in the job search), and 87 'never', 74 'rarely', 35 'often' and 2 'regularly' (for unfair treatment at the workplace). Because of the small number of both employed and unemployed participants endorsing the 'regularly' response, this response category was integrated with the 'often' category to form a single 'often/regularly' category of the highest self-reported frequency of unfair treatment in the given context (i.e. job search or workplace). Thus, the 'frequency of unfair treatment' variable in all the analyses has three levels.

To assess the *responses to a particular experience of unfair treatment*, participants who indicated that they had experienced such treatment at least rarely were asked to recall one particular experience of unfair treatment, and to report their reactions to the event by responding to a set of rating scales. (a) *Intensity of discontent* was assessed by ratings of three negative emotions that may have been experienced in the situation: anger, disappointment and resentment. Previous research and theorising on reactions to injustice indicates that these emotions are frequently associated with perception of injustice (Hafer and Olson, 1998; Mikula, 1998a). The intensity of these emotions was rated on a six-point scale, ranging from 1 ('not at all') to 6 ('absolutely'). The three items were significantly correlated in both samples (from 0.79 to 0.87 in the unemployed participants; from 0.76 to 0.80 in the employed participants). Thus, these items were collapsed to form a scale describing the intensity of discontent (unemployed: *alpha* = 0.94; employed: *alpha* = 0.91). (b) Three further rating scales examined the perceived *unfairness* and *undeservedness* of the treatment and the *lack of justification* for it. The latter two refer to judgements that are considered constitutive elements of the perception of injustice (Mikula, 1993). That is, they should be related to judgements of unfairness, and show similar patterns of relationships with other reactions to the unjust event. These three ratings were treated separately in the statistical analyses. As for the intensity of negative emotions, a six-point rating scale was used. (c) *Self-blame* was assessed as the perceived degree of *personal responsibility* for causing the event and *personal control* over the situation.

198   *Vera Cubela Adoric*

That is, the tendency to blame oneself was defined as the tendency to see the event as partly self-inflicted, by causing it oneself or missing the opportunity to prevent it. Again a six-point rating scale was used, with higher ratings indicating a stronger tendency to blame oneself. Since the two items were only moderately correlated (unemployed: $r = 0.49$, $p < 0.001$; employed: $r = 0.57$, $p < 0.001$), they were used as two separate indices of self-blame in further analyses.

For employed participants, the mean ratings on these variables did not differ by gender and education (all $p > 0.05$). The same was true for the unemployed participants, with the exception of the personal control ratings, which were higher in males than in females (for males: $M = 3.1$, $SD = 1.29$; for females: $M = 2.6$, $SD = 1.36$; $t = 2.038$, $p = 0.04$).

Results

Before analysing the BJW's relationships with employment status, unemployment duration and responses to experience of injustice, I explored the reliability and the latent structure of the BJW scales in the groups of employed and unemployed participants. These analyses showed that in both groups the Personal BJW Scale is a unidimensional measure with satisfactory internal consistency (employed participants: $alpha = 0.73$; unemployed participants: $alpha = 0.71$). The General BJW Scale also showed acceptable internal consistency in both groups (employed participants: $alpha = 0.68$; unemployed participants: $alpha = 0.72$). It is of note, however, that in the unemployed group, the principal component analysis of this scale resulted in two factors with eigenvalues greater than 1 (see Table 12.1).

The obtained matrix of factor loadings is in fact similar to the one Dalbert and Katona-Sallay (1996) found in groups of Hungarian and Slovenian students, in that the general BJW breaks down into distinct factors for present- and future-oriented beliefs. However, the fact that some items have substantial loadings on both factors indicates that they are not completely independent. This is corroborated by the results of the hierarchical analysis of oblique factors, which revealed one second-order factor on which all items had a substantial loading (0.39 or higher). The correlation between the oblique factors was 0.38.

BJW's relationship with employment status, length of unemployment and number of rejections

The endorsement of the general and personal BJWs in the two groups of participants was compared using a two-way ANOVA with employment status as between-subjects factor and the type of BJW as within-subjects factor. The two main effects were significant (effect of employment status: $F = 8.862$, $df = 1/396$, $p < 0.01$; effect of BJW type: $F = 38.608$, $df = 1/396$,

Table 12.1 Factor structure of the General Belief in a Just World Scale in employed and unemployed participants

Item	Employed	Unemployed	
	Loading 1	Loading 1	Loading 2
I think basically the world is a just place	0.62	0.74	0.21
I believe that, by and large, people get what they deserve	0.65	0.67	0.40
I am confident that justice always prevails over injustice	0.72	0.14	0.83
I am convinced that in the long run people will be compensated for injustices	0.55	0.09	0.81
I firmly believe that injustices in all areas of life (e.g. professional, family, politics) are the exception rather than the rule	0.56	0.79	−0.05
I think that people try to be fair when making important decisions	0.59	0.40	0.43
Eigenvalue	2.301	1.799	1.761
% of explained variance	38.3	30.0	29.3

$p < 0.001$), whereas the interaction effect was not significant ($F = 1.537$, $df = 1/396$, $p = 0.22$). In general, the participants endorsed the personal BJW more strongly than the general BJW (personal BJW: $M = 3.69$, $SD = 0.74$; general BJW: $M = 3.48$, $SD = 0.83$). The effect of employment status indicates that the unemployed participants were weaker believers in a just world than the employed participants. As indicated by the insignificant interaction effect, this is a general tendency, independent of the type of BJW and/or employment status.

In the group of unemployed participants, both BJWs correlated with the length of unemployment in the expected direction (general BJW: $r = -0.28$, $p < 0.001$; personal BJW: $r = -0.34$, $p < 0.001$). The analysis of partial correlations showed that when controlling for the other BJW dimension, only the relationship between personal BJW and length of unemployment remained significant (general, controlled for personal: $r_{12.3} = -0.07$, $p > 0.05$; personal, controlled for general: $r_{12.3} = = 0.21$, $p > 0.001$).

A significant correlation with the number of failed job applications was obtained for the general BJW ($r = -0.25$, $p < 0.001$) but not for the personal BJW ($r = -0.11$, $p = 0.20$). To compare the two BJWs at various levels of failure, I divided the unemployed group into four categories (see Method section) and examined the effect of the number of rejections on the two BJWs using a two-way ANOVA, with the number of failed applications as between-subjects factor and the type of BJW as within-subjects factor. In addition to the main effect of the BJW type (described earlier in this chapter), the main effect of the number of rejections was significant ($F = 3.386$, $df = 3/125$, $p = 0.02$). Post-hoc comparisons (Tukey HSD test for unequal sample sizes) showed that this applies to the difference between the groups with the lowest and highest frequencies of failed applications ($p < 0.05$).

Both main effects were qualified by a significant interaction between the BJW type and the number of applications ($F = 3.531$, $df = 3/125$, $p = 0.02$). The Tukey HSD test for unequal sample sizes showed several significant differences. Although the personal BJW is quite stable across the groups with different numbers of failed applications (see Figure 12.1),

Belief in a Just World

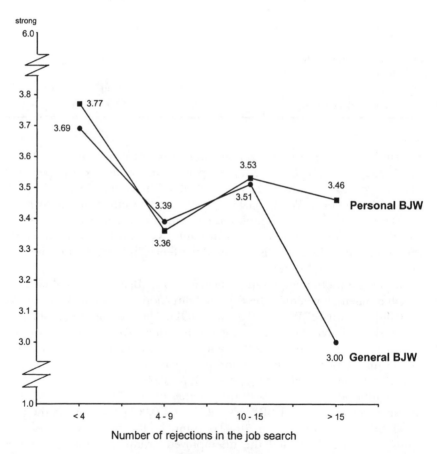

Figure 12.1 General and personal BJW in unemployed individuals with differing numbers of unsuccessful job applications.

BJW, unemployment and the job search 201

it is more strongly endorsed by the group with 'less than four' applications than by the group with 'four to nine' applications ($p = 0.02$). The general BJW was significantly lower in those who had submitted more than 15 applications than in any of the other groups of unemployed participants (all $p < 0.05$). The difference between the personal and general BJWs was significant only in the group with more than 15 applications ($p = 0.004$).

BJW and frequency of unfair treatment

The effect of the reported frequency of unfair treatment on the BJW was examined separately for injustices experienced in the job search and at the workplace (i.e. in the groups of unemployed and employed participants) using a two-way ANOVA with the frequency of unfair treatment as between-subjects factor and the type of BJW as within-subjects factor. In addition to the already observed main effect of the type of BJW, a significant main effect of the 'frequency of unfair treatment' was obtained in both samples (injustices at the workplace: $F = 8.459$, $df = 2/195$, $p = 0.0003$; injustices in the job search: $F = 5.656$, $df = 2/194$, $p = 0.004$), whereas the interaction effects were not significant (injustices at the workplace: $F = 0.10$, $df = 2/195$, $p = 0.90$; injustices in the job search: $F = 1.118$, $df = 2/194$, $p = 0.33$).

As can be seen from Figure 12.2, the pattern of means for both BJWs that was obtained in the group of *employed* participants is in line with the assumption that the BJW does not begin to accommodate to experiences of injustice until the frequency of these experiences exceeds some subjectively high level (indicated here by the 'often' and 'regularly' ratings). Specifically, in the post-hoc analysis of this main effect, two significant differences were obtained, both applying to the lower levels of BJW in the group with the highest subjective level of unfair treatment at the workplace compared to those who had never or rarely experienced such a treatment (both $p < 0.001$). It should be noted that this effect applies equally to both BJWs, and that the personal BJW is stronger than the general BJW in all groups of employed participants, irrespective of the subjective frequency of unfair treatment. In the group of *unemployed* participants, both BJWs tend to decrease with the frequency of unfair treatment in job search. Post-hoc tests of the main effect of the frequency of unfair treatment showed that only the differences between the two extreme groups reached significance (both $p < 0.001$).

The reported frequency of unfair treatment in job search correlated positively with the length of unemployment ($r = 0.28$, $p < 0.001$) and the number of failed applications ($r = 0.56$, $p < 0.001$), which were also significantly interrelated ($r = 0.32$, $p < 0.001$). It also correlated negatively with personal BJW ($r = -0.25$, $p < 0.001$) and general BJW ($r = -0.19$, $p < 0.01$). However, when entered in a multiple regression simultaneously

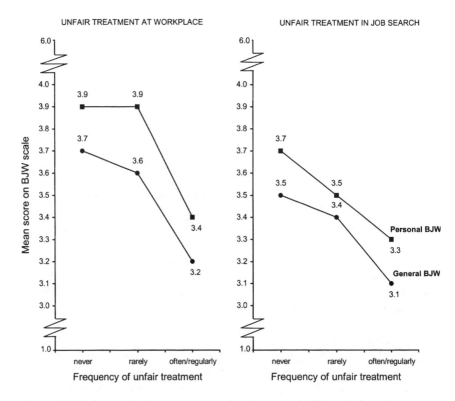

Figure 12.2 Relationship between general and personal BJW and the self-reported frequency of unfair treatment at the workplace and in the job search.

with the length of unemployment and the number of job applications, the frequency of unfair treatment made no unique contribution to explaining the variance of these two just world beliefs. Specifically, the results of the standard multiple regression analyses, which were performed separately for the general and personal BJWs as criteria, showed that these three variables explained about 12 per cent of the variance in the general BJW ($F = 5.483$, $df = 3/122$, $p < 0.001$; length of unemployment: $p = 0.03$; applications: $p = 0.22$; unfair treatment: $p = 0.20$) and 16 per cent of the variance in the personal BJW ($F = 7.622$, $df = 3/122$, $p < 0.001$; length of unemployment: $p = 0.001$; applications: $p = 0.09$; unfair treatment: $p = 0.83$).

BJW and responses to particular unfair treatment

Table 12.2 presents the correlations between the BJWs and responses to a particular experience of unfair treatment in the job search or at the workplace. As expected, the BJW (especially in the personal domain) is associ-

BJW, unemployment and the job search 203

Table 12.2 Correlations of the BJW with reactions towards unfair treatment in the job search (unemployed) and at the workplace (employed)

Response to unfair treatment	Unemployed		Employed	
	General BJW	Personal BJW	General BJW	Personal BJW
Intensity of discontent	−0.22**	−0.32**	−0.13	−0.24**
Unfairness	−0.15	−0.19*	−0.02	−0.34**
Lack of justification	−0.17*	−0.22**	0.05	−0.19*
Undeservedness	−0.17*	−0.22**	0.07	−0.17*
Personal control	−0.11	0.15	0.10	0.05
Personal responsibility	0.11	0.09	−0.01	−0.09

Notes
* $p < 0.05$.
** $p < 0.01$.

ated with lower endorsements of unfairness, undeservedness and lack of justification for the unfair treatment, and less discontent with the experienced injustice in both contexts. The BJW's relationship with the indicators of self-blame was not significant, however.

Further analyses showed, however, that the general frequency of unfair treatment in the job search moderates the personal BJW's relationship with the tendency to blame oneself. Specifically, among unemployed participants who reported a high level of such treatment (i.e. 'often/ regularly'), the personal BJW was significantly (albeit weakly) associated with judgements of personal responsibility for the unfair treatment ($r = 0.28$, $p < 0.05$), whereas in those who rarely experienced such treatment, this relationship was not significant ($r = −0.08$, $p > 0.05$). No similar moderating effect of the frequency of unfair treatment was found for employed participants (i.e. for injustices at the workplace).

To examine the BJW's impact on the relationships between diverse responses to the unfair treatment, the participants in both samples were divided into two BJW groups using the middle of the six-point rating scale (i.e. 3.5) as a cutting-point. The correlation matrices obtained are presented in Tables 12.3 and 12.4, separately for the two BJWs and the two contexts of unfair treatment. In short, for participants strong in a BJW, nearly all correlations between the aspects of self-blame and the other responses to unfair treatment were insignificant. On the other hand, in participants (especially unemployed ones) with a weak BJW (especially a weak personal BJW), self-blame covaried with the other responses to the unfair treatment. This latter pattern is in line with the assumption that, in weak believers, self-blame reflects a tendency that is in fact the reverse of external attribution of the event, so the higher the perceived unfairness (and presumably the stronger the external attribution of the event), the weaker the tendency to blame oneself.

Some support for this interpretation is also provided by the analyses of

Table 12.3 Correlations between reactions towards unfair treatment in the job search, separately for participants low and high in general and personal BJW

Response to unfair treatment	Personal BJW						General BJW					
	1	2	3	4	5	6	1	2	3	4	5	6
1 Intensity of discontent	–	0.81**	0.71**	0.69**	–0.23	–0.15	–	0.81**	0.63**	0.64**	–0.21	–0.09
2 Unfairness	0.59**	–	0.77**	0.61**	–0.15	–0.24	0.69**	–	0.73**	0.50**	–0.22	–0.19
3 Lack of justification	0.50**	0.69**	–	0.75**	–0.10	–0.22	0.63**	0.74**	–	0.64**	–0.18	–0.22
4 Undeservedness	0.40**	0.66**	0.75**	–	0.01	–0.12	0.53**	0.68**	0.80**	–	0.03	–0.02
5 Personal control	–0.36**	–0.28*	–0.32**	–0.19	–	0.49**	–0.35**	–0.23*	–0.27**	–0.21	–	0.45**
6 Personal responsibility	–0.23	–0.34**	–0.34**	–0.35**	0.47**	–	–0.26*	–0.28**	–0.25**	–0.30**	0.53**	–

Notes

Above diagonal: high BJW (personal: $n = 115$; general: $n = 83$); below diagonal: low BJW (personal: $n = 85$; general: $n = 102$).

* $p < 0.05$.

** $p < 0.01$.

Table 12.4 Correlations between reactions towards unfair treatment at the workplace, separately for participants low and high in general and personal BJW

Response to unfair treatment	Personal BJW						General BJW					
	1	2	3	4	5	6	1	2	3	4	5	6
1 Intensity of discontent	–	0.71**	0.64**	0.75**	0.05	–0.04	–	0.59**	0.62**	0.67**	–0.22	–0.16
2 Unfairness	0.34*	–	0.76**	0.72**	0.06	0.10	0.68**	–	0.76**	0.75**	–0.32**	–0.16
3 Lack of justification	0.57**	0.74**	–	0.81**	0.09	0.03	0.68**	0.86**	–	0.69**	–0.17	–0.09
4 Undeservedness	0.55**	0.75**	0.77**	–	0.07	–0.02	0.78**	0.79**	0.85**	–	–0.27	–0.18
5 Personal control	–0.49**	–0.16	–0.17	–0.41**	–	0.56**	–0.01	0.16	0.11	–0.01	–	0.52**
6 Personal responsibility	–0.30	–0.22	–0.14	–0.31	0.62**	–	–0.04	0.02	0.01	–0.05	0.59**	–

Notes
Above diagonal: high BJW (personal: $n = 138$; general: $n = 95$); below diagonal: low BJW (personal: $n = 62$; general: $n = 87$)
* $p < 0.05$.
** $p < 0.01$.

206   *Vera Cubela Adoric*

the contribution that self-blame makes to explaining the variance in discontent independently of perceived unfairness. In a series of standard multiple regression analyses, which were performed independently for the two types of injustice, the relative efficacy of self-blame and perception of unfairness in predicting discontent was explored separately for strong and weak believers in a just world. In short, these analyses showed that, in weak believers in a just world (whether general or personal), the self-blame dimensions make no significant contribution to explaining the variance in the negative emotional response to the treatment independently of the portion already explained by perceived unfairness (see Table 12.5 for the results obtained in groups of strong and weak believers in a *personal* just world). A similar pattern, indicating that the self-blame dimensions made no unique contribution to explaining the variance of discontent, was also obtained for the strong believers' reactions to unfair treatment at the workplace. Given that the correlations between self-blame and other reactions to unfair treatment were not significant in this group, this really is not surprising. It is of note, however, that in the group of unemployed participants (i.e. for unfair treatment in the job search) who strongly believe in a *personal* just world, personal control appeared to be a significant negative predictor of the intensity of discontent, which contributed to the explanation independently of the perceived unfairness. This is not surprising given that personal control showed a negative association with the intensity of discontent in this group (see the corresponding column in the left-hand part of Table 12.3), which approached significance ($p = 0.07$). The correlations of discontent with unfairness-related ratings were insignificant (all $p > 0.22$).

Thus, the results of these analyses show that – at least under some conditions – strong BJW can promote some tendencies (in this case, the perception of control over the event) that contribute to attenuation of the negative emotional consequences of a personally unjust event. This function of BJW was observed here only for the BJW in the personal domain and for responses to unfair treatment in the job search.

Discussion

As expected, the present results showed that, relative to their employed counterparts, long-term unemployed young adults who are still looking for their *first* job believe less strongly that they live in a just world. Moreover, the longer they have been unemployed and the more injustices they have experienced in job search, the lower their personal and general BJW. A negative association with the number of rejections in the job search was also found, but this held only for the general BJW.

These findings provide rather compelling evidence for the hypothesis that endorsement of the belief in a just world reflects, at least partly, one's experiences (see Schmitt, 1998, for a detailed review of this 'knowledge

Table 12.5 Beta weights of perceived unfairness and self-blame in explaining discontent with unfair treatment in the job search (unemployed) and at the workplace (employed) in the groups of participants high and low in personal BJW

Predictors	Unemployed		Employed	
	High BJW	Low BJW	High BJW	Low BJW
Unfairness	0.56**	0.49**	0.42**	−0.26
Lack of justification	0.08	0.16	−0.07	0.60**
Undeservedness	0.23	0.03	0.48**	0.12
Personal control	−0.25**	−0.18	0.10	−0.17
Personal responsibility	0.13	0.01	−0.11	−0.01
	$R^2 = 0.71$ $F_{\text{total}}(5/56) = 34.148,$ $p < 0.001$	$R^2 = 0.44$ $F_{\text{total}}(5/56) = 8.819,$ $p < 0.001$	$R^2 = 0.61$ $F_{\text{total}}(5/51) = 16.068,$ $p < 0.001$	$R^2 = 0.51$ $F_{\text{total}}(5/22) = 4.560,$ $p < 0.001$

Note
** $p < 0.01$.

208   *Vera Cubela Adoric*

hypothesis'). Although the proportion of the BJW's variance explained by the three 'experience' variables (i.e. length of unemployment, number of failed job applications and subjective frequency of unfair treatment in job search) is in fact modest, it should be noted that only one domain of experience was examined. Furthermore, this is rare empirical evidence for the negative impact of unemployment on the absolute endorsement of the BJW.

The failure of previous research with unemployed people to provide evidence for the impact that the (length of) unemployment status has on the endorsement of the BJW (e.g. Dzuka and Dalbert, 2002) is probably due to the relatively short unemployment durations and restricted range of jobless spells in their samples. It appears that in designing a study aiming to gather evidence of the effects of unemployment on the BJW, one should take into account that the process of accommodation probably does not begin until the unemployment duration exceeds a critical point and/or until the level of failures and of experienced injustices in the job search surpasses one's threshold of negativity. As already noted, most individuals entering the job market expect a certain period of unemployment. If the unemployment duration is still within one's expectations, it may not seriously threaten one's BJW. Furthermore, it usually takes more than one violation of justice standards to trigger an evaluation of unfairness (Gilliland *et al.*, 1998), and probably more than one evaluation of unfairness to represent a serious threat to one's BJW. Unless the number and importance of these violations of justice standards and of injustice judgements are above a certain subjectively critical point, they can be assimilated to the schema of a just world, presumably using some of the various means of neutralising the anger and anxiety generated by the injustice that are identified by the justice motive theory (e.g. Lerner, 1998).

This reasoning is in line with the finding that the subjective frequency of unfair treatment at which a decline in the BJW can be expected depends on the context. For unfair treatment in the job search, both personal and general BJW showed a tendency to decrease continuously with the frequency of such treatments. For unfair treatments at the workplace, a decline in BJW was observed only at a relatively high frequency of such treatments. These findings suggest that unfairness experienced in the job search poses a more serious threat to the BJW than unfairness experienced at the workplace, meaning that even rare exposure to unfair treatment in the job search may be enough for the process of BJW accommodation to begin. On the other hand, unfairness experiences at the workplace seem to be less severe instances of injustice, likely to prompt such a process only if they become too frequent.

If the BJW declines with prolonged unemployment and negative experiences in the job search, what are the implications for the assumed adaptive function of the BJW? First, it should be noted that the mean

BJW, unemployment and the job search 209

scores on the BJW scales obtained in the unemployed sample and the groups with relatively frequent negative experiences in the job search are located around the middle point of the six-point rating scale. That is, although their BJW is relatively weak compared to employed participants and those with no experiences of injustice, these groups do not actually reject the notion of a just world. The mean values obtained are within the range of those obtained in my previous studies with Croatian subjects (see Cubela Adoric, 2003, for a review). Moreover, they are higher than those obtained in samples from some other countries (see Schmitt, 1998, for a detailed review). Since it is generally assumed that the endorsement of the BJW at least partly reflects the strength of the justice motive, this may indicate a stronger need to protect the BJW in Croatian subjects. This seems plausible considering the depth of the economic and social crisis Croatia is going through in the decade after the war (the high unemployment rate is one indicator of this), which may pose a serious challenge to one's belief in the justness of the world. As postulated by the justice motive theory, it is precisely under conditions of high threat that people are motivated to protect and maintain this basic world schema (Lerner, 1998).

One might argue that, if this interpretation is correct, we would expect a pattern of differences with regard to employment status and frequency of negative experiences that is quite the reverse of the one obtained in this study. Such an interpretation of the 'delusional hypothesis' about the BJW is not uncommon, but has little empirical support (Schmitt, 1998). It also implies that the endorsement of items claiming that the world is just simply reflects the strength of the justice motive, and should thus be higher, the more unjust experiences one has. Considering the empirical data, including those obtained in this study, such a position is difficult to sustain. How, then, can the 'knowledge' interpretation of the observed difference in BJW by employment status and frequency of unjust experiences be reconciled with the 'delusional' interpretation of the generally stronger endorsement of the BJW in Croatian subjects relative to subjects from some other countries? One solution to this conundrum may be to consider the referents people use for the 'world' in evaluating the justness of the world (is it, perhaps, one's society rather than the world in general?) and the comparison standards used in the evaluation of one's position in that world. Although these issues have been recognised in social justice research (e.g. Crocker *et al.*, 1998; Mikula, 1998b; Montada, 1998), to my knowledge they have not yet received attention in BJW research.

Furthermore, the weaker endorsement of the BJW in unemployed participants and participants with a relatively high frequency of unjust experiences does not necessarily mean that they are generally less motivated to defend the basic schema of a just world than employed participants and those who have not experienced injustices. As indicated by the

210 *Vera Cubela Adoric*

analysis of the BJW's relationship with the number of failed job applications, the personal BJW is quite stable across the groups of unemployed participants who have submitted various numbers of applications. Indeed, after a slight initial decrease, there is no significant change in this aspect of the BJW as the number of failures rise. In contrast, the general BJW shows a remarkable decline when rejections become very frequent. The stability of the personal BJW, which is probably due to its adaptive importance, suggests that, as evidence seriously threatening one's belief in a personal just world mounts up, individuals apply strategies aimed at protecting this belief. One of these can be detachment of the personal BJW from outcomes in the domain in which one is repeatedly experiencing failure or injustice, with the result that the negative impact of such experiences is less pronounced in the endorsement of this aspect of the BJW than in the endorsement of the general BJW or the belief in the justness of the world in the particular domain in which the injustice is experienced. Whereas this explanation is in line with Dalbert's (2001) elaboration of the development of the personal BJW and parallels the mechanism of psychological disengagement that is identified as a self-protecting strategy of coping with self-esteem threatening information in members of socially disadvantaged groups (e.g. Crocker *et al.*, 1998), one would be more confident in making this interpretation if a longitudinal design were used. The assumed stability of the personal BJW and the hypothesised process of its detachment from a particular domain of potentially threatening experiences certainly need to be examined in a study with such a design.

The sensitivity of the general BJW to the threatening experience of unemployment is also indicated by the finding that this belief broke down into relatively distinct present- and future-oriented beliefs in the group of unemployed participants. As already noted, Dalbert and Katona-Sallay (1996) observed a similar phenomenon in groups of Slovenian and Hungarian students during a period of war in the neighbouring country (Croatia, which happens to be the homeland of the participants in this study). It appears, then, that some differentiation of the facets of general BJW is a more common phenomenon, to be expected in people who are facing a high level of perceived threat and uncertainty caused by socio-political changes and war or other extremely adverse and threatening conditions, such as being out of work for several years. Separating the belief in just compensation in the future from the perception of the unjustness of the present situation to some extent may well help them to endure the adverse conditions without giving up their fundamental belief in the justness of the world.

In this study, another strategy that supposedly contributes to the maintenance of the BJW was also examined. This is the tendency to see a personal misfortune in which one had actually no substantial causal contribution as at least partly self-inflicted and, thus, deserved. In this study, two aspects of this tendency towards unrealistic self-blame (perception of personal responsibility for and personal control over the unjust event) were assessed for the two different contexts. The expected positive relationship, which presumably reflects the function of the causal self-attribution in protecting one's BJW, was found only between the personal BJW and perceived personal responsibility for unfair treatment in the job search under the condition of generally high frequency of such experiences. Thus, it appears that the function of self-blame is activated when an event (i.e. unfair treatment in the job search) poses a serious threat to one's personal BJW, and when one's BJW is already seriously challenged by a subjectively high level of similar, highly threatening events. Note that the obtained correlation is modest, which may be partly due to the restricted range of the personal responsibility ratings. Further research is certainly needed to establish the strength of this association as well as the replicability of this finding.

The same holds for the findings referring to my second hypothesis about the BJW's relationship with self-blame, which proposed that, in strong believers in a just world, such a tendency contributes to the attenuation of the negative emotional impact of the injustice. As expected, self-blame (in terms of ratings of personal control) contributed to the explanation of the intensity of discontent independently of perceived unfairness, but only for injustices in the job search and with regard to the personal BJW. In weak believers in a just world, self-blame for both types of injustices was related to discontent, but made no predictive contribution to explaining discontent when considered simultaneously with perceived unfairness. This finding in fact suggests that, in weak believers in a just world, self-blame merely reflects an aspect of the perception of unfairness (presumably the attribution component identified by Mikula, 1993). The same holds for strong believers' tendency to blame themselves for injustices at the workplace. As indicated by insignificant relationships between self-blame and perceived unfairness, however, in the case of what can be assumed to be a more serious injustice (i.e. unfair treatment in job search), self-blame is unrealistic and, as already noted, appears to neutralise the negative emotions.

Finally, it should be noted that the BJW, especially in the personal domain, was negatively associated with the intensity of these emotions and the unfairness-related ratings for both types of injustice. That is, the stronger the personal BJW, the lower the intensity of discontent, perceived unfairness, undeservedness and lack of justification for the treatment. Thus, these results provide support for Hafer and Olson's (1998) conclusion that the relationship is a quite robust one, probably due to the tendency of strong believers to accept or justify personal misfortune more readily than weak believers in a just world. Since it was left to the participants to decide which experience was to be described, it is also possible that strong believers chose less severe occurrences of injustice than did weak

212 *Vera Cubela Adoric*

believers in a personal just world. This does not invalidate Hafer and Olson's interpretation, however.

Conclusion

In this chapter, I have attempted to give an overview of the empirical findings and theoretical considerations that are relevant to the BJW's relationship with the experience of unemployment. The study that was presented in the second part of the chapter was based on my observation that young people who have experienced long-term unemployment while looking for their *first* job have been almost completely ignored in previous research in this domain.

The results of this study undoubtedly show that the endorsement of the BJW is negatively associated with the unemployment status, the length of unemployment and the level of failures and injustices experienced in job search. They also indicate that young people in long-term unemployment might still have a strong need to maintain the fundamental belief in the justness of their world. The personal BJW, for example, which is generally assumed to be of more adaptive importance than the general BJW, remains rather stable across various levels of rejection and, under condition of serious threat (as indicated by a high frequency of injustices in the job search), contributes to the attenuation of the negative emotional impact of personally unjust events in the job search.

Based on these and other findings, I proposed some strategies that the long-term unemployed probably use to protect their basic schema of a just world, such as detachment of their personal BJW from the domain in which they are repeatedly faced with contradicting evidence. These findings and claims must be qualified, however, by some limitations of my data. The data were collected from young people in Croatia and perhaps reflect specific concerns with the justness of *their* world. Although studies with long-term unemployed young people from other countries are certainly needed to test the generalisability of these findings, longitudinal studies are also required to demonstrate the proposed BJW-protecting strategies at work.

References

Benson, D.E. and Ritter, C. (1990) 'Belief in a just world, job loss, and depression', *Sociological Focus*, 23: 49–63.

Crocker, J., Major, B. and Steele, C. (1998) 'Social stigma', in Gilbert, D.T., Fiske, S.T. and Lindzey, G. (eds), *The Handbook of Social Psychology* (Vol. 2), Boston: McGraw-Hill.

Cubela, V. and Ivanov, L. (2000) 'Vjerovanja u (ne)pravedan svijet i centralnost pravde: Relacije s osjecajem koherentnosti i generaliziranim ocekivanjima u pogledu buducnosti [Beliefs in a (un)just world and the centrality of justice:

BJW, unemployment and the job search 213

Their relations to the sense of coherence and generalized future expectancies]', *Radovi Filozofskog fakulteta u Zadru*, 39: 33–51.

Cubela, V., Prorokovic, A. and Gregov, Lj. (1999) 'Neki aspekti valjanosti i pouzdanosti dviju skala vjerovanja u pravedan svijet' [Some aspects of validity and reliability of two belief in a just world scales], *Radovi Filozofskog fakulteta u Zadru*, 38: 133–48.

Cubela Adoric, V. (2003) Iluzija pravednog svijeta [Just-World Illusion], *manuscript under review*.

Dalbert, C. (1998) 'Belief in a just world, well-being, and coping with an unjust fate', in Montada, L. and Lerner, M.J. (eds), *Responses to Victimizations and Belief in a Just World*, New York: Plenum Press.

Dalbert, C. (1999) 'The world is more just for me than generally: About the Personal Belief in a Just World Scale's validity', *Social Justice Research*, 12: 79–98.

Dalbert, C. (2000) 'Beliefs in a Just World Questionnaire', in Maltby, J., Lewis C.A. and Hill, A. (eds), *Commissioned Reviews of 250 Psychological Tests*, Lampeter, Wales: The Edwin Mellen Press.

Dalbert, C. (2001) *The Justice Motive as a Personal Resource: Dealing with Challenges and Critical Life Events*, New York: Kluwer Academic/Plenum Publishers.

Dalbert, C. and Katona-Sallay, H. (1996) 'The belief in a just world construct in Hungary', *Journal of Cross-Cultural Psychology*, 27: 293–314.

Dalbert, C. and Maes, J. (2002) 'Belief in a just world as a personal resource in school', in Ross, M. and Miller, D.T. (eds), *The Justice Motive in Everyday Life*, Cambridge: Cambridge University Press.

Dalbert, C., Montada, L. and Schmitt, M. (1987) 'Glaube an eine gerechte Welt als Motiv: Validierungskorrelate zweier Skalen' [Belief in a just world as motive: Validation correlation of two scales], *Psychologische Beiträge*, 29: 596–615.

Dzuka, J. and Dalbert, C. (2002) 'Mental health and personality of Slovak unemployed adolescents: About the beliefs in just world's impact', *Journal of Applied Social Psychology*, 4: 732–57.

Gilliland, S.W., Benson, L. and Schepers, D.H. (1998) 'A rejection threshold in justice evaluations: Effects on judgment and decision-making', *Organizational Behavior and Human Decision Processes*, 76: 113–31.

Hafer, C.L. and Olson, J.M. (1998) 'Individual differences in the belief in a just world and responses to personal misfortune', in Montada, L. and Lerner, M.J. (eds), *Responses to Victimizations and Belief in a Just World*, New York: Plenum Press.

Lackovic-Grgin, K. (2000) *Stres u djece i adolescenata* [Stress in children and adolescents], Jastrebarsko: Naklada Slap.

Lambert, A.J., Burroughs, T. and Chasteen, A.L. (1998) 'Belief in a just world and right-wing authoritarianism as moderators of perceived risk', in Montada, L. and Lerner, M.J. (eds), *Responses to Victimizations and Belief in a Just World*, New York: Plenum Press.

Lerner, M.J. (1998) 'The two forms of belief in a just world: Some thoughts on why and how people care about justice', in Montada, L. and Lerner, M.J. (eds) *Responses to Victimizations and Belief in a Just World*, New York: Plenum Press.

Lerner, M.J. (2002) 'Pursuing the justice motive', in Ross, M. and Miller, D.T. (eds), *The Justice Motive in Everyday Life*, Cambridge: Cambridge University Press.

Lipkus, I.M., Dalbert, C. and Siegler, I.C. (1996) 'The importance of distinguishing the belief in a just world for self versus for others: Implications for psychological well being', *Personality and Social Psychology Bulletin*, 22: 666–77.

214 *Vera Cubela Adoric*

McFadyen, R.G. and Thomas, J.P. (1997) 'Economic and psychological models of job search behavior of the unemployed', *Human Relations*, 50: 1461–84.

Meeus, W., Dekovic, M. and Iedema, J. (1997) 'Unemployment and identity in adolescence', *The Career Development Quarterly*, 45: 369–80.

Mikula, G. (1993) 'On the experience of injustice', *European Review of Social Psychology*, 4: 223–44.

Mikula, G. (1998a) 'The role of injustice in the elicitation of differential emotional reactions', *Personality and Social Psychology Bulletin*, 24: 769–83.

Mikula, G. (1998b) 'Division of household labor and perceived justice: A growing field of research', *Social Justice Research*, 11: 215–41.

Montada, L. (1996) 'Mass unemployment under perspectives of justice', in Montada, L. and Lerner, M.J. (eds), *Current Societal Concerns About Justice*, New York: Plenum Press.

Montada, L. (1998) 'Belief in a just world: A hybrid of justice motive and self-interest?', in Montada, L. and Lerner, M.J. (eds), *Responses to Victimizations and Belief in a Just World*, New York: Plenum Press.

Patton, W. and Donohue, R. (1998) 'Coping with long-term unemployment', *Journal of Community and Applied Social Psychology*, 8: 331–43.

Schmitt, M.J. (1998) 'Methodological strategies in research to validate measures of belief in a just world', in Montada, L. and Lerner, M.J. (eds), *Responses to Victimizations and Belief in a Just World*, New York: Plenum Press.

Tomaka, J. and Blascovich, J. (1994) 'Effects of justice beliefs on cognitive appraisals of and subjective, physiological, and behavioral responses to potential stress', *Journal of Personality and Social Psychology*, 67: 732–40.

13 Entering the job market

Belief in a just world, fairness and well-being of graduating students

Hedvig Sallay

Graduation from university can be considered a decisive point in the life course, a marker of the end of student life. Two of the possibilities awaiting graduating students are securing a promising job and becoming unemployed. The threat of unemployment may be especially critical for these young people, because the lack of a workplace is not compensated by an established familial or professional biography or a stable personal identity.

After the rapid socio-political changes of 1990, Hungarian society is still in the process of transformation, and the outcome of these gradual processes of change is still uncertain and unpredictable. Although the new market economy seems to be a very promising environment for young people, they also voice concerns about finding a stable and well-paid job, becoming financially independent of their parents and establishing a basis for their own professional career.

Sociologists have shown that 73 per cent of Hungarian respondents from a representative sample agreed with the bitter statement that 'in this country one can achieve material success only by dishonest/illegal means' (Kolosi *et al.*, 1999: 521). In the same study it was also demonstrated that Hungarians are in fact satisfied with their jobs, but not with their standard of living or their income situation. Moreover, all respondents firmly believed that the Euro-Atlantic integration of the country would have a favourable influence on the job market. In general, the chances of getting a good job depend on a wide variety of factors, including the kind of training received. For example, there are fewer job opportunities for teachers than for computing and IT experts. Given these facts on the societal level, the job prospects of graduating students must differ on the individual level. This can be expected to impact on their well-being. In particular, the well-being of those who were able to find a job before graduating should differ from that of those who are still looking for a job. Beliefs in a just world and fairness perceptions are considered to represent a resource for individuals facing the threat of unemployment, and may have remained stable or even increased over the last few years in Hungary. Thus, the present study explored subjective well-being (SWB),

216   *Hedvig Sallay*

beliefs in a just world (BJW) and anticipated fairness in the workplace of Hungarian students graduating at two different time points, in 1999 and 2001.

The impact of time, job-situation and gender on well-being, fairness and just world beliefs

Different approaches to the definition of subjective well-being (SWB) can be found in the literature. The present study is based on the conceptualisation by Grob (1995), who defined well-being as a positive attitude towards life, a generally positive sense of self-esteem, an enjoyment of life, a low level of depressed mood, and a lack of serious personal problems and somatic complaints. The implications of SWB are twofold. (a) It has a motivational component. This means that if people feel bad, they attempt to change this state into a positive one. However, if they feel good, they try to maintain this state. (b) SWB is an important global indicator of psychological health (Taylor and Brown, 1988). The key factors influencing SWB are the accomplishment of age-related specific developmental tasks (Brim, 1992), pursuing meaningful life-goals (Emmons, 1992) and perceived control. Besides these, Havighurst (1984) suggested that, for young adults, normative life-events include the aspiration to a satisfying career. Critical life-events like entering the labour market and searching for a first job put people under severe emotional strain. The particular socio-historical and economic situation, the individual standard of living, the resources provided by society, and individual biographies and characteristics all contribute to the level of well-being felt by individual members of society (Moscovici, 1984).

I would like to argue that by 2001 Hungarians had a more realistic view of the socio-political changes and their consequences than in 1999, having experienced hardships such as strong rivalry for good jobs at first hand, and graduating students' well-being has generally decreased over this time. In order to become independent of their parents, both financially and emotionally, young adults need to find employment immediately after their student years. The tight labour-market situation has made it more important for them to start looking for jobs before they even graduate. The likelihood of finding a good job has decreased, however. Before the socio-political changes, it was not simply the qualification earned, but the wider range of possibilities open to them that made the life of graduating students easier. Membership of the Socialist Party opened more doors for job seekers. Once employed, moreover, party members' work was evaluated more favourably than that of non-members. Thus, there was a low level of fairness at the workplace. Nowadays, however, it has become more common in Hungary for work to be evaluated on a more competitive basis, in terms of effort, knowledge and hard-working attitudes. Consequently, work should now be evaluated more fairly. In sum, well-being

Entering the job market: graduating   217

was expected to decrease from 1999 to 2001, while anticipated fairness at the workplace is expected to increase.

There are a number of psychological theories relating well-being to employment status. For example, the functional model focuses on the latent functions of employment (Jahoda, 1982), the agency theory emphasises the individual's ability to influence events (Freyer, 1986) and the 'vitamin model' stresses the aspects of the environment surrounding the individual (Warr, 1987). Theories focusing on individuals highlight their ability to cope with different situations, while environmentally oriented theories emphasise the features of the situation the individuals find themselves in. The latter are particularly pertinent to the impact of employment status, and the factors listed in the vitamin model are fairly representative of the type of environmental aspects related to mental health, e.g. opportunity for control, physical security, externally generated goals, opportunity for interpersonal contact and valued social position. These environmental features also suggest that labour market policies, or on a general level societal factors, may have an effect on well-being. There is evidence from different countries and time periods, from cross-sectional and also longitudinal studies, unambiguously showing that unemployed individuals show lower levels of well-being than employed individuals (e.g. Dooley et al., 1996; Kasl et al., 1998). Furthermore, reduced occupational aspirations of unemployed young people may lead to negative attitudes towards work and life in general (e.g. Banks and Ullah, 1988). Gender differences are also observable; it seems that the negative association between unemployment and well-being is stronger among men (Korpi, 1977). The present study focuses on university students at the end of their studies, and is aimed at comparing young adults who have already secured a job with those who have not yet found work and who thus face a very real threat of unemployment. The job seekers, and in particular the males, are expected to reveal a lower level of SWB than those who have already found work (the 'employed').

Besides the employment status, several studies suggest that perceptions of the workplace also contribute to well-being (e.g. Roberts and Markel, 2001). For example, Saathoff (2001) found that satisfaction with social support resources, level of education and perceptions of the daily work environment significantly affected the life satisfaction of workers. In the same study, he also showed that job satisfaction was significantly affected by level of education, positive perceptions of the daily work environment, and positive perceptions of organisational fairness. Perceived fairness at the workplace can thus also be expected to strengthen well-being at the workplace. Antalovits (2000) proposes that the process of workplace socialisation includes a pre-job phase with two parallel tracks. One involves conscious preparation for the new sphere of work (as opposed to student life), and the active search for information about different work places, organisations and the demands associated with them. The other is

218   *Hedvig Sallay*

based on the influences of parents, peers and anyone else with work-related experience. These indirect influences help to build up the representations that students develop about their future workplace. These representations consist of anticipations about working conditions, including workplace fairness. In this study, I would like to show that anticipated fairness at the workplace might differ for those who are still looking for a job and those who have already secured one. It can be assumed that those who have not yet gained any personal work experience have more positive illusions and, consequently, anticipate a future workplace that is fairer than those with personal work experiences. The belief in fairness at the workplace may help students to be even more motivated in the process of finding a job. Moreover, anticipated fairness was expected to increase in 2001 due to the socio-economic changes described above.

Besides the impact of socio-political changes and employment status on well-being, previous studies have also demonstrated the impact of gender on several components of SWB. For example, males show a lower level of depression on various scales than females (Baron and Campbell, 1993; McCauley *et al.*, 1993), and usually have fewer somatic complaints (Gannon *et al.*, 1992). In a study conducted by Lewin (1989), it was also demonstrated that work-related attributes were related to somatic complaints among women. The self-esteem also shows gender differences, with generally higher levels for males than for females (DuBois and Tevendale, 1999). Overall, levels of SWB have proved to be higher among males than among females.

A questionnaire study was thus conducted with students entering the job market to test the following hypotheses in relation to socio-political changes, the job situation and gender. (a) Students graduating in 2001 were expected to anticipate more fairness at the workplace than those graduating in 1999. (b) Graduating students' well-being was expected to be lower in 2001 compared to 1999. (c) A higher level of anticipated fairness is expected for those who are still job seekers. (d) Job-seeking students, especially males, are expected to reveal lower levels of SWB. (e) Overall, females are expected to have lower SWB than males. Additionally, I will explore whether the BJW remains stable from 1999 to 2001.

Subjects and procedure

In 1999, 115 subjects took part in a questionnaire study (40 males and 75 females; mean age: 23.9 years), of whom 42 had already found a job, while 73 were still job seekers. In 2001, 101 students participated (40 males and 61 females; mean age: 23.5 years). This time, only 26 respondents had already found a job before graduation, and 75 were job seekers. Their level of SWB, general and personal beliefs in a just world and anticipations of workplace fairness were assessed in questionnaire studies after lectures.

Entering the job market: graduating 219

Instruments

SWB was measured using the Hungarian version of the Berne Questionnaire of Subjective Well-being (Grob, 1995), with the following six dimensions: positive attitude towards life (8 items, Alpha = 0.84), personal problems (8 items, Alpha = 0.71), somatic complaints (8 items, Alpha = 0.77), self-esteem (5 items, Alpha = 0.77), depressive mood (5 items, Alpha = 0.70), joy in life (4 items, Alpha = 0.71). *Anticipated fairness at the workplace* was assessed with a 5-item scale (sample item 'Bosses always profit from their employees in an unjust way'; Alpha = 0.71). Two dimensions of the *belief in a just world* were measured. The general BJW was measured with six items of the General Belief in a Just World Scale (Alpha = 0.70; Dalbert *et al.*, 1987). The Hungarian version of this scale had already been implemented successfully in a previous study (Dalbert and Katona-Sallay, 1996). The personal BJW was measured with the Hungarian version of seven items of the Personal Belief in a Just World Scale (Alpha = 0.75; Dalbert, 1999). Subjects responded to all items on a 6-point Likert scale ranging from 1 ('totally disagree') to 6 ('totally agree'). Demographic data were collected at the end of the questionnaire.

Results

In order to explore the possible impact of time point, job situation and gender on SWB, anticipated fairness at the workplace and just world beliefs, 3-way ANOVAs were conducted on each variable. Where the dimensions of SWB were concerned, job situation revealed main effects for positive attitude towards life and self-esteem. Those who had already found a job showed a more positive attitude towards life ($F_{(1,215)} = 9.563$; $p \leqslant 0.002$, $M = 4.54$, $SD = 0.66$) than job seekers ($M = 4.16$, $SD = 0.90$). Surprisingly, however, the self-esteem of students who had secured jobs was lower $F_{(1,215)} = 6.685$; $p \leqslant 0.010$, $M = 4.39$, $SD = 0.96$) than that of job seekers ($M = 4.75$, $SD = 0.84$). Significant main effects of gender were found for personal problems and self-esteem. Females had more personal problems ($F_{(1,212)} = 6.225$; $p \leqslant 0.013$, $M = 3.44$, $SD = 0.98$) as compared to males ($M = 3.10$, $SD = 0.99$). Females also proved to have a lower level of self-esteem ($F_{(1,215)} = 3.891$; $p \leqslant 0.050$, $M = 4.40$, $SD = 0.94$) than males ($M = 4.67$, $SD = 0.94$). Main effects of gender ($F_{(1,214)} = 8.345$; $p \leqslant 0.004$) and time point ($F_{(1,213)} = 8.968$; $p \leqslant 0.003$) were observed for somatic complaints, but these were qualified by an interaction of gender by time point ($F_{(1,215)} = 8.845$; $p \leqslant 0.003$). This interaction of gender by time point clearly showed that females in 2001 suffered more somatic complaints ($M = 2.17$, $SD = 0.72$) than females in 1999 ($M = 1.67$, $SD = 0.55$), and than males in either 1999 ($M = 1.62$, $SD = 0.58$) or 2001 ($M = 1.73$, $SD = 0.53$).

Regarding the anticipated fairness of the workplace, a significant

220   *Hedvig Sallay*

impact of time was observed, indicating – as expected – a higher level of fairness in 2001 ($F_{(1,214)} = 3.968$; $p \leqslant 0.048$, $M = 3.80$, $SD = 0.77$) than in 1999 ($M = 3.64$, $SD = 0.82$). No significant effects were found for either dimension of BJW.

Discussion

The hypothesis that SWB should decline as a result of the ongoing socio-economic transitions in Hungary, was not supported. The only significant change in the components of SWB over time was that women revealed more somatic complaints in 2001. The respondents' employment status had an impact on two of the six well-being dimensions. Relative to the job seekers, those who had found a job had a more positive attitude towards life, but a lower level of self-esteem. The more positive attitude of these students can be attributed to the prospect of a stable future after graduation, which seems to strengthen their positive attitude towards life. However, the reverse effect on self-esteem was not expected. I can only speculate as to why this occurred. It may be that some of the students accepted jobs that did not match their qualifications and aspirations, simply to avoid unemployment. Accepting a job that does not necessarily live up to one's ideals, aspirations or wishes may decrease the level of self-esteem. Only a few gender differences were observed. In line with previous studies (e.g. DuBois and Tevendale, 1999; Josephs *et al.*, 1992; Grob *et al.*, 2001), women reported more personal problems and lower self-esteem than men. The impact of socio-economic changes on anticipated fairness at the workplace was in line with the hypotheses. Students anticipated a higher level of fairness in 2001 than in 1999. This seems to indicate that by this time students expected the evaluation of their work to be determined by personal abilities, knowledge and efficacy, rather than by political factors. The hypothesised effect of the job situation on anticipated fairness in the workplace was not confirmed, however. Time, job situation and gender had no impact on either BJW in this study.

Taken together, the SWB – in terms of a positive attitude towards life, fewer personal problems and high self-esteem – was more stable than hypothesised. The hypothesis that women have lower SWB was partially supported. However, anticipated fairness at the workplace, but not the BJW, revealed an effect of societal change. Overall, the impact of the job situation was weak.

Relations between just world beliefs, anticipated fairness at the workplace and SWB

The adaptive functions of beliefs in a just world (BJW) have been studied in great breadth and depth in past years (e.g. Dalbert, 1996; Tomaka and Blascovich, 1994), and the BJW has been shown to be a personal resource

Entering the job market: graduating   221

that helps individuals by protecting their mental health, providing a buffer against stress and enabling investment in long-term goals. In general, BJW has been shown to be positively correlated with well-being (Dalbert, 1998; Lipkus *et al.*, 1996). Moreover, Dalbert (1996) found that subjects high in BJW evaluate their fates to be less unfair than do individuals low in BJW, and this held for very different samples, including unemployed workers. Thus, I will now explore the relationship between the BJW, anticipated fairness at the workplace and SWB.

Perceptions of the self, the world and the future are essential for the maintenance of mental health. Yet, considerable research suggests that exaggerated perceptions of control and unrealistic optimism are characteristics of normal human thought (Taylor and Brown, 1988). These positive illusions appear to promote mental health, including the ability to care about others and to engage in productive and creative work. People estimate their chances of experiencing a wide variety of pleasant events, such as liking their first job, getting a good salary, or having a gifted child, to be higher than those of their peers (Weinstein, 1980). Evidence from other sources suggests that positive illusions about the self, control and the future may be especially apparent and adaptive under adverse conditions, that is, in circumstances that might be expected to produce depression or a lack of motivation. Under such circumstances, the belief in oneself as a competent, efficacious actor may be especially helpful in overcoming setbacks and potential blows to self-esteem.

The belief in a just world has also been conceptualised as a positive illusion (Dalbert, 1992, 1993), as it encourages people to see the world around them as orderly, meaningful and predictable. The positive relationship between the belief in a just world and mental health is supported by the following arguments. (a) The belief in a just world encourages people to see the world as meaningful, and this increases their feelings of competence and control, making it possible to have a positive outlook on the future (Lerner, 1978). These feelings foster a high level of self-esteem and well-being. (b) The belief in a just world is considered an important precondition for investment in long-term goals (Dalbert, 1996; Hafer, 2000). This is a significant adaptive function, not only for the well-being of the individual but also for the stability of groups and whole societies (Platt, 1973). Moreover, BJW encourages individuals to invest in their plans by using just means (Hafer, 2000). (c) Furthermore, some of the coping reactions motivated by the just world belief can also sustain well-being. For example, Dalbert (1997) demonstrated that unemployed women with a strong BJW avoided the 'Why me?' question, which is a maladaptive coping reaction.

The present study thus goes on to explore relationships between general and personal belief in a just world and anticipated fairness at the workplace of graduating students on the one hand and dimensions of

222   *Hedvig Sallay*

SWB on the other. More precisely, I was interested in whether the job situation of students (job seekers vs. employed), their gender and the time points investigated (1999 vs. 2001) had any significant impact on the relationship between BJW, anticipated fairness at the workplace and well-being. Experiences of unfairness, such as becoming unemployed, threaten the BJW. According to Dalbert (1999), people tend to deny injustice on a personal level more than unfairness on a general level. As a corollary, fairness is attributed more to one's own actions than to the actions of others (Messick *et al.*, 1985). General BJW is a good index of fairness considerations in the broad societal context, whereas personal BJW seems to be a good indicator of individual considerations. Because the job seekers are still faced with the threat of unemployment, I expect job-seeking students to be more motivated to protect their BJW, particularly the personal BJW. Moreover, I expect personal BJW to correlate more strongly with anticipated fairness at the workplace than general BJW. As subjects in the present study were still in the phase of pre-job socialisation, their anticipations of workplace fairness as well as just world beliefs might also contribute to their well-being. The impact of BJW on SWB is thus expected to be mediated by anticipated fairness at the workplace. Students with a strong just-world belief and a positive anticipation of workplace fairness are expected to show a higher level of well-being than those who are weak believers and/or do not expect to experience fairness at the workplace.

In the present study, the relationship between just world beliefs and SWB is expected to strengthen with time, as the chances of getting a job seemed to be lower in 2001 than in 1999. Consequently, students searching for a job in 2001 were faced with a more serious threat of unemployment. They can thus be expected to be in greater need of a buffer to protect their SWB, and to ensure they have a positive attitude towards life, fewer personal problems, a high level of self-esteem, a low level of depression and few somatic complaints, as well as more joy in life. Moreover, the relationships between BJW and SWB are expected to vary by gender. It is well known that women doing the same jobs as men tend to earn less and to have lower status. Men and women are offered different career opportunities, thus strengthening gender stereotypes, and in turn leading to more somatic complaints in women (e.g. Brown, 1979; Eagly and Steffen, 1984). It was thus expected that women would be in greater need of a buffer such as the BJW. According to previous studies, women usually show lower levels of self-esteem and higher levels of depression, have more personal problems, and suffer more somatic complaints than men (e.g. Grob *et al.*, 2001). In the stressful situation of entering the labour market, females can be expected to be more sensitive and to feel more pressure to find a job.

In sum, the following hypotheses are tested. (a) Personal BJW correlates more strongly than general BJW with anticipated fairness at the work-

Entering the job market: graduating 223

place. (b) Subjects with a strong just world belief and a positive anticipation of workplace fairness show a higher level of well-being than those who are weak believers or do not expect fairness at the workplace. Regarding job seekers, it is hypothesised that (c) they are motivated to protect their BJW, particularly their personal BJW. High belief in a just world motivates them to anticipate a higher level of fairness at the workplace and the association between BJW and fairness should thus be stronger for job seekers than for those who have already secured a job. (d) The relationship between just world beliefs and SWB is expected to be stronger in 2001 than in 1999. (e) The relationship between BJW and SWB is expected to be stronger for women than for men.

In order to explore the inter-relatedness of just world beliefs, anticipated fairness at the workplace and SWB, their correlations were studied (see Table 13.1). As expected, both BJWs correlated positively with fairness at the workplace, and all dimensions of SWB (except general BJW and problems) and fairness also correlated significantly with all dimensions of SWB.

In order to explore the unique contributions of BJW and anticipated fairness at the workplace to well-being, moderated multiple regressions were run for each of the six well-being dimensions separately. Variables were entered stepwise within blocks; the significance level was fixed to $p < 0.05$. Dummies for time point ($0 = 1999$; $1 = 2001$), gender ($0 = $ male; $1 = $ female) and job situation ($0 = $ employed; $1 = $ job seeker) were entered in the first block, BJW and anticipated fairness at the workplace were entered in the second block, and the three two-way interaction terms amongst the dummies as well as the nine two-way interaction terms of the dummies with the BJW and anticipated fairness were entered in the third block. Interaction terms which were not significant and variables which were not part of a significant interaction or which revealed no significant main effect were deleted from the regression. The accepted models are shown in Table 13.2.

A stepwise multiple regression analysis on positive attitude towards life showed a significant impact of the job situation, personal and general BJW, and anticipated fairness at the workplace, explaining a total of 29 per cent of the variance. The more the students believed in a personal and in a general just world, and the more fairness they anticipated at the workplace, the more positive their attitude towards life. Students who had already found a job also had a more positive attitude to life. Gender and fairness at the workplace proved to be significant to personal problems. The more fairness the respondents anticipated at the workplace, the fewer personal problems they reported; females also reported fewer personal problems. Time point, gender and personal BJW predicted somatic complaints, with respondents surveyed in 2001 and females reporting more complaints. Furthermore, the more they endorsed the personal BJW, the fewer somatic complaints the students reported. The job situation,

Table 13.1 Means (*M*), standard deviations (*SD*) and bivariate correlations for BJW and SWB

	M	SD	1	2	3	4	5	6	7	8	9	10	11
1 Time point	–	–	–	–	–	–	–	–	–	–	–	–	–
2 Gender	–	–	-0.04	–	–	–	–	–	–	–	–	–	–
3 Job situation	–	–	0.12	0.06	–	–	–	–	–	–	–	–	–
4 General belief in a just world	3.25	0.85	-0.01	0.14*	-0.08	–	–	–	–	–	–	–	–
5 Personal belief in a just world	4.15	0.82	-0.14*	-0.07	-0.09	0.49**	–	–	–	–	–	–	–
6 Anticipated fairness at the workplace	4.27	0.85	0.09	-0.00	-0.02	0.31**	0.46**	–	–	–	–	–	–
7 Positive attitude towards life	3.31	0.99	0.02	-0.07	-0.20**	0.38**	0.48**	0.33**	–	–	–	–	–
8 Personal problems	4.50	0.94	-0.08	0.16*	-0.02	-0.05	-0.16*	-0.26**	-0.24**	–	–	–	–
9 Self-esteem	2.05	0.88	-0.01	-0.13*	-0.18**	0.29**	0.34**	0.28**	0.72**	-0.28**	–	–	–
10 Depressive mood	1.81	0.64	-0.10	0.01	0.05	-0.18**	-0.24**	-0.23**	-0.59**	0.18**	-0.61**	–	–
11 Somatic complaints	2.96	0.59	0.27**	0.16*	0.12	-0.13	-0.32**	-0.18**	-0.31**	0.32**	-0.27**	0.21**	–
12 Joy in life	3.72	0.79	-0.11	0.00	-0.09	0.22**	0.30**	0.19**	0.39**	-0.07	0.30**	-0.32**	0.19**

Notes

* *p* ≤ 0.05.

** *p* ≤ 0.01.

Time point (0 = 1999; 1 = 2001); Gender (0 = males; 1 = females); Job situation (0 = employed; 1 = job seeker).

Entering the job market: graduating 225

Table 13.2 Regression of SWB on BJW, anticipated fairness at the workplace, time point, gender and job situation and their interactions (multiple regression, accepted models; $p<0.05$)

Predictor	R	R^2	B	t	p
Positive attitude towards life ($F_{total} = 20.401$; $df= 4/200$; $p<0.000$)					
Job situation	0.21	0.04	−0.25	−2.23	0.027
Personal BJW	0.50	0.25	0.33	4.27	0.000
General BJW	0.53	0.28	0.18	2.57	0.011
Anticipated fairness at the workplace	0.54	0.29	0.15	2.05	0.042
			1.92		
Personal problems ($F_{total} = 11.233$; $df= 2/210$; $p= 0.000$)					
Gender	0.17	0.03	0.33	0.16	0.016
Anticipated fairness at the workplace	0.31	0.10	−0.33	−0.27	0.000
			4.34		
Somatic complaints and reactions ($F_{total} = 15.703$; $df= 3/210$; $p<0.000$)					
Time point	0.29	0.08	0.33	4.03	0.000
Gender	0.34	0.11	0.19	2.32	0.021
Personal BJW	0.43	0.19	−0.21	−4.27	0.000
			2.40		
Self-esteem ($F_{total} = 12.550$; $df= 4/211$; $p<0.000$)					
Job situation	0.19	0.03	0.29	−2.34	0.020
Gender	0.23	0.05	−0.33	−2.68	0.008
General BJW	0.40	0.16	0.31	4.12	0.000
Anticipated fairness at the workplace	0.44	0.20	0.23	2.92	0.004
			3.07		
Depressive mood ($F_{total} = 8.853$; $df= 2/207$; $p= 0.000$)					
Personal BJW	0.24	0.06	−0.18	−2.23	0.027
Anticipated fairness at the workplace	0.28	0.08	−0.18	−2.17	0.031
			3.49		
Joy in life ($F_{total} = 8.749$; $df= 4/207$; $p<0.000$)					
Time point	0.13	0.02	0.78	–	–
Personal BJW	0.32	0.10	0.20	3.62	0.000
General BJW	0.33	0.11	0.19	–	–
Time point × General BJW	0.38	0.15	−0.27	−3.02	0.003
			1.61		
Anticipated fairness at the workplace ($F_{total} = 33.573$; $df= 2/209$; $p<0.000$)					
Time point	0.10	0.01	0.28	2.88	0.004
Personal BJW	0.50	0.25	0.47	8.02	0.000
			1.62		

gender, general BJW and anticipated fairness at the workplace revealed significant main effects on self-esteem, explaining a total of 20 per cent of the variance. Self-esteem was higher among males and those still seeking a job. Furthermore, the more strongly students endorsed the general BJW and the more fairness they anticipated at the workplace, the higher their self-esteem. Depressive mood was predicted by personal BJW and fairness

226   *Hedvig Sallay*

at the workplace, explaining 8 per cent of the variance. The more subjects endorsed the personal BJW, and the fairer they expected their workplace to be, the less depressed they were. Joy in life was predicted by a main effect of personal BJW and by an interaction effect of general BJW with time point, explaining a total 15 per cent of the variance. The more subjects endorsed the personal and the general BJW, the more they enjoyed life. However, the positive association between general BJW and joy in life held only for 2001 ($b = 0.19$) and not for 1999 ($b = -0.08$). Finally, anticipated fairness at the workplace was predicted by time point and personal BJW. Those surveyed in 2001 and those with a strong personal BJW anticipated more fairness at the workplace than those surveyed in 1999 and those with a weak personal BJW.

Discussion

The results of our study unambiguously support the hypothesis that the belief in a general and a personal just world is an important resource for graduating students. As predicted by the justice motive theory, BJW had a considerable impact on four of six well-being dimensions as well as on anticipated fairness at the workplace. Personal BJW was in fact the most important predictor for most dependent variables, while other observed variables – such as general BJW, time point, gender and job situation – merely coloured the results. In addition, the anticipated fairness of the workplace was predicted by personal BJW and, in turn, directly contributed to all dimensions of SWB except somatic complaints and joy in life. In sum, personal BJW consistently showed a direct and an indirect impact on SWB, the latter mediated by anticipated fairness at the workplace. General BJW had an additional positive impact on positive attitudes towards life, self-esteem and, for those surveyed in 2001, on joy in life.

Conclusion

The process of pre-job socialisation is an integral part of general, workplace and organisational socialisation. Consequently, it is important to explore the factors that may play a role in this process. Results from this study support the view that expectations about fairness at the workplace constitute one of the factors that influence later career aspirations and socialisation at the workplace, as Maanen (1977) suggested. In this study it was clearly shown that the fairer students anticipate their workplace to be, the more positive their attitude towards life, the fewer problems they report, the higher their self-esteem and the less depressed they are.

Besides anticipated fairness at the workplace, the job situation of graduating students (job seeker vs. employed) also had an impact on their subjective well-being; however, it was only observed for two of the dimensions of well-being under investigation. First, students who had already obtained a job had a more positive attitude towards life. It is easy to understand this attitude, because having secured a job is a justifiable source of satisfaction. On the other hand, students still looking for a job had a less positive attitude towards life, which can be explained by the ongoing stress of seeking work and stable living standards. Self-esteem was the second component of SWB affected by the job situation. However, contrary to expectations, students who had already found a job reported lower self-esteem than their peers who were still looking for one. This may indicate that they have accepted a job that did not correspond to their qualifications or aspirations. On the other hand, maintaining a high level of self-esteem has an important adaptive role for the future as well. If job seekers succeed in maintaining a high level of self-esteem, they will also be more likely to make a good impression in the job-search process and find gainful employment.

Another main effect on self-esteem was observed for gender, with women reporting lower levels of self-esteem. Gender also produced a significant main effect on personal problems and somatic complaints. Again, it was the women who reported more personal problems and somatic complaints. These gender differences might indirectly reflect that women expect to have fewer job opportunities than men, and tend to manifest their problems on these dimensions of SWB. However, this is merely speculation, as attributions for job search and finding a job were not investigated in this study. These results are in line with previous studies comparing gender characteristics of well-being (e.g. Visser *et al.*, 1999).

In this study, the impact of the socio-economic changes that occurred between 1999 and 2001 were rather minor. The developing individual, entering into cultural understanding and participation in the community, is both a crucible and a mirror of such changes. Although two years seems to be a relatively short period, the speed of change became faster than ever before during these years, and the consequences more pronounced. Economic problems were evident, and the widening gap between rich and poor was apparent at all levels of everyday life. A comparative study conducted by Van Hoorn *et al.* (2000) demonstrated that Hungarian youngsters show a dialectical developmental process when they go through a transformation via their personal experiences and those of their families. In line with my hypotheses, the socio-economic changes did have an observable impact on anticipated workplace fairness, which was higher in 2001 than in 1999. However, apart from this effect, the transformation process is only partially reflected in their levels of well-being. Graduating female students had more somatic complaints in 2001. Where women are concerned, my interpretation is consistent with that of Diener *et al.* (1995; Diener and Diener, 1995), who found that economic development affects the level of well-being even beyond the effects of personality. However, it can be assumed that males also react to these changes, but in different

228 Hedvig Sallay

ways that were not examined in this study. Young adults' BJWs have an adaptive role in helping them to adjust to the demands of a given socio-political and socio-historical context; this function is reflected in different components of well-being. To gain a more detailed impression of the impact of socio-political changes on the well-being of graduating students and how BJW works as a buffer in this process, however, longitudinal studies should be conducted with more time points.

In sum, the work presented here lends support to the theory that the personal BJW functions as an especially effective buffer. Students high in personal BJW are motivated to protect their trust that injustice is the exception rather than the rule in their own lives. Hopefully, this trust will also help students graduating in the coming years to overcome the difficulties they encounter when they leave student life to enter the world of earners.

References

Antalovits, M. (2000) 'Munkaköri- és munkahelyi szocializáció' [Socialisation for sphere and place of work], in Meszáros, A. (ed), *Work Psychology*, Gödöllö: Szent István University, pp. 65–79.

Banks, M.H. and Ullah, P. (1988) *Youth Unemployment in the 1980s. Its Psychological Effects*, London: Croom Helm.

Baron, P. and Campbell, T.L. (1993) 'Gender differences in the expression of depressive symptoms in middle adolescents: An extension of earlier findings', *Adolescence*, 28: 903–11.

Brim, O.G. Jr. (1992) *Ambition: How We Manage Success and Failure Throughout Our Lives*, New York: Basic Books.

Brown, L.K. (1979) 'Women and business management', *Journal of Women in Culture and Society*, 5: 266–88.

Dalbert, C. (1992) 'Subjektives Wohlbefinden junger Erwachsener: Theoretische und empirische Analysen der Struktur und Stabilitat' [Subjective well-being of young adults: theoretical and empirical analyses of structure and stability], *Zeitschrift für Differentielle und Diagnostische Psychologie*, 13: 207–20.

Dalbert, C. (1993) 'Gefahrdung des Wohlbefindens durch Arbeitsplatzunsicher-heit: Eine Analyse der Einflussfaktoren Selbstwert und Gerechte-Welt-Glaube' [Endangering subjective well-being by job insecurity: An analysis of the impact of self-esteem and belief in a just world], *Zeitschrift für Gesundheitspsychologie*, 1: 235–53.

Dalbert, C. (1996) *Über den Umgang mit Ungerechtigkeit. Eine psychologische Analyse* [Dealing with injustice. A psychological analysis], Bern: Huber.

Dalbert, C. (1997) 'Coping with an unjust fate: The case of structural unemploy-ment', *Social Justice Research*, 10: 175–89.

Dalbert, C. (1998) 'Belief in a just world, well-being, and coping with an unjust fate', in Montada, L. and Lerner, M.J. (eds), *Responses to Victimizations and Belief in a Just World*, New York: Plenum Press.

Dalbert, C. (1999) 'The world is more just for me than generally: About the Per-sonal Belief in a Just World Scale's validity', *Social Justice Research*, 12: 79–98.

Entering the job market: graduating 229

Dalbert, C. and Katona-Sallay, H. (1996) 'The "belief in the just world" construct in Hungary', *Journal of Cross-Cultural Psychology*, 27: 293–314.

Dalbert, C., Montada, L. and Schmitt, M. (1987) 'Glaube an eine gerechte Welt als Motiv: Validierungskorrelate zweier Skalen', *Psychologische Beitrage*, 29: 596–615.

Diener, E. and Diener, M. (1995) 'Cross-cultural correlates of life satisfaction and self-esteem', *Journal of Personality and Social Psychology*, 68: 653–63.

Diener, E., Diener, M. and Diener, C. (1995) 'Factors predicting the subjective well-being of nations', *Journal of Personality and Social Psychology*, 69: 851–64.

Dooley, D., Fielding, J. and Levi, L. (1996) 'Health and unemployment', *Annual Review of Public Health*, 17: 449–65.

DuBois, D.L. and Tevendale, H.D. (1999) 'Self-esteem in childhood and adolescence: Vaccine or epiphenomenon?', *Applied and Preventive Psychology*, 8: 103–17.

Eagly, A.H. and Steffen, V.J. (1984) 'Gender stereotypes stem from the distribution of women and men into social roles', *Journal of Personality and Social Psychology*, 46: 735–54.

Emmons, R.A. (1992) 'Abstract versus concrete goals: Personal striving level, physical illness, and psychological well-being', *Journal of Personality and Social Psychology*, 62: 292–300.

Freyer, D.M. (1986) 'Employment deprivation and personal agency during unemployment: A critical discussion of Jahoda's explanation of the psychological effects of unemployment', *Social Behaviour*, 1: 3–23.

Gannon, L., Vaux, A., Rhodes, K. and Luchetta, T. (1992) 'A two-domain model of well-being: Everyday events, social support, and gender-related personality factors', *Journal of Research in Personality*, 26: 288–301.

Grob, A. (1995) 'Subjective well-being and significant life-events across the life-span', *Swiss Journal of Psychology*, 54: 3–18.

Grob, A., Lemler-Lauerbach, A., Rietz, C. and Weisheit, W. (2001) 'Subjektives Wohlbefinden von drei Generationen derselben Familie' [Subjective well-being of three generations in the same family], paper presented at 6th Workshop for Differential, and Personality Psychology and Psychological Diagnostics of the German Psychological Society, Leipzig, Germany, September.

Hafer, C.L. (2000) 'Investment in long-term goals and commitment to just means drive the need to believe in a just world', *Personality and Social Psychology Bulletin*, 26: 1059–73.

Havighurst, R.J. (1984) *Developmental Tasks and Education*, New York: McKay.

Jahoda, M. (1982) *Employment and Unemployment: A Social Psychological Analysis*, Cambridge: Cambridge University Press.

Josephs, R.A., Markus, H.R. and Tafarodi, R.W. (1992) 'Gender and self-esteem', *Journal of Personality and Social Psychology*, 63: 391–402.

Kasl, S.V., Rodriguez, E. and Lasch, K.E. (1998) 'The impact of unemployment on health and well-being', in Dohrenwend, B.P. (ed.), *Adversity, Stress, and Psychopathology*, New York: Oxford University Press, pp. 111–31.

Kolosi, T., Tóth, I.Gy. and Vukovich, Gy. (1999) 'Social Report 1998', *Budapest: TÁRKI Social Research Informatics Center*, 519–40.

Korpi, T. (1997) 'Is utility related to employment status? Employment, unemployment, labor market policies and subjective well-being among Swedish youth', *Labour Economics*, 4: 125–47.

Lerner, M.J. (1978) ' "Belief in a just world" versus "authoritarianism" syndrome . . . but nobody liked the Indians', *Ethnicity*, 5: 229–37.

230 Hedvig Sallay

Lewin, E.N. (1989) 'Work characteristics and ill health: Gender differences in Israel', *Work and Occupations*, 16: 80–104.

Lipkus, I.M., Dalbert, C. and Siegler, I.C. (1996) 'The importance of distinguishing the belief in a just world for self versus others', *Personality and Social Psychology Bulletin*, 22: 666–77.

Maanen, J.V. (1977) 'Experiencing organization: Notes on the meaning of careers and socialization', in Maanen, J.V. (ed.), *Organizational Careers: Some New Perspectives*, New York: Wiley.

McCauley, E., Myers, K., Mitchell, J. and Calderon, R. (1993) 'Depression in young people: Initial presentation and clinical course', *Journal of the American Academy of Child and Adolescent Psychiatry*, 32: 714–22.

Messick, D.M., Bloom, S., Boldizar, J.P. and Samuelson, C.D. (1985) 'Why we are fairer than others?', *Journal of Experimental Social Psychology*, 21: 480–500.

Moscovici, S. (1984) *Social Representations*, Cambridge: Cambridge University Press.

Platt, J. (1973) 'Social traps', *American Psychologist*, 28: 641–51.

Roberts, K. and Markel, K.S. (2001) 'Claiming the name of fairness: Organizational justice and the decision to file for workplace injury compensation', *Journal of Occupational Health Psychology*, 6: 332–47.

Saathoff, W.T.S. (2001) 'Development of a theoretical model using social support and workplace fairness as factors in the subjective well-being of American expatriates', *Dissertation Abstracts International Section A: Humanities and Social Sciences*, 61: 3787.

Taylor, S. and Brown, J. (1988) 'Illusion and well-being: A social-psychological perspective on mental health', *Psychological Bulletin*, 103: 193–210.

Tomaka, J. and Blascovich, J. (1994) 'Effects of justice beliefs on cognitive, psychological, and behavioral responses to potential stress', *Journal of Personality and Social Psychology*, 67: 732–40.

Van Hoorn, J.L., Komlosi, A., Suchar, E. and Samelson, D. (2000) *Adolescent Development and Rapid Social Change*, Albany, NY: SUNY Press.

Visser, J.J., van der Ende, J., Koof, H.M. and Verhulst, F.C. (1999) 'Continuity of psychopathology in youths referred to mental health services', *Journal of the American Academy of Child and Adolescent Psychiatry*, 38: 1560–8.

Warr, P. (1987) *Work, Unemployment and Mental Health*, Oxford: Clarendon Press.

Weinstein, N.D. (1980) 'Unrealistic optimism about future life events', *Journal of Personality and Social Psychology*, 39: 806–10.

14 Belief in a just world and adolescents' vocational and social goals

Dorothea Dette, Joachim Stöber and Claudia Dalbert

Introduction

Suppose you are a teenager about to start your final year of school. You need to think about what you want to do with the rest of your life and what professional training to go for. What would you base your decision on? Of course, it is important to do something you enjoy – so how about becoming a professional football player, a rock star or supermodel? It's a nice idea, but you also need to consider your chances of success. Can you really make it in your chosen profession? Because if you discover too late that you cannot, you will have lost precious time.

The 'Can I make it?' question, the estimated 'probability of success', has indeed proved to be a valid predictor of goal-related decisions and goal commitment, and it is important to identify the potential determinants of this subjective estimation of success. Previous research has shown that, besides situational influences, stable dispositional factors and personality variables such as the 'big five' personality factors and self-efficacy are of importance. Moreover, the belief in a just world (BJW) has emerged to be relevant to many areas of daily life (for a comprehensive review, see Dalbert, 2001). However, the direct influence of the BJW on specific aspects of personal goals has, as yet, rarely been investigated (cf. Otto and Dalbert, in this volume).

The present chapter presents results from a study on the relationship between the BJW and the personal goals of adolescents. Specifically, the aim of the study was to shed some light on the relationship between the BJW and a central aspect of two important classes of personal goals, namely the probability of success in vocational and social personal goals. We will focus on adolescence, a potentially turbulent time, in which the formation of personal goals plays an important role (Nurmi, 1993; Oerter and Dreher, 1995). In the first part of the chapter, we will describe the BJW and its two facets, the general BJW and the personal BJW. Thereafter, we will outline research on personal goals in which the probability of success has emerged as a central variable. In the second part, we will present findings from a questionnaire study with students attending the

232   *D. Dette, J. Stöber and C. Dalbert*

9th grade of high school.[1] Specifically, we will show that both the personal and the general BJW have significant and different influences on the estimated probability of success in adolescents' social and vocational goals. In the third and final part, we will integrate our findings, discuss limitations of our study and suggest future research directions.

Belief in a just world

According to the just world hypothesis (Lerner, 1965), people are motivated to believe in a just world where people generally get what they deserve and deserve what they get. To put it simply, good behaviour gets rewarded, and bad guys get punished. This BJW helps people to orientate themselves in a complex social and physical world by assuming that their environment is reliable and orderly (Lerner and Miller, 1978). Not everyone has the same amount of trust in the world's justice, however. The strength of the BJW varies between individuals (Rubin and Peplau, 1973, 1975). The stronger a person's BJW, the more justice-motivated his or her reactions. This often leads to positive outcomes, such as enhanced coping behaviour and hence better well-being (Dalbert, 2002). In addition, the BJW serves other useful adaptive functions (Dalbert, 2001, 2002). It provides people with the confidence that they will be treated fairly and will not fall victim to an unforeseen and unjust fate. Thus, individuals high in BJW place more trust in others (Zuckerman and Gerbasi, 1977) and show more dyadic trust in times of need (Dalbert, 2001). This trust in fairness allows them to assume that today's investments will be fairly rewarded in the future. If I promise to behave according to certain standards, a good return on my investments is certain. The reasoning behind this is that if everyone behaves fairly, the world will be a just place. Consequently, the BJW may foster goal-directed behaviour such as investments in long-term goals (Hafer, 2000). Moreover, it may promote unspecific investments in times of need, for example, engaging in prosocial behaviour with the aim of earning a positive outcome for oneself when it is needed most (Zuckerman, 1975).

At first, the construct of the BJW was defined and measured in very broad terms and consisted mainly of beliefs about the world in general being a just place. With a greater focus on the individual, however, the view became more detailed. Several researchers argued that the BJW should be differentiated into a general and a personal BJW (Furnham and Procter, 1989; Hafer and Olson, 1993; Lerner and Miller, 1978). In addition to the general BJW, which reflects the belief that the world in general is a just place, a personal BJW has been conceptualised, reflecting the belief that one's own fate is just and that events in one's life are deserved. Lipkus *et al.* (1996) and Dalbert (1999) provided empirical evidence for the need to differentiate between general and personal BJW. They showed the personal BJW was stronger than the general BJW, as well as being a better predictor of mental health and more closely related to self-esteem.

Personal goals

According to Brunstein *et al.* (1996: 1006), 'personal goals are the consciously accessible and personally meaningful objectives people pursue in their daily life. Personal goals indicate what individuals are striving for in their current life situations and what they try to attain or avoid in various life domains.' The term 'personal goals' thus serves as an umbrella term for four different research traditions, namely research on current concerns (Klinger, 1977), personal projects (Little, 1983), personal strivings (Emmons, 1986) and life tasks (Cantor and Kihlstrom, 1987). On a rather abstract level, personal strivings are defined as patterns of goals that represent what a person typically tries to accomplish (Emmons, 1989). According to this definition, a striving can be achieved through a series of concrete, smaller goals. Thus, according to Emmons, strivings are a more abstract form of personal goals and do not include ways of reaching a certain goal. The concept of life tasks is more specific in this regard (Cantor and Kihlstrom, 1987). Here, goals do not remain static over the life course, but change with life situations and developmental phases. Every life task contains both the desired outcome and ideas and problem-solving strategies that help to fulfil it. Still more concrete are current concerns (Klinger, 1977). These result from the commitment a person has formed towards a desired state, and they are very difficult to relinquish. Moreover, current concerns are not only representations of the desired outcome, but also include plans and ideas on how to reach this outcome. The most concrete form of personal goals is the concept of personal projects (Little, 1983). Personal projects are seen as a set of interrelated acts that continue over time and are carried out to reach a desired end-state.

Despite these differences, the four concepts have been subsumed under the common term 'personal goals', mainly because they all follow what is called an 'idiographic–nomothetic approach' to assessment (Klinger, 1987; see also Brunstein and Maier, 1996). First, participants are asked to write down their own personal goals in a free format. Hence, the content of the goals reported may be different for each participant. This represents the idiographic part of the approach. Subsequently, participants are asked to rate their individual goals along a set of given dimensions (e.g. estimated probability of success). Thus, despite their individually differing content, the personal goals may be compared on common dimensions. This represents the nomothetic part of the approach. If the researchers did not specify particular categories of individual goals *a priori*, external raters categorise the goals reported so that it is also possible to compare categories of goals on common dimensions.

234   *D. Dette, J. Stöber and C. Dalbert*

Research on classifying goals has shown that most goals can be subsumed into two broad categories, namely vocational/academic goals and social/interpersonal goals (Little *et al.*, 1992; Pöhlmann, 2001; Wentzel, 1991). Moreover, these two goal domains represent the main topics that adolescents across different socio-cultural backgrounds mention when asked about their hopes and fears (e.g. Lanz and Rosnati, 2002; Nurmi *et al.*, 1994). Consequently, these two categories were also adopted in the present research.

Of course, it does not suffice to have set oneself certain goals. The goals also have to be pursued actively. Innumerable goals – New Year's resolutions, for example – never get accomplished. Why? Because if people are not committed, they do not invest in these goals, and therefore never achieve them except by chance or luck. Commitment is of pivotal importance to goal success. So what determines which goals are pursued with commitment?

We do not usually have just one goal, but strive toward many goals at a time. Some are more important than others; some are equally important but differ in content; some are far-reaching whereas others are only important in the short term; some are more difficult, some easier and so on. However many goals there might be, ideally, every one of them should be pursued. An individual only has limited resources, however. Hardly anyone has the wherewithal to go for every single one of their goals. Therefore, a decision must be made on which goals to invest in and which to postpone or to drop. This decision is based on the comparison of two or more goals, and determines which goal is to be given commitment. Multiple factors influence the decision-making process, including the personality of the person involved and the characteristics of the goal itself.

The personal importance of goals and the estimated probability of success are central goal dimensions that most researchers have included in their assessment of personal goals (for an overview, see Emmons, 1997). According to Hollenbeck and Klein (1987) – who referred to these two factors as 'attractiveness of goal attainment' and 'expectancy of goal attainment' – they are also the two factors that lead to goal commitment. To our knowledge, the Hollenbeck and Klein model has only been partially tested empirically. One study examined the relationship of goal attractiveness and probability of success with commitment, and found both factors to have a significant influence on goal commitment (Metz-Göckel and Leffelsend, 2001). These results clearly show that probability of success is a major predictor of goal commitment. In the present chapter, we thus focus on the expectancy of goal attainment, or as we term it, the estimated probability of success in a given goal.

Adolescence and personal goals

Personal goals are important throughout life. However, they are especially important in times of rapid changes, when the individual has to find new perspectives, search for new challenges and choose new orientations. One such time is adolescence. Indeed, the development and successful pursuit of personal goals are central to adolescents' personality development (see Nurmi, 1991, 1993).

In developmental terms, adolescence can be a very turbulent time. Rapid biological, intellectual and social changes require swift adaptation and quick reactions. Adolescents often feel trapped between the expectations of others and their own desires, and only gradually adapt to their new role (Oerter and Dreher, 1995). In classical developmental psychology, adolescence is one of several major stages of individual development throughout life (e.g. Erikson, 1959; Havighurst, 1948). In each of these stages, specific developmental tasks have to be fulfilled. In adolescence, self-definition is a major concern. The young person has to find a position in life, to feel a purpose and identify a direction for the life course. Another major task is the formation of stable social networks outside the family. Friends become especially important in adolescence because – unlike family members – they are not given, but can be freely chosen. Another objective, and one that is closely related to social network building, is the adolescents' individuation from their parents (Dreher and Dreher, 1985). In short, adolescents face the challenge of setting the stage for their own life course.

One of the most important tasks here is the choice of a vocational career (Erikson, 1959; Havighurst, 1948; Marcia, 1966). This major step precedes entry into the job market, a pivotal point in every adolescent's life. The decision for a profession is one of the most important decisions in life. Moreover, it is one of the earliest decisions, if not *the* earliest, with a huge impact on the rest of the life course. As such, it is often a difficult decision, and one that is even more difficult to make at a point in life at which one is still very ignorant of the job market. It is almost impossible to make a truly informed decision, because life at school bears little resemblance to what awaits them on the job market. Still, the decision must be made even before the final exams are taken. Thus, the adolescents must rely on the resources they have and the help they are offered.

Another developmental task facing adolescents is the formation of a stable social network within, and more importantly, outside the family. Good relationships with relatives and peers are the primary source of social support and facilitate problem solving and promote health (Scholte et al., 2001). Thus, both vocational and social goals are of central importance in adolescence, and it is essential for young people to pursue and achieve both categories of goals.

Therefore, in order to gain a better understanding of goal pursuit in

236　D. Dette, J. Stöber and C. Dalbert

adolescence, it would be interesting to be able to predict the probability of success in personal goals. This would also provide an insight into why some people stick to their goals and succeed in reaching them, while others fail again and again. Some predictors of the probability of success have already been identified, namely personality, self-efficacy and situation-specific influence.

Personality and other predictors of the probability of success in personal goals

As the term 'personal' goals implies, personality is an important influencing factor here. The dominant model for capturing broad dimensions of personality is the five-factor model of personality. Its 'big five' dimensions have been labelled (a) neuroticism or, its opposite, emotional stability, (b) extraversion or surgency, (c) agreeableness, (d) conscientiousness or dependability and (e) openness, culture, or intellect (John, 1990). Though there has been – and still is – considerable debate as to whether these five dimensions constitute an adequate and comprehensive description of personality (e.g. Block, 1995; McAdams, 1992), the five-factor model of personality represents an established base from which one may start to explore potential relationships between personality and personal goals.

Thus far, however, only a limited number of studies have dealt with the relations between the 'big five' and personal goals. Two studies (Little, 1989; Little et al., 1992) reported correlations between the Big Five personality factors and participants' ratings of their personal projects. Although the patterns for academic (vocational) and interpersonal (social) personal projects were somewhat different, the studies found that the Big Five personality traits influenced most of the goal dimensions in both domains. For example, neuroticism showed significant correlations with several goal dimensions related to the probability of success, and was positively correlated with estimations of stress and difficulty, and negatively correlated with control. Moreover, extraversion and conscientiousness showed correlations with success-related dimensions. Extraversion showed positive correlations with estimated efficacy, and conscientiousness with enjoyment and control. It thus seems likely that the Big Five personality traits will also influence a person's estimated probability of success.

Besides the broad, general 'big five' personality factors, more specific predictors of specific goal contents have also been identified. Higher self-efficacy has been shown to be related to goal pursuit (Locke and Latham, 1990; Vrugt et al., 2002). The construct of self-efficacy was introduced by Bandura and represents a core aspect of his social-cognitive theory (Bandura, 1977, 1995). Self-efficacy refers to the belief of being able to exert control and influence events in the desired direction. It is commonly understood to be domain-specific; that is, the expected control over events varies across situations. We can thus assume that social self-efficacy will be an influential predictor of the estimated probability of success in attaining one's social goals. Finally, whether or not action has already been taken to attain a certain goal may also play a role. The more people have invested in a goal, the higher the probability that they will eventually attain it. Preparations for vocational training should thus be another potential predictor of the probability of success in vocational goals. Moreover, we expect the BJW to be a relevant personality factor in the prediction of personal goals.

The belief in a just world and personal goals

The BJW serves important adaptive functions and has positive effects on mental health and well-being (Dalbert, 1997, 1999, 2001). Moreover, a recent study by Hafer (2000) suggests that the BJW may also be related to the pursuit of personal goals. People with a strong BJW assume that the world is a reliable and orderly place where everyone gets what they deserve (Dalbert, 2001). Based on this assumption, they can be confident that their current work and investments will pay off and be of benefit to them in the future. This is a basic condition for the formation and pursuit of personal goals. Personal goals, particularly high-level goals, may comprise numerous subgoals that need to be attained in preparation for the overarching goal (Emmons, 1989). Moreover, many important personal goals – especially vocational goals, but also social goals related to marriage and family life – are long-range goals that will not be attained for many years to come (e.g. Nurmi, 1989). Consequently, a considerable amount of time may elapse between today's efforts and future outcomes. Thus, it is crucial to believe that the world is a just place and that one will eventually be able to reap the rewards of one's effort. If the world were not just, it might well be that undeserving others benefit from one's investments. Indeed, Hafer (2000) showed a relationship between the BJW and personal goals. The more strongly participants focused on their long-term goals, the more they tried to protect their BJW. Clearly, then, the BJW is an important precondition for investment in long-term goals. This finding supports the idea that the BJW helps motivate investment in long-term goals, particularly as the BJW has been shown to be a rather stable personality trait (Dalbert, 2001) whereas personal goals are more situationally variable and thus less stable. Consequently, it seems likely that the BJW should be a potential predictor of the estimated probability of success in personal goals.

Aims of the present study

In the following study, we aim to explore the relationship between the BJW and the expected probability of success in adolescents' vocational

238   *D. Dette, J. Stöber and C. Dalbert*

and social goals. Specifically, we investigate whether general and personal BJW are still predictive of higher probability of success in personal goals after controlling for the Big Five personality factors. Moreover, we examine whether general and personal BJW show specific relationships with estimated success in the two different goal domains after domain-specific predictors – i.e. preparation for vocational training (for vocational goals) and social self-efficacy (for social goals) – are introduced as concurrent predictors.

Our study

Sample and procedure

The sample consisted of 392 adolescents attending the 9th grade of 12 German secondary schools of the *Realschule* type.[2] Gender was equally distributed, with 195 girls and 196 boys (one person did not indicate their gender). The mean age was 15.1 years ($SD = 0.61$; range 14–17 years). The assessment was conducted in the classroom during lesson time. Written consent was obtained from students, parents and teachers prior to data collection.

Measures

Probability of success in vocational and social goals

First, participants were asked to list their two most important vocational goals and their two most important social goals in a free format. They were then instructed to estimate the subjective probability of success in each goal with the following instruction: 'Please indicate the probability of success in your goals'. The answer format was a 6-point Likert-type scale ranging from 6 ('very high probability of success') to 1 ('very low probability of success'). The mean of the two vocational goals ratings was used as a measure of the probability of success in vocational goals, and the mean of the two social goals ratings as a measure of the probability of success in social goals.

General and personal BJW

To measure the personal BJW, we used the Personal Belief in a Just World Scale (Dalbert, 1999). The scale consists of seven items (e.g. 'I believe that, by and large, I deserve what happens to me'). The reliability was Alpha = 0.83. For the general BJW, we used the General Belief in a Just World Scale (Dalbert *et al.*, 1987). The scale comprises six items (e.g. 'I think basically the world is a just place'). The reliability was Alpha = 0.75. Both scales employed a 6-point Likert-type answer format ranging from 6

BJW and vocational and social goals 239

('totally agree') to 1 ('totally disagree'). As with all other scales, scores were calculated by averaging across items.

Big Five personality factors

The Big Five personality factors were measured with a 30-item short form of the NEO Five Factor Inventory (Costa and McCrae, 1992; German version: Borkenau and Ostendorf, 1993) as developed by Trautwein *et al.* (2004). The inventory captures individual differences on the five personality traits: neuroticism (Alpha = 0.70), extraversion (Alpha = 0.57), openness (Alpha = 0.52), agreeableness (Alpha = 0.56) and conscientiousness (Alpha = 0.67). The scale consisted of five items for the subscale openness (one item had to be excluded due to low item-total correlation) and six items for each of the other subscales. The answer format was a 4-point Likert-type scale ranging from 4 ('totally agree') to 1 ('totally disagree').

Social self-efficacy

Social self-efficacy was measured with the 8-item social self-efficacy scale developed by Satow and Mittag (1999). The scale captures participants' feelings of competence in difficult social situations (e.g. 'I easily find friends after moving to a new school'). Reliability was Alpha = 0.66. The answer format was the same 6-point scale as for the BJW scales.

Preparations for vocational training

These were measured with 10 statements describing activities involved in the preparation for vocational training. (e.g. 'I have gathered information about schools offering vocational training'). The participants were asked to indicate whether or not they had already undertaken each action (dichotomous answer format), and positive responses were summed to give a score between 0 and 10. This measure was designed specifically for the purposes of the present study.

Results

First, we looked at the goal contents of the adolescents. The most frequent vocational goals were education-related (e.g. 'become a mechanic') or concerned the later work life (e.g. 'find a full-time job'). The social goals mostly dealt with family and friends (e.g. 'be on good terms with my parents' or 'have a romantic relationship'). As we did not find any gender differences except for the preference of specific professions (e.g. more boys than girls wanted to become a mechanic), data were collapsed across gender. Then we inspected the resulting correlations (Table 14.1). The

Table 14.1 Means, standard deviations and bivariate correlations

	M	SD	Correlation									
			1	2	3	4	5	6	7	8	9	10
1 Probability of success in vocational goals	4.24	1.01	–	–	–	–	–	–	–	–	–	–
2 Probability of success in social goals	4.83	0.95	0.21***	–	–	–	–	–	–	–	–	–
3 General BJW	3.70	1.00	0.14**	0.14**	–	–	–	–	–	–	–	–
4 Personal BJW	4.13	0.90	0.15***	0.16**	0.63***	–	–	–	–	–	–	–
5 Neuroticism	2.43	0.60	-0.20***	-0.09	0.07	-0.08	–	–	–	–	–	–
6 Extraversion	3.11	0.48	0.10	0.13*	0.03	0.11*	-0.17**	–	–	–	–	–
7 Openness	2.54	0.56	0.10*	-0.04	0.01	0.11*	0.03	0.01	–	–	–	–
8 Agreeableness	2.60	0.46	0.01	0.04	0.01	0.01	-0.17**	0.15**	-0.06	–	–	–
9 Conscientiousness	3.01	0.54	0.26***	0.12*	0.20***	0.27***	-0.16**	0.25***	0.15**	-0.00	–	–
10 Social self-efficacy	4.72	0.71	0.20***	0.20***	0.21***	0.27***	-0.15**	0.38***	0.17**	0.05	0.35***	–
11 Preparations for vocational training	3.57	1.91	0.14**	0.05	-0.07	-0.02	-0.05	0.11*	0.02	0.04	0.18***	0.14**

Notes

$N = 392$. BJW = belief in a just world.

* $p < 0.05$.

** $p < 0.01$.

*** $p < 0.001$.

BJW and vocational and social goals 241

general as well as the personal BJW correlated significantly and in the expected direction with the probability of success in both vocational and social goals. Furthermore, preparations for vocational training, neuroticism, openness and conscientiousness correlated significantly with the probability of success in vocational goals. Social self-efficacy also correlated significantly with the probability of success in vocational goals, and this correlation was of the same magnitude as that between social self-efficacy and the probability of success in social goals. Besides social self-efficacy, extraversion and conscientiousness showed significant correlations in the expected direction with the probability of success in social goals. We did not find a significant correlation between the probability of success in social goals and preparations for vocational training.

Bivariate correlations do not allow conclusions to be drawn on the relative importance of variables, however. Thus, we computed two separate multiple regression analyses to further test our assumptions. To prevent the accumulation of suppressor effects, only the variables that showed significant correlations with the criterion were entered in the regression equation and accepted as significant predictors if $p < 0.05$. This procedure allows the stable effects to be more pronounced and the unstable effects to be less important. The results of these regression analyses are shown in Figure 14.1. For the vocational goals, both beliefs in a just world, social self-efficacy, preparation for vocational training, neuroticism, openness and conscientiousness were entered into the regression procedure. Four significant predictors emerged from the regression. The more the adolescents endorsed the general BJW, the less neurotic and the more conscientious they were, and the more preparations they had made for vocational training, the higher the estimated probability of success in their vocational goals (see Figure 14.1). Together, the predictor variables explained 12 per cent of the variance. For the social goals, both beliefs in a just world, social self-efficacy, extraversion and conscientiousness were entered in the regression procedure. Two significant predictors emerged from the regression. The more the adolescents believed in a personal just world and the stronger their social self-efficacy, the higher their estimated probability of success in social goals (see Figure 14.1). Together, the two predictors explained 5 per cent of the variance.

Discussion

In sum, the present findings show that the general and the personal BJW are significant predictors of social and vocational goals, specifically of the probability of success in these goals. Adolescents with stronger beliefs in a just world assign a higher probability of success to their goals than do adolescents with a weaker BJW. This holds true even when concurrent predictors are entered into the regression equation. Furthermore, an important

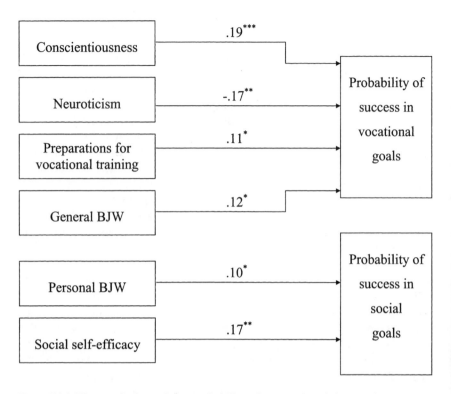

Figure 14.1 The prediction of the probability of success in adolescents' vocational and social goals (BJW = belief in a just world; standardised regression coefficients; $*p<0.05$; $**p<0.01$; $***p<0.001$).

new finding emerged. Although both BJWs correlated with both goals to a comparable degree, the multiple regression revealed that the personal and general BJW were predictive of different goal contents: the general BJW was related to vocational goals and the personal BJW to social goals. This supports the need for a distinction between a personal and general domain of the BJW and adds to the specific description of the two goal contents.

The probability of success in vocational goals was enhanced by the general BJW and additionally by intense preparation for vocational training, low neuroticism and high conscientiousness. This is in line with previous studies (Little, 1989; Little *et al.*, 1992). Personality, measured in terms of conscientiousness and neuroticism, predicted the probability of success in vocational goals. Furthermore and as expected, investments in goal attainment – here, preparations for vocational training – seem to increase the probability of success in vocational goals. In addition to all these factors, adolescents were most likely to believe that they would be able to achieve their goals if they had a strong general BJW, and if the impact of this general BJW was of a similar magnitude to that of their preparations for vocational training. Finally, on the bivariate level, social self-efficacy had shown a significant correlation with the probability of success in vocational goals, of the same magnitude as that with social goals. Although it is plausible to assume that social self-efficacy is also important in the vocational realm, in the multiple regression, the relation was no longer significant. Social self-efficacy showed a significant correlation with conscientiousness and neuroticism. This suggests that personality and social self-efficacy might explain the same portion of variance in the criterion. Thus, the multiple regression for the probability of success in vocational goals revealed only conscientiousness and neuroticism, but not social self-efficacy, to be influential.

The probability of success in social goals was enhanced by a strong personal BJW and additionally by strong social self-efficacy. The more the adolescents believed that the world is fair for them personally, and the more convinced they were that they can actively influence the outcomes of social situations, the higher their expectations of success in their personal goals. In addition to these two predictors, we had expected that strong extraversion would significantly increase the probability of success of social goals. Extraversion, shown to be related to social goals in prior research (Little *et al.*, 1992), displayed a significant bivariate correlation with the probability of success in social goals, but had no such effect in the multiple regression. The reason for this could be the comparatively high correlation of extraversion with social self-efficacy. As both constructs were related, they might explain the same portion of variance in the criterion, meaning that only one predictor has a significant influence.

The limitations of the present study relate to three main points. First, we conducted our research with German high school students attending the 9th grade of *Realschule* (see Note 2). Therefore, it is questionable if our findings can be generalised to adolescents of other age groups, school education, or nationality. Second, although we have presented our findings in a way that suggests causality, our conclusions must remain preliminary, because our data were cross-sectional in nature. Future studies may profit from replicating the present findings in a longitudinal design to test the causal nature of the relationships reported here. Third, our study focused on one goal dimension only, namely the subjective probability of success. Even though this dimension has been shown to be intimately associated with a person's commitment to his or her personal goals, future studies should include additional goal dimensions associated with commitment, such as goal importance (Metz-Göckel and Leffelsend, 2001), or include direct measures of goal commitment (e.g. Brunstein, 1993) in the assessment of adolescents' vocational and social goals.

Our data provide a further piece of evidence indicating that the distinction between the general and personal BJW is indeed useful and justified. Both the general and the personal BJW were predictive for the probability

244   D. Dette, J. Stöber and C. Dalbert

of success. On the bivariate level, both BJWs showed significant correlations with the probabilities of success in each content area. Interestingly, however, in the multiple regression, the general and personal belief were predictive of different goal contents. This finding is quite new, but is compatible with recent research (Dalbert, 1999, 2001). In our sample of school students, vocational goals were predicted by the general BJW. A possible explanation for this could be that vocational goals, which are still somewhat abstract for the students, are less closely related to their personal experiences. This corresponds with the general BJW, which is more distant from personal experience. Social goals, on the other hand, are probably closer and more familiar to the students. These were related to the personal BJW, which is likewise closer to personal experience. Thus far, the BJW has seldom been included in personal goal research (e.g. Hafer, 2000). Our results provide useful information in this respect. The belief in a just world fosters a positive evaluation of the probability of success, which in turn strengthens goal commitment.

Conclusion

These results have several theoretical and practical implications. The BJW with its two facets, general and personal BJW, showed significant relations to personal goals, specifically to the probability of success in vocational and social goals. Moreover, the general and personal BJW were predictive for different areas of goal content. Thus, the theoretical distinction between a general and a personal BJW also seems to be useful in relation to personal goals, and should be examined in more detail in further research. The practical implications of our study are of equal importance. At the start of this chapter, we asked how adolescents could be helped to select and pursue their personal goals. In order to assist adolescents to master their transition into adulthood, it may be useful not only to support their efforts for goal attainment, but also to strengthen their belief in a just world.

Acknowledgements

Parts of the results described in this chapter were presented at the 8th Biennial Conference of the European Association for Research on Adolescence, 3–7 September 2002, Oxford, UK, and at the 43rd Conference of the Deutsche Gesellschaft für Psychologie [German Psychological Society], 22–26 September 2002, Berlin, Germany.

Notes

1 In Germany, school grades are counted consecutively. Thus, '9th grade of high school' refers to the 9th year from the start of schooling.

BJW and vocational and social goals   245

2 Germany has a three-tier system of secondary school education, with the *Realschule* representing the middle level. Many students attending *Realschule* leave secondary school education after 10th grade to begin vocational training. Thus, for *Realschule* students, the 9th grade is the year before graduation, and the time when choices about future professions have to be made.

References

Bandura, A. (1977) 'Self-efficacy: Toward a unifying theory of behavioral change', *Psychological Review*, 84: 191–215.

Bandura, A. (1995) *Self-efficacy: The Exercise of Control.* New York: Freeman.

Block, J. (1995) 'A contrarian view of the five-factor approach to personality description', *Psychological Bulletin*, 117: 187–215.

Borkenau, P. and Ostendorf, F. (1993) *NEO-Fünf-Faktoren Inventar (NEO-FFI)* [NEO Five Factor Inventory (NEO-FFI)], Göttingen: Hogrefe.

Brunstein, J.C. (1993) 'Personal goals and subjective well-being: A longitudinal study', *Journal of Personality and Social Psychology*, 65: 1061–70.

Brunstein, J.C. and Maier, G.W. (1996) 'Persönliche Ziele: Ein Überblick zum Stand der Forschung [Personal goals: An overview of the current state of research], *Psychologische Rundschau*, 47: 146–60.

Brunstein, J.C., Dangelmayer, G. and Schultheiss, O.C. (1996) 'Personal goals and social support in close relationships: Effects on relationship mood and marital satisfaction', *Journal of Personality and Social Psychology*, 71: 1006–19.

Cantor, N. and Kihlstrom, J.F. (1987) *Personality and Social Intelligence*, Englewood Cliffs, NJ: Prentice-Hall.

Costa, P.T., Jr. and McCrae, R.R. (1992) *Revised NEO Personality Inventory (NEO PI-R) and NEO Five Factor Inventory: Professional Manual*, Odessa, FL: Psychological Assessment Resources.

Dalbert, C. (1997) 'Coping with an unjust fate: The case of structural unemployment', *Social Justice Research*, 10: 175–89.

Dalbert, C. (1999) 'The world is more just for me than generally: About the Personal Belief in a Just World Scale's validity', *Social Justice Research*, 12: 79–98.

Dalbert, C. (2001) *The Justice Motive as a Personal Resource: Dealing with Challenges and Critical Life Events*, New York: Kluwer Academic/Plenum Publishers.

Dalbert, C. (2002) 'Beliefs in a just world as a buffer against anger', *Social Justice Research*, 15: 123–45.

Dalbert, C., Montada, L. and Schmitt, M. (1987) 'Glaube an eine gerechte Welt als Motiv: Validierungskorrelate zweier Skalen' [The belief in a just world as a motive: Validation of two scales], *Psychologische Beiträge*, 29: 596–615.

Dreher, E. and Dreher, M. (1985) 'Entwicklungsaufgaben im Jugendalter: Bedeutsamkeit und Bewältigungskonzepte' [Developmental tasks of adolescence: Importance and coping concepts], in Liepmann, D. and Stiksrud, A. (eds), *Entwicklungsaufgaben und Bewältigungsprobleme in der Adoleszenz*, Göttingen: Hogrefe.

Emmons, R.A. (1986) 'Personal strivings: An approach to personality and subjective well-being', *Journal of Personality and Social Psychology*, 51: 1058–68.

Emmons, R.A. (1989) 'The personal striving approach to personality', in Pervin, L.A. (ed.) *Goal Concepts in Personality and Social Psychology*, Hillsdale, NJ: Erlbaum.

246   *D. Dette, J. Stöber and C. Dalbert*

Emmons, R.A. (1997) 'Motives and life goals', in Hogan, R., Johnson, J. and Briggs, S. (eds), *Handbook of Personality Psychology*, San Diego, CA: Academic Press.

Erikson, E.H. (1959) Identity and the life cycle. *Psychological Issues, 1 (Monographs No. 1).*

Furnham, A. and Procter, E. (1989) 'Belief in a just world: Review and critique of the individual difference literature', *British Journal of Social Psychology*, 28: 365–84.

Hafer, C.L. (2000) 'Investment in long-term goals and commitment to just means drive the need to believe in a just world', *Personality and Social Psychology Bulletin*, 26: 1059–73.

Hafer, C.L. and Olson, J.M. (1993) 'Beliefs in a just world, discontent, and assertive actions by working women', *Personality and Social Psychology Bulletin*, 19: 30–8.

Havighurst, R.J. (1948) *Developmental Tasks and Education*, New York: Longman.

Hollenbeck, J.R. and Klein, H.J. (1987) 'Goal commitment and the goal-setting process: Problems, prospects, and proposals for future research', *Journal of Applied Psychology*, 72: 212–20.

John, O.P. (1990) 'The "Big Five" factor taxonomy: Dimensions of personality in the natural language and in questionnaires', in Pervin, L.A. (ed.), *Handbook of Personality: Theory and Research*, New York: Guilford.

Klinger, E. (1977) *Meaning and Void: Inner Experience and the Incentives in People's Lives*, Minneapolis, MN: University of Minnesota Press.

Klinger, E. (1987) 'The Interview Questionnaire technique: Reliability and validity of a mixed idiographic–nomothetic measure of motivation', in Butcher, J.N. and Spielberger, C.D. (eds), *Advances in Personality Assessment*, 6: 31–48, Hillsdale, NJ: Erlbaum.

Lanz, M. and Rosnati, R. (2002) 'Adolescents' and young adults' construction of the future: Effects of family relations, self-esteem, and sense of coherence', in Trempala, J. and Malmberg, L.E. (eds), *Adolescents' Future-orientation: Theory and Research*, Frankfurt am Main: Peter Lang.

Lerner, M.J. (1965) 'Evaluation of performance as a function of performer's reward and attractiveness', *Journal of Personality and Social Psychology*, 1: 355–60.

Lerner, M.J. and Miller, D.T. (1978) 'Just world research and the attribution process: Looking back and ahead', *Psychological Bulletin*, 85: 1030–51.

Lipkus, I.M., Dalbert, C. and Siegler, I.C. (1996) 'The importance of distinguishing the belief in a just world for self versus others', *Personality and Social Psychology Bulletin*, 22: 666–77.

Little, B.R. (1983) 'Personal projects: A rationale and method for investigation', *Environment and Behavior*, 15: 273–309.

Little, B.R. (1989) 'Personal project analysis: Trivial pursuits, magnificent obsessions, and the search for coherence', in Buss, D.M. and Cantor, N. (eds), *Personality Psychology: Recent Trends and Emerging Directions*, New York: Springer.

Little, B.R., Lecci, L. and Watkinson, B. (1992) 'Personality and personal projects: Linking Big Five and PAC units of analysis', *Journal of Personality*, 60: 501–25.

Locke, E.A. and Latham, G.P. (1990) *A Theory of Goal Setting and Task Performance*, Englewood Cliffs, NJ: Prentice-Hall.

Marcia, J.E. (1966) 'Development and validation of ego-identity status', *Journal of Personality and Social Psychology*, 3: 551–8.

McAdams, D.P. (1992) 'The five-factor model in personality: A critical appraisal', *Journal of Personality*, 60: 329–61.

BJW and vocational and social goals 247

Metz-Göckel, H. and Leffelsend, S. (2001) 'Motivationale Determinanten der Zielbindung im Studium' [Motivational determinants of goal commitment at university], *Zeitschrift für Psychologie*, 209: 153–73.

Nurmi, J.-E. (1989) 'Development of orientation to the future during early adolescence: A four-year longitudinal study and two cross-sectional comparisons', *International Journal of Psychology*, 24: 195–214.

Nurmi, J.-E. (1991) 'How do adolescents see their future? A review of the development of future orientation and planning', *Developmental Review*, 11: 1–59.

Nurmi, J.-E. (1993) 'Adolescent development in an age-graded context: The role of personal beliefs, goals, and strategies in the tackling of developmental tasks and standards', *International Journal of Behavioral Development*, 16: 169–89.

Nurmi, J.-E., Poole, M.E. and Kalakoski, V. (1994) 'Age differences in adolescent future-oriented goals, concerns, and related temporal extension in different sociocultural contexts', *Journal of Youth and Adolescence*, 23: 471–87.

Oerter, R. and Dreher, E. (1995) 'Jugendalter' [Adolescence], in Oerter, R. and Montada, L. (eds), *Entwicklungspsychologie*, Weinheim: PVU.

Pöhlmann, K. (2001) 'Agency- and communion-orientation in life goals: Impacts on goal pursuit strategies and psychological well-being', in Schmuck, P. and Sheldon, K.M. (eds), *Life Goals and Well-being: Towards a Positive Psychology of Human Striving*, Seattle: Hogrefe and Huber.

Rubin, Z. and Peplau, L.A. (1973) 'Belief in a just world and reactions to another's lot: A study of participants in the national draft lottery', *Journal of Social Issues*, 29: 73–93.

Rubin, Z. and Peplau, L.A. (1975) 'Who believes in a just world?', *Journal of Social Issues*, 31: 65–89.

Satow, L. and Mittag, W. (1999) 'Selbstwirksamkeitserwartung im Umgang mit sozialen Anforderungen (WIRKSOZ) [Self-efficacy when facing social demands], in Schwarzer, R. and Jerusalem, M. (eds), *Skalen zur Erfassung von Lehrer-und Schülermerkmalen*, Berlin: Free University of Berlin and Humboldt University of Berlin.

Scholte, R.J.H., van Lieshout, C.F.M. and van Aken, M.A.G. (2001) 'Perceived relational support in adolescence: Dimensions, configurations, and adolescent adjustment', *Journal of Research on Adolescence*, 11: 71–94.

Trautwein, U., Watermann, R.R., Maaz, K., Nagy, G., Köller, O., Lüdtke, O. and Baumert, J. (2004) 'Bildungsverläufe und psychosoziale Entwicklung im Jugend- und jungen Erwachsenenalter (BIJU)', Dokumentation Welle 6 [Educational course and psychosocial development in adolescence and early adulthood (BIJU) Wave 6 Working Paper: Unpublished manuscript], Berlin: Max-Planck-Institut für Bildungsforschung: Unveröffentlichtes Manuskript.

Vrugt, A., Oort, F.J. and Zeeberg, C. (2002) 'Goal orientations, perceived self-efficacy and study results amongst beginners and advanced students', *British Journal of Educational Psychology*, 72: 385–97.

Wentzel, K.R. (1991) 'Social and academic goals at school: Motivation and achievement in context', *Advances in Motivation and Achievement*, 7: 185–212.

Zuckerman, M. (1975) 'Belief in a just world and altruistic behavior', *Journal of Personality and Social Psychology*, 31: 972–6.

Zuckerman, M. and Gerbasi, K.C. (1977) 'Belief in a just world and trust', *Journal of Research in Personality*, 11: 306–17.

15 Developmental trajectories and developmental functions of the belief in a just world

Some concluding remarks

Claudia Dalbert and Hedvig Sallay

All studies in this volume address the belief in a just world construct introduced by Melvin J. Lerner (e.g. 1980). The volume stands out from the majority of previous justice psychology publications in two ways: (a) it brings together studies from different European countries, (b) it fuses justice psychology and developmental psychology. Furthermore, picking up on recent theorising, it describes the three – mostly adaptive – functions of the belief in a just world (Dalbert, 2001), focusing on its developmental functions in adolescence and young adulthood. In this concluding chapter, we would like to summarise some of the findings presented in this volume, guided by the following questions. (a) What are the developmental trajectories of the belief in a just world (BJW)? (b) Which conditions impact on its development? (c) What can we learn about the nature of the BJW? (d) How does the BJW shape development during adolescence and young adulthood? (e) Is the justice motive theory cross-culturally valid?

Developmental trajectories

The age curve

During late childhood, the childish belief in immanent justice – i.e. the belief that justice emanates from events and occurrences themselves – transforms into the belief in a just world, the strength of which differs individually, but which is upheld across the life-span. Maes and Schmitt (Chapter 5) describe a U-shaped age curve for the general BJW, which corresponds perfectly to a comparable age curve described by Dalbert (2001), also observed in Germany. The belief in a generally just world, a world which is essentially just, decreases significantly during adolescence and young adulthood, remains relatively stable during adulthood, and increases again slightly in late adulthood and old age. Because these data were gained by cross-sectional comparison of different age groups, however, these mean differences may not mirror a developmental trajectory, but a cohort effect, with people born at different times adapting to

Some concluding remarks   249

the zeitgeist of their childhood and youth in different ways. Maes and Schmitt discuss this point carefully. One important argument they make concerns the BJW's relationships with fascism and authoritarianism. BJW and authoritarianism are positively correlated (Furnham and Procter, 1989). If the zeitgeist explanation were true, these relationships should be especially strong among those who grew up in Germany during the fascist era and, thus, may explain the higher BJW in old age. However, the correlations of BJW with fascism and authoritarianism observed by Maes and Schmitt (Chapter 5) were equally high for all adult age groups, independent of whether they were born during or after the fascist period. We thus agree with their conclusion that the differences observed between the age groups can be interpreted as developmental differences.

The transition from adolescence to adulthood is characterised by the school-to-work transition and by a change in the family situation (e.g. leaving the family of origin; starting a family of one's own), often accompanied by a geographical move. Overall, this transition process forces young adults to widen their social experiences. However, the wider the social environment, the more opportunity young people have to observe or experience unfairness. In the long run, this confrontation with injustice may prompt a steady decrease in the BJW (Dalbert, 2001). Even so, the BJW remains capable of enhancing the prospects for positive action. Youth and adulthood are developmental periods during which individuals are challenged to actively influence the life course and to try to get a just share of life. The results presented by Maes and Schmitt (Chapter 5) demonstrate this function of the BJW for adolescents and young adults. Later in life, however, as prospective life-span shortens, people feel compelled to make peace with their lives. They need a psychological buffer to help them find meaning in their – more or less irreversible – life course. BJW can be seen as such a buffer, and this may explain why BJW increases again in late adulthood and old age (Dalbert, 2001).

Developmental sequence of the personal and the general belief in a just world

The belief in a just world can be differentiated into the belief in a general just world, in which everybody is treated justly, and the belief in a personal just world, where events in one's own life tend to be just. We do not yet know in which sequence the two beliefs develop, or indeed whether there is a fixed sequence of development. However, two studies presented in this book reveal that adolescents (aged around 16 to 17 in the study by Dalbert and Dzuka [Chapter 7] and 15 in the study by Dette *et al.*, [Chapter 14]) already differentiate between the two beliefs. In both studies, the correlations between the two beliefs were of medium magnitude ($0.33 \leqslant r \leqslant 0.63$), and each belief was shown to perform different

250   *C. Dalbert and H. Sallay*

functions. The results presented by Dalbert and Radant (Chapter 2) do allow us to speculate about the developmental sequence of general and personal BJW, however. Personal BJW revealed stable relationships with parenting, and a huge overlap with the perception of a just family climate. This relationship was even stronger for young adolescents than for university students. Although the two BJWs tend to be positively correlated, general BJW was unrelated to parenting and only weakly correlated with the perception of a just family climate. Thus, the general BJW seems to be less closely linked to experiences in the family than the personal BJW. Furthermore, abstract reasoning develops during adolescence and the general BJW consists of more abstract representations of the world. Taken collectively, it seems that children first transform their childish belief in immanent justice into the belief in a personal just world and later, during adolescence, differentiate the general BJW from this personal BJW.

Developmental conditions

According to Piaget (1932/1997), young children believe in immanent justice. Once the belief in a (personal) just world has emerged during late childhood, the BJW shows remarkable inter-individual differences. This raises the question of which developmental conditions produce these individual differences. Studies in this volume identify at least four developmental conditions that result in individually varying BJW: transmission within the family, neuroticism, parenting and family structure.

Parent–offspring transmission

Schönpflug and Bilz (Chapter 4) observed a direct transmission of the BJW from parents to their children. The more the parents believed in a just world, the stronger their children's BJW. In contrast, Dalbert and Radant (Chapter 2) did not observe direct transmission from parents to their offspring. This may be due to several differences between the two studies. The Schönpflug and Bilz study (Chapter 4) was conducted in East Germany, using the general BJW scale and spanning the 14–24 age group. The Dalbert and Radant study (Study 2, Chapter 2) was conducted in southern West Germany, using the personal BJW scale and spanning the 10–14 age bracket. In line with Schönpflug and Bilz, we suspect that the observed difference in direct transmission may be due to the age difference in the two samples. The direct relationship between the BJWs of parents and their offspring seems to become stronger as the children get older. Social attitudes involve genetic as well as environmental variance. The impact of hereditary factors increases with age, presumably because individuals entering adolescence and adulthood are granted more freedom to seek out environments that are compatible with their own genetic predispositions, and hence to develop along these lines. As far as

Some concluding remarks 251

direct transmission indicates biological transmission, it should thus increase with age. Schönpflug and Bilz argue that social transmission should also increase with age: while adolescents strive for individuation and autonomy and thus shy away from parental influences, these attitudes may have stabilised by young adulthood, meaning that young adults are more likely to accept parental influences.

It is not only the offspring's age that shapes direct transmission, however. Schönpflug and Bilz examined the transmission channels – i.e. the conditions intensifying the transmission process – and identified three transmission channels for the BJW. These are: (a) similarity of the parental BJWs, i.e. if both parents are high in BJW, their children are also likely to develop a strong belief in a just world, (b) children's acceptance of their parents as role models, and (c) parents' positive evaluation of their own adaptation to the labour market: the more the offspring accepted their parents as role models, and the more the parents considered themselves to be positively adapted to the labour market, the stronger the direct transmission of the BJW. The latter was especially true of fathers, but not of mothers. Overall, however, fathers and mothers had an equal impact on transmission. In sum, direct parent–offspring transmission of the BJW seems to be more likely in young adulthood than in adolescence. Furthermore, it becomes stronger when efficient transmission channels are in place.

Neuroticism

Systematic research has shown that BJW reveals adaptive relationships with global personality dimensions. In particular, non-neurotic persons develop stronger beliefs in a personally just world than neurotic persons. Dalbert and Dzuka (Chapter 7) reviewed studies on this topic and confirmed this relationship for Slovakian and German adolescents. Personality is hierarchically structured. Global personality dimensions such as neuroticism are thought to be the highest and most stable level of personality and, as such, to determine lower-level personality dimensions, such as the BJW. We can thus conclude that neuroticism shapes the BJW's development. The unpredictability and over-sensitivity of neurotic persons may make them susceptible to different experiences during childhood and adolescence. For example, they may be more likely to feel unjustly treated, and thus to develop a weaker BJW than their non-neurotic counterparts. We would like to recommend including neuroticism in future developmental studies on BJW and investigating how the effect of neuroticism on BJW is mediated.

252   *C. Dalbert and H. Sallay*

Parenting

The influence of parenting was investigated in two studies in this volume (Dalbert and Radant, Chapter 2; Sallay and Dalbert, Chapter 3). Both studies implemented the same approach, comparing nurture, restriction and the perception of the family climate as just. Nurture was reflected by a family orientation with a low rate of conflict, manipulation and inconsistent parenting, and restriction was defined as a family with a strong rule orientation, a constant parenting attitude and the parenting aim of conformity. Both studies revealed similar patterns of results. The more nurture the offspring experienced and the more they perceived the climate of their family of origin to be just, the stronger their beliefs in a just world. Moreover, parenting and just family climate were more closely associated with the personal, than with the general BJW. Restriction, the family structure (intact vs. one-parent family, see below), and the gender of the child or parent made little or no difference. In other words, the pattern of results held for Hungarian and German subjects; for those growing up with both parents or with lone mothers; for boys and girls; for fathers and mothers. The more nurture parents can provide, the stronger the BJW developed by their children, i.e. the more strongly they believe that they will be treated justly in life.

Family structure

Finally, Sallay and Dalbert (Chapter 3) revealed an effect of family structure. Whether a person grows up with both parents or with their mother only has little effect on the relationship between parenting and BJW, but it does seem to affect the strength of the BJW. People who grew up with only their mother have a weaker belief in a personal just world, but a stronger belief in a general just world, than those who grew up with both parents. Because this study into the impact of family structure was conducted in retrospect, it is unclear whether the differences in BJW were already present in late childhood, or developed later in adolescence or young adulthood. However, there were no systematic differences in the parenting styles described by children brought up in the two family structures. Thus, we do not know what triggers these differences. It seems likely that children in one-parent families feel deprived about growing up with just one parent and are thus less convinced that the world is fair to them personally, or that they usually get what they deserve. But why do they develop a stronger belief in a general just world? Several explanations are possible. (a) There may be a direct causal link between the personal and the general BJW, resulting in compensating beliefs. The weaker the personal BJW becomes, the stronger the general BJW will grow, and vice versa. This kind of equilibrium between the two beliefs has already been observed in groups of adolescents with different cognitive abilities

Some concluding remarks   253

(Dalbert, 2001). (b) The world outside the family may appear more just than the world within the one-parent family. Growing up in one-parent families may generate some kind of contrasting comparison phenomenon, leading to an overestimation of injustice in one's own world and an underestimation of justice problems in the world at large. Further research is needed to cast light on the causal mechanisms producing this family structure effect.

About the nature of the belief in a just world

Can the BJW be seen as a stable personality dimension which can be differentiated from specific justice perceptions and, if so, does it represent a justice motive or does it imply a socially learned attitude, namely self-interest (Montada, 1998)? Several studies described in this volume address this question. In particular, two studies present findings to suggest that the BJW indicates a justice motive, at least in adolescence, while two further studies substantiate the notion that BJW is a relatively stable construct that can be differentiated from specific justice perceptions.

BJW as a justice motive

Dalbert and Radant's parenting study (Chapter 2) revealed a strong and unique relationship between nurture in the family and the BJW. The more nurture parents can provide, the stronger the belief in a just world developed by their children, and the deeper their trust in being treated fairly in life. In contrast, restriction in the family, although significantly associated with the perception of a just family climate, does not affect the BJW. This pattern of results seems to indicate that BJW is not socially learned – i.e. by a strong rule-orientation in the family – but is shaped by early emotional experiences. Motives are typically learned by early emotional experiences (McClelland et al., 1989; Spangler, 1992). Thus, the results of this study are in line with the view that the BJW is indicative of a justice motive.

Maes and Schmitt (Chapter 5) compared correlational patterns concerning BJW for different age groups and came to a similar conclusion. In adolescence and young adulthood, BJW correlates with an idealistic worldview, i.e. with the aspiration to work towards a good life and to identify with one's work. In adulthood and old age, BJW is associated with conservative socio-political ideologies. Maes and Schmitt conclude that the correlational pattern in the younger age group is more in line with the notion of a justice motive, while the correlational pattern in the older age groups is more consistent with the adoption of a conservative socio-political ideology as a result of secondary socialisation. In sum, we may conclude that the BJW is indicative of a justice motive, which is promoted by nurture in the family. Later in life, BJW may be transformed by

254   C. Dalbert and H. Sallay

experiences in the working life, which is more strongly governed by the myth of self-interest (Miller, 1999). In this stage of life, BJW may indicate a justice motive as well as a social attitude.

In young adulthood, direct transmission can be observed from the parents' to their children's BJW. At the same time, BJW as a justice motive may begin to fuse with BJW as a social attitude – presumably reflecting mainly self-interest. In the course of development, this fusion in the meaning of the BJW may broaden, prompted by secondary socialisation in the working life. Cubela Adoric (Chapter 12) provides us with further insight into this process. It is not so much the number of critical experiences *per se* – e.g. rejections of unemployed individuals' job applications – that seems to shape the BJW. Rather, the relationship between BJW and injustice experiences seems to be more important. Individuals who feel that they are regularly treated unjustly at their workplace or that they are often treated unfairly during their job search reveal a diminished BJW, and vice versa. As yet, the direction of the causal relationship is unclear. However, this finding lends support to Maes and Schmitt's notion that secondary socialisation in the professional life impacts on the BJW and triggers the fusion of its meaning as a justice motive with that of a socially learned attitude.

BJW and justice perceptions

The study by Dalbert and Radant (Chapter 2) provides insights into the nature of BJW and its relationship with justice perceptions. In early childhood, it seems that the belief in immanent justice and justice perceptions of different domains cannot be differentiated. Justice is assumed to originate from events and occurrences themselves and thus all domains in the childish world are seen as just, particularly the family. In early adolescence, the personal belief in a just world and the perception of a just family climate can be differentiated, although there is still a huge overlap. For young adults, this overlap between the personal BJW and the perception of a just family climate is still large, but no longer as pronounced. This finding supports the hypothesis that BJW and justice perceptions do not represent the same construct. With ongoing development, the BJW and justice perceptions seem to become increasingly disentangled. Two more results point in this direction. A just family climate was associated with both restriction and nurture in the family, but personal BJW only revealed a direct association with nurture. It seems that all experiences in the family impact on the perception of a just family climate, but that only experiences of nurture shape the personal BJW. Furthermore, Sallay (Chapter 13) investigated the impact of BJW and anticipated justice at the workplace on the mental health of young adults about to enter the job market. It emerged that both BJW and anticipated justice at the workplace shaped the young adults' mental health, again suggesting that justice

Some concluding remarks   255

perceptions and the BJW carry different meanings. Justice perceptions are evidently based on concrete experiences and observations within a given field such as the family or the workplace, whereas the BJW is more of a general trust in justice, formed by early experiences in life.

Cubela Adoric's findings (Chapter 12) lend further support to the notion that BJW is a highly stable personality characteristic, and that only enduring experiences such as long-term unemployment – the subjects in her study had been unemployed for an average of eight years – seem to have the potential to shape it. Sallay's study (Chapter 13) points in the same direction. Sallay compared anticipated justice at the workplace and BJW at two points in time, 1999 and 2001 in Hungary. Young adults entering the Hungarian job market were found to have higher expectations of justice at the workplace in 2001 than in 1999, but there was no change in either the general or the personal BJW over this time. This again reflects the overall stability of the BJW.

Developmental functions in adolescence and young adulthood

Besides the developmental trajectory of the BJW and the conditions shaping it, the functions of the BJW in adolescence and young adulthood were closely investigated. Dalbert (2001) has identified three main functions of the BJW: (a) it endows individuals with the confidence that they will be treated justly by others and will not fall victim to an unforeseeable disaster, (b) it provides a conceptual framework which helps individuals to interpret the events of their personal life in a meaningful way, and (c) it is indicative of the personal contract and the obligation to behave justly. Although the first two functions are highlighted in several of the studies described in this book, the third function is only investigated by Otto and Dalbert (Chapter 10), who found that the stronger young male prisoners' belief in a personal just world, the more likely they are to stick to prison rules. In the following section, we focus on results concerning the other two functions and on the BJW's impact on mental health.

Belief in a just world, trust and BJW's developmental consequences

The association between BJW and trust was investigated directly, and by focusing on the consequences of this trust. The hypothesis that BJW strengthens trust in others is supported by Correia and Vala (Chapter 6). In a representative sample of Portuguese young adults, they found the expected positive relationship between BJW and institutional, but not interpersonal trust. The more the individuals believed in a just world, the more trust they revealed in 15 institutions, from the church to the United Nations. Contrary to expectations, the expected association between BJW and interpersonal trust was not confirmed (e.g. Dalbert, 2001; Zuckerman

256   C. Dalbert and H. Sallay

and Gerbasi, 1977). However, this may be due to the low reliability of the interpersonal trust variable, which was measured with a one-item rating only.

One important developmental consequence of BJW and the trust it provides is the impact on legal socialisation. Developing a positive attitude towards institutional authorities such as the school, the police and the law is an important developmental task in adolescence. Adolescents have to learn that institutions and the persons representing them place legitimate restrictions on individual behaviour (e.g. Emler and Reicher, 1987). This seems to be an important precondition for developing the intrinsic motivation to obey the law and institutional rules. Dalbert (Chapter 8) summarises studies showing that justice experiences in school are a crucial factor in the development of positive attitudes towards the school authorities, which in turn foster a positive attitude towards other institutional authorities. BJW promotes justice perceptions in school where grades or general teacher behaviour are concerned, and thus – directly or mediated by these justice perceptions – fosters the development of institutional trust, which in turn seems to promote behaviour compliant with legal and institutional rules.

The BJW's function of providing trust also has adaptive consequences for the school career itself. Maes and Kals (Chapter 9) identify a whole set of school-related variables that are associated with the BJW and, in particular, the belief that injustices will be compensated (belief in ultimate justice). A strong belief in ultimate justice enables students to develop a strong learning motivation and to take pride in their achievements. Furthermore, Dalbert (Chapter 8) summarises studies evidencing a positive association between BJW and school-related self-efficacy. Students with a strong BJW feel better able to cope with school-related challenges, and there is much evidence to show that self-efficacy is conducive to a successful school career. In all, BJW seems to be a useful resource for a successful school career, and its effects appear to be mediated by factors such as academic motivation, pride and school-related self-efficacy.

Furthermore, because BJW endows individuals with the confidence that they will be treated fairly in life, it enables them to invest in their vocational career and social life course. Other important developmental tasks during adolescence include the school-to-work transition and first moves towards starting a family of one's own. By supporting individual trust in institutions and in others, BJW gives people confidence in being treated justly by others and getting what they deserve. An important consequence of this kind of trust is the belief that personal goals can be attained. Otto and Dalbert and Dette et al. (Chapters 10 and 14) evidenced a positive relationship between BJW and the belief in successful goal attainment for groups of adolescents as diverse as school leavers and juvenile prisoners. The more these adolescents believed in a personal just world, the more convinced they were that they could achieve their personal goals, such as

Some concluding remarks   257

going unpunished in the future, coming off drugs, finding a full-time job, becoming a mechanic, having a romantic relationship, getting married, or starting a family. It is well documented that the belief in successful goal attainment is a major predictor of goal commitment. Furthermore, by providing trust, BJW strengthens self-efficacy in different domains (e.g. social, school-specific). In particular, the stronger their BJW, the better adolescents are able to cope with social demands (Dette *et al.*, Chapter 14). Mediated by the belief in goal attainment and social self-efficacy, BJW can thus be seen as an important resource for adolescents and young adults, allowing them to invest in their personal social and vocational goals, the two most important goal domains for adolescents and young adults (e.g. Nurmi *et al.*, 1994).

Belief in a just world, assimilation of injustice and its developmental consequences

The second function of the BJW – providing individuals with a conceptual framework that helps them to interpret the events of their personal life in a meaningful way – is best illustrated by the association between BJW and the assimilation of injustice. The more individuals believe in a just world, the more they evaluate events in their life as just. In this volume, this hypothesis is confirmed in three domains of life (legal, vocational, scholastic). The more juvenile prisoners believed in a just world (Otto and Dalbert, Chapter 10), the more they evaluated their trial and their sentence as just and, in consequence, the more guilty they felt. Moreover, a strong BJW and, presumably, the ability to cope better with injustice, seems to strengthen young prisoners' ability to control their feelings of anger and outburst behaviour. This holds especially for those with a less serious criminal background. In the same vein, Cubela Adoric (Chapter 12) revealed an adaptive association between BJW and justice perceptions in the vocational domain in her investigation of long-term unemployed individuals and working young adults. Those with a high BJW rarely felt unjustly treated at the workplace or while looking for a job, they experienced fewer negative emotions, and were more likely to justify their experiences than those low in BJW. The vocational domain was also the focus of Sallay's study (Chapter 13). She found a similar pattern of results for university students entering the job market. The more the young adults believed in a personal just world, the more they anticipated their future workplace to be a just one. Both a strong belief in a personal BJW and the anticipation of a just workplace increased their subjective wellbeing. Moreover, this pattern of results held for both those young adults who had already found a job and those who where still seeking for one, and at different points in time (1999, 2001). Within the school domain, the same relationships were observed in several studies, summarised by Dalbert (Chapter 8). School students with a strong BJW, and those who

258   C. Dalbert and H. Sallay

perceived their teachers as treating them fairly, experienced school as less stressful than those with a weak BJW and those who felt that they were treated unjustly by their teachers. It was this deep-rooted belief in justice – rather than receiving poor or unfair grades – that explained distress in school.

In sum, the studies presented in this volume demonstrate that BJW facilitates the assimilation of injustice experiences – BJW and justice perceptions are consistently positively associated. Moreover, a very similar pattern of results is observed in different domains of life. Therefore, we would like to conclude that BJW helps people to cope with injustice experiences by finding meaning in their life and thus easing legal (re-)socialisation, facilitating a promising school career, and buffering the difficult school-to-work transition during adolescence and young adulthood.

BJW and mental health

The three functions of the BJW – endowing individuals with the trust in justice, enabling them to assimilate injustices and to avoid committing injustices themselves – all have the potential to strengthen individual mental health. The association between BJW and two dimensions of mental health – life satisfaction and self-esteem – is further clarified by various studies in this volume.

First, the well-documented relationship between BJW and life satisfaction (e.g. Dalbert, 1998) was thoroughly investigated and further validated. Correia and Vala (Chapter 6) revealed in two studies that the positive relationship between BJW and life satisfaction holds when controlled for dispositional optimism and internal locus of control, both of which are positively correlated with BJW and life satisfaction. Dalbert and Dzuka (Chapter 7) controlled this relationship for global personality factors – particularly neuroticism, which is negatively correlated with both BJW and subjective well-being and may thus be the cause of the positive association between the two – and evidenced the expected adaptive relationship between BJW and life satisfaction in three samples. Furthermore, they observed a similar pattern of results for positive, but not negative, affect. Finally, Maes and Kals (Chapter 9) complete this picture by providing evidence for a positive association between several satisfaction dimensions and the belief that injustice will be compensated among German school students. Overall, this volume presents evidence for a positive association between BJW and life satisfaction for Portuguese, Slovakian and German adolescents and young adults. Taken collectively, we can thus assume that the more individuals believe in a just world, the more satisfied they are with their life.

Second, self-esteem can also be regarded as an important dimension of mental health. The relationship between BJW and self-esteem seems to be complex. In two studies, Correia and Vala (Chapter 6) observed a positive

Some concluding remarks 259

bivariate correlation between self-esteem and BJW, but when controlled for optimism and internal locus of control – both of which were positively correlated with BJW and self-esteem – this relationship was no longer significant. In sum, no unique relationship was found between BJW and self-esteem. Maes and Schmitt (Chapter 5) cast further light on this relationship. They compared the correlational patterns between BJW and self-esteem for different age groups and showed that this relationship was only significant in the two oldest age groups, particularly in the oldest group of those aged over 65. In contrast, a global mental health scale correlated significantly with BJW in all age groups. The observations of Maes and Schmitt and Correira and Vala (Chapters 5 and 6) converge in the notion that BJW and self-esteem do not share a unique relationship during adolescence and young adulthood. In adulthood and old age, however, there may be a positive association between BJW and self-esteem. As one explanation for this phenomenon, Maes and Schmitt hypothesise that older people tend to interpret their personal experiences in a more consistent manner, aligning them with their fundamental beliefs like BJW. The more old adults believe in a just world, the less likely they are to see themselves as having been discriminated against earlier in life (for example, Lipkus and Siegler, 1993). This and other mechanisms may enable old adults with a strong BJW to strengthen their self-esteem.

Taken collectively, the pattern of results for BJW and mental health indicates that this relationship is mediated by different mechanisms at different ages. The functions of providing trust and encouraging people to behave fairly may produce the adaptive relationship between BJW and mental health, namely subjective well-being, in adolescence and young adulthood. The function of supporting the assimilation of unfairness by finding meaning in one's life seems to mediate the adaptive association between BJW and mental health, including self-esteem, particularly in old age and when coping with critical life-events (Dalbert, 2001).

Cross-cultural validity

All of the studies described in this book were conducted in Europe by experienced justice researchers, but for the most part in countries that had not previously been very visible in international justice psychology. In particular, BJW was investigated in Croatia, in different parts of Germany (including East and West Germany), in Hungary, Portugal and Slovakia. We can learn two important lessons from these cross-cultural comparisons.

All the results presented are consistent with justice motive theory and indicate that this theory – and, more precisely, the three functions of the belief in a just world – holds not only in North America and Germany, where most previous studies have been conducted, but in large parts of Europe, from Portugal to Slovakia. Cultural differences are apparently

260   *C. Dalbert and H. Sallay*

very small or non-existent. This finding of global validity corresponds with observations concerning simple mean differences in BJW in different countries. Cross-cultural studies have identified few significant differences in mean BJW. India and Israel have been rare exceptions (e.g. Furnham, 1993; for a review, see Dalbert, 1996). Combining these earlier results with the findings of this volume, we would like to conclude that justice motive theory is homogeneously valid, in most parts of North America and Europe, at least.

There is a second lesson to be learned from the present studies: European countries seem to be getting closer to one another. Dalbert and Katona-Sallay (1996) summarised studies conducted between 1991 and 1994 in Hungary, Slovenia, Slovakia and East Germany. Some of these studies revealed structural problems with the BJW construct – i.e. the BJW items did not form a homogeneous scale – immediately after the political transformations in Hungary and Slovenia. No such problems were observed in East Germany or Slovakia, however. The results from Slovenia and Hungary indicated that, after the dramatic political changes in Central Europe and the societal turmoil resulting from these societal transformation processes, the BJW construct seemed to collapse or to split into a belief in a just world and a belief in compensating justice. It may be that people living in times of great political and societal turmoil have difficulty believing in a just world and may accommodate their belief system by developing a belief that injustices will be compensated in the future and splitting this belief off from the belief that the world is basically a just place. Daily functioning now seems to have returned to normal in these countries, however. With the exception of the study on long-term unemployed individuals in Croatia, none of the recent studies conducted in Croatia, East Germany, Hungary and Slovakia described in this volume encountered problems with the BJW construct itself. This indicates that European countries are growing closer together.

Perspectives

The studies presented in this volume portray the belief in a just world as an important developmental resource in adolescence and young adulthood. The BJW's function of providing trust in the fairness of the world seems to be of particular importance during this stage of development. It enables adolescents and young adults to actively shape their development, i.e. their school and vocational career, and thus to attain their vocational and social goals. Thus far, however, more is known about the BJW as a resource for mental health, and its positive impact on coping and justice perceptions, than about the BJW as a resource for problem-focused coping. We need to find out more about the action-oriented potential of the BJW. For example, Dalbert (Chapter 11) evidenced its shortcomings with respect to coping with unemployment and Cubela Adoric (Chapter

Some concluding remarks 261

12) described the ambivalence between BJW and job search behaviour. Future studies need to shed further light on the action-oriented implications of the BJW, in and beyond the occupational domain.

Parenting, the family structure, global personality dimensions and direct parent–offspring transmission all seem to be factors simultaneously affecting the development of the BJW. Thus far, the few developmental studies on BJW have focused on just one or two of these developmental conditions. It is vital that the interplay of these different developmental conditions be explored in future studies.

Finally, further evidence needs to be provided for the developmental trajectory described in this book. In late childhood, the childish belief in immanent justice is transformed into a more mature belief in a personal just world which, later in adolescence and young adulthood, is differentiated into a personal and a general BJW. The meaning of the BJW also seems to change during the course of development. Whereas the BJW seems to indicate a justice motive in adolescence, it seems later to become a blend of a justice motive and socially learned attitudes – in response to diverse and decisive experiences in the vocational domain in particular. This fusion of different meanings underlying the BJW requires further investigation. Hence, studies are needed to disentangle the justice motive from a socially learned attitude and to test the assumption that they emerge at different points of development, prompted by divergent conditions.

Taken collectively, we hope to have shown that the justice motive and (in)justice experiences are important aspects of individual development in adolescence and young adulthood and that development cannot be fully understood without taking the justice motive into account. We hope that this synthesis of justice psychology and developmental psychology will be a productive one. In a recent review, Furnham (2003) predicted that just world research will survive for many years to come. Our hope is that these future investigations will provide further insights into the developmental trajectories and developmental functions of the belief in a just world.

References

Dalbert, C. (1996) *Über den Umgang mit Ungerechtigkeit. Eine Psychologische Analyse* [Dealing with injustice. A psychological analysis], Bern: Huber.

Dalbert, C. (1998) 'Belief in a just world, well-being, and coping with an unjust fate', in Montada, L. and Lerner, M.J. (eds), *Responses to Victimizations and Belief in a Just World*, New York: Plenum Press.

Dalbert, C. (2001) *The Justice Motive as a Personal Resource: Dealing with Challenges and Critical Life Events*, New York: Plenum Press.

Dalbert, C. and Katona-Sallay, H. (1996) 'The "belief in a just world" construct in Hungary', *Journal of Cross-Cultural Psychology*, 27: 293–314.

Emler, N. and Reicher, S. (1987) 'Orientations to institutional authority in adolescence', *Journal of Moral Education*, 16: 108–16.

Furnham, A. (1993) 'Just world beliefs in twelve societies', *Journal of Social Psychology*, 133: 317–29.

Furnham, A. (2003) 'Belief in a just world: Research progress over the past decade', *Personality and Individual Differences*, 34: 795–817.

Furnham, A. and Procter, E. (1989) 'Belief in a just world: Review and critique of the individual difference literature', *British Journal of Social Psychology*, 28: 365–84.

Lerner, M.J. (1980) *The Belief in a Just World. A Fundamental Delusion*, New York: Plenum Press.

Lipkus, I.M. and Siegler, I.C. (1993) 'The belief in a just world and perceptions of discrimination', *Journal of Psychology*, 127: 465–74.

McClelland, D.C., Koestner, R. and Weinberger, J. (1989) 'How do self-attributed and implicit motives differ?', *Psychological Review*, 96: 680–702.

Miller, D.T. (1999) 'The norm of self-interest', *American Psychologist*, 54: 1053–60.

Montada, L. (1998) 'Belief in a just world: A hybrid of justice motive and self-interest?', in Montada, L. and Lerner, M.J. (eds), *Responses to Victimizations and Belief in a Just World*, New York: Plenum Press.

Nurmi, J.-E., Poole, M.E. and Kalakoski, V. (1994) 'Age differences in adolescent future-oriented goals, concerns, and related temporal extension in different sociocultural contexts', *Journal of Youth and Adolescence*, 23: 471–87.

Piaget, J. (1932/1997) *The Moral Judgment of the Child*, Glencoe, IL: Free Press.

Spangler, W.D. (1992) 'Validity of questionnaire and TAT measures of need for achievement: two meta-analyses', *Psychological Bulletin*, 112: 140–54.

Zuckerman, M. and Gerbasi, K.C. (1977) 'Belief in a just world and trust', *Journal of Research in Personality*, 11: 306–17.

Index

Aboud, F. 59
abstract reasoning 22
acceptance 193
accident victims 157
achievement: motivation 123, 127;
    school student 127–9; situations
    141–8
actions: justice-motivated 3
adolescence 3, 16, 101–13, 153, 168,
    253; attitude towards authority
    124–5; experienced culture 78; late
    189; and personal goals 235–6;
    transition to adulthood 249
adolescents 11–23, 117, 241, 243;
    criminality 153; German 105;
    German and Slovakian 5; mental
    health of young unemployed 175;
    Slovakian 105
Adorno, T. *et al.* 65
adult life: experienced culture 78
age curve 248
agreeableness 236
AIDS 91
alcohol abuse 176
Almeida, D. and Larson, R. 56
anger 102, 129–30, 153; control 5, 156;
    overt 5
Antalovits, M. 217
anxiety 193
aspiration level 143
attributions: behavioural 180; internal
    180
Australia 65
authoritarianism 65, 72–4, 91, 249
authoritative parenting 28

Bandura, A. 48
Baumeister, R. 87
Beck Depression Inventory 69

Becker, P. 74
Bègue, L. 88
behaviour: coping 3; unjust 3
belief in immanent justice (BIJ) 139–49
*Belief in a just world: A fundamental
    delusion* (Lerner) 90
belief in a just world (BJW) 1; 1990s
    research 2; achievement situations
    141–8; achievement-oriented
    emotions 144; action-oriented
    implications 261; adaptation to
    discontinuous social context 55;
    adaptive function 208–9, 232;
    attributions for success and failure
    146–7; and authoritarianism 13;
    believers 3; as buffer for graduating
    students 228; as buffer for prisoners
    158–69; as buffer for unemployed
    177; buffering effect 109–13;
    children's 19; concordance of
    parental belief as transmission
    mechanism 53–4, 251; consequences
    of (un)just experiences in school
    123–31; and criminality 154–8; cross-
    cultural validity 259–60; cultural
    transmission 45; and derogation of
    victims 139; development 4, 11–23,
    26–40, 43–4; development during
    socialisation process 3, 27–9;
    developmental consequences and
    trust 255–8; developmental sequence
    249–50; developmental trajectories
    and functions 248–61; eight stages of
    development 1; emotion-focused
    coping with unemployment 179–82;
    environmental influence 12;
    experiences in school 121–32;
    familial influences on 12–14; and
    frequency of unfair treatment 201–2;

264 Index

belief in a just world *continued*
function of 2–3; general 23, 27, 31, 108, 198, 212, 238–9, 242, 261; general and personal dimension 14, 27, 40, 101–2; genetic influence 12; global personality dimensions 109–11; graduating and entering the job market 215–28; history 1–2; impact on career development 5; impact of non cognitive development-related factors 44–5; importance as developmental resource 260; importance for educational psychology 135–8; indirect effect of family climate 44; interpersonal and institutional trust 87–8; and its correlates in different age groups 64–78; as a justice motive 253–4; and justice perceptions 254–5; learning aims and aspiration levels 143; and life satisfaction 86–7; life satisfaction 148; and locus of control 88–90; and mental health 85–98, 102–3, 258–9; mental health in anger-evoking situations 129–30; and mental health during unemployment 176–86; motivational basis for 77; motivational force of 64; motivational origin of 66; nature of 253–5; non-genetic transmission 45; and optimism 90–1; origins 76; parental 18–19, 251; parental and filial 44; parenting 11–23; patterns in different age groups 66–79; and perception of injustice 88; personal 15, 101–2, 156–7, 193, 203, 219, 238–9, 243–4; and personal goals 237; personal misfortune 3; and personality 103–5; personality and well-being of adolescents 101–13; pilot study on relationship with parenting 14–17, 19, 20, 21; positive impact on well-being 6; and problem-focused coping 182–4; and Protestant work ethic 76; as resource for young prisoners 153–69; as resource for the young unemployed 175–86; responses to unfair treatment 202–6; role of transmission mechanisms 45–8, 56, 57; and school achievement behaviour 135–49; self-ascribed capabilities and learning styles 145; and self-esteem 5, 90, 102,

125, 149, 178–9, 210, 225, 258; social victims 3; socialisation of the two facets 141; as socio-political ideology 64; stability of 6; study into intensity of belief in groups 51–3; subjective well-being and anticipated workplace fairness 220–6; subjective well-being and trust 85–98; three functions of 85, 86; transmission in the family 43–61; transmission process 45–8, 251; two facets of 135–49; unemployment and the job search 189–212; vocational and social goals 231–44; and well-being 140–1; young adolescents' 11–23

Belief in a Just World Scale 43; *see also* General Belief in Just World Scale; Personal Belief in Just World Scale

belief in ultimate justice (BUJ) 139–49

beliefs: present and future-oriented 198

Bengtson, V. and Troll, L. 61

Benson, D. and Ritter, C. 177

Berne Questionnaire of Subjective Well-being 219

between-profession mobility (BPM) 183

Bible 138

Bilz, L. 50

Bissonnette, V. and Lipkus, I. 87, 88, 97

blaming the victim phenomenon 136

Blascovich, J. and Tomaka, J. 2, 128, 130, 136

Boyd, R. and Richerson, P. 45

Brinton, M. 45

Brunstein, J.: Dangelmayer, G. and Schultheiss, O. 233

Canada 185

cancer 91; study on 139

career development 7

Carlstone, J. and Finamore, F. 65, 88, 97

Carver, C. and Sheier, M. 90

causality 11; in random events 101

Cavalli-Sforza, L. 45; and Feldman, M. 48, 53, 60

Central Europe 175

Chan, S. and Fan, R. 117, 125

child monitoring 28

children 11; justice beliefs of 11–12; psychological development 26; relationship between education and BJW 57; school track 57

Clayton, S. 97

cognitive development 29, 40, 59, 101
cognitive maturity 101, 102
college students 51
commitment 234
communism 58
Connors, J. and Heaven, P. 65, 104
conscientiousness 236, 242
conservatism 7, 65, 66, 72; political and economical 87
Conservative Party 65
conservative socio-political ideology 75, 78, 253
control: locus of 90, 91, 92, 97, 259; personal 197
coping behaviour 3
Correia, I. 4
Correy, B. and Hafer, C. 86, 121, 123, 130, 136
Costa, P. and McCrae, R. 104
couples: dating 88; married 88
Creed, P. and Reynolds, J. 175
crime: long-term prisoners 161–2; sex 157, 159; violent 168
criminal behaviour 153
criminal career 153, 158, 159, 164; nine characteristics of 168
criminal justice system 169
criminality: anger expression style 153; disciplinary problems during imprisonment 154; moral justification of the crime 153; perceived justice of sentence 153; perceived justice of trial 153, 159, 163, 164; perceived prospects after release 154; relapsing into 166
Croatia 6, 192, 195, 209, 212, 260; adults 197; school-leavers 194; students 197
cross-cultural studies 12, 259–60
Cubela Adoric, V. 6
Cubela, V. 87, 88, 97
cultural capital: transmission 46
cultural dimension: of power-distance 44
cultural world view: Western society 77

Dalbert, C. 2, 44–5, 85, 90, 103, 177, 194, 222; and Dzuka, J. 104, 178, 193; and Katona-Sallay, H. 87, 198, 210; and Maes, J. 87, 123, 137, 141, 143, 144, 146; and Sallay, H. 44; and Wolfradt, U. 104; and Yamauchi, L. 97

Dangelmayer, G.: Brunstein, J. and Schultheiss, O. 233
Darling, N. and Steinberg, L. 47
depression 69, 193
depressive mood 225
depressive symptoms 181
despair 193
detention centre: German 5
Dette, D. 6
development: cognitive 29, 40, 59, 101
developmental process: dialetical 227
developmental psychology 1, 7
Dickinson, J. and Dittmar, H. 65, 76, 77
Diener, E. et al. 92, 227
Diener, E. and Fujita, F. 105
disabled children: mothers of 86
discontent: intensity of 197
Dittmar, H. and Dickinson, J. 65, 76, 77
divorce 26, 27
Donohue, R. and Patton, W. 193
Dzuka, J. and Dalbert, C. 104, 178, 193

East Germany 67, 175, 177, 179, 183, 260; value transmission study 49–61; workers 180
economic liberalism 72–4
educational level: of employment sample group 195
educational psychology 135, 137
Emler, N. et al. 124
emotion-focused coping 185
employment: gender differences 227
empowerment 123; belief in successful goal attainment 126; dimensions of 126; school student 126–7
environmentalism 11, 72–4
equality principle 119–20
ethnicity 118
Europe 3, 260
European Association for Research on Adolescence 244
European Values Survey 94
events: non-causal contingent 43; random 11
evil 101
exhaustion 193
experienced culture: adolescence 78; adult life 78
experiences: unfair 6
extraversion 104–13, 176, 236, 243
Eysenck, H. 104

266 *Index*

fairness 13; anticipated workplace 219, 220–6; at the workplace 6
fairy tales 29
families: conflict-ridden 19; fairness perception in 30; harmonious 30; immigrant 49; middle-class 28; nuclear 28; one-parent 252; rule-oriented 13, 16, 19
family climate 4, 13; conflict-ridden 14–15, 31, 32, 34, 36–7, 39; harmonious 37; impact of just 23; indirect effect 44; just 17, 19, 21, 22, 31, 250; perception of just 14; perception of the 16; rule-oriented 14–15, 18, 28, 31, 33
family life: patterns 26
family role 55; effect of 51, 52; gender effect 53
Family Socialisation Questionnaire 14, 31
family structure 252–3
family types and gender 34–7
Fan, R. and Chan, S. 117, 125
fascism 72–4
father 28, 51; job adaptation 55, 59; socio-economic status 60
Feather, N. 87
Feldman, M. and Cavalli-Sforza, L. 48, 53, 60
Finamore, F. and Carlstone, J. 65, 88, 97
first job 177, 183, 184, 186, 194, 206, 212, 221
forgetfulness 182
Freiburg Personality Inventory 105
Fujita, F. and Diener, E. 105
Furnham, A. 1–2, 43, 79; and Gunter, B. 65
futility 193

gender 55, 107; impact on well-being 216–20
gender effect: family role 53
General Belief in Just World Scale 31, 50, 92, 94, 95, 105, 196
General Satisfaction with Life Scale 105
Gerbasi, K. and Zuckerman, M. 87, 89, 97
German machiavellianism scale 71
Germany 5, 6, 51, 111, 119, 182–3, 185, 248; fascist era 249; grammar school students 142; high school students 243; psychological consequences of

reunification 66–79; *Realschule* secondary schools 238, 243, 245; school-leavers 6, 184; secondary school students 123, 126, 128, 131, 258; secondary schools 120, 122, 123; study 4
global personality dimensions 6, 261
goal attainment 244; attractiveness of 234; expectancy of 234; successful 257
goal-related decisions 231
goal-specific predictors 6
goals: commitment 231, 257; importance 243; innumerable 234; personal importance of 234; pursuit 235; social 242, 244, 260; success 234; vocational 260
good behaviour: relationship with good luck 5
Goodnow, J. and Grusec, J. 29, 44, 47, 61
Gouveia-Pereira, M. *et al.* 125
grades: justice of 122, 125
grading: distributive justice of 118–20
graduating: and entering the job market 215–28
Green, D. and Smith, K. 65
Grob, A. 216
Grusec, J. and Goodnow, J. 29, 44, 47, 61
guilt 156, 162, 163, 164, 168
Gunter, B. and Furnham, A. 65

Hafer, C. 136, 237; and Correy, B. 86, 121, 123, 130, 136; and Olson, J. 191, 194, 211
Halle (East Germany) 49
happiness 95
Havighurst, R. 216
health 175–6; *see also* mental health
Heaven, P. and Connors, J. 65, 104
Henning, H. and Six, B. 71
hepatitis 91
Hepburn, J. and Stratton, J. 169
heteronomous morality 29
heterosexuality 169
Hofstede, G. 44
Hollenbeck, J. and Klein, H. 234
Hong Kong 120
Hotard, S. *et al.* 104
Hungary 6, 27, 220, 255, 259, 260; Euro-Atlantic integration 215; job market 255; political and societal

Index 267

changes 6; Socialist Party 216; society 215; socio-economic changes 227; socio-political changes 216; students 198, 210; study 4; youngsters 227

idealistic world views 71–2, 75
idiographic-nomothetic assessment 233
Ihinger, M. 29
illness-related emotions 139
immanent justice 5, 11, 29, 43, 67, 101, 135, 261
immanent and ultimate justice 138–9; school-specific questionnaire for assessment 140
immigrant families 49
imprisonment: length of 169
individualism 44
injustice 103, 177, 222; experiences of 126, 137, 194, 195, 198; negative emotional impact 211
institutional trust 256
interpersonal trust 255
invulnerability 190
Israel 118, 120
Israelashvili, M. 118

job loss: self-attribution of 192
job market 179, 208, 235, 257; entering the 215–28
job perspectives: Croatian students 192
joblessness *see* unemployment
jobs: applications 202; failed applications 199, 210, 254; impact on well-being 216–20; right to have 191; satisfaction 26
Judaeo-Christian culture 138
Just Family Climate Scale 14, 19, 31
Just School Climate Scale 122
just world: hypothesis 232; research 64–6; resource literature 74
justice 2, 11, 13, 17, 101, 103, 232; belief in compensating 260; beliefs 22; constructs 31; culture of 78; distributive 121; faith in 137; in the family 29; of grading 118–20; immanent 5, 11, 69, 101, 135, 248, 261; individual needs for 79; perceptions 253, 256, 258, 260; perceptions in school 130; personal experience of 13; procedural 124–5; social constructions of 79; trust in 131; ultimate 5, 67, 68, 69, 131, 135, 256

justice beliefs: role of 135–49
justice motive: transformation of 64–78
justice motive theory 1, 135, 167, 182, 259, 261
justice psychology 77, 261
justice-motivated actions 3

Kals, E. 5; and Maes, J. 131, 140, 142, 149
Katona-Sallay, H. and Dalbert, C. 87, 198, 210
Klein, H. and Hollenbeck, J. 234
Knafo, A. and Schwarz, S. 46
Kowal, A. *et al.* 30
Kraus, L. 169
Krettenauer, T. 71
Kuczynski, L.: Marshall, S. and Schnell, K. 61

labour market 49, 216, 251; adaptation after reunification of Germany 50–1, 57; policies 217
Lambert, A. *et al.* 91
language: acquisition of pronunciation 48
Larson, R. and Almeida, D. 56
legal socialisation 5, 124–6
legal system 124
Lerner, M. 1, 26, 64, 85, 90, 135, 191, 248; and Simmons, C. 26, 138; and Somers, D. 177
leukaemia 91
Lewin, E. 218
libertarianism 65
Life Orientation Test 92, 94
life philosophy 16
life satisfaction 5, 86–7, 91, 102–3, 109, 178–9, 193, 258
Lipkus, I.: and Bissonnette, V. 87, 88, 97; *et al.* 104, 232; and Siegler, I. 121

Maanen, J. 226
Maass, A. and Martella, D. 175
McCrae, R. and Costa, P. 104
McFadyen, R. and Thomas, J. 191, 193
McFatter, R. 105
Machievellianism 71
McLanahan, S. and Sandefur, G. 27
Maes, J. 1, 4, 5, 89, 91; and Dalbert, C. 87, 123, 137, 141, 143, 144, 146; and Kals, E. 131, 140, 142, 149

268 *Index*

manslaughter 153
marital status: of employment sample group 195
Marshall, S.: Kuczynski, L. and Schnell, K. 61
Martella, D. and Maass, A. 175
maternal parenting 30, 34
maternal restriction 38
maternal support 37, 39
meaning in life 2
mental health 3, 91, 102–3, 175, 192, 221, 237; different dimensions 74; dimensions of 177
Miller, D. and Ratner, R. 77, 78
Moffitt, T. 153, 168
Montada, L. 3
moral attitudes: young prisoners 168, 169
moral individualism 66
moral realism 29
moral reasoning: of juvenile delinquents 159
morality: autonomous concept of 29; heteronomous 29
mother-father differences 28
mothers 51; of disabled children 86; job adaptation 55, 61; single 28
murder 153

need principle 119–20
negative outcomes 3
neuroticism 7, 104–13, 236, 242, 250, 251, 258
New Year's Resolutions 234
Nixon, President R. 65
non-interventionist: economy 65
non-victim group 178
non-victimised individuals 86
North America 259, 260
Northern Ireland 192
nuclear families 28
nurture 4, 12, 17, 22, 30, 33, 252, 254

offenders 155, 157; recurrent 165
Olkin, I. 142
Olson, J. and Hafer, C. 191, 194, 211
one-parent families 27–9; *see also* single mothers
openness 236
optimism 5, 92, 93, 94, 97, 259; dispositional 190
Otto, K. 5
overt anger 5

parent: as role model 4
parental attitudes 48
parental education styles 141
parental experience 49
parental norms 26, 29
parental remarriage 26
parental schooling 118
parental standards 29; internalisation of 29
parental treatment 30; legitimacy of 30
parenting 4, 11–23, 261; acceptance as models 50, 58; acceptance as models as moderator of BJW transmission 56–8, 60, 61; with aim of autonomy 12, 14–15, 18, 32, 34, 37; with aim of conformity 15, 18, 20, 32, 33, 34, 36; authoritative 28; and belief in a just world (BJW) 26–40; consistency 38; construct validity of 18; dimensions 12, 20; experiences 17; Hungarian questionnaire study 30–40; impact of one-parent or 'intact' family 26–40; maternal 30, 34; second study 17–23; styles 28, 29; three-factor model of 17
parenting attitude 14–15, 18, 20, 31; manipulative 14–15, 17, 18, 20, 31, 37
parenting patterns 37–40; in one-parent and 'intact' families 32–3
parenting style: inconsistent 32; reproving 32; supportive 32
parenting within intact families 36–8, 44; main differences between mother and father 34
paternal restriction 38
patients: cancer 89; hospitalised in intensive care units 89
Patton, W. and Donohue, R. 193
peer contacts 22; impact of just 23
penal system 169
Peplau, L. and Rubin, Z. 43, 65
Personal Belief in a Just World Scale 122, 155, 196, 219
personal contract: concept of 137, 157, 183
personal development 17
personal goals 231, 233–7, 244; personality and other predictors of success 236–7
personal worries 178–9
personality: 'Big Five' factors 239; development 5; dimensions 251; five-factor model 236; questionnaire

(Becker) 74; theories 103; and well-being 104–5
pessimism 193
Piaget, J. 29, 40, 67, 250
police 124
Portugal 95, 259; annual national attitude survey 94–8; study 4
poverty 65
power-distance: cultural dimension of 44
prejudice 64
prisoners: belief in a just world (BJW) 153–69; moral attitudes 168, 169; moral justification of short/long-term 161–2; rehabilitation after release 166; young male 125
problem-focused coping 185, 260
problem-solving strategies 233
procrastination 182
psychological buffer 249
psychological health 216
psychological theories: well-being/employment status 217
psychology: developmental 1, 7, 248, 261; educational 135, 137; international justice 259; social 7

Quirk, M. and Wagstaff, G. 65

Radant, M. 4, 58
randomness 11
Ratner, R. and Miller, D. 77, 78
re-employment 184
reasoning: abstract 22
religious attributions 146
resignation 193
responsibility: personal 197
restriction 12, 14, 23, 28, 252, 253, 254
Reynolds, J. and Creed, P. 175
Rhineland-Palatinate (Germany) 142
Richerson, P. and Boyd, R. 45
right-wing: ideology 71, 72; political orientation 65
Rim, Y. 104
Ritter, C. and Benson, D. 177
Rosenberg Self-Esteem Scale 69, 92
Rotter, J. 88, 89, 92
Rubin, Z. and Peplau, L. 43, 65
rule-orientation: in the family 13, 253
rumination: self-focused 102

Saathof, W. 217

Sallay, H. 6; and Dalbert, C. 44
Sandefur, G. and McLanahan, S. 27
Satisfaction with Life Scale 92, 94
Scheffé Test 54, 55, 68
Schmitt, M. 4
Schnell, K.: Marshall, S. and Kuczynski, L. 61
school 256, 257, 258, 260; academic motivation 130; anxiety 140; aversion to 140; distress in 128–31; euphoria 140; fear of other people 140; implications and functions of (un)just experiences 117–32; justice in 117; perceptions of justice 130; school-related self-efficacy 126, 127–8; student achievement 127–9; student empowerment 126–7; see also Germany
school context 5, 117, 125; immanent and ultimate justice 139–40
Schultheiss, O.: Dangelmayer, G. and Brunstein, J. 233
Schwartz, S. 71; and Knafo, A. 46
Schwenkmezger, P. 104
security 89
self: perceptions of the 221
self-blame 102, 194, 195, 197, 198, 203, 206; unrealistic 211
self-defeating behaviour 182
self-efficacy 126, 236; school-related 256; social 238, 239, 241, 243
self-esteem 5, 87, 102, 149, 178–9, 184, 210, 225; youth 75
self-interest 77–8
sex crimes 157, 159
Sheier, M. and Carver, C. 90
Siegler, I. and Lipkus, I. 121
Simmons, C. and Lerner, M. 26, 138
single mothers 28
Six, B. and Henning, H. 71
Slovakia 6, 111, 185, 259, 260
Slovenia 260; students 198, 210
Smith, K. and Green, D. 65
smoking 176
social attitudes 250; variance in 11
social environment 249
social goals 6
social justice: perceptions of 94
social learning theory (Bandura) 48
social orientations 49
social psychology 7, 88
social sciences 77
social self-efficacy 6

270   *Index*

socialisation 26, 117, 141, 176; in
    childhood 78; legal 5, 123, 124–6;
    one-parent families 27–9;
    organisational 226; of a political
    ideology 78; pre-job 226; Western
    137
socialism 58, 65, 72–4
socio-economic changes 227
socio-politics 210, 215, 216, 218;
    context 228; ideologies 76–7;
    orientations 72–4
sociologists 215
Somers, D. and Lerner, M. 177
Steensma, H. *et al.* 89
Steinberg, L. and Darling, N. 47
Stöber, J. 6
Stratton, J. and Hepburn, J. 169
stress 138
students 14, 117; achievement 127–9;
    Chinese secondary school 117;
    German 65, 123, 126, 128, 131, 258;
    Hungary 198, 210; Slovenia 198, 210
support: maternal 37

teachers 117; fairness 122, 128;
    interpersonal treatment 121; justice
    122; Spanish 65
Ter Bogt, T. *et al.* 46
Thomas, J. and McFadyen, R. 191, 193
time: impact on well-being 216–20
tolerance 7
Tomaka, J. and Blascovich, J. 2, 128,
    130, 136
training: vocational 237, 238, 239, 241
transmission: age-specificity 48; of BJW
    in the family 43–61; carriers of 46;
    contents of 46; of cultural capital 46;
    developmental perspective on 47–8;
    direct 56, 254; directions of 46; East
    German value transmission study
    49–61; horizontal (via peers) 47, 48;
    hypotheses 48–9; intergenerational
    46; intergenerational gaps 58; parent
    as moderator 56–8; rate 48; recipient
    of 46; selectivity of 46; of social
    orientation of BJW 57; vertical
    (parent to child) 46, 48, 58; vertical
    transmission of religious and political
    attitudes 48
Trier Personality Questionnaire 69
Troll, L. and Bengtson, V. 61
trust 2, 4, 5, 6, 13, 30, 64, 232; in
    fairness 126; in fellow people 136; in

government actions 88; institutional
    96, 256; interpersonal 88, 96, 255;
    interpersonal and institutional 87–8;
    in justice 131; in politicians 87; in
    social institutions 136; of young
    adults 85–98
Turkey HSD test 200
Tyler, T. 124

ultimate and immanent justice
    138–9; school-specific questionnaire
    140
ultimate justice 5, 67, 68, 69, 131, 135,
    256
undeservedness 197
unemployment 5, 6, 175–6, 184, 215;
    BJW as resource 175–86; coping with
    193, 260; duration 190, 195, 202, 212;
    gender difference in length of 196;
    long-term 192, 212, 255; negative
    impact of 208; negative psychological
    impact 194; peer 190; personal 191;
    predicting one's own 190;
    psychological consequences 175, 177,
    184, 186, 191; rate 192; short-term
    192; stage theories 193
unfair treatment 203; responses to
    particular experience 197
unfairness 102, 197, 249; perceived
    206; perception 194; self-experienced
    180
university students: female 14
unjust behaviour 3
unjust experiences: frequency of 197

Vala, J. 4, 95, 98
values 26
Van Hoorn, J. *et al.* 227
victim 64, 86, 139, 179; derogation 138;
    innocent 136, 138; studies 177
Villaverde Cabral, M. 95, 98
violent crimes 153, 159, 168
vocational training 237; preparation for
    238, 239, 241

Wagstaff, G. and Quirk, M. 65
war 210
well-being 4, 5, 69–70, 89, 104, 216–20,
    232; dimensions 223, 226; and
    employment status 217; impact of
    employment status 218; and
    personality 104–5; physical 90;
    psychological 87; socio-emotional 30;

subjective (SWB) 85–98, 102, 111, 140, 149, 215, 220–6
West Germany 67, 250
Western society 77
Why Me? Question 180–2, 192, 221
wishful thinking 182
Wolfradt, U. and Dalbert, C. 104
women: labour force participation 27; unemployed 182; university students 14

workplace 226; anticipated fairness at 219, 220–6; just 257
world beliefs 26

Yamauchi, L. and Dalbert, C. 97
youth: self-esteem 75; *see also* adolescence; adolescents

Zuckerman, M. and Gerbasi, K. 87, 89, 97

eBooks – at www.eBookstore.tandf.co.uk

A library at your fingertips!

eBooks are electronic versions of printed books. You can store them on your PC/laptop or browse them online.

They have advantages for anyone needing rapid access to a wide variety of published, copyright information.

eBooks can help your research by enabling you to bookmark chapters, annotate text and use instant searches to find specific words or phrases. Several eBook files would fit on even a small laptop or PDA.

NEW: Save money by eSubscribing: cheap, online access to any eBook for as long as you need it.

Annual subscription packages

We now offer special low-cost bulk subscriptions to packages of eBooks in certain subject areas. These are available to libraries or to individuals.

For more information please contact webmaster.ebooks@tandf.co.uk

We're continually developing the eBook concept, so keep up to date by visiting the website.

www.eBookstore.tandf.co.uk